海南经贸职业技术学院"中国特色高水平高职学校与专业建设计划"提升国际化水平项目
Internationalization Level Improvement Project under the "High-Level Higher Vocational Schools and Majors Construction Program with Chinese Characteristics" of Hainan College of Economics and Business

国际贸易系列教材

INTERNATIONAL
TRADE PRACTICE

国际贸易实务中英双语教程

覃 娜　符白薇 ◎主编
尤一帆　李晓欢 ◎副主编

浙江大学出版社
·杭州·

图书在版编目（CIP）数据

国际贸易实务中英双语教程 / 覃娜，符白薇主编. -- 杭州：浙江大学出版社，2025.1
ISBN 978-7-308-24456-5

I. ①国… II. ①覃… ②符… III. ①国际贸易－贸易实务－教材－汉、英 IV. ①F740.4

中国国家版本馆 CIP 数据核字(2023)第 235019 号

国际贸易实务中英双语教程
GUOJI MAOYI SHIWU ZHONGYING SHUANGYU JIAOCHENG

主 编　覃　娜　符白薇

策划编辑	李　晨
责任编辑	高士吟
责任校对	郑成业
封面设计	春天书装
出版发行	浙江大学出版社
	（杭州市天目山路148号　邮政编码310007）
	（网址：http://www.zjupress.com）
排　　版	杭州林智广告有限公司
印　　刷	杭州高腾印务有限公司
开　　本	787mm×1092mm　1/16
印　　张	18.25
字　　数	547千
版 印 次	2025年1月第1版　2025年1月第1次印刷
书　　号	ISBN 978-7-308-24456-5
定　　价	58.00元

版权所有　侵权必究　　印装差错　负责调换

浙江大学出版社市场运营中心联系方式：0571 - 88925591；http://zjdxcbs.tmall.com

前言

PREFACE

  党的二十大报告提出,要推进高水平对外开放,推动货物贸易优化升级,创新服务贸易发展机制,发展数字贸易,加快建设贸易强国。① 作为开放型经济和国际贸易的坚定支持者,中国和世界各国(地区)的贸易往来日益频繁,国内外市场对具备国际视野和国际竞争力的外向型人才的需求不断增加,对外贸从业人员的综合素质和业务能力提出了更高的要求。同时具备专业技能和外语知识,并能将专业技能融会贯通的应用型、复合型人才越来越受用人单位的欢迎和重用。

  The Report to the 20th National Congress of the Communist Party of China proposes to promote high-standard opening up, upgrade trade in goods, develop new mechanisms for trade in services, and promote digital trade, in order to accelerate China's transformation into a trader of quality. As a staunch supporter of an open economy and international trade, China's trade exchanges with other countries (regions) are becoming increasingly frequent. The demand for export-oriented talents with international vision and competitiveness in domestic and foreign markets is increasing, which puts forward higher requirements on the comprehensive quality and business ability of foreign trade practitioners. Application-oriented interdisciplinary talents with professional skills and foreign language expertise are increasingly favored and valued by employers.

  为适应经济全球化对外贸从业人员的需求,培养高职院校学生的外贸业务能力,提高学生的外贸综合素质,满足共建"一带一路"国家国际商务及相关专业留学生学习和教学的需要,本着"理实一体、工学结合"的方针和"实用、应用、够用"的原则,我们组织编写了这本双语教材。

  In order to adapt foreign trade practitioners to economic globalization, foster the foreign trade business ability of higher vocational college students, improve the students' comprehensive quality in foreign trade, and meet the learning and teaching requirements of international business and related majors in Belt and Road partner countries, we have prepared this bilingual textbook based on the policy of

---

① 习近平. 高举中国特色社会主义伟大旗帜　为全面建设社会主义现代化国家而团结奋斗:在中国共产党第二十次全国代表大会上的报告[N]. 人民日报,2022-10-26(1).

"integrating theory with practice and combining work and learning" and the principle of "practicability, application and sufficiency".

本教材的特色与优势体现在以下几个方面：第一，汉英双语。教材内容采用中英文对照，详细、系统地介绍了国际贸易业务的相关知识和操作流程。第二，校企合编。教材由教学水平高的双师教学团队、从业经验丰富的行业专家、外语扎实的留学教师等共同研究编写，确保了教材内容的前瞻性、科学性和实用性。第三，案例丰富。教材应用当前外贸企业前沿的货物进出口案例和外贸单据，帮助学生实现专业学习和工作岗位的近距离对接。

The characteristics and advantages of this textbook are reflected in the following aspects. First, Chinese-English bilingual compilation. The textbook is compiled in Chinese and English to introduce the knowledge and operation process of international trade business in detail and systematically. Second, school-enterprise co-compilation. The textbook is co-compiled by a high-level co-teaching team, experienced industry experts, and returnee teachers proficient in English, so as to ensure forward-looking, scientific and practical content. Third, abundant cases. The textbook uses the cutting-edge import and export cases and foreign trade documents of current foreign trade enterprises to help students align professional learning with working.

本教材便于教师双语教学和学生学习阅读，使学生掌握专业知识的同时，提高学生的英语运用能力，体现双语教学的效果。同时，每章开始有导读，结尾的二维码中有知识拓展、专业词汇和练习，提高学生学习兴趣，帮助学生进行知识总结，提高学生实务操作能力。为支持本课程的教学，方便教师授课，教材编写组还配套了教学课件、案例和练习题等教学资源。

This textbook is convenient for teachers to conduct bilingual teaching and for students to read and learn. It enables students to master professional knowledge while improving their English application ability, ensuring the effect of bilingual education. In addition, each chapter of the textbook starts with a knowledge guide and ends with a QR code containing knowledge expansion, terminology, and exercises, so as to arouse students' interest in learning, help them summarize what they have learned, and improve their practical operation abilities. To facilitate course teaching, supporting resources such as courseware, cases, and exercises are also made available by the compilation group.

本教材由海南经贸职业技术学院的覃娜、符白薇主编，并负责全书的策划和统稿。具体编写分工如下：覃娜编写了第一、二、三、七、十章，李晓欢编写了第四、五、六、十一章，尤一帆编写了第八、九、十二章，符白薇负责全书的英文翻译。

The editors-in-chief of the textbook are Qin Na and Fu Baiwei from Hainan College of Economics and Business, who are also responsible for the planning and finalization of the textbook. The specific division of work is as follows: Qin Na complied Chapters 1, 2, 3, 7 and 10; Li Xiaohuan Chapters 4, 5, 6 and 11; You Yifan Chapters 8, 9 and 12; Fu Baiwei is responsible for the English translation of the entire book.

本教材的出版得到了海南经贸职业技术学院"中国特色高水平高职学校与专业建设计划"提升国际化水平项目的支持。感谢浙江大学出版社为本教材的编辑出版提供的优质服务。

The publication of this textbook is supported by the International Level Improvement Project under the "High-level Higher Vocational Schools and Majors Construction Program with Chinese Characteristics" of Hainan College of Economics and Business. We are grateful to Zhejiang University Press for providing quality services for the editing and publication of thistextbook.

本教材如有不足之处，敬请读者批评指正。

If there are any shortcomings in this textbook, we welcome the readers' criticism and suggestions for improvement.

目 录
CONTENTS

第一章 国际贸易概述
Chapter 1 Overview of International Trade

第一节 国际贸易的基本概念 … 002
Section 1 Basic Concepts of International Trade … 002

第二节 国际贸易的分类 … 003
Section 2 Classification of International Trade … 003

第三节 国际贸易的作用和特点 … 008
Section 3 Role and Characteristics of International Trade … 008

第二章 交易磋商与签订合同
Chapter 2 Business Negotiation and Contract Signing

第一节 交易磋商 … 014
Section 1 Business Negotiation … 014

第二节 签订合同 … 029
Section 2 Contract Signing … 029

第三章 国际贸易术语
Chapter 3 International Trade Terms

第一节 贸易术语及其国际贸易惯例 … 037
Section 1 Trade Terms and International Trade Customs … 037

第二节 六种主要的贸易术语 … 044
Section 2 Six Major Trade Terms … 044

第三节 其他五种贸易术语 … 069
Section 3 Five Other Trade Terms … 069

第四章 商品的名称和质量
Chapter 4 Name and Quality of Commodity

第一节 品名、品质的含义 … 073
Section 1 Meaning of Commodity and Quality … 073

1

第二节　品质的表示方法　　　　　　　　　　　　　　　　074
Section 2　Representation of Quality　　　　　　　　　074

第三节　合同中的品名、品质条款　　　　　　　　　　　081
Section 3　Commodity and Quality Clause in the Contract　081

第五章　商品的数量
Chapter 5　Quantity of Goods

第一节　商品数量的含义　　　　　　　　　　　　　　　087
Section 1　Meaning of Commodity Quantity　　　　　　087

第二节　计量单位与计重方法　　　　　　　　　　　　　087
Section 2　Unit and Method of Measurement　　　　　　087

第三节　合同中的数量条款　　　　　　　　　　　　　　091
Section 3　Quantity Clause in the Contract　　　　　　091

第六章　商品的包装
Chapter 6　Packing of Goods

第一节　商品包装的含义与意义　　　　　　　　　　　　094
Section 1　Meaning and Significance of Commodity Packing　094

第二节　包装的种类　　　　　　　　　　　　　　　　　095
Section 2　Types of Packing　　　　　　　　　　　　　095

第三节　运输包装的标志　　　　　　　　　　　　　　　100
Section 3　Transport Packing Marks　　　　　　　　　　100

第四节　合同中的包装条款　　　　　　　　　　　　　　101
Section 4　Packing Clause in the Contract　　　　　　　101

第七章　商品的价格
Chapter 7　Price of Goods

第一节　出口商品的价格构成与计算　　　　　　　　　　104
Section 1　Price Composition and Calculation of Export Goods　104

第二节　六种贸易术语价格的构成及换算　　　　　　　　112
Section 2　Price Composition and Conversion of Six Trade Terms　112

第三节　定价原则和报价时应考虑的因素　　　　　　　　113
Section 3　Pricing Principles and Factors to be Considered in Quotation　113

第四节　合同中的价格条款　　　　　　　　　　　　　　116
Section 4　Price Clause in the Contract　　　　　　　　116

第八章　国际货物运输
Chapter 8　International Carriage of Goods

第一节　国际货物运输方式　123
Section 1　International Transportation Mode of Goods　123

第二节　国际货物运输单据　144
Section 2　International Goods Transport Documents　144

第三节　合同中的装运条款　158
Section 3　Shipment Clause in the Contract　158

第九章　国际货物运输保险
Chapter 9　International Cargo Insurance

第一节　海运货物保险的承保范围　168
Section 1　Coverage of Marine Cargo Insurance　168

第二节　中国海运货物保险条款　172
Section 2　China Marine Cargo Insurance Clauses　172

第三节　伦敦保险协会海运货物保险条款　178
Section 3　Institute Cargo Clauses　178

第四节　我国其他货运险别　181
Section 4　Other Cargo Risks in China　181

第五节　保险实务　183
Section 5　Insurance Practice　183

第六节　合同中的保险条款　189
Section 6　Insurance Clause in the Contract　189

第十章　货款的支付
Chapter 10　Payment for Goods

第一节　支付工具　191
Section 1　Payment Instruments　191

第二节　信用证支付　213
Section 2　L/C Payment　213

第三节　汇付　231
Section 3　Remittance　231

第四节　托收　235
Section 4　Collection　235

第五节　合同中的支付条款　245
Section 5　Payment Terms in the Contract　245

第十一章 商品检验、索赔、不可抗力与仲裁
Chapter 11 Commodity Inspection, Claim, Force Majeure and Arbitration

第一节 商品检验   247
Section 1 Commodity Inspection   247

第二节 索赔   256
Section 2 Claim   256

第三节 不可抗力   261
Section 3 Force Majeure   261

第四节 仲裁   265
Section 4 Arbitration   265

第十二章 进出口合同的履行
Chapter 12 Performance of Import and Export Contract

第一节 出口合同的履行   274
Section 1 Performance of Export Contract   274

第二节 进口合同的履行   277
Section 2 Performance of Import Contract   277

参考文献   280
References   280

第一章 国际贸易概述
Chapter 1　Overview of International Trade

导　读
Introduction

　　在奴隶社会，第三次社会大分工诞生了商人阶层，随着社会生产力的发展，私有制和阶级出现，国家产生，并且有了更多可供交换的剩余产品，国际贸易开始产生。初时的国际贸易主要集中在欧洲的迦太基（腓尼基人建立的古国）、希腊和罗马等地，交换的商品主要是各种奢侈品（珠宝、丝绸、香料）。封建社会的国际贸易主要集中在地中海东部，阿拉伯民族扮演着世界商人的角色。公元11世纪后，随着意大利北部和波罗的海沿岸城市的兴起，国际贸易的范围扩大至地中海、北海、波罗的海和黑海沿岸。

　　In slave society, the third great social division of labor gave birth to the merchant class. With the development of the productive forces of society, private ownership and classes emerged, and the state arose. There were more surplus products for exchange, and international trade began to emerge. In the beginning, international trade was concentrated in Carthage (an ancient state founded by the Phoenicians), Greece and Rome, and the commodities exchanged were mainly luxuries (jewelry, silk and spices). International trade in feudal society was mainly concentrated in the eastern Mediterranean, with the Arabs playing the role of world merchants. After the 11th century, with the rise of cities in northern Italy and the Baltic Sea, the scope of international trade was expanded to cover the coastal areas of the Mediterranean Sea, North Sea, Baltic Sea, and Black Sea.

　　公元前2世纪，汉使张骞出使西域，开辟了丝绸之路。自丝绸之路开辟以来，中国的对外贸易源远流长，四大发明以及丝绸、茶叶、瓷器等奢侈品通过贸易运往欧洲各国，而外国的毛织品、香料、贵金属、农产品等也传至中国。例如，西瓜原产于埃及，后经欧洲和西亚，于五代时期传入中国；西红柿、辣椒原产于美洲，于明代经欧洲传入中国；苹果原产于欧洲，于元代末期引入中国。

　　In the 2nd century BC, Zhang Qian, an envoy of the Han Dynasty, went to the Western Regions and opened up the Silk Road. China has enjoyed a long history of foreign trade since the initiation of the Silk Road. The four great inventions and luxuries such as silk, tea, and porcelain have been shipped to European countries through trade, while foreign wool fabrics, spices, precious metals, and agricultural products have also been introduced to China. For example, watermelons were native to Egypt and later introduced into China via Europe and West Asia during the Five Dynasties; tomatoes and chili peppers were native to America and introduced into China via Europe in the Ming Dynasty; apples were native to Europe and introduced into China in the late Yuan Dynasty.

第一节　国际贸易的基本概念
Section 1　Basic Concepts of International Trade

一、国际贸易的含义
I. Meaning of International Trade

（一）国际贸易 (International Trade)

国际贸易又称世界贸易，是指世界各国（地区）之间所进行的以货币为媒介的商品交换活动。它既包含有形商品（货物）的交换，也包含无形商品（服务、技术等）的交换。

International trade, also known as world trade, refers to the exchange of commodities across countries (regions) with currency as the medium. It includes both the exchange of tangible commodities (goods) and the exchange of intangible commodities (services, technology, and so on).

（二）对外贸易 (Foreign Trade)

对外贸易又称进出口贸易，是指国际贸易活动中的一国（地区）同其他国家（地区）所进行的货物、服务、知识等的交换活动。这是立足于一个国家或地区去看待它与其他国家或地区的商品贸易活动。某些海岛国家，如英国、日本等，也将其对外贸易称为海外贸易（overseas trade）。

Foreign trade, also known as import and export trade, refers to the exchange of commodities, services, and knowledge between a country (region) and other countries (regions) in international trade activities. It is an approach that focuses on the trade of commodities of a particular country or region with other countries or regions. Some island countries, such as the United Kingdom and Japan, also refer to foreign trade as overseas trade.

二、国际贸易产生与发展的基本条件
II. Basic Conditions for the Emergence and Development of International Trade

国际贸易是一个历史的范畴，是在一定的历史条件下产生的，是社会生产力发展到一定阶段的产物。可以说人类历史上的三次大分工使国际贸易产生的必要条件一步步得以满足。原始社会末期出现了阶级和国家。商品交换一旦超出国家界限，就出现了最早的国际商品交换的萌芽。

International trade is a historical concept that has emerged under certain historical conditions and is a product of the development of social productive forces to a certain stage. The necessary conditions for the emergence of international trade have been met step by step through the three social divisions of labor in human history. Classes and states emerged at the end of primitive society. The exchange of commodities across national boundaries led to the formation of the earliest international commodity exchange.

所以，国际贸易是随着国际分工的出现和世界市场的形成而产生和发展起来的。从根本上讲，社会生产力的发展和社会分工的扩大是国际贸易产生和发展的基础和前提，自然条件的不同使得国际贸易出现多样化。

Therefore, international trade has emerged and developed with the appearance of the international division of labor and the formation of world markets. Fundamentally, the development of social productive forces and the expansion of social division of labor are the basis and premise for the emergence and development of international trade.

第二节　国际贸易的分类
Section 2　Classification of International Trade

国际贸易的范围广泛，种类繁多，交易方式千差万别，但我们可以从不同角度对其进行分类，使各种交易的脉络更加明晰和规范。

International trade covers a wide range and involves various types and transaction methods. However, we can classify it from different perspectives to provide a clearer and more standardized framework for various types of transactions.

一、按商品流向分类
I. Classification by Commodity Flow

按商品流向分类，国际贸易可分为出口贸易、进口贸易和过境贸易等。

International trade can be classified into export trade, import trade, and transit trade according to the flow of commodities.

（一）出口贸易 (Export Trade)

出口贸易又称输出贸易，简称出口，是指一国（地区）生产或加工的商品输往他国（地区）市场销售。

Export trade, or export, refers to commodities produced or processed in one country (region) and sold to another country (region) markets.

（二）进口贸易 (Import Trade)

进口贸易又称输入贸易，简称进口，是指将其他国家（地区）的商品输入本国（地区）市场销售。

Import trade, or import, refers to commodities purchased into one country (region) from another country (region).

（三）过境贸易 (Transit Trade)

过境贸易又称通过贸易，是指A国（地区）的出口商品经由B国（地区）输往C国（地区）销售，对B国（地区）而言即为过境贸易。因为对B国（地区）来说，这种贸易既不是进口，也不是出口，仅仅是商品过境而已。过境贸易为内陆国家（地区）提供了与其他国家（地区）进行贸易的便利，在欧洲大陆国家较为流行。过境贸易商品在过境国（地区）一般无须缴纳关税，只需支付少量的过境费。

Transit trade refers to the export of commodities from Country (Region) A to Country (Region) C via Country (Region) B. For Country (Region) B, this is transit trade as it is neither import nor export, but only transit of commodities. Transit trade facilitates trade between landlocked countries (region) and other countries (region) and is popular in continental European countries. In transit trade, commodities are generally not subject to tariffs and only a small amount of transit fees will be charged by the transit country (region).

二、按商品形态分类
II. Classification by Commodity Form

按商品形态分类，国际贸易可分为货物贸易和服务贸易。

International trade can be classified into trade in goods and trade in services according to the form of commodities.

（一）货物贸易 (Trade in Goods)

货物贸易是指实物形态商品的进出口活动。由于实物形态的商品看得见、摸得着，因此货物贸易也称为有形贸易（visible trade or tangible trade）。

Trade in goods refers to the import and export of physical commodities. As such commodities are visible and tangible, this kind of trade is also called visible trade or tangible trade.

（二）服务贸易 (Trade in Services)

服务贸易是指一国（地区）的法人或自然人在其境内或进入他国境内向外国（地区）的法人或自然人提供服务的贸易行为。服务贸易大体相当于无形贸易（invisible trade or intangible trade），但不包括无形贸易中的投资收益，即国（地区）与国（地区）之间因资本借贷或投资等所产生的利息、股息、利润收支。按照世界贸易组织于1994年签署的《服务贸易总协定》，服务贸易有四种提供方式。

Trade in services refers to the trade activity in which the legal or natural person of one country (region) provides services to the legal or natural person of another country (region), either within its own territory or by entering the territory of another country. Trade in services is generally equivalent to invisible trade or intangible trade. However, it does not include investment income, that is, the interest, dividends, and profits generated from capital borrowing or investment between countries (regions). According to the General Agreement on Trade in Services, a treaty signed by WTO in 1994, there are four modes of supplying services.

（1）跨境交付：指服务的提供者在一成员方的领土内，向另一成员方领土内的消费者提供服务的方式（如在中国境内通过电信、邮政、计算机网络等手段实现对境外的消费者的服务）。

Cross-border supply: It refers to the supply of services from the territory of one member into the territory of any other member (e.g. services supplied to overseas foreigners via telecommunications, mail, or computer networks in the territory of China).

（2）境外消费：指服务提供者在一成员方的领土内，向来自另一成员方的消费者提供服务的方式（如中国公民在境外短期居留期间，享受境外的医疗服务）。

Consumption abroad: It refers to situations where a service consumer moves into another member's territory to obtain a service (e.g. Chinese citizens enjoying medical services abroad during their short-term stay).

（3）商业存在：指一成员方的服务提供者在另一成员方领土内设立商业机构，在后者领土内为消费者提供服务的方式（如外国服务类企业在中国设立公司为中国企业或个人提供服务）。

Commercial presence: It implies that a service supplier of one member establishes a commercial presence in another member's territory to provide services for the consumers in that territory (e.g. foreign service enterprises establish companies in China to provide services for Chinese enterprises or individuals).

（4）自然人流动：指一成员方的服务提供者以自然人的身份进入另一成员方的领土内提供服务的方式（如某外国律师作为外国律师事务所的驻华代表到中国境内为消费者提供服务）。

Presence of natural persons: It implies that the service provider of one member enters the territory of another member to provide services as a natural person (e.g. a foreign lawyer providing services for consumers in China as the representative of a foreign law firm in China).

三、按贸易有无第三方参加分类
III. Classification by the Presence of the Third Party

按贸易有无第三方参加分类，国际贸易可分为直接贸易、间接贸易和转口贸易。

International trade can be classified into direct trade, indirect trade, and entrepot trade according to whether the third party participates in the trade.

（一）直接贸易 (Direct Trade)

直接贸易是指商品生产国（地区）与商品消费国（地区）直接买卖商品的行为，即由进出口两国（地区）直接完成的交易。

Direct trade refers to the act of directly buying and selling commodities between the producing country (region) and the consuming country (region). It involves transactions that are directly conducted between the importing and exporting countries (regions).

（二）间接贸易 (Indirect Trade)

间接贸易是指商品生产国（地区）不直接向消费国（地区）出口，商品消费国（地区）也不直接从生产国（地区）进口，而由第三国（地区）贸易商完成的交易。

Indirect trade refers to situations where commodities are neither exported directly to the consuming country (region) nor imported directly from the producing country (region), and the transaction is completed by the trader of a third country (region).

（三）转口贸易 (Entrepot Trade)

转口贸易又称中转贸易（intermediary trade），指商品生产国（地区）和消费国（地区）通过第三国（地区）进行的贸易，对第三国（地区）而言就是转口贸易。贸易的货物能够由出口国（地区）运往第三国（地区），在第三国（地区）不通过加工（转换包装、分类、选择、收拾等不作为加工论）再销往消费国（地区）；也能够不通过第三国（地区）而直接由生产国（地区）运往消费国（地区），但生产国（地区）与消费国（地区）之间并不发生贸易联系，而是由中转国（地区）分别同生产国（地区）和消费国（地区）发生贸易。

Entrepot trade, also known as intermediary trade, refers to trade in which commodities are transferred between the producing country (region) and the consuming country (region) through a third country (region). From the perspective of the third country (region), this trade is considered entrepot trade. The traded goods can be transported from the exporting country (region) to a third country (region), where they are not processed (excluding activities like repackaging, categorizing, selecting, or tidying), and then sold to the consuming country (region). Alternatively, goods can be transported directly from the producing country (region) to the consuming country (region) without direct trade relations between the two countries (regions), but instead involving an intermediary country (region) that engages in trade separately with the producing and consuming countries (regions).

四、按贸易方式分类
IV. Classification by Trade Mode

按贸易方式分类，国际贸易可分为一般贸易和加工贸易。

International trade can be classified into common trade and processing trade according to the trade mode.

（一）一般贸易 (Common Trade)

一般贸易是指中国境内有进出口经营权的企业单边进口或单边出口的贸易，按一般贸易交易方式进出口的货物即为一般贸易货物。一般贸易货物在进口时可以按一般进出口监管制度办理海关手续，这时它就是一般进出口货物；也可以享受特定减免税优惠，按特定减免税监管制度办理海关手续，这时它就是特定减免税货物；也可以经海关批准保税，按保税监管制度办理海关手续，这时它就是保税货物。

Common trade refers to the trade conducted by enterprises in China's territory that possess the import and export right, involving either unilateral imports or unilateral exports. The goods imported or exported through common trade transactions are referred to as common trade goods. During import, common trade goods can be subject to customs procedures under the general import and export control system, in which case they are considered common import and export goods. They can also enjoy specific tax reliefs and undergo customs procedures under the specific tax relief control system, in which case they are considered specific tax relief goods. Furthermore, they can be approved by the customs for bonded status and undergo customs procedures under the bonded supervision system, in which case they are considered bonded goods.

（二）加工贸易 (Processing Trade)

加工贸易是指经营企业进口全部或者部分料件（原辅材料、零部件、元器件、包装物料），经加工或装配后，将制成品复出口的经营活动，包括进料加工、来料加工、装配业务和协作生产。

Processing trade refers to the business activity of enterprises importing all or part of the materials (raw materials, parts, components, and packaging materials), and after processing or assembling, re-exporting the finished products. It includes the processing of imported materials, processing of supplied materials, assembly operations, and cooperative production.

五、按清偿工具分类
V. Classification by Liquidation Instrument

按清偿工具分类，国际贸易可分为现汇贸易和易货贸易。

International trade can be classified into trade by current exchange and barter according to the liquidation instrument.

（一）现汇贸易 (Trade by Current Exchange)

现汇贸易又称自由结汇贸易，是用国际货币进行商品价款结算的一种贸易方式。买卖双方按国际市场价格水平议价，按国际贸易惯例议定具体交易条件。交货完毕以后，买方按双方商定的国际货币付款。现汇贸易的特点表现在买卖行为是各自独立的单向贸易。它非常方便，是国际贸易中使用最多、最普遍的贸易方式。然而，在当代国际贸易中，使用外汇现金结算的交易已罕见。随着汇票、支票等信用工具的广泛使用，贸易结算已基本采用非现金结算。

Trade by current exchange, also known as free-liquidation trade, is a way of trading in international currency for commodity price settlement. The buyer and the seller negotiate based on international market price levels and agree upon specific transaction conditions according to international trade customs. After the delivery is completed, the buyer makes payment in the international currency agreed upon by both parties. The characteristics of trade by current exchange lie in that buying and selling actions are independent and unilateral. It is very convenient and is the most widely used and common trade method in international trade. However, in contemporary international trade, transactions using cash settlement in foreign exchange are becoming increasingly rare. With the widespread use of credit instruments such as drafts and checks, trade settlement has shifted towards non-cash methods.

（二）易货贸易 (Barter)

易货贸易是指不以货币为媒介，或只以货币计价，直接以货物相交换的贸易活动。易货贸易的特点是进出口直接挂钩，进出平衡，不必动用外汇。

Barter refers to trade activities where goods are exchanged directly without the use of currency as a medium or where goods are only priced in currency. The characteristics of barter trade include a direct link between imports and exports, which ensures a balanced trade without the use of foreign exchange.

六、按运输方式分类
VI. Classification by Transportation Mode

按运输方式分类，国际贸易可分为陆路贸易、海运贸易、空运贸易、邮购贸易和多式联运贸易。

International trade can be classified into trade by roadway, trade by seaway, trade by airway, trade by mail order, and trade by multimodal transport according to the mode of transportation.

（一）陆路贸易 (Trade by Roadway)

货物通过陆地运输的国际贸易称为陆路贸易。陆地毗邻国家（地区）之间的贸易多采用陆路贸易方式，主要运输工具是火车和卡车，约占国际贸易量的8%。

International trade involving the transportation of goods through land routes is referred to as trade by roadway. This method is often adopted for the trade between land-adjacent countries (regions), which involves the use of trains and trucks as the main means of conveyance. This type of trade accounts for approximately 8% of international trade volume.

（二）海运贸易 (Trade by Seaway)

货物通过海上运输的国际贸易称为海运贸易。运输工具主要是各类船舶，这是国际贸易最主要的运输方式，约占国际贸易量的90%。

International trade involving the transportation of goods through sea routes is referred to as trade by seaway, and the main means of conveyance include various ships. It is the most important transportation mode in international trade, accounting for about 90% of the international trade volume.

（三）空运贸易 (Trade by Airway)

货物通过航空运输的国际贸易称为空运贸易。对单位价值较高或需求紧迫的货物，为争取时效，往往采用空运贸易方式，约占国际贸易量的1.2%。

International trade involving the transportation of goods through air routes is referred to as trade by airway. For goods with a higher unit value or urgent demand, trade by airway is often employed to ensure timely delivery. It accounts for approximately 1.2% of international trade volume.

（四）邮购贸易 (Trade by Mail Order)

货物采用邮政包裹或其他寄送方式交付的国际贸易称为邮购贸易。对订货数量很少的商品通常使用邮购贸易，如个人自用品、公司样品等。

International trade in which goods are delivered through postal parcels or other mailing methods is referred to as trade by mail order. This type of trade is commonly used for goods that have a small order quantity, such as personal items for individual use or company samples.

（五）多式联运贸易 (Trade by Multimodal Transport)

多式联运是指海陆空各种运输方式结合运送货物的行为。国际物流业的迅猛发展促进了这种方式的贸易。

Trade by multimodal transport refers to the practice of combining various modes of transportation, including sea, land, and air, to transport goods. The rapid development of international logistics has facilitated this type of trade.

七、按国境与关境划分
VII. Classification by National Territory and Customs Territory

（一）总贸易 (General Trade)

总贸易是"专门贸易"的对称，是指以国境为标准划分的进出口贸易。凡进入国境的商品一律列为总进口；凡离开国境的商品一律列为总出口。在总出口中又包括本国产品的出口和未经加工的进口商品的出口。总进口额加总出口额就是一国的总贸易额。美国、日本、英国、加拿大、澳大利亚等国家采用这种划分标准。

General trade is the symmetry of "special trade", which refers to import and export trade classified by the national territory. All commodities entering the national territory are classified as general imports, while all commodities leaving the national territory are classified as general exports. General exports encompass exports of domestic products and re-exports of imported goods without processing. The sum of general imports and general exports is known as a country's total trade volume. This classification criterion is used in the United States, Japan, the United Kingdom, Canada, Australia.

（二）专门贸易 (Special Trade)

专门贸易是"总贸易"的对称，是以关境为标准划分的进出口贸易。只有从外国进入关境的商品以及从保税仓库存提出进入关境的商品才列为专门进口。当外国商品进入国境后，暂时存放在保税仓库，未进入关境，不列为专门进口。从国内运出关境的本国产品以及进口后经加工又运出关境的商品，则列为专门出口。专门进口额加专门出口额称为专门贸易额。中国、欧盟等国家和地区采用这种划分标准。

Special trade is the symmetry of "general trade", which refers to import and export trade classified by the customs territory. Special imports refer specifically to commodities that enter the customs territory of one country from another country or are picked up from the bonded warehouse to enter the customs territory. When foreign commodities entering a national territory are temporarily stored in the bonded warehouse without entering the customs territory, they are not classified as special imports. Domestic products that are transported out of the customs territory as well as imported commodities that are re-exported out of the customs territory after processing are classified as special exports. The sum of special imports and special exports is known as the special trade volume. This classification criterion is used in countries and regions like China and the European Union.

第三节 国际贸易的作用和特点
Section 3　Role and Characteristics of International Trade

一、国际贸易的作用
I. Role of International Trade

国际贸易对参与贸易的国家（地区）乃至世界经济的发展具有重要作用，具体表现在以下几方面。

International trade plays an important role in the development of countries (regions) participating in trade and even the world economy, which is reflected in the following aspects.

(一)国际贸易使世界各国(地区)互通有无,弥补资源短缺,满足国民经济发展需要 [International Trade Facilitates the Exchange of Goods and Services Between Countries (Regions), Bridging Resource gaps and Meeting the Economic Development Needs of Nations]

世界上不同的国家(地区),由于所处的地理位置不同,所拥有的自然条件不同,自然资源的禀赋也不尽相同。如中东地区盛产石油,热带、亚热带地区的国家(地区)盛产可可、天然橡胶、咖啡等,这些因地域及自然条件的不同导致的资源差异,往往影响各国(地区)的经济发展。由于各国(地区)科技发展水平不同,许多工业化发展水平低的国家(地区),既不能生产高技术产品,也无法生产普通技术产品,因而不能满足本国(地区)消费者的正常需要。在这些情况下,通过对外贸易,可以弥补本国(地区)资源的短缺,填补本国(地区)技术产品的空白,从而调整本国(地区)市场的供求,满足国民经济发展的需要。

Due to different geographical locations, countries (regions) in the world possess different natural conditions and resources. For example, the Middle East is rich in petroleum, while countries (regions) in tropical and subtropical regions are abundant in cocoa, natural rubber, coffee, and so on. These differences in resources, resulting from different geographical and natural conditions, often have an impact on the economic development of countries (regions). Due to the varying levels of technological development among countries (regions), many nations with lower levels of industrialization are unable to produce high-tech or even basic technological products, thus failing to meet the normal needs of their local consumers. In such situations, foreign trade can help bridge the local resource shortage and fill the gap in local technological products, thereby adjusting the supply and demand in the local market and meeting the needs of national economic development.

(二)国际贸易有利于世界各国(地区)利用国际分工,发挥比较优势,获得比较利益 [International Trade Allows Countries (Regions) Worldwide to Leverage International Division of Labor and Exploit Comparative Advantages to Obtain Comparative Benefits]

在国际经济联系日益紧密的今天,由于各国(地区)的自然条件、生产力水平、经济结构、科学技术水平等方面的差异,以及历史和社会等多方面的原因,有些国家(地区)对某些商品的生产有利,而对某些商品的生产不利。此外,任何一个国家(地区)也不可能生产自己所需要的一切物品,同时也不可能完全消费掉自己所生产的一切物品。这些矛盾只能通过参与国际分工、进行商品交换得以解决。通过参与国际分工,各国(地区)可以充分利用本国(地区)的生产要素优势,发展那些本国(地区)条件相对优越的产业部门,从而节约社会劳动时间,促进本国(地区)经济增长。

Today, international economies are becoming increasingly interconnected. National differences in natural conditions, productivity levels, economic structures, and scientific and technological capabilities, as well as various historical and social factors, contribute to the situation where some countries (regions) have an edge in the production of certain commodities while being disadvantaged in the production of others. Furthermore, no country (region) can produce all the goods it needs, nor can it consume all the goods it produces. These contradictions can only be solved by participating in the international division of labor and conducting commodity exchanges. By participating in the international division of labor, countries (regions) can make full use of their own advantages in production factors and develop those industrial sectors with relatively superior conditions, thus saving social labor time and promoting domestic economic growth.

(三)国际贸易有利于世界各国(地区)提高生产技术水平 [International Trade Is Conducive to Improving the Production Technology Level in All Countries (Regions)]

当代世界各国(地区)经济发展所取得的成就表明,劳动生产率的提高已在越来越大的程度上依靠科学技术的进步。所以，经济竞争的实质是科学技术的竞争。哪个国家（地区）在科学技术上领先，并能有效地把技术应用到生产实践中，该国（地区）的经济增长就会在世界上处于领先地位。这就要求世界各国（地区）在技术上进行相互交流，通过这个重要途径去改造现有企业，进行全行业的技术改造，提高本国（地区）产品的技术质量和整体科学技术水平，从而缩短同外国科学技术水平的差距。但在现代条件下，科学技术水平又是一种特殊的商品，它的使用与转让也要像其他商品一样，必须通过市场与贸易，以等价交换的方式进行。这种技术贸易的发展，已成为当代国际贸易的一个重要组成部分，也成为各国（地区）提高生产技术水平的一条重要捷径。

The current achievements made by countries (regions) around the world in economic development indicate that the improvement in labor productivity increasingly relies on advancements in science and technology. Therefore, the essence of economic competition lies in the competition of science and technology. The country (region) that leads in science and technology and effectively applies technology to production practices will spearhead the world in economic growth. This requires countries (regions) all over the world to exchange technologies with each other, so as to transform existing enterprises, carry out industry-wide technological transformation, and improve the technological quality of their own products as well as their overall scientific and technological expertise, thus narrowing the gap with other countries (regions) in science and technology. However, in modern times, scientific and technological expertise is a unique commodity. Its utilization and transfer, like other commodities, must be carried out under the principle of equal exchange through market and trade. The development of technology trade has become an integral part of contemporary international trade and an important shortcut for countries (regions) to enhance their production technology levels.

（四）国际贸易有利于世界各国（地区）增加财政收入和就业 [International Trade Can Help Countries (Regions) Around the World Increase Fiscal Revenue and Employment]

国际贸易可以提高一国（地区）财政收入，其作用表现在两个方面：一方面是通过国际分工和国际商品交换可以使各国（地区）节约一定的社会劳动耗费，节约原材料耗费，创造更多的价值，从而间接地增加一国（地区）的财政收入；另一方面是通过对外贸易，通过各国（地区）从事进出口的企业上缴的各种税收以及国家征收的关税，能直接增加一国（地区）的财政收入，尤其是能增加国家（地区）经济与发展过程中急需的外汇收入。根据中国海关和国家统计局相关统计数据测算，在不减免税收和不退税的条件下，中国每出口1亿元人民币收入的工业总产品，国家可得税利3500万元左右。

International trade contributes to enhancing a country's (region's) fiscal revenue, which is mainly manifested in two aspects: First, the international division of labor and exchange of commodities allow countries (regions) to save on social labor costs and raw material consumption and create more value, thus indirectly increasing their fiscal revenue; second, by engaging in foreign trade, a country (region) can directly increase its fiscal revenue through the collection of taxes from import and export enterprises as well as through the imposition of tariffs, which can directly increase the country's (region's) fiscal revenue, especially foreign exchange income urgently needed in the country's (region's) economy and during its development. Calculated on the basis of relevant statistics from China Customs and the National Bureau of Statistics, under the condition of no tax exemptions or refunds, China registers approximately RMB 35 million worth of taxes and profits for every RMB 100 million worth of industrial products exported.

实现劳动力充分就业，是一个国家（地区）发展经济、实现内部均衡的重要内容。世界各国（地区）由于各种原因都在不同程度上存在着失业或就业不足，这必然会造成劳动力资源的浪费，对外贸易为各国（地区）解决劳动力就业开辟了新途径。对外贸易不仅维持了一部分人就业，而且可以通过扩大出口，增加一部分就业，使闲置的劳动力得到安置，增加国民收入。根据中国海关和国家统计局相关统计数据测算，每出口 1 亿元人民币的工业品，一年就能够提供 1.2 万人的就业机会。可见，对外贸易对解决劳动力就业来说，作用是极为显著的。

Achieving full employment of the labor force is an important aspect of a country's (region's) economic development and internal equilibrium. Due to various reasons, countries (regions) around the world experience varying degrees of unemployment or underemployment, leading to wastage of labor resources. Foreign trade provides new pathways for countries (regions) to address employment issues. Foreign trade not only sustains a portion of employment but also generates additional employment by expanding exports, allowing the placement of unemployed labor and increasing national income. Calculated on the basis of relevant statistics from China Customs and the National Bureau of Statistics, 12000 jobs can be created annually for every RMB 100 million worth of industrial products exported. Therefore, foreign trade plays a significant role in addressing labor force employment.

二、国际贸易的特点
II. Characteristics of International Trade

（一）国际贸易具有广泛性 (International Trade Is Extensive)

1. 市场空间的广泛性 (Extensive Market Space)

在国际贸易中，对贸易商来说，世界有多大，市场就有多大，贸易就可以做多大。第二次世界大战以后，随着贸易全球化的不断深入，贸易活动日益突破国内市场和区域市场的狭窄界限，在全球范围内展开，为贸易商开展贸易活动提供了前所未有的广阔空间。

In international trade, for traders, the size of the world determines the size of the market and how much trade can be conducted. After World War II, with the continuous deepening of trade globalization, trade activities have surpassed the boundaries of domestic and regional markets and expanded globally. This has provided unprecedented opportunities and broad space for traders to engage in trade activities on a global scale.

2. 法律适用的广泛性 (Extensive Scope of Law Application)

国际贸易涉及大量的国际、国内和国外法律，但至今世界上没有一部完整统一的国际贸易法。由于各国的法律体系制度不尽相同，贸易商必须了解相关的国际贸易法律法规和国际贸易惯例。

International trade involves a myriad of international, domestic, and foreign laws. However, there is no comprehensive and unified international trade law in the world. Due to variations in legal systems across different countries, traders must familiarize themselves with relevant international trade laws, regulations, and customs.

3. 贸易障碍的广泛性 (Extensive Trade Barriers)

为了争夺市场，维护本国（地区）利益，各国（地区）或多或少地都采取关税壁垒和非关税壁垒限制外国（地区）商品的进口，从而给国际贸易造成了许多障碍。

In order to compete for markets and safeguard their own interests, countries (regions), to a greater or lesser extent, impose tariff and non-tariff barriers to restrict imports of commodities of other countries (regions), thereby creating numerous obstacles to international trade.

4. 交易接洽的广泛性 (Extensive Transaction Engagement)

除了国际展会，电子商务还为世界各地贸易商开展贸易提供了更为广泛的交流平台。

In addition to international exhibitions, e-commerce provides a more extensive exchange platform for traders from all over the world to engage in trade activities.

（二）国际贸易具有更大的风险性 (International Trade Is More Risky)

1. 自然风险 (Natural Risks)

在国际贸易中，自然力导致的突发性灾难事故时有发生，如地震、瘟疫等，这些风险必然会给国际贸易带来许多意想不到的困难。

In international trade, unforeseen natural disasters such as earthquakes and epidemics often occur. These risks inevitably bring about numerous unexpected challenges to international trade.

2. 社会风险 (Social Risks)

社会风险包括政治风险、价格风险、商业风险、信用风险、汇兑风险、运输风险等。国际贸易的交易双方必然有一方要以外币计价和付款，但由于世界主要结算货币实行的都是浮动汇率制，汇率变化，稍不留神就会出现汇兑风险。一些贸易商明明在商品生产和经营上技高一筹，本应获得更多的贸易利益，但由于未能正确把握汇率变动趋势而吃了亏。例如，中国一家企业向美国出口 100 万美元的商品，签约时人民币兑美元汇率为 USD 1=CNY 6.7，收到 100 万美元货款时，人民币兑美元汇率升值为 USD 1=CNY 6.3，则该企业这笔交易的人民币收入减少了 40 万元。

Social risks include political risks, price risks, commercial risks, credit risks, foreign exchange risks, and transportation risks. In international trade, one of the parties involved is inevitably required to price and make payments in a foreign currency. However, due to the implementation of floating exchange rates for major currencies of settlement worldwide, exchange rate fluctuations may lead to foreign exchange risks. Some traders, despite being more skilled in product manufacturing and operations, should have gained more from trade. However, due to their failure to correctly grasp the trend of exchange rate fluctuations, they suffered losses. For example, a Chinese company exported USD 1 million worth of commodities to the United States, and at the time of the contract signing, the exchange rate was USD 1 = CNY 6.7. However, when they received the payment of USD 1 million, the exchange rate became USD 1 = CNY 6.3, and the company's income from this transaction decreased by RMB 400000.

贸易政策突变的风险案例：2018 年初，中国某出口企业将以 CIF 术语成交的一个集装箱的蚕豆出口到墨西哥，船离港后业务员才接到进口商的通知，说墨西哥海关正在调整进口政策，即日起蚕豆一类的农产品暂停入关。由于货物已经发运，业务员只能被动等待事情出现转机。20 天过去了，墨西哥的政策没有变化，而货物已运抵墨西哥。中国的出口企业不得不电告船公司，在返航时将原货带回。两个月后墨西哥进口政策才有所松动，出口商得以将该批蚕豆复出口，但白白浪费了一个来回的运费和保险费，以及资金的超时占压。

There is the case of risks resulting from a such change in the trade policy: In early 2018, a Chinese exporting company entered into a CIF transaction to export a container of fava beans to Mexico. After the vessel departed, the company's salesperson received a notification from the importer that the Mexican customs authority was adjusting their import policies, which included a temporary suspension of fava beans and similar agricultural products. Since the shipment was already en route, the salesperson had no choice but to wait for an upturn. After 20 days, with no changes in Mexico's policy, the goods arrived in Mexico. The Chinese exporter had to inform the shipping company in a telegram that the goods needed to be returned with the returning vessel. It took another two months for Mexico to relax the import policy, allowing the exporter to reship the fava beans. However, this incident resulted in the waste of freight charges and premiums for a round trip, as well as extended holding of funds.

（三）国际贸易具有复杂性 (International Trade Is Complex)

国际贸易的交易程序、度量衡制度、贸易结算、海关制度、运输手续、商业习惯、语言文字等都具有复杂性。

International trade is complex in aspects such as trade procedures, systems of weights and measures, trade settlement, customs regime, transportation formalities, business habits, and language.

第一章拓展知识、专业词汇和练习

第二章　交易磋商与签订合同
Chapter 2　Business Negotiation and Contract Signing

导　读
Introduction

交易磋商工作的好坏直接影响合同的签订及履行，直接关系将来买卖双方的权利、义务和经济利益，是做好进出口贸易的关键所在。因此，在磋商之前，进出口双方都应当做好准备工作；在磋商的过程中，进出口商不仅要注意磋商的合理形式和表达方法，更应当注意每一个步骤的作用和法律效果。

Business negotiations are key to import and export trade as they directly impact the signing and performance of contracts and are directly related to the rights, obligations, and economic interests of the buyer and the seller. Therefore, both the importer and the exporter should make adequate preparations before the negotiation, and during the negotiation, they should not only pay attention to the appropriate form and expression, but also be aware of the function and legal effect of each procedure.

第一节　交易磋商
Section 1　Business Negotiation

交易磋商（business negotiation）是指在国际贸易中，进出口双方就商品的各项交易条件进行谈判，以期达成一致的过程。

Business negotiation refers to the process in international trade where the importer and the exporter negotiate various transaction conditions with the aim of reaching a consensus.

一、交易磋商的形式
I. Forms of Business Negotiation

交易磋商从形式上可分为口头磋商和书面磋商两种。

Business negotiations can be divided into two forms: verbal negotiation and written negotiation.

（一）口头磋商 (Verbal Negotiation)

口头磋商，如各种交易会或洽谈会上的谈判，以及贸易小组出访、国外客户来华洽谈等。此外，还包括双方通过聊天软件、视频会议、电话等方式进行的交易磋商。口头磋商的特点是直接交流，便于了解对方的态度，采取相应的对策，并根据进展情况及时调整策略，以达到预期的目的。口头磋商比较适合谈判内容复杂、涉及问题较多的业务，如大型成套设备交易的谈判。

Verbal negotiations include talks conducted during trade fairs or meetings, as well as discussions carried out during trade delegations' visits to foreign countries and foreign clients' visits to China. In addition, they involve business negotiations conducted through chat software, video conferences, and phone calls. Verbal negotiation is characterized by direct communication, which facilitates understanding of the trading partner's attitude, enables the implementation of corresponding measures, and allows for timely adjustments of strategies based on the progress of the negotiation, so as to achieve the desired objectives. Verbal negotiation is more suitable for business with complex negotiation content and involves numerous issues, such as negotiations for the transaction of large complete equipment.

（二）书面磋商 (Written Negotiation)

书面磋商指通过信件、传真、电子邮件等通信方式来洽谈交易。书面磋商成本费用低廉、简便易行，是买卖双方通常采用的方式。

Written negotiation refers to the process of negotiating transactions through written communication methods such as letters, faxes, and emails. Written negotiation has the advantage of being cost-effective, convenient, and easily accessible, making it the preferred method for buyers and sellers.

在国际贸易中，进出口双方通常采用书面形式磋商交易。鉴于多数情况下交易磋商需要一个较长时间过程，因此对一份合同的磋商往往需要结合使用多种磋商形式。此外，交易磋商的形式还有拍卖、招投标、期货等特殊形式。

In international trade, the two parties involved in import and export typically negotiate transactions in written form. Considering that most business negotiations require a lengthy process, it is often necessary to combine multiple negotiation forms when negotiating a contract. In addition, business negotiation also takes special forms such as auctions, bidding and tendering, and futures.

在外贸实践中，交易磋商形式的选择要结合合同的金额大小、商品的技术复杂程度和国家相关政策的规定。一般情况下，小金额合同的交易磋商主要采用函电磋商和电话磋商；大金额合同、技术复杂商品的交易磋商主要采用函电磋商、电话磋商和口头磋商相结合；国际招标主要适用于国家规定必须采用国际招标的机电产品。

In international trade practice, the choice of business negotiation forms should be based on factors such as the contract amount, technical complexity of commodities, and relevant policies and regulations of the countries involved. In general, for small-amount contracts, correspondence and telephone negotiations are mainly adopted for business negotiations. For large-amount contracts or transactions involving technically complex goods, a combination of correspondence, telephone negotiations, and face-to-face negotiations is often used. International bidding is primarily applicable to electromechanical products where it is required by national regulations to use international bidding.

二、交易磋商的内容
II. Content of Business Negotiation

进出口交易磋商的内容，主要是围绕买卖某种商品的各项交易条件，如合同的标的（货物的品名、品质、数量、包装）、价格与支付条款、交货条件（运输、保险）、预防与解决争议的条款（检验、索赔、不可抗力和仲裁）等进行协商。其中，品名、品质、数量、包装、价格、装运、支付等七项为主要内容或主要交易条件（main terms and conditions）。买卖双方欲达成交易、订立合同，至少须就这七项交易条件进行磋商并取得一致意见。至于其他交易条件，如检验、索赔、不可抗力和仲裁等条款，它们虽然不是合同成立不可缺少的内容，但是为了防止或减少纠纷，解决可能发生的争议，买卖双方在交易磋商时也不应忽视。

The content of import and export business negotiations mainly revolves around the transaction conditions related to buying and selling a particular commodity. This includes the subject matter of the contract (the name, quality, quantity, and packing of the goods), price and payment clauses, delivery conditions (transportation and insurance), provisions for prevention and resolution of disputes (inspection, claims, force majeure, and arbitration), and other aspects. Among them, the commodity name, quality, quantity, packing, price, shipment, and payment are the main content or main terms and conditions of business negotiations. In order for the buyer and the seller to reach a transaction and conclude a contract, they need to negotiate and reach a consensus on at least these above seven conditions. As for other transaction conditions regarding inspection, claims, force majeure, and arbitration, although they are not essential for a contract, they should not be overlooked during business negotiations in order to prevent or reduce disputes and resolve potential conflicts.

在实际业务中，并非每笔交易都要将全部的交易条件一一列出、逐条进行商讨。因为，在普通商品交易中，一般都使用固定格式的合同。而检验、索赔、不可抗力和仲裁条款通常作为一般交易条件印就在格式合同中，只要对方没有异议，就不必重新协商，这些条件也就成为双方进行交易的基础。有经验的外贸业务员往往在进行正式磋商之前，先就一般交易条件与对方达成一致，以简化磋商内容，提高磋商效率，降低磋商成本。

In practical business operations, it is not necessary to list and discuss all conditions for every transaction. This is because standardized contract templates are generally used in ordinary commodity trades. Inspection, claims, force majeure, and arbitration clause are usually included as general terms and conditions in the standardized contracts. Unless the other party objects, there is no need to renegotiate these conditions, and they become the foundation for the transaction between the two parties. Experienced foreign trade salespersons often reach an agreement with the other party on the general terms and conditions before engaging in formal negotiations. This helps simplify the negotiation process, improve efficiency, and reduce associated costs.

一般交易条件（general terms and conditions）的内容因经营商品的不同而不同，通常包括以下几个方面：①有关争议的预防和处理条件（如检验、索赔、不可抗力和仲裁的有关规定）；②有关主要交易条件的补充说明（如品质机动幅度、分批装运、保险险别等）；③个别主要交易条件的习惯做法（如通常的包装方式、付款方式等）。

The content of general terms and conditions may vary depending on the nature of the traded commodities. It generally includes several aspects: ① Conditions for prevention and handling of disputes (such as inspection, claims, force majeure, and arbitration); ② Supplementary explanations regarding main terms and conditions (such as quality latitude, partial shipments, and types of insurance coverage); ③ Common practices for specific main terms and conditions (such as typical packing methods and payment terms).

三、交易磋商的一般程序
III. General Procedures for Business Negotiation

在外贸业务中，交易磋商的程序一般包括询盘、发盘、还盘和接受四个环节。其中，发盘和接受是达成交易、合同成立不可缺少的两个基本环节和必经的法律步骤。

In international trade, the general procedures for business negotiations usually include inquiry/enquiry, offer, counter-offer, and acceptance. Among them, offer and acceptance are two essential and necessary steps in finalizing a transaction and establishing a contract from a legal perspective.

（一）询盘 (Inquiry/Enquiry)

询盘，也称询价，是指交易一方欲购买或出售某种商品而向交易的另一方询问买卖该种商品的有关交易条件。

Inquiry/enquiry refers to one party in a transaction expressing interest in purchasing or selling a specific commodity and asking the other party for the relevant terms and conditions.

1. 询盘的内容及其法律效力（Content and Legal Effect of Inquiry）

在外贸业务中，询盘多由进口方向出口方发出，因此这种买方询盘也称"邀请发盘"，是买方对所要购买的商品向卖方做出的探询。

In international trade, an inquiry is often initiated by the importer to the exporter. Therefore, the inquiry initiated by the buyer is also called an "invitation to offer", where the buyer seeks information from the seller regarding the desired commodities.

询盘的内容包括商品的品质、规格、数量、包装、价格、装运等成交条件或索取样品。在实际业务中，询盘的内容可繁可简，可只询问价格，也可询问其他有关的交易条件。

The content of an inquiry typically includes the quality, specification, quantity, packing, price, shipment, and other transaction conditions, or a request for samples. In actual business operations, the content of an inquiry can be elaborate or concise. It can solely inquire about prices or ask about other related transaction conditions.

询盘只是探询买或卖的可能性，所以不具有法律上的约束力，询盘的一方对能否达成协议不负有任何责任。询盘也不是每笔业务的必经程序。如交易双方彼此都了解情况，不需要向对方探询成交条件或交易的可能性，就不必进行询盘，可直接向对方发盘。

An inquiry is merely about the possibility of buying or selling and therefore is not legally binding. The party initiating the inquiry is not responsible for whether an agreement can be reached or not. An inquiry is not a mandatory procedure for every business transaction. If both parties are aware of each other's situation and do not need to inquire about the transaction conditions or the possibility of a deal, it is not necessary to initiate an inquiry. Instead, they can directly make an offer.

2. 询盘的种类（Types of Inquiry）

根据询盘的性质和意图，询盘可分为一般询盘和具体询盘。

Based on the nature and intention of the inquiry, it can be classified into general inquiry and specific inquiry.

（1）一般询盘（general inquiry）。一般询盘并不一定立即触及具体交易，一般属摸底性质。其内容包括：请寄某种商品的样品、目录及/或价格表；探询某种商品的品质、价格、数量、交货期等。

General inquiry: a general inquiry does not necessarily involve an immediate transaction and is generally diagnostic in nature. The content of a general inquiry may include: requesting samples, catalog, and/or price list of a commodity; inquiring about the quality, price, quantity, and time of delivery of a commodity.

（2）具体询盘（specific inquiry）。具体询盘实际上就是请求对方报盘，也就是说，买方已经准备购买某种商品，或已有现成买主，请卖方就这一商品报价。

Specific inquiry: it is actually a request for an offer. That is to say, the buyer is ready to purchase a commodity, or the commodity has a potential buyer, so the seller is requested to make an offer for this commodity.

3. 询盘的注意事项（Precautions for Inquiry）

（1）询盘虽然可同时向一个或几个交易对象发出，但不应在同时期集中对外询盘，以防止暴露销售或购买心切。

Although inquiries can be sent to one or several potential trading partners simultaneously, it is not advisable to concentrate inquiries in the same period. This is to prevent exposing eagerness to sell or buy.

（2）在询盘时，不仅限于询问价格，也可以询问其他交易条件。

An inquiry is not limited to asking about the price only; other transaction conditions can also be inquired about.

（3）询盘是交易洽商的第一步，在法律上对询盘人和被询盘人均无约束力，即买方询盘后无购买货物的义务和卖方询盘后无出售货物的责任。

An inquiry is the first step in business negotiations and is not legally binding for both the inquirer and the respondent. This means that the buyer has no obligation to purchase goods after making an inquiry, and the seller has no responsibility to sell goods after receiving an inquiry.

（4）被询盘人可以及时发价回答询盘，也可以拖延一段时间发盘，还可以拒绝回答询盘。不过在交易习惯上要尊重对方，无论是否出售或购买均以及时回复为宜。

The recipient of an inquiry can respond promptly with an offer, delay making an offer, or even refuse to respond to the inquiry. However, it is customary in business transactions to show respect for the other party by providing a timely response, regardless of whether to sell or make a purchase.

（5）询盘虽然对双方无约束力，但是，双方在询盘的基础上经过多次洽商，最后达成交易，如果履约时发生争议，那么原询盘的内容也成为洽商成交文件的不可分割部分，同样可以作为处理争议的依据。

Although inquiries are not legally binding for both parties, if they engage in rounds of negotiations based on the inquiry and eventually reach a transaction, the content of the original inquiry may become an integral part of the negotiated agreement. In case of disputes arising during the performance of the agreement, the content of the original inquiry can be used as a basis for resolving the disputes.

（二）发盘 (Offer)

发盘，又称发价，在法律上称为"要约"，是买方或卖方向对方提出各项交易条件，并愿意按照这些条件达成交易、订立合同的一种肯定的表示。在实际业务中，发盘通常是一方收到对方询盘后提出的，但也可不经对方询盘而直接向对方发盘。发盘人可以是卖方，也可以是买方。前者又称为售货发盘（selling offer）；后者又称购货发盘（buying offer）或递盘（bid）。

An offer is a positive expression made by the buyer or seller to the other party, presenting various trading conditions and indicating a willingness to enter into a transaction and establish a contract based on these conditions. In actual business practice, an offer is typically made by one party in response to an inquiry from the other party. However, it is also possible to make an offer directly without the other party's inquiry. The offeror can be either the seller or the buyer. If the offeror is the seller, the offer is referred to as a selling offer; otherwise, it is known as a buying offer or a bid.

发盘是对发盘人具有法律约束力的"要约"，发盘人在发盘的有效期限内不得任意撤销或修改发盘的内容。发盘一经对方在有效期限内表示无条件接受，发盘人将受其约束并承担按发盘条件与对方签订合同的法律责任。

An offer is legally binding for the offeror. The offeror is not allowed to arbitrarily revoke or modify the content of the offer within the specified validity period of the offer. Once the offer has been unconditionally accepted by the other party within the specified validity period, the offeror becomes bound by the offer and assumes the legal responsibility to enter into a contract with the other party based on the conditions stated in the offer.

1. 构成发盘的必要条件 (Requirements for Constituting an Offer)

《联合国国际货物销售合同公约》（以下简称《公约》）第十四条第一款对发盘做了如下定义："向一个或一个以上特定的人提出的订立合同的建议，如果十分确定并且表明发价人在得到接受时承受约束的意旨，即构成发价。一个建议如果写明货物并且明示或暗示地规定数量和价格或规定如何确定数量和价格，即为十分确定。"《公约》第十五条第一款规定："发价于送达被发价人时生效。"据此，构成一项法律上有效的发盘须具备四个条件。

Article 14 (1) of the United Nations Convention on Contracts for the International Sale of Goods (CISG) defines that "A proposal for concluding a contract addressed to one or more specific persons constitutes an offer if it is sufficiently definite and indicates the intention of the offeror to be bound in case of acceptance. A proposal is sufficiently definite if it indicates the goods and expressly or implicitly fixes or makes provision for determining the quantity and the price." Article 15 (1) of CISG further stipulates that an offer becomes effective when it reaches the offeree. On this basis, four conditions must be met to constitute a legally valid offer.

（1）发盘必须向一个或一个以上特定的人提出。

(1) An offer must be addressed to one or more specific persons.

发盘必须向一个或一个以上特定的人提出。《公约》第十四条第二款规定："非向一个或一个以上特定的人提出的建议，仅应视为邀请做出发价，除非提出建议的人明确地表示相反的意向。"所谓"特定的人"，是指发盘中指明个人姓名或企业名称的收盘人。这一规定的目的是将向特定对象做出的发盘与在报刊上刊登广告、向国外客商寄发商品目录、价目单和其他宣传品的行为区分开来。在后一种情况下，广告的对象是广大社会公众，商品目录、价目表和宣传品是普遍寄发给为数众多的客商的。这些对象都不属于特定的人。因此，这类行为一般不能构成发盘，而仅能视为发盘邀请。但是，如果广告内容十分具体、明确和肯定，在一定事实情况下，也可能构成一项发盘，一旦见到广告的人做出接受的行为，该刊登广告者即须按广告中所提出的条件，履行其诺言。至于向国外众多客商大量寄发商品目录、价目表等宣传商品，谨慎的出口商往往在宣传品上注明"所列价格仅供参考"，"价格需经确认为准"或"价格可不经事先通知而予以变动"等，以免因市价上涨而收件人要求按宣传品上所列价格订约，使自己处于被动的境地，或由此造成经济损失。

An offer must be addressed to one or more specific persons. According to Article 14 (2) of CISG, a proposal other than one addressed to one or more specific persons is to be considered merely as an invitation to make offers, unless the contrary is clearly indicated by the person making the proposal. The term "specific person" refers to the offeree whose name, being either an individual's name or a company's name, is stated in the offer. The purpose of this provision is to distinguish between making offers to specific objects and actions such as advertising in newspapers, mailing commodity catalogs, price lists, and other promotional materials to foreign merchants. In the latter case, the target audience of the advertisement is the general public, and the commodity catalogs, price lists, and promotional materials are generally sent to a large number of merchants. None of them are specific persons. Therefore, such actions generally do not constitute an offer, but rather should be considered as an invitation to make offers. However, if the content of the advertisement is specific, clear, and definite, under certain factual circumstances, it may also constitute an offer. Once a person who sees the advertisement performs an act of acceptance, the advertiser must fulfill the promises stated in the advertisement according to the conditions proposed. As for sending commodity catalogs, price lists, and other promotional materials to a large number of foreign merchants, cautious exporters often include disclaimers in the promotional materials such as "prices listed are for reference only", "prices are subject to confirmation", or "prices are subject to change without prior notice". This is to prevent the exporter from suffering financial losses and being caught in a disadvantageous situation where the recipients of the promotional materials require the contract to be concluded based on the prices listed despite fluctuations in the market price.

（2）发盘的内容必须十分确定。

(2) The content of the offer must be sufficiently definite.

按《公约》规定，一项订立合同的建议"如果写明货物，并且明示或暗示地规定数量和价格或如何确定数量和价格，即为十分确定"。按此规定，一项订约建议只要列明货物、数量和价格三项条件，即可构成一项有效发盘。如该发盘为受盘人接受，即可成立合同。但为了防止误解和可能发生的争议，在外贸实践中，我国外贸企业在对外发盘时，应明示或暗示的交易条件主要有六项：货物的品质（质量）、数量、包装、价格、交货和支付条件。此外，发盘中的交易条件不可含糊、模棱两可，不能使用诸如"大约""左右""参考价"等字眼。

According to CISG, "for the proposal to be sufficiently definite, it must indicate the goods and expressly or implicitly fix or make provision for determining the quantity and the price". Under this provision, a proposal for concluding a contract constitutes a valid offer if it sets out the goods, quantity, and price. If the offer is accepted by the offeree, a contract can be concluded. However, in order to prevent misunderstandings and potential disputes, in foreign trade practice, Chinese foreign trade enterprises should explicitly or implicitly specify at least six main terms and conditions when making offers to foreign parties, including the quality, quantity, packing, price, delivery, and payment terms of the goods. In addition, the terms and conditions stated in an offer must be clear and unambiguous, avoiding using vague terms such as "approximately," "around," or "reference price".

（3）发盘必须表明订约意旨。

(3) An offer must indicate the intention to conclude a contract.

一项发盘必须表明订约意旨，即表明在发盘被接受时承受约束的意旨。换言之，发盘中的交易条件是终局性的，一旦被受盘人接受，合同就此达成。如果一方当事人在他所提出的售货或购货的建议中未表明在被接受时承受约束的意旨，或者附有保留或限制性的条件，如"经确认为准""以未售出为准""以我方认可样品为准""以领得许可证为准"等，则该项建议就不能构成发盘，而仅应被视为邀请做出发盘。

It means the offer must indicate the intention of the offeror to be bound in case of acceptance. In other words, the terms and conditions in the offer are final, and once they are accepted by the offeree, the contract is considered concluded. If a party concerned does not indicate in its proposal for sale or purchase the intention to be bound in case of acceptance, or includes ambiguous or restrictive conditions such as "subject to confirmation", "subject to availability", "subject to our approved sample", and "subject to the permit obtained", then such a proposal cannot constitute an offer but rather should be regarded as an invitation to make offers.

（4）发盘必须传达到受盘人。

(4) An offer must reach the offeree.

《公约》和我国法律都要求，发盘无论是口头的还是书面的，只有被传达到受盘人时才生效。例如，发盘人用信件或电报发盘，如该信件或电报因错误投递或在传递途中遗失，以致受盘人没有收到，则该发盘无效。

Both CISG and China's law require that an offer, whether oral or written, becomes effective only when it reaches the offeree. For example, if an offeror sends an offer through a letter or telegram, and if that letter or telegram is misdelivered or lost during transmission, resulting in the offeree not receiving it, then that offer will be considered invalid.

2. 发盘的有效期 (Validity Time of an Offer)

在国际贸易的交易磋商中，有效的发盘一般都有有效期。发盘的有效期（validity time）是指可供受盘人对发盘做出接受的时间或期限。这一含义有两层意思：一是发盘人在发盘有效期内受约束，即如果受盘人在有效期内将接受通知送达发盘人，发盘人承担按发盘条件与之订立合同的责任；另一层意思是指超过有效期，发盘人将不再受约束。因此，发盘的有效期，既是对发盘人的一种限制，也是对发盘人的一种保障。

In international business negotiations, a valid offer generally has validity time. The validity time of an offer refers to the time or period within which the offeree is able to accept the offer. This has two implications: First, the offeror is bound by the offer during its validity time. If the offeree dispatches a notice of acceptance to the offeror within the validity time, the offeror is obligated to enter into a contract with the offeree on the terms and conditions of the offer. Second, once the validity time expires, the offeror is no longer bound by the offer. Therefore, the validity time of an offer serves as both a limitation and a safeguard for the offeror.

发盘人对发盘有效期可做明确的规定，也可不做明确的规定。明确规定有效期并不是构成发盘的必要条件，不明确规定有效期的发盘，按法律在"合理时间"内有效。何谓"合理时间"，需视交易的具体情况而定，一般按惯例处理。根据《公约》规定，采用口头发盘时，除非发盘人发盘时另有声明外，受盘人只能当场表示接受，方为有效。

The offeror may or may not explicitly specify the validity time of an offer. Explicitly specifying the validity time is not a requirement for constituting an offer. If the offeror does not explicitly specify the validity time, then the offer is considered valid for a "reasonable period of time" as determined by law. The length of the "reasonable period of time" depends on the specific transaction and is generally determined according to customs. According to CISG, an oral offer must be accepted immediately unless the circumstances indicate otherwise.

采用函电发盘时，常见的明确规定有效期的方法主要有以下两种：一是规定最迟接受的期限，如"限某年某月某日复到此地"；二是规定一段接受的期限，如"此发盘的有效期为5天"。规定一段接受的期限，需明确发盘有效期计算的起讫问题。《公约》第二十条规定：发盘人在电报或信件内规定的接受期间，以信上载明的发信日期起算；如信上未载明发信日期，则从发盘送达受盘人时起算。如接受期限的最后一天是发盘人营业地的正式假日或非营业日，则应顺延至下一个营业日。

When making an offer through a telegram or telex, there are two common methods for explicitly specifying the validity time: stipulating a deadline for acceptance, such as "send a reply to this address no later than MM/DD/YY"; or specifying a period of time for acceptance, such as "the validity time of this offer is 5 days". When specifying a period of time for acceptance, it is necessary to clarify the starting and ending points for calculating the validity time of the offer. According to Article 20 of CISG, the period of acceptance specified by the offeror in the telegram or letter begins to run from the date shown on the letter or, if no such date is shown, from the moment that the offer reaches the offeree. If the last day of the acceptance period falls on an official holiday or a non-business day at the place of business of the offeror, the period is extended until the first business day which follows.

3. 发盘生效的时间 (Effective Time of an Offer)

发盘生效的时间有不同的情况：以口头方式做出的发盘，其法律效力自对方了解发盘内容时生效。以书面形式做出的发盘，关于其生效时间，主要有两种不同的观点与做法。一是发信主义，又称投邮主义，即认为发盘人将发盘发出的同时，发盘就生效；另一种是受信主义，又称到达主义，即认为发盘必须到达受盘人时才生效。《公约》和《中华人民共和国合同法》（以下简称《合同法》）都是采用到达主义。

The effective time of an offer varies depending on the circumstances. In the case of an offer made verbally, it becomes effective when the offeree is aware of the content of the offer. For offers made in written form, there are two different viewpoints and practices regarding their effective time. One is the Mailbox Rule, which holds that an offer becomes effective as soon as it is dispatched by the offeror. Another is the Arrival Rule, which asserts that an offer becomes effective only when it reaches the offeree. Both CISG and the Contract Law of the People's Republic of China are governed by the Arrival Rule.

4. 发盘的撤回和撤销（Withdrawal and Revocation of an Offer）

发盘的撤回与撤销是两个不同的概念。前者是在发盘送达受盘人之前将其撤回，以阻止其生效；后者是指发盘已送达受盘人，即发盘生效后将发盘取消，使其失去效力。

The withdrawal and revocation of an offer mean two different things. The former refers to retracting an offer before it reaches the offeree in order to stop it from taking effect. The latter, on the other hand, is to invalidate an offer that has reached the offeree.

发盘的撤回（withdrawal）是指发盘人将尚未被受盘人收到的发盘予以取消的行为。按照《公约》第十五条第二款规定："一项发盘，即使是不可撤销的，得予撤回，如果撤回通知于发盘送达被发盘人之前或同时，送达被发盘人。"这一规定是基于发盘到达受盘人之前对发盘人未产生约束力，所以发盘人可以将其撤回。可见，"撤回"的实质是阻止发盘生效。

The withdrawal of an offer refers to the act of canceling an offer before it reaches the offeree. According to Article 15 (2) of CISG, "An offer, even if it is irrevocable, may be withdrawn if the withdrawal reaches the offeree before or at the same time as the offer." This provision is based on the fact that the offeror is not bound before the offer reaches the offeree and is thus entitled to withdraw the offer. It can be seen that the essence of "withdrawal" is to prevent the offer from becoming effective.

在业务实践中，发盘人如果发现发盘中内容有误或市场情况有变，可争取在发盘到达受盘人之前，立即以更快速的通信方式撤回该项发盘。需要注意的是，第一，现代通信方式快捷无比，电传、传真、电子邮件等，在发出的同时对方已收到，已没有余地撤回。因此，发盘人发盘之前要研究妥当，以免到时无法撤回，产生麻烦。第二，发盘人应估计到有时撤回通知未能如愿在发盘送达受盘人之前或同时送达受盘人，此时该发盘已生效，对发盘人已产生约束力，如果取消该发盘，就不是撤回的问题。

In practical business operations, if the offeror discovers any errors in the content of the offer or if there are changes in the market conditions, the offeror may endeavor to withdraw the offer immediately using a faster mode of communication before it reaches the offeree. There are two things to be noted: First, modern communication methods, such as telex, fax, and email, are incredibly fast, and once they are sent, the other party receives them almost instantly, leaving no room for withdrawal. Therefore, it is necessary to carefully study the offer before sending it, so as to avoid trouble arising from failure in withdrawal. Second, it should be anticipated that there may be occasions when the withdrawal fails to reach the offeree before or at the same time as the offer. In such cases, the offer has already become effective and the offeror is bound by it, and then the cancellation of the offer is not a matter of withdrawal.

发盘的撤销（revocation）是指发盘人将已经为受盘人收到的发盘予以取消的行为。《公约》第十六条规定："在未订立合同之前，发盘得予撤销，如果撤销通知在受盘人发出接受通知之前送达受盘人。但在下列情况下发盘不得撤销：(a)发盘表明接受期限，或以其他方式表示发盘是不可撤销的；(b)受盘人有理由信赖该发盘是不可撤销的，并且已本着对该项发盘的信赖行事。"

The revocation of an offer refers to the act of canceling an offer after it reaches the offeree. According to Article 16 of CISG, "Until a contract is concluded an offer may be revoked if the revocation reaches the offeree before he has dispatched an acceptance. However, an offer cannot be revoked: (a) if it indicates, whether by stating a fixed time for acceptance or otherwise, that it is irrevocable; or (b) if it was reasonable for the offeree to rely on the offer as being irrevocable and the offeree has acted in reliance on the offer."

上述规定表明，发盘在一定条件下可以撤销，而在有些情况下不可撤销。可以撤销的条件是在受盘人发出接受通知之前将撤销通知传达到受盘人。而一旦受盘人发出接受通知，则发盘人无权撤销该发盘。发盘不可撤销的情况有：一是发盘规定了有效期，在有效期内不能撤销，如果没有明确规定有效期，但以其他方式表示发盘不可撤销，如在发盘中使用了"此发盘不可撤销""在未获贵公司答复前不另向其他人发盘"等字样，那么在合理时间内该项发盘不能撤销；二是受盘人有理由信赖该发盘是不可撤销的，并采取了一定的行动，如受盘人曾发出询盘，称某工程需要某设备，在收到发盘后，本着对该发盘的信赖，与该工程联系洽谈，那么这项发盘就不能撤销。

The aforementioned provision indicates that an offer can be revoked under certain conditions, while in some situations, it is irrevocable. An offer can be revoked under the condition that the revocation reaches the offeree before he has dispatched an acceptance. However, once the offeree has dispatched an acceptance, the offeror does not have the right to revoke the offer. An offer cannot be revoked in the following situations: First, the offer specifies a validity time during which it cannot be revoked, or if there is no such a validity time, the offer indicates that it is irrevocable by other means such as using phrases like "this offer is irrevocable" or "no other offers will be made until we receive a response from your company", in which case the offer cannot be revoked within a reasonable time. Second, it was reasonable for the offeree to rely on the offer as being irrevocable and the offeree has acted in reliance on the offer. For example, if the offeree has made an inquiry stating that particular equipment is required for a certain project, and after receiving the offer, he has initiated negotiations in reliance on the offer, then the offer cannot be revoked.

5. 发盘的失效 (Invalidation of an Offer)

发盘的失效（invalidation）是指发盘失去法律效力，它有两方面的含义：一是发盘人不再受发盘的约束；二是受盘人失去了接受该发盘的权利。《公约》第十七条规定："一项发盘，即使是不可撤销的，于拒绝通知送达发盘人时终止。"这就是说，当受盘人不接受发盘的内容，并将拒绝的通知送到发盘人手中时，即使发盘的有效期尚未届满，原发盘也失去效力，发盘人不再受其约束。除了明确拒绝发盘会导致发盘失效，还盘也会使发盘失效。根据《公约》第十九条第一款规定："对发盘表示接受但载有添加、限制或其他更改的答复，即为拒绝该项发盘，并构成还盘。"据此，有条件的接受属于还盘，还盘是对原发盘的拒绝，原发盘即失效。如果受盘人拒绝发盘后又反悔，重新表示接受，即使发盘的有效期尚未届满，合同也不能成立，除非原发盘人对该"接受"（实际是原受盘人做出的一项新发盘）予以确认。

The invalidation of an offer refers to the loss of legal effect of the offer. Its significance lies in two aspects: First, the offeror is no longer bound by the offer; second, the offeree loses the right to accept the offer. According to Article 17 of CISG, "An offer, even if it is irrevocable, is terminated when a rejection reaches the offeror." That is, when the offeree does not accept the content of the offer and dispatches a rejection to the offeror, the original offer loses its effect and the offeror is no longer bound by it even if the validity time has not expired. In addition to explicit rejection of an offer, a counter-offer will also result in the invalidation of the offer. According to Article 19 (1) of CISG, "A reply to an offer which purports to be an acceptance but contains additions, limitations or other modifications is a rejection of the offer and constitutes a counteroffer." Based on this, a conditional acceptance is considered a counter-offer, which is a rejection of the original offer and invalidates the original offer. If the offeree rejects an offer and later changes his mind, re-expressing the intention of acceptance, even if the validity time of the original offer has not expired, a contract cannot be established unless the original offeror confirms this "acceptance" (which is essentially a new offer made by the original offeree).

此外，在业务实践中还有以下几种情况造成发盘失效：①受盘人拒绝发盘或做出还盘；

②发盘人依法撤销发盘；③发盘规定的有效期届满；④人力不可抗拒事件造成发盘的失效，如发盘后，发盘人的工厂厂房和仓库在地震中被毁，无法提供发盘中的商品；⑤在发盘被接受前，当事人丧失行为能力（如自然人死亡、法人破产等）。

In addition, in business practice, there are several situations that can cause an offer to become invalid: ① The offeree rejects the offer or makes a counter-offer; ② The offeror revokes the offer in accordance with the law; ③ The validity time specified in the offer has expired; ④ The offer becomes invalid due to an event of force majeure, such as if the offeror's factory and warehouse are destroyed in an earthquake, making it impossible to provide the commodities mentioned in the offer; ⑤ One or both parties lose legal capacity before the offer is accepted, such as the death of a natural person or the bankruptcy of a legal entity.

6. 发盘的注意事项（Precautions for Offers）

（1）对外发盘应该符合国际公约和国内外法律的相关规定。

(1) When making an offer, one should comply with the relevant provisions of international conventions and domestic and foreign laws.

（2）要正确理解和掌握发盘的有效期。

(2) One should properly understand and grasp the validity time of an offer.

（3）发盘要慎重，不能盲目对外发盘。

(3) An offer must be made with caution.

（4）要学习和掌握发盘的技巧和策略。

(4) One should learn and master the skills and strategies of making an offer.

（5）学会判断发盘的有效性，即判断发盘是实盘还是虚盘。

(5) One should learn to determine the effectiveness of an offer.

（6）贸易实践中，常用报价单、价目表和形式发票进行发盘。其中，价目表除买卖双方另有规定外，一般不具有约束力。

In trade practice, offers are commonly made in such forms as quotation sheets, price lists, and proforma invoices. Among them, price lists are generally not binding unless otherwise specified by the buyer and the seller.

（三）还盘 (Counter-offer)

还盘，又称还价，在法律上称为反要约，是指受盘人不同意或不完全同意发盘提出的各项条件，对发盘提出修改意见发送原发盘人的行为。

A counter-offer refers to the act of the offeree rejecting or partially accepting the terms and conditions of the offer and proposing modifications to the offer, which is then sent back to the original offeror.

1. 还盘的法律意义（Legal Significance of Counter-offers）

还盘是对原发盘的拒绝，也是受盘人向原发盘人提出的一项新的发盘。在交易磋商中，一经还盘，原发盘即失去效力，发盘人不再受其约束，即使在发盘的有效期内，对发盘人也不再具有法律上的约束力。《公约》第十九条第一款规定："对发盘表示接受但载有添加、限制或其他更改的答复，即为拒绝该项发盘，并构成还盘。"

A counter-offer is both a rejection of the original offer and a new offer made by the offeree to the original offeror. In business negotiations, once a counter-offer is made, the original offer loses its validity, and the offeror is no longer bound by the original offer even if it is still within the validity time. According to Article 19 (1) of CISG, "A reply to an offer which purports to be an acceptance but contains additions, limitations or other modifications is a rejection of the offer and constitutes a counteroffer."

2. 还盘的判定标准 (Criteria for Determining a Counter-offer)

还盘可以明确使用"counter-offer"字样，也可以不使用，只是在内容中表示对发盘的修改。《公约》第十九条第三款规定，对"有关货物的价格、付款、货物质量和数量、交货地点和时间、一方当事人对另一方当事人的赔偿责任范围或解决争端等等的添加或不同条件，均视为在实质上变更发盘的条件"，属于还盘。不属于这些实质上变更原发盘的条件之外的其他情况，除发盘人在不过分迟延的时间内以口头或书面通知表示反对外，不算还盘，仍构成接受，合同的条件就以原发盘的条件以及接受通知内所载的更改为准。

A counter-offer may be explicitly indicated using the term "counter-offer", or it may express the modifications to the original offer within its content. According to Article 19 (3) of CISG, "Additional or different terms relating, among other things, to the price, payment, quality and quantity of the goods, place and time of delivery, extent of one party's liability to the other or the settlement of disputes are considered to alter the terms of the offer materially," which is deemed a counter-offer. Other situations where the terms of the offer are not materially altered still constitute an acceptance, unless the offeror objects orally or in writing without undue delay. If he does not so object, the terms of the contract are the terms of the original offer and the modifications contained in the acceptance.

3. 还盘的注意事项 (Precautions for Counter-offers)

（1）要识别还盘的形式，有的明确使用"还盘"字样，有的则不使用。

(1) It is important to recognize a counter-offer, which may or may not be explicitly indicated using the term "counter-offer".

（2）接到还盘后，要与原还盘进行核对，找出还盘中提出的新内容，然后结合市场变化情况和销售意图，认真予以区别对待。

(2) Upon receiving a counter-offer, one should compare it with the original offer, identify any new content proposed, and carefully differentiate and consider the counter-offer in light of market changes and sales intentions.

（3）还盘是对原还盘的拒绝，原还盘人可以就此停止洽商。如果原还盘人继续与受盘人进行还盘或反还盘，一旦达成协议，在履约中发生争议，所有交易洽商全过程的函电或谈判记录即为解决争议的依据。

(3) A counter-offer is a rejection of the original offer, and the original offeror thus has the option to cease the negotiation. If the original offeror continues to engage with the offeree by making further counter-offers, once an agreement is eventually reached, all correspondence and records throughout the business negotiation will serve as the basis for resolving any disputes that may arise during the performance of the contract.

（4）在表示还盘时，一般只针对原还盘提出不同意或需要修改的部分，已同意的内容在还盘中可以省略。

(4) Generally, a counter-offer may only address the parts of the original offer that are disagreed with or need modifications, and the agreed terms can be omitted.

（四）接受 (Acceptance)

接受，在法律上称"承诺"，指受盘人在发盘规定的有效期内或合理时间内，以声明或行动的方式，无条件同意发盘提出的各项条件，并愿意按这些条件同发盘人达成合同的一种意思表示。一项发盘经过受盘人接受后，交易即告达成，合同即告成立。

Acceptance, legally referred to as "assent", means that the offeree, within the validity time or a reasonable time as specified in the offer, unconditionally agrees to all the terms of the offer and expresses the intent to enter into a contract with the offeror based on these terms by means of a statement or other conduct. Once an offer is accepted by the offeree, the transaction is reached, and the contract is established.

1. 构成接受的条件 (Conditions Constituting an Acceptance)

《公约》第十八条第一款对接受做了如下定义:"被发价人声明或做出其他行为表示同意一项发价,即是接受。缄默或不行动本身不等于接受。"根据《公约》的规定,构成一项法律上有效的接受,必须具备四个条件。

According to Article 18 (1) of CISG, "A statement made by or other conduct of the offeree indicating assent to an offer is an acceptance. Silence or inactivity does not in itself amount to acceptance." According to CISG, there are four conditions that must be met to constitute a legally effective acceptance.

(1) 接受必须由特定的受盘人做出。

(1) Acceptance must be made by specific offeree(s).

一项有效的发盘必须是向一个或一个以上特定的人做出的,因此对发盘表示接受,也必须是发盘中所指明的特定的受盘人,而不能是其他人。如果其他人通过某种途径获悉非向他做出的发盘,而向发盘人表示接受,该"接受"只是其他人向原发盘人做出的一项发盘。

An effective offer must be made to one or more specific persons. Therefore, acceptance of the offer must also be made by the specific offeree(s) mentioned in the offer, and not by any other person. If someone else learns of an offer that was not made to him and indicates an acceptance to the offeror, that "acceptance" will be considered an offer made by that person to the original offeror.

(2) 接受必须表示出来。

(2) Acceptance must be indicated.

接受必须由受盘人以某种方式向发盘人表示出来。如果受盘人在思想上愿意接受对方的发盘,但默不作声或不做出任何其他行动表示其对发盘的同意,那么,在法律上并不存在接受。按《公约》的规定,受盘人表示接受的方式有两种:①用"声明"(statement)做出表示。即受盘人用口头或书面形式向发盘人表示同意发盘。这是国际贸易中最常用的表示方法,如受盘人用"接受"或"同意"即可明确地表达受盘人同意发盘的意思。②用"做出行为"(performing an act)来表示。《公约》规定,如根据发盘或依照当事人业已确定的习惯做法或惯例,受盘人可以做出某种行为来表示接受,而无须向发盘人发出接受通知。例如,发盘人在发盘中要求"立即装运",受盘人可做出立即发运货物的行为对发盘表示同意,而且这种行为表示的接受,在装运货物时立即生效,合同即告成立,发盘人就应受其约束。但在外贸实践中,一般不建议这样做。我国外贸企业应以书面通知的形式表示对发盘的接受。

Acceptance must be indicated by the offeree to the offeror in some manner. If the offeree mentally intends to accept the offer but remains silent or does not take any other action to indicate their assent to the offer, then legally there is no acceptance. According to CISG, there are two ways for the offeree to indicate an acceptance: ① Statement. That is, the offeree communicated to the offeror orally or in writing, indicating his assent to the offer. This is the most common method of indicating an acceptance in international trade, where the offeree can clearly express his assent to the offer by using words such as "accept" or "assent". ② Performing an act. According to CISG, by virtue of the offer or as a result of practices which the parties have established between themselves or of usage, the offeree may indicate assent by performing an act without notice to the offeror. For example, if the offeror requests "immediate shipment" in the offer, the offeree can indicate their assent to the offer by performing the act of immediately shipping the goods. Such acceptance becomes effective at the moment the act is performed, the contract is established accordingly, and the offeror is bound by the contract. However, in foreign trade practice, it is generally not recommended to proceed do so. Chinese foreign trade enterprises should indicate their acceptance of an offer in written form.

（3）接受必须在发盘的有效期内传达到发盘人。

(3) Acceptance must reach the offeror within the validity time of the offer.

根据法律的一般要求，接受必须在发盘的有效期内被传达到发盘人方能生效。《公约》采用到达生效的原则，对于口头发盘必须立即接受。即表示接受的函电必须在发盘有效期内到达发盘人，接受才生效。如果表示接受的函电，在邮寄途中延误或遗失，合同不能成立，其传递延误或遗失的风险由受盘人承担。

According to the general legal requirements, acceptance must reach the offeror within the validity time of the offer in order to be effective. CISG follows the Arrival Rule, which means an oral offer must be accepted immediately. In other words, the letter or telegram containing acceptance must reach the offeror within the validity time of the offer for it to be effective. If the letter or telegram containing acceptance is delayed or lost during delivery, the contract cannot be established, and the risk of such delay or loss is borne by the offeree.

（4）接受必须与发盘相符。

(4) Acceptance must be consistent with the offer.

如要达成交易，成立合同，根据传统的法律规则，受盘人必须无条件地、全部同意发盘的条件。因此，若对发盘表示接受但附有添加、限制或其他更改的答复，即为拒绝该项发盘，并构成还盘。

In order to reach an agreement and establish a contract, according to traditional legal rules, the offeree must fully and unconditionally accept all the terms of the offer. Therefore, a reply to an offer which purports to be an acceptance but contains additions, limitations or other modifications is a rejection of the offer and constitutes a counter-offer.

但是，在国际贸易的实际业务中，受盘人在表示接受时，往往对发盘做出某些添加、限制或其他更改。《公约》将接受中对发盘的条件所做的变更分为：实质性变更（对货物的价格、付款、质量和数量、交货地点和时间、赔偿责任范围或解决争端等的添加、限制或更改，有的国家的法律还包括对包装条件的变更）和非实质性变更（如要求提供重量单、装箱单、商检证和产地证等单据、关于分批装运、刷制指定的唛头等）。表示接受但含有实质性变更，无疑构成还盘。发盘人对此不予确认，合同不能成立。对于含有非实质性变更的接受，除发盘人及时向受盘人表示反对其间差异外，仍构成接受，合同得以成立，并且合同的条件以该项发盘的条件以及在接受中所载的变更为准。

However, in the practical business of international trade, the offeree often makes certain additions, limitations or other modifications to the offer when indicating an acceptance. CISG categorizes alterations to the terms of an offer contained in an acceptance as material alterations (such as additions, limitations or modifications related to the price, payment, quality and quantity of the goods, place and time of delivery, extent of one party's liability to the other or the settlement of disputes; in some countries, these also include changes in packing conditions) and non-material alterations (such as requesting weight lists, packing lists, inspection certificates, and certificates of origin, or specifying partial shipments or specific markings). A reply to an offer which purports to be an acceptance but contains content that materially alters the terms of the offer constitutes a counter-offer. Unless the offeror confirms this acceptance, the contract is not established. A reply to an offer which purports to be an acceptance but contains content that does not materially alter the terms of the offer, unless the offeror timely objects to the discrepancy and communicate this objection to the offeree, still constitutes an acceptance and the contract is established. The terms of the contract are the terms of the original offer and the modifications contained in the acceptance.

2. 逾期接受 (Late Acceptance)

如果接受通知超过发盘规定的有效期限，或发盘未具体规定有效期限而超过合理时间才传达到发盘人，这就构成一项逾期接受（late acceptance），或称迟到的接受。逾期接受在一般情况下无效。但是，按《公约》规定，如果发盘人于收到逾期接受后，毫不延迟地通知受盘人，确认其为有效，则该逾期接受仍有接受的效力。另一种情况是，一项逾期接受，从它使用的信件或其他书面文件表明，在传递正常的情况下，本能及时送达发盘人，由于出现传递不正常的情况而造成了延误，这种逾期接受仍可被认为是有效的，除非发盘人毫不延迟地用口头或书面形式通知受盘人，他认为他的发盘已经失效。

If an acceptance is dispatched after expiration of the validity time specified in the offer, or, if the offer does not explicitly specify a validity time, the acceptance reaches the offeror beyond a reasonable period of time, it constitutes a late acceptance. A late acceptance is generally not effective. However, according to CISG, a late acceptance is nevertheless effective as an acceptance if without delay the offeror orally so informs the offeree or dispatches a notice to that effect. Alternatively, if a letter or other writing containing a late acceptance shows that it has been sent in such circumstances that if its transmission had been normal it would have reached the offeror in due time, the late acceptance is effective as an acceptance unless, without delay, the offeror orally informs the offeree that he considers his offer as having lapsed or dispatches a notice to that effect.

3. 接受的撤回 (Withdrawal of Acceptance)

接受于表示同意的通知送达发盘人时生效。因此在接受通知送达发盘人之前，受盘人可随时撤回接受，即阻止接受生效，但以撤回通知先于接受或与接受通知同时到达发盘人为限。

An acceptance of an offer becomes effective at the moment the indication of assent reaches the offeror. Therefore, before the notice of acceptance reaches the offeror, the offeree can withdraw the acceptance at any time to prevent it from taking effect. However, the withdrawal must reach the offeror before or at the same tine as the acceptance.

如接受已经送达发盘人，则接受一旦生效，合同即告成立，就不能再撤回或修改其内容，因为这样做无异于撤销或修改合同，所以接受是不能撤销的。

If the acceptance has reached the offeror and become effective, the contract is considered established. In this case, the acceptance cannot be revoked or modified, or it would be deemed as revoking or modifying the contract.

4. 接受的注意事项 (Precautions for Acceptance)

（1）进口方表示接受时，应注意以下几个问题。

(1) The importer should pay attention to the following matters regarding the indication of an acceptance.

①在表示接受时应该慎重地对洽商的函电或谈判记录进行认真核对，经核对认为对方提出的各项主要交易条件已明确、完整、无保留条件和肯定时，才能表示接受。

①When indicating an acceptance, the exporter should carefully review the correspondence or negotiation records with the other party. Upon careful review, if it is determined that all the main terms and conditions proposed by the other party are clear, complete, without any reservations, and affirmative, then an acceptance can be made.

②表示接受应在对方报价规定的有效期之内进行，并应严格遵守有关时间的计算规定。

②Acceptance should be indicated within the validity time specified by the other party's offer, and it should strictly adhere to the relevant rules for calculating time.

③在表示接受之前，应该详细分析对方的报价，准确识别是发价还是询价。如果将对方

的询价误认为发价表示接受，可能暴露己方接受的底价和条件，使己方处于被动地位；如果将对方的发价误认为询价，可能误失成交良机。

③Before indicating an acceptance, it is important to carefully analyze the other party's offer and identify whether it is a firm offer or a mere inquiry. Mistaking the other party's inquiry as a firm offer and indicating an acceptance may expose the exporter's bottom price and conditions, putting the exporter in a disadvantageous position. Conversely, mistaking the other party's firm offer as an inquiry may result in missing out on a favorable business opportunity.

（2）出口方表示接受时，应注意以下几个问题。

(2) The exporter should pay attention to the following matters regarding the indication of an acceptance.

①要认真分析客户表示的接受是一项有效的接受，还是一项有条件的接受（还盘）。

①The importer should carefully analyze whether the acceptance indicated by a client is an effective acceptance or a conditional acceptance (a counter-offer).

②在对待客户的接受时，要坚持"重合同、守信用"的原则。如果发生出口货物价格上涨或支付货币汇率下浮等对我方不利的情况，我方仍应同客户达成交易，订立合同，维护己方公司的信誉。

②When dealing with clients' acceptances, it is important to adhere to the principle of "respect contracts and maintain credibility". In the case of an unfavorable circumstance such as an increase in the export price or a decrease in the currency exchange rate, the importer should still proceed with the transaction and enter into a contract with the client to uphold the company's reputation.

③在客户接受我方发盘时，对一些非重要条件或者是轻微的改动，按照国际贸易惯例，应视为有效的接受，但发盘人有权拒绝此项轻微改动的要求。如发价人并未及时提出反对其间的差异，则不影响对方接受的有效性，仍然有订立合同的义务。

③If a client accepts an offer with additional non-essential conditions or minor modifications, it constitutes an effective acceptance according to international trade customs. However, the offeror has the right to refuse such minor modifications. If the offeror does not object to the discrepancy in a timely manner, it does not affect the effectiveness of the other party's acceptance, and the offeror is still obliged to enter into a contract.

第二节　签订合同
Section 2　Contract Signing

买卖双方经过磋商，一方的发盘被另一方有效接受，交易即告达成，合同即告成立。但在实际业务中，买卖双方达成协议后，通常还要制作书面合同将各自的权利与义务以书面的形式加以明确，这就是合同的签订。

After negotiations between the buyer and the seller, if one party's offer is effectively accepted by the other party, the transaction is concluded and the contract is established. However, in actual business operations, after reaching an agreement, it is customary for the buyer and the seller to create a written contract that clearly outlines their respective rights and obligations. This process is known as contract signing.

一、合同有效成立的条件
I. Conditions for Valid Establishment of the Contract

国际货物买卖合同（contract for international sale of goods）是营业地在不同国家（地区）

的当事人之间为买卖一定货物所达成的协议。国际货物买卖合同以营业地为标准来判定合同的国际性。依法成立的合同具有法律约束力，合同自成立时生效。根据各国合同法的规定，一项合同还需具备以下条件，才是一项有效的合同，才能得到法律的保护。

A contract for international sale of goods is an agreement reached between parties with their places of business in different countries (regions) for the sale of specific goods. The international nature of the contract is determined based on the places of business of the parties involved. The contract established in accordance with the law is legally binding and becomes effective from the moment of its formation. According to the provisions of contract laws in various countries, a contract must meet the following conditions to be considered effective and entitled to legal protection.

（一）当事人必须在自愿和真实的基础上达成协议(The Parties Concerned Must Reach an Agreement in Volunteer and True Willingness)

各国法律都认为，签订合同必须是双方自愿的，当事人的意思表示必须是真实的才能构成一项有约束力的合同，否则合同无效。若一方以欺诈、胁迫的手段或者乘人之危，使对方在违背真实意思情况下订立的合同，受害方有权请求人民法院或者仲裁机构变更或者撤销。

Laws in all countries hold that, to constitute a binding contract, both parties concerned should be voluntary and their intentions must be true. Otherwise, the contract would be considered invalid. If one party uses means such as deception or coercion or takes advantage of the other party's difficulties to cause him to conclude or amend a contract contrary to his true intention, the injured party has the right to petition a people's court or an arbitral institution to modify or revoke the contract.

（二）当事人应具备签订合同的行为能力(The Parties Concerned Must Be with the Conduct Capacity to Sign a Contract)

合同双方当事人应具备签订国际货物买卖合同的合法资格，具体要求是：若签订合同的当事人为企业法人，则该企业法人必须是依法注册成立的合法组织，有关业务应当属于其法定经营范围，负责磋商和签约者应为其法定代表人或合法授权人；若签订合同的当事人为自然人，则该自然人必须是精神正常的成年人，神志不清、未成年人等都不具有签订合同的合法资格。

The contracting parties should have the legal qualification to enter into a contract for international sale of goods. The specific requirements are as follows: If the contracting party is a legal entity, it must be a legal organization registered and established in accordance with the law, the business concerned should fall within its authorized scope of operations, and the individuals responsible for negotiations and contract signing should be its legal representatives or authorized persons; if the contracting party is a natural person, he must be a mentally sound adult. Individuals who are not being in their right mind or underage do not possess the legal qualification to enter into a contract.

（三）合同的标的和内容必须合法(The Subject Matter and Content of the Contract Must Be Lawful)

合同的标的是指交易双方买卖的客体。签订合同时，合同的标的和内容必须符合双方国家法律的规定，才是有效的合同。关于"合同内容必须合法"的解释，许多国家法律都规定，合同内容不得违反法律，不得违反公共秩序或公共政策，以及不得违反良好的社会风俗或道德。

The subject matter of a contract refers to the object being bought or sold between the parties involved in the transaction. When signing a contract, the subject matter and content of the contract must comply with the laws and regulations of both parties' respective countries in order to be considered an effective contract. The requirement for a contract to have lawful content is stipulated in many countries' laws, which state that the content of a contract must not violate any legal provisions, public order, or public policy, and should not go against good social customs or morals.

（四）合同必须有对价或约因 (A Contract Must Be with Consideration)

英美法系认为，对价是指当事人为了取得合同利益所付出的代价。大陆法系认为，约因是指当事人签订合同所追求的直接目的。按照英美法系和大陆法系的规定，合同只有在有对价或约因时，才是法律上有效的合同，无对价或无约因的合同，是得不到法律保护的。

In the Anglo-American law system, consideration is the price paid by the parties concerned in order to obtain the benefits of the contract. In the civil law system, consideration refers to the direct purpose pursued by the parties concerned when signing a contract. According to the provisions of Anglo-American law system and civil law system, a contract is legally valid only when there is consideration. A contract without consideration cannot be protected by law.

（五）合同形式必须符合法律规定的要求 (The Form of the Contract Must Comply with Provisions of Law)

世界上大多数国家和地区只对少数合同要求必须按法律规定的特定形式订立，而大多数合同，一般不从法律上规定应当采取的形式。我国《合同法》第十条规定："当事人订立合同，有书面形式、口头形式和其他形式。"

In most countries and regions in the world, only a few contracts are required to be formed in specific legally prescribed forms. For the majority of contracts, there are no specific legal requirements regarding the form that should be followed. According to Article 10 of the Contract Law of the People's Republic of China, "The parties may conclude their contract in writing, orally or in another form."

二、书面形式合同的签订
II. Signing of the Contract in Writing

（一）书面合同的意义 (Significance of Written Contracts)

在国际贸易中，买卖双方最好能签订书面形式的合同，书面合同具有以下意义。

In international trade, it is best for both the buyer and the seller to sign a contract in writing. The significance of written contracts are reflected in the following aspects.

1. 书面合同是合同成立的证据 (A Written Contract Is the Evidence of the Formation of the Contract)

根据法律的要求，凡是合同必须能得到证明，提供证据，包括人证和物证。在用信函或函电磋商时，往来函电就是证明。口头合同成立后，如不用一定的书面形式加以确定，那么它将由于不能被证明而不能得到法律的保障，甚至在法律上成为无效。

As required by law, all contracts must be provable and supported by evidence, including human evidence and physical evidence. When negotiations are conducted by letter or telegram, the letters and telegrams exchanged are evidence. After an oral contract is established, if it is not confirmed in written form, it will lack legal protection and even become invalid in law because it cannot be proven.

2. 书面合同是合同生效的条件 (A Written Contract Is a Condition for the Contract to Become Effective)

一般情况下，合同的成立是以接受的生效为条件的。但在有些情况下，签订书面合同却成为合同生效的条件。我国《合同法》第十条规定："法律、行政法规规定采用书面形式的，应当采用书面形式。当事人约定采用书面形式的，应当采用书面形式。"

In general, the formation of a contract is conditional on the acceptance taking effect. However, in some cases, signing a written contract becomes a condition for the contract to become effective. According to Article 10 of the Contract Law of the People's Republic of China, "The written form shall be adopted if laws or administrative regulations so require. The written form shall be adopted if the parties so agree."

3. 书面合同是合同履行的依据 (A Written Contract Is the Basis for Contract Performance)

国际货物买卖合同的履行涉及很多部门，如以分散的函电为依据，将给履行合同造成很多不便。所以买卖双方不论通过口头，还是信函、函电磋商在达成交易后将谈定的完整的交易条件，全面清楚地列明在一个书面文件上，对进一步明确双方的权利和义务，以及为合同的履行提供更好的依据，具有重要意义。

The performance of a contract for international sale of goods involves many sectors. Taking scattered letters and telegrams as the basis can cause great inconvenience to contract performance. Therefore, regardless of whether the buyer and the seller have negotiated orally or through letters and telegrams, they should clearly specify all the agreed terms in a written document after reaching a transaction. This is of great significance to the further clarification of both parties' rights and obligations and provision of a better basis for the performance of the contract.

（二）书面合同的形式 (Forms of Written Contracts)

在国际贸易中，买卖双方签订的书面合同可采用合同、确认书、协议、备忘录等形式。在中国的进出口业务中，书面合同主要采用以下两种形式。

In international trade, the written contract entered into by the buyer and the seller can take various forms, such as a contract, confirmation letter, agreement, memorandum, and so on. In China's import and export business, written contracts mainly take the following two forms.

1. 合同 (Contract)

合同或称正式合同，其内容比较全面详细，除了包括交易的主要条件如品名、规格、数量、包装、价格、装运、支付、保险外，还包括商检、异议索赔、仲裁和不可抗力等一般条款。出口商拟定提出的合同称为销售合同（sales contract），进口商拟定提出的合同称为购货合同（purchase contract），使用的文字是第三人称的语气。这种合同形式的特点是内容比较全面，对双方的权利和义务以及发生争议的处理均有详细规定，适合于大宗货物或成交金额较大的交易。

A contract, or a formal contract, is more comprehensive and elaborate. In addition to the main terms and conditions such as the commodity name, specification, quantity, packing, price, shipment, payment, and insurance, it also includes general clauses regarding inspection, discrepancy and claim, arbitration, and force majeure. The contract proposed by an exporter is called as a sales contract, while that proposed by an importer is called a purchase contract. Both are drafted using the third-person perspective. The characteristic of this contract form is that it contains comprehensive provisions regarding the rights, obligations of both parties, and the resolution of disputes. It is suitable for the trading of bulk commodities or high-value transactions.

2. 成交确认书 (Confirmation)

成交确认书是合同的简化形式，其内容一般包括货物名称、品质规格、数量、包装、单价、总值、交货期、装运港和目的港、支付方式、运输标志、商品检验等条款，对于异议索赔、仲裁、不可抗力等一般条款都不予列入。成交确认书也可分为售货确认书（sales confirmation）和购货确认书（purchase confirmation）两种。无论是合同还是成交确认书在法律上具有同等的效力。成交确认书一般适用于成交金额不大、批次较多的轻工日用品、土特产品或者已有包销、代理等长期协议的交易。

A confirmation is a simplified form of a contract. It generally includes clauses related to the commodity name, quality, specification, quantity, packing, unit price, total amount, time of delivery, port of shipment, port of destination, payment method, shipping mark, and commodity inspection. However, it excludes clauses regarding discrepancy and claim, arbitration, force majeure, and other general terms. Confirmations can also be divided into sales confirmations and purchase confirmations. Both contracts and confirmations have equal legal validity. Confirmation generally suitable for transactions of light industry daily necessities and local specialties with small transaction amount and many batches, or transactions that already have long-term agreements such as bought deals and agency.

在我国进出口业务中，一般均由我方根据双方约定的条件制成一式两份的正式合同或成交确认书，先由我方签字，再寄给对方。对方审核无误签字后，保留其中一份，将另一份寄还给我方。若对方在寄回的正式合同或成交确认书上更改或附加条款，并与原本达成的协议内容有冲突时，我方应及时加以拒绝。

In China's import and export business, it is common practice for the Chinese party to create two copies of a formal contract or confirmation based on the agreed conditions, which will be signed by the Chinese party and then sent to the other party. After the other party reviews and signs the contract or confirmation, they keep one copy for themselves and send the other copy back to the Chinese party. If the other party makes changes or adds clauses to the returned contract or confirmation that conflict with the original agreement, the Chinese party should promptly refuse to accept them.

（三）书面合同的内容 (Content of Written Contracts)

书面合同的内容一般由三个部分组成。国际货物销售合同的书面合同样本可参考合同样本 2.1。

The content of a written contract generally consists of three parts. Refer to Contract Sample 2.1 for the sample of the written contract for international sale of goods.

1. 约首 (Preamble)

约首是合同的首部，包括合同的名称、合同号码、订约日期、订约地点、买卖双方的名称和地址以及序言等内容。序言主要是写明双方订立合同的意义和执行合同的保证，对双方都有约束力等。双方的名称应用全称，不能用简称，地址要详细列明，因涉及法律管辖权问题，所以不能随便填写。在我国出口业务中，除在国外签订的合同外，一般都是以我出口公司所在地为签约地址。

The preamble is the first part of a contract, including the name of the contract, contract number, date of execution, place of execution, names and addresses of the buyer and the seller, as well as the foreword. The preamble primarily clarifies the significance of the contract being entered into by both parties and provides assurance regarding the execution of the contract. It is binding on both parties. The full names, instead of short names, of both parties should be used. The addresses should be clearly specified, as it relates to issues of legal jurisdiction. In China's export business, except for contracts signed abroad, the signing address is generally the location of the export company.

2. 正文 (Body)

正文是合同的主体部分，规定了双方的权利和义务，包括合同的各项交易条款，如商品名称、品质规格、数量包装、单价和总值、交货期限、支付条款、保险、检验、索赔、不可抗力和仲裁条款等，以及根据不同商品和不同的交易情况加列的其他条款，如保值条款、溢短装条款和合同适用的法律等。

The body of the contract sets forth the rights and obligations of both parties. It includes various transaction clauses of the contract, such as the commodity name, quality, specification, quantity, packing, unit price and total amount, time of delivery, payment clause, insurance, inspection, claims, force majeure, and arbitration clause. Additionally, it may contain additional clauses specific to different commodities and transactions, such as the proviso clause and more or less clause, as well as the applicable law of the contract.

3. 约尾 (Witness Clause)

约尾是合同的尾部，包括合同文字的效力、份数、订约的时间和地点及生效的时间、附件的效力以及双方签字等，这也是合同不可缺少的重要组成部分。合同的订约地点往往要涉及合同依据法的问题，因此要慎重对待。我国的出口合同的订约地点一般都写在我国。也有的合同将订约的时间和地点在约首订明。

The witness clause is the final part of a contract, which includes the effectiveness of the contract, the number of copies, the date and place of signing, the effective date, the validity of attachments, and the signatures of both parties. It is also an integral part of the contract. The selection of the place of contract signing often involves issues related to the governing law of the contract, and therefore should be handled with caution. For China's export contacts, the place of contract signing is generally within China. Some contracts include the time and place of contract signing in the preamble.

合同样本 2-1

Contract Sample 2-1

销售确认书

SALE CONFIRMATION

合同号：2022903012

CONTRACT NO: 202203012

日期：2022 年 3 月 20 日

DATE: March 20, 2022

卖方：海南博通商贸有限公司

SELLERS: Hainan Botong International Trade Co.

地址（ADDRESS）：15 Liufang Road, Qiongshan District, Haikou, China

买方（BUYERS）：Online Am International Trading Co.

地址（ADDRESS）：1150 Wall Street, New York, the U.S. 传真（FAX）：001-212-666666

货号 Art NO.	品名及规格 Description	数量 Quantity	单价 Unit Price	金额 Amount	总值 Total Value
ART NO. WM1048	"TAOTAO" BRAND BOOTS OF LADY'S STYLE SIZE:36–41	4000 PAIRS	USD 17.80/PR	USD 71200.00	USD 71200.00
USD17.80/PR CFR Oakland (INCOTERMS® 2020) AMOUNT: SAY U.S.DOLLARS SEVENTY-ONE THOUSAND TWO HUNDERD ONLY					

兹经买卖双方同意按下列条款成交。

The undersigned sellers and buyers have agreed to close the following transactions.
According to the terms and conditions stipulated below:

1. 包装（Packing）：1 PAIR TO BE PACKED IN A BOX, 20 PAIRS IN A CARTON
SIZE ASSORTED/CTN: 2/36　3/37　5/38　5/39　3/40　2/41
Total 200 CARTONS

2. 运输标志（Shipping Marks）：ON AM/202203012/OAKLAND/CTN NO.1-200

3. 装运期（Time of Shipment）：不迟于六月（NOT LATER THAN JUNE, 2022）

4. 装运港和目的港（Loading & Destination）：海运广州到奥克兰（FROM GUANGZHOU TO OAKLAND BY VESSEL）

5. 付款条件（Payment）：买方须于 2022 年 5 月 20 日前将即期信用证开到卖方。信用证议付有效期至货物装运后 21 天在中国到期。卖方必须于装船后 48 小时内向买方发出装船通知。IRREVOCABLE L/C TO BE AVAILABLE BY SIGHT DRAFT TO REACH THE SELLERS BEFORE 20 MAY, 2022 AND TO REMAIN VALID FOR NEGOTIATION IN CHINA UNTIL 21 DAYS AFTER THE DATE OF SHIPMENT. THE SELLER MUST SEND THE SHIPMENT ADVICE TO THE BUYER WITHIN 48 HOURS AFTER THE SHIPMENT.

6. 保险（Insurance）：由买方负责。（TO BE EFFECTED BY BUYER.）

7. 品质（Quality）：卖方保证商品品质与样品相一致。（COMPORT WITH THE SAMPLES.）

8. 仲裁条款（Arbitrate Clauses）：凡因本合同引起的或与本合同有关的争议，均应提交中国国际经济贸易委员会，按照申请仲裁时该会现行仲裁规则进行仲裁，仲裁地点在 中国 北京，仲裁裁决是终局，对双方均有约束力。（Any dispute arising out of in connection with this contract shall be referred to China International Economic and Trade Arbitration Commission for arbitration in accordance with its existing rules of arbitration. The place of arbitration shall be BEIJING CHINA. The arbitral award is final and binding upon the two parties.）

9. 不可抗力条款（Force Majeure）卖方不承担因以下自然灾害、战争或其他的不可抗力事件造成的无法交付或迟延交付的责任。（The sellers shall not hold liable for non-delivery or delay in delivery of the entire lot or a portion of the goods hereunder by reason of natural disasters, war or other cause of force majeure.）

备注（Remark）：合同一式两份，买卖双方各执一份。
THE CONTRACT IS MADE OUT IN TWO PRIGINAL COPIES, ONE COPY TO BE HELD BY EACH PARTY.

卖方（Sellers）：　　　　　　　　　　　　　　　买方（Buyers）：

三、签订合同应注意的问题
III. Precautions for Contract Signing

（1）合同的内容必须体现我国平等互利的对外贸易原则和有关方针政策，必须对双方都有约束力。

(1) The content of the contract must reflect the principles of equality and mutual benefit in China's foreign trade as well as relevant policies guidelines, and should be binding on both parties.

（2）必须符合合同有效成立的要件，即双方当事人的意思表示必须一致和真实；当事人都有订约行为能力；合同标的、内容必须合法等。

(2) It must comply with the essential requirements for the valid formation of a contract. That is, the intentions of both parties must be consistent and true, the parties concerned must be with the conduct capacity to sign a contract, and the subject matter and content of the contract must be lawful.

（3）合同的各项条款必须与双方通过发盘和接受所达成的协议一致，同时在条款的规定上必须严密，要明确责任、权利义务对等。

(3) All the clauses of the contract must be consistent with the agreement reached between both parties through the offer and acceptance process. Additionally, these clauses must be stringent, clearly defining responsibilities and ensuring equal rights and obligations.

（4）合同各条款间必须协调一致，不能相互矛盾。如单价与总价的货币名称要一致；价格条款中贸易术语后接的装运港/地或目的港/地要与装运条款中的装运港/地或目的港/地一致，价格条款与保险条款要一致；合同多次出现的商品名称要一致等。

(4) The clauses of the contract must be coordinated and consistent with each other, without any contradictions. For example, the currency name for unit price and total value should be the same; the port of shipment or destination following the trade terms in the price clause should match the port of shipment or destination specified in the shipment clause; the price clause should align with the insurance clause; the commodity name should be consistent throughout the contract if mentioned multiple times.

（5）合同条款要完整、肯定，防止错列或漏列主要事项。合同词句要准确、严谨，切忌模棱两可或含糊不清，不要使用"大约""可能"等词句。

(5) Contract clauses should be complete and affirmative, avoiding misplacement or omission of major items. Contractual terms should be accurate and precise, avoiding ambiguity or vagueness. Words or phrases such as "approximately" and "may" should not be used.

第二章拓展知识、专业词汇和练习

第三章　国际贸易术语
Chapter 3　International Trade Terms

导　读
Introduction

在国际货物买卖中，买卖双方的基本义务分别是：卖方提交合格的货物和单据，买方受领货物和支付货款。但在交易中仅仅明确双方的基本义务是不够的，在货物的交接过程中，有关责任、费用和风险也必须在买卖双方之间加以划分，而这些划分必然会影响商品的价格。在实际业务中，买卖双方往往通过贸易术语确定上述问题。因此，学习和掌握国际贸易中现行的各种贸易术语及其相关的国际贸易惯例，对于明确双方各自承担的责任、费用和风险，以及合理确定商品价格具有十分重要的意义。

In international trade of goods, the basic obligations of the buyer and the seller are as follows: The seller should deliver qualified goods and provide the necessary documents, and the buyer should take delivery of the goods and make the corresponding payment. However, merely defining the basic obligations of the buyer and the seller is not enough in a transaction. In the process of goods delivery, it is necessary to allocate responsibilities, costs, and risks between the parties involved, and such allocations will inevitably impact the commodity price. In practical business operations, the aforementioned issues are addressed between the buyer and the seller through trade terms. Therefore, it is of great importance to learn and master various trade terms and international trade customs, which helps to clarify the parties' respective responsibilities, costs, and risks and determine the commodity price reasonably.

第一节　贸易术语及其国际贸易惯例
Section 1　Trade Terms and International Trade Customs

一、贸易术语的含义和作用
I. Meaning and Role of Trade Terms

（一）贸易术语的含义 (Meaning of Trade Terms)

贸易术语（trade terms）被称为"国际贸易的语言"，它是指用三个英文大写字母缩写或一个简短的概念，说明交货地点，表示商品的价格构成，以及买卖双方在货物交接中的责任、费用和风险划分的专门用语。对贸易术语的含义须从以下几个方面理解。

Trade terms, also known as "the language of international trade", refer to a specialized vocabulary used to indicate the place of delivery, specify the pricing structure of commodities, and allocate responsibilities, costs, and risks between the buyer and the seller in the process of goods delivery. A trade term is typically represented by a three-letter acronym or a concise concept. The meaning of trade terms should be understood from the following aspects.

1. 三个英文大写字母缩写或一个简短的概念 (A Three-letter Acronym or A Concise Concept)

贸易术语"FOB"为三个英文大写字母的缩写,其简短概念为"船上交货(注明指定装运港)"。

The trade term "FOB" is an acronym and its concise concept is "free on board (indicating the port of shipment)".

2. 说明交货地点 (Indicate the Place of Delivery)

Incoterms® 2020 中的 11 个贸易术语,其交货地点不尽相同。卖方在产地交货的合同属启运合同;卖方在出口国或出口地交货属装运合同;卖方在进口国或进口地交货的合同属到达合同。

The 11 trade terms in Incoterms® 2020 indicate different places of delivery. If the seller delivers the goods at the place of origin, it is considered a departure contract. If the seller delivers the goods in the exporting country or place, it is considered a shipment contract. If the seller delivers the goods in the importing country or place, it is considered an arrival contract.

3. 表示商品的价格构成 (Specify the Pricing Structure of Commodities)

商品的FOB仅包含商品的出口成本,而商品的CIF不仅包含商品的出口成本,还包括商品出口的海运费和保险费。按FOB报价,因卖方承担的责任、费用和风险小,所以商品报价低;按CIF报价,因卖方承担的责任、费用和风险大,所以商品报价高。

The trade term FOB only includes the export cost of the goods, while CIF includes not only the export cost but also the shipping cost and premium. Under FOB pricing, the seller assumes less responsibility, costs, and risks, which results in a lower-price offer. Under CIF pricing, the seller assumes more responsibility, costs, and risks, resulting in a higher-price offer.

4. 表明买卖双方在货物交接过程中的责任、费用和风险划分 (Allocate Responsibilities, Costs, and Risks between the Buyer and the Seller in the Process of Goods Delivery)

在此处,"责任"是指卖方和买方之间各需履行哪些义务,如谁来组织货物的运输或保险,谁来获取装运单据和进出口许可证;"费用"在此为买卖双方各自承担哪些费用,如运输、包装或装卸费用,以及货物查验或与安全有关的费用;而"风险"表示货物灭失或损坏的危险。

In this context, "responsibilities" refer to the obligations that the seller and buyer need to fulfill, such as who is responsible for organizing the transportation or insurance of the goods, and who obtains the shipping documents and import/export licenses; "costs" refer to the expenses borne by the buyer and the seller, such as transportation, packing, or handling fees, as well as costs related to goods inspection or security; "risks" refer to the danger of the goods being lost or damaged.

总之,不同的贸易术语表明买卖双方各自承担不同的责任、费用和风险,而责任、费用和风险的大小又影响成交商品的价格。由此可见,贸易术语具有两重性,它一方面表示交货条件;另一方面表示成交商品的价格构成,且这两方面是密切相关的。

In summary, different trade terms indicate that the buyer and the seller assume different responsibilities, costs, and risks, and the magnitude of these responsibilities, costs, and risks affects the price of the traded goods. Therefore, trade terms have a dual nature—they indicate delivery conditions while representing the pricing structure of the traded goods, and these two traits are closely related to each other.

(二)贸易术语的作用 (Role of Trade Terms)

1. 有利于买卖双方洽商交易和订立合同 (Facilitate Negotiations and Contract Formation between the Buyer and the Seller)

每种贸易术语都有特定的含义,买卖双方只要商定按何种贸易术语成交,即可明确彼此在货物交接过程中的主要责任、费用和风险。因此，贸易术语的使用大大简化了交易磋商的手续，缩短了洽商时间，节省了交易费用，从而有利于买卖双方达成交易和签订合同。

Each trade term has a specific meaning. Once the buyer and the seller agree on which trade term to transact under, they can be clear about their respective responsibilities, costs, and risks during the process of goods delivery. Therefore, the use of trade terms greatly simplifies the procedures of business negotiations, reduces negotiation time, and saves transaction costs, which is beneficial for both the buyer and the seller to reach an agreement and sign the contract.

2. 有利于买卖双方核算价格和成本 (Help the Buyer and the Seller Calculate the Price and Costs)

贸易术语表示了进出口商品价格的构成，买卖双方在确定成交价格时，可通过贸易术语明确成交商品的价格构成。因此，买卖双方可以根据报价中的贸易术语迅速进行价格、成本和盈亏核算，对对方的报价做出准确的反应。

Trade terms indicate the pricing structure of imported and exported goods. When determining the transaction price, the buyer and the seller can specify the pricing structure of the traded goods through a trade term. Therefore, the buyer and the seller can quickly calculate the price, costs, profit and loss based on the trade term in the offer, so as to make accurate responses to each other's offer.

3. 有利于买卖双方解决履约中的争议 (Conducive to the Settlement of Disputes during Contract Performance)

国际贸易中的买卖双方在货物交接中产生争议时，可援引交易采用的贸易术语的一般解释来处理。其一般解释已成为国际贸易惯例，是大家所遵循的一种类似行为规范的准则。

In international trade, when disputes arise between the buyer and the seller during the delivery of goods, they can refer to the general interpretation of the trade terms governing their transaction. Such general interpretation has become international trade customs that are followed by everyone as a guideline or something similar to a code of conduct.

总之，贸易术语与国际货物买卖合同密切相关。就国际货物买卖合同的成立而言，买卖双方以贸易术语作为报价与接受的基准；就合同的履行而言，买卖双方以所选用的贸易术语作为各自履行义务、享受权利的依据；就合同的纠纷而言，买卖双方以所选用的贸易术语作为解决纠纷、划分责任的准则。因此，贸易术语自然而然地具有了合同的主要特征，一般合同也常以其所选用的贸易术语称呼，如人们对以 FOB 术语成交的合同，称为 FOB 合同，对以 CIF 术语成交的合同，称为 CIF 合同。

In conclusion, trade terms are closely related to contracts for international sale of goods. Regarding the formation of contracts for international sale of goods, trade terms serve as the basis for the offer and acceptance between the buyer and the seller. In terms of contract performance, both parties rely on the chosen trade term to fulfill their respective obligations and exercise their rights. In case of disputes arising from the contract, the chosen trade term serves as a guideline to resolve the dispute and allocate responsibilities. Therefore, trade terms naturally have the primary features of a contract, and general contracts are often referred to by the trade terms used. For example, contracts concluded using the term FOB are called FOB contracts, while those concluded under the term CIF are referred to as CIF contracts.

二、有关贸易术语的国际贸易惯例
II. International Trade Customs on Trade Terms

早在 19 世纪，在国际贸易中就已开始使用贸易术语。1812 年，世界上第一个贸易术语

FOB 在英国利物浦出现，50 年后的 1862 年，CIF 术语也在英国产生了。在后来的 100 多年时间里，随着国际贸易的扩大和深化，贸易术语的种类不断增加，新的问题也产生了，那就是不同国家（地区）和不同业务中，对同一个贸易术语可能存在不同解释。因此，人们在使用贸易术语时，可能会因对术语的理解不同而引起矛盾和分歧。为了解决此类矛盾和分歧，统一对贸易术语的解释和做法，国际商会和某些国家（地区）的商业团体分别制定了解释国际贸易术语的规则。这些规则在国际上被广泛采用，形成了有关国际贸易术语的国际贸易惯例。目前在国际上影响较大的有关贸易术语的国际贸易惯例有三种。

As early as the 19th century, trade terms began to be used in international trade. In 1812, the world's first trade term, FOB, emerged in Liverpool, the United Kingdom. Fifty years later, in 1862, the term CIF was brought forth in the same country. Over the next 100 years, with the expansion and deepening of international trade, the variety of trade terms continued to increase and a new problem arose: Different countries (regions) and industries might have different interpretations for the same trade term. Therefore, people might have conflicts and disagreements when using trade terms due to different understandings of the terms. To address such conflicts and disagreements, rules have been established by the International Chamber of Commerce (ICC) and business organizations of some countries (regions) to provide unified interpretations and practices for international trade terms. These rules have been widely adopted internationally, forming international trade customs on trade terms. At present, there are three international trade customs on trade terms that have great international influence.

（一）《1932 年华沙—牛津规则》(Warsaw-Oxford Rules 1932)

《华沙—牛津规则》是国际法协会专门为解释 CIF 合同而制定的。19 世纪中叶，CIF 术语开始在国际贸易中被广泛采用，而对使用这一术语时买卖双方各自承担的具体义务并没有统一的规定和解释。对此，国际法协会于 1928 年在波兰首都华沙开会，制定了关于 CIF 合同的统一规则，称为《1928 年华沙规则》，共包括 22 条。其后，将此规则修订为 21 条，并更名为《1932 年华沙—牛津规则》，沿用至今。这一规则对于 CIF 的性质、买卖双方所承担的风险、责任和费用的划分以及所有权转移的方式等问题都做了比较详细的解释。

The Warsaw-Oxford Rules were developed by the International Law Association specifically for the interpretation of CIF contracts. In the mid-19th century, the term CIF started to be widely used in international trade. However, there was no uniform provision or interpretation regarding the specific obligations undertaken by the buyer and the seller when using this term. In this regard, the International Law Association convened a meeting in Warsaw, the capital of Poland, in 1928 and set unified rules for CIF contracts. These rules, known as the Warsaw Rules, 1928, consisted of 22 articles. Later, the rules were revised to encompass 21 articles and renamed the Warsaw-Oxford Rules 1932, which are still used today. These rules provide a detailed explanation regarding the nature of CIF contracts, the allocation of risks, responsibilities, and expenses between the buyer and the seller, as well as the method of transferring ownership.

（二）《1990 年美国对外贸易定义修订本》(Revised American Foreign Trade Definitions 1990)

《1990 年美国对外贸易定义修订本》是由美国 9 个商业团体制定的。它最早于 1919 年在纽约制定，原称为《美国出口报价术语定义》，后来于 1940 年在美国第 27 届全国对外贸易会议上做了修订，并于 1941 年 7 月定稿，命名为《1941 年美国对外贸易定义修订本》，简称《美国定义》。至 1990 年又加以修订，改称《1990 年美国对外贸易定义修订本》，该修订本中所解释的贸易术语共有 6 种（见表 3-1）。

The Revised American Foreign Trade Definitions 1990 was developed by nine business groups in the US. It was initially formulated in 1919 in New York, originally known as The U.S. Definitions of Export Quotations.

It was later revised at the 27th National Foreign Trade Convention in 1940 in the US and finalized in July 1941, named Revised American Foreign Trade Definitions 1941, or American Definitions for short. In 1990, it was revised again and renamed Revised American Foreign Trade Definitions 1990, which includes the interpretations of six trade items (see Table 3-1).

表3-1 《1990年美国对外贸易修订本》6种贸易术语一览
Table 3-1　List of Six Trade Terms in Revised American Foreign Trade Definitions 1990

英文缩写与名称 Acronym and Description	中文名称 Chinese
EXW（Ex Works-named Place）	产地交货
FOB（Free on Board）	运输工具上交货
FAS（Free Along Side）	运输工具边交货
CFR（Cost and Freight）	成本加运费
CIF（Cost, Insurance, Freight）	成本、保险费加运费
DEQ［(Delivered Ex Quay（duty paid）］	目的港码头交货并完税

《1990年美国对外贸易定义修订本》的修改幅度很小，且影响力有限。早期，美国将对外贸易定义修订本的内容并入了《统一商法典》（UCC）专门的一个章节——Delivery Terms（交货条件）。由于国际贸易中大多数国家（地区）均采用国际商会定义的Incoterms®，因此美国在2004年修订UCC时将有关贸易术语的规则删除了。这意味着美国无论是国际贸易还是国内贸易，均倾向采用国际商会定义的贸易术语，放弃了其本国的定义。

The modifications in the Revised American Foreign Trade Definitions 1990 were minimal with limited impact. Early on, the US incorporated the content of the Revised American Foreign Trade Definitions into a specific chapter, Delivery Terms, of the Uniform Commercial Code (UCC). However, as most countries (regions) in international trade used the Incoterms® defined by the International Chamber of Commerce (ICC), the rules on trade terms were removed from UCC in the revision in 2004. This revealed the US preferred trade terms defined by ICC for both international and domestic trade, thereby abandoning its own domestic definitions.

（三）《国际贸易术语解释通则2020》(Incoterms® 2020)

《国际贸易术语解释通则》（Incoterms®）是国际贸易中应用最为广泛的国际商事规则。第一版Incoterms®由国际商会（ICC）于1936年正式发布，并先后于1953年、1967年、1976年、1980年、1990年、2000年、2010年和2020年进行了修订和补充。Incoterms® 2020（又称《2020通则》，国际商会第723E号出版物），是为适应国际贸易实务的最新发展，在Incoterms® 2010的基础上修订产生的，并于2020年1月1日起生效。Incoterms® 2020解释的贸易术语共有11种，并将它们按照适用的运输方式不同分为两大类（见表3-2）。

The International Rules for the Interpretation of Trade Terms (Incoterms®) are the most widely used international commercial rules in international trade. The first edition was officially released by ICC in 1936. Subsequently, revisions and amendments were made in 1953, 1967, 1976, 1980, 1990, 2000, 2010, and 2020. Incoterms® 2020, ICC Publication No. 723E, was revised from Incoterms® 2010 to adapt to the latest developments in international trade practice and became effective on January 1, 2020. Incoterms® 2020 contains the interpretations of 11 trade terms, which are divided into two categories according to the applicable mode of transportation (see Table 3-2).

表3-2 《国际贸易术语解释通则2020》（Incoterms® 2020）中的贸易术语
Table 3-2　Trade Terms in Incoterms® 2020

术语缩写 Acronym	贸易术语全称 Full Description	适用运输方式 Applicable Mode of Carriage
EXW	Ex Works 工厂交货（注明指定交货地）	任一或多种运输方式 Any one or more modes of transportation
FCA	Free Carrier 货交承运人（注明指定交货地）	任一或多种运输方式 Any one or more modes of transportation
CPT	Carriage Paid to 运费付至（注明指定目的地）	任一或多种运输方式 Any one or more modes of transportation
CIP	Carriage and Insurance Paid to 运费、保险费付至（注明指定目的地）	任一或多种运输方式 Any one or more modes of transportation
DAP	Delivered at Place 目的地交货（注明指定目的地）	任一或多种运输方式 Any one or more modes of transportation
DPU	Delivered at Place Unloaded 目的地卸货后交货（注明指定目的地）	任一或多种运输方式 Any one or more modes of transportation
DDP	Delivered Duty Paid 完税后交货（注明指定目的地）	任一或多种运输方式 Any one or more modes of transportation
FAS	Free Alongside Ship 船边交货（注明指定装运港）	海运和内河水运 Ocean and inland waterway transportation
FOB	Free on Board 船上交货（注明指定装运港）	海运和内河水运 Ocean and inland waterway transportation
CFR	Cost and Freight 成本加运费（注明指定目的港）	海运和内河水运 Ocean and inland waterway transportation
CIF	Cost Insurance and Freight 成本、保险费加运费（注明指定目的港）	海运和内河水运 Ocean and inland waterway transportation

《2020通则》通过一套10个条款规定了每种贸易术语对买卖双方在货物买卖中的主要责任、费用和风险，按照A1/B1等排序，A条款代表卖方的义务，B条款代表买方的义务（见表3-3）。

The Incoterms® 2020 consists of a set of 10 rules that specify the main responsibilities, costs, and risks for both the buyer and the seller. They are organized in order from A1/B1, where the A terms are the seller's obligations and the B terms are the buyer's obligations (see Table 3-3).

表3-3　Incoterms® 2020所规定的买卖双方的主要义务
Table 3-3　Obligations of the Buyer and the Seller Under Incoterms® 2020

义务编号 Obligation No.	义务名称 Description
A1/B1	general obligations 一般义务
A2/B2	delivery /taking delivery 交货/提货
A3/B3	transfer of risks 风险转移
A4/B4	carriage 运输
A5/B5	insurance 保险

续表

义务编号 Obligation No.	义务名称 Description
A6/B6	delivery /transport document 交货单据/运输单据
A7/B7	export /import clearance 出口/进口清关
A8/B8	checking /packaging /marking 查验/包装/标记
A9/B9	allocation of costs 费用划分
A10/B10	notices 通知

三、国际贸易惯例的适用性
III. Applicability of International Trade Customs

国际贸易惯例（international trade customs），是指国际商业组织根据国际贸易实践中逐渐形成的一般贸易习惯做法而制定为成文的规则。这些规则根据当事人意思自治的原则，被国际上普遍接受和广泛使用，从而被公认为贸易惯例。国际贸易惯例是国际贸易法律的重要渊源之一，在国际贸易中具有非常特殊的地位，由于所具有的非主权性、任意选择性以及直接来自国际贸易的实践等属性，大大增强了在国际贸易中的普遍适用性。贸易惯例不是强制性规则，而是任意选择性规则。只有当事人各方一致同意采用某惯例，该惯例才具有约束力。

International trade customs refer to the written rules established by international business organizations based on common trade practices gradually formed in international trade. These rules, based on the principle of party autonomy, are widely accepted and extensively used internationally, thus recognized as trade customs. International trade customs are one of the important sources of international trade law and hold a very unique position in international trade. The nature of being non-sovereign, discretionary, and directly derived from international trade practices has greatly enhanced its universal applicability in international trade. Trade customs are not mandatory rules but rather discretionary rules. A trade custom only becomes binding when all parties involved agree unanimously to adopt it.

国际贸易惯例本身并不是法律，它以当事人的自愿为基础，对当事人不具有强制性约束力。买卖双方有权在合同中做出与惯例不符的规定，只要合同有效，双方均要履行合同规定的义务，一旦出现争议，法院或仲裁机构将依据合同条款进行判决或裁决。

An international trade custom itself is not a law. It is based on the willingness of the parties involved and shall not be mandatorily binding on the parties. The buyer and the seller have the right to include in the contract provisions that deviate from customs. As long as the contract is effective, both parties are obligated to fulfill their obligations thereunder. In the event of a dispute, the court or arbitration institution will make a judgment or arbitration based on the terms of the contract.

所以，当买卖双方发生争议时，如果：①合同的规定与惯例矛盾，则法院或仲裁机构以合同的规定为准；②合同的规定与惯例不抵触，则法院或仲裁机构以国际惯例的规定为准；③合同中明确规定采用某种惯例，则这种惯例就有其强制性。

Therefore, when a dispute arises between the buyer and the seller, if: ① the provisions of the contract are contradictory to customs, the court or arbitration institution will apply the provisions of the contract; ② the provisions of the contract do not contradict customs, the court or arbitration institution will apply the provisions of international customs; ③ the contract explicitly stipulates the adoption of a certain custom, that custom will be binding.

上述有关贸易术语的国际贸易惯例都是由非政府组织制定的，它们既非某国的法律，也非国际法律或协定，因此这些解释规则不具有法律强制性。只有当事人在合同中明确约定采用某项惯例时，它才对当事人具有法律约束力。同时，这些惯例对同一写法的贸易术语的解释不尽相同，有时甚至出入较大。为避免争议，建议贸易商在其所订立的买卖合同中订明采用规则的具体名称和版本年份。假如合同中未约定适用何种解释规则而发生争议，鉴于国际商会制定的Incoterms®被广泛使用，影响力最大，如当事人无特别约定，各国法院或仲裁机构往往推定当事人适用Incoterms®。

The aforementioned international trade customs concerning trade terms are established by non-governmental organizations. They are neither the laws of any specific country nor international laws or agreements. Therefore, these interpretive rules are not legally mandatory. Only when the parties concerned explicitly agree to adopt a specific custom in the contract, is that custom legally binding on the parties. In addition, these customs may interpret the same trade term in different ways, and sometimes even have significant variations. To avoid disputes, it is recommended that traders specify the specific name and edition year of the rules adopted in their contracts. If the contract does not specify which interpretive rules to apply in case of dispute, considering that the Incoterms® established by the International Chamber of Commerce are widely used and have the greatest impact, courts or arbitration institutions in various countries often presume that the parties concerned have applied Incoterms® unless otherwise agreed between them.

此外，买卖双方商定适用某惯例解释的贸易术语，并不意味着其买卖合同绝对受该贸易术语的约束。若合同有与该贸易术语解释冲突的特别规定，则合同的规定将优先适用。并且，买卖双方也可以通过合同对某惯例的贸易术语的规则进行修改，但当事人需要在合同中非常清晰地明确此类修改欲达到的效果。

Furthermore, when the buyer and the seller agree to apply a customary interpretation to a trade term, it does not necessarily mean that their contract is absolutely bound by that trade term. If the contract contains special provisions that contradict the interpretation of that trade term, the provisions of the contract shall prevail. Moreover, the buyer and the seller can also modify the rules of a customary trade term through the contract. However, the parties concerned must clearly and explicitly indicate in the contract the intended effect of such modifications.

第二节　六种主要的贸易术语
Section 2　Six Major Trade Terms

《2020通则》解释的11种贸易术语，对买卖双方在货物交接中的责任、费用和风险划分做出了不同规定，适于不同交易条件下买卖双方选用。根据它们被使用的频率，可将这11种贸易术语分为"常用的6种贸易术语"和"其他5种贸易术语"。

The 11 trade terms in the Incoterms® 2020 make different provisions on the allocation of responsibilities, costs, and risks between the buyer and the seller during the delivery of goods, which can be selected by the parties concerned under different trading conditions. Based on their frequency of use, these 11 trade terms can be categorized into "six commonly used trade terms" and "five other trade terms".

一、FOB
I. FOB

（一）FOB的含义 (Meaning of FOB)

FOB [Free on Board (insert named port of shipment)，船上交货（填入指定装运港）]，是指卖方以在指定装运港将货物装上船（该船舶由买方指定），或取得已经如此交付的货物（常见于大宗商品的链式销售）即完成交货，货物灭失或损坏的风险在货物交到船上时发生转移，同时，买方承担自那时起的一切费用。

FOB [Free on Board (insert named port of shipment)] means that the seller delivers the goods on board the vessel nominated by the buyer at the named port of shipment or procures the goods already so delivered (commonly seen in the chain sale of bulk commodities). The risk of loss of or damage to the goods passes when the products are on board the vessel. The buyer bears all costs from that moment onwards.

该术语仅适用于海运或内河水运，不适合于货物在交到船上之前已经移交给承运人的情形，如在集装箱终端被交给承运人。在此种情况下，双方应考虑采用FCA。

The FOB rule applies only to sea or inland waterway transportation and is not appropriate where goods are handed over to the carrier before they are on board the vessel, for example where goods are handed over to a carrier at a container terminal. Where this is the case, parties should consider using the FCA rule rather than the FOB rule.

从商品的价格构成上看，FOB=EXW+货物装上船前的一切费用+出口清关的费用+出口方政府规定的装船前检验费用。

In terms of the pricing structure of commodities, FOB can be explained as the sum of EXW (Ex Works) price, all costs incurred before the goods are on board the vessel, export clearance fees, and pre-shipment inspection fees as required by the exporting government.

在合同中正确使用FOB的方法是，将FOB订入合同的价格条款，如"USD 50.00 /CARTON FOB HAIKOU INCOTERMS® 2020"，FOB后应填入具体的装运港，并注明适用的规则及版本。因为海口的货运港口只有秀英港一个，所以可以写海口。但像上海有多个货运港口的，最好在FOB后注明具体的港口名称，如上海外高桥、上海洋山等。

The correct way to use FOB in the contract is to include FOB in the price clause of the contract, such as "USD 50.00 /CARTON FOB HAIKOU INCOTERMS® 2020". The specific port of shipment shall be filled in after FOB with applicable rules and versions indicated. As Xiuying Port is the only cargo port in Haikou, it can be stated as Haikou. However, for cities like Shanghai with multiple cargo ports, it is preferable to specify the exact port name after FOB, such as Shanghai Waigaoqiao and Shanghai Yangshan.

（二）FOB对买卖双方主要义务的划分 (Main Obligations of Buyers and Sellers under FOB)

根据《2020通则》规定，FOB下买卖双方的主要义务如表3-4所示。

According to Incoterms® 2020, the main obligations of the buyer and the seller under FOB are as follows (Table 3-4).

表3-4 FOB下买卖双方的主要义务
Table 3-4 Main Obligations of Buyers and Sellers under FOB

项目 Item	卖方 Seller	买方 Buyer
责任 Responsibilities	1. 必须提供符合销售合同约定的货物和商业发票，及合同可能要求的其他与合同相符的证据，以及交货的通常证明 The seller must provide goods and commercial invoices conforming to the provisions of the sales contract and any other evidence of conformity that may be required by the contract, as well as general proof of delivery	1. 必须按销售合同约定支付货物价款，提取货物，接受交货证明 The buyer must pay the price of goods, take delivery of goods and accept proof of delivery as agreed in the sales contract

续表

项目 Item	卖方 Seller	买方 Buyer
责任 Responsibilities	2. 必须在约定日期或买方通知的约定期限内在买方指定的装运港内的装货点（如有），按照该港口的习惯方式，以将货物置于买方指定的船上，或以取得已经如此交付的货物的方式交货，并给予买方充分通知 The seller must, on the agreed date or within the agreed period notified by the buyer, deliver the goods either by placing them on board the vessel nominated by the buyer at the loading point, if any, indicated by the buyer at the named port of shipment or by procuring goods so delivered in the manner customary at the port, and provide the buyer with sufficient notice 3. 必须提供其所拥有的买方安排运输和保险所需的信息，遵守与运输有关的安全要求 The seller must provide the buyer with any information in their possession that the buyer needs for arranging carriage and insurance and comply with any carriage-related security requirements 4. 如需要，必须办理出口国（地区）要求的所有清关手续并支付费用，如出口许可证、出口安检清关、装运前检验及任何其他官方授权 The seller must complete all customs clearance formalities required by the exporting country (region), such as export licenses, export security clearance, pre-shipment inspection and any other official authorization and pay for them if necessary 5. 必须以适合该货物运输的方式对货物进行包装和标记 The seller must pack and mark the goods in a manner appropriate to the carriage	2. 必须自付费用订立自指定装运港起的货物运输合同，并就任何运输相关的安全要求、船舶名称、装货点以及约定期限内所选择的交货时间给予卖方充分通知 The buyer must contract or arrange at its own cost for the carriage of the goods from the named port of shipment, and provide the seller with sufficient notice regarding any carriage-related security requirements, the vessel name, the loading point, and the selected time of delivery within the agreed period 3. 如需要，必须办理任何过境国和进口国（地区）要求的所有手续并支付费用，如进口许可及过境所需的任何许可、进口及任何过境安检清关、装运前检验及任何其他官方授权 The buyer must complete and pay for all formalities required by any transit and importing country (region), if necessary, such as import licenses and any permits required for transit, import and any transit security clearance, pre-shipment inspection and any other official authorization
费用 Costs	1. 货物在指定装运港装上船之前的一切费用 All costs relating to the goods before they are on board the vessel at the named port of shipment 2. 如需要，办理出口清关的关税、税款和任何其他费用 Customs duty, tax and any other charges for export clearance if required	1. 货物在指定装运港装上船之后的一切费用 All costs relating to the goods after they are on board the vessel at the named port of shipment 2. 如需要，办理过境或进口清关的关税、税款和任何其他费用 Customs duty, tax and any other charges for transit or import clearance if required

续表

项目 Item	卖方 Seller	买方 Buyer
风险 Risks	承担货物在指定装运港装上船之前的一切风险 The seller bears all risks relating to the goods before they are on board the vessel at the named port of shipment	承担货物在指定装运港装上船之时起的一切风险 The buyer bears all risks relating to the goods from the time they are on board the vessel at the named port of shipment

（三）按FOB成交应注意的问题 (Precautions for FOB)

1. 明确风险分界点 (Identify the Point of Risk Transfer)

FOB的风险分界点为卖方交货点，是在指定装运港卖方将货物装上买方指定的船舶时，即货交船上时，此点也是买卖双方的费用分界点。在实践中，买方或银行一般要求卖方提交清洁已装船的提单，故卖方要将货物安全完好地装船。

Under FOB, the point of risk transfer is the delivery point of the seller, which is the point when the seller loads the goods onto the buyer's designated vessel at the named port of shipment, or when the goods are on board the vessel. This is also the point when costs are transferred from the seller to the buyer. In practice, the buyer or the bank typically requires the seller to submit a clean bill of lading, so the seller shall load the goods onto the vessel safely and in good condition.

买卖双方应在订立销售合同时，应在FOB后填入明确具体的交货点和适用规则版本。此外，应谨慎使用各种变形条件，如FOB Liner Terms，FOB Under Tackle，FOBST，因为《2020通则》中并未对FOB的变形条件做出任何具体的规定，若买卖双方未明确上述变形条件有无改变贸易术语的交货点和风险转移点，很容易引起争议。

The buyer and the seller should clearly specify the delivery point and the version of the applicable rule after FOB when entering into a sales contract. Furthermore, the variants of FOB such as FOB Liner Terms, FOB Under Tackle, and FOBST should be used with caution because the Incoterms® 2020 does not provide any specific regulations on the variants of FOB. If the buyer and the seller do not clearly specify whether the above-mentioned variants have altered the delivery point and the point of risk transfer under the trade term, disputes can occur easily.

2. 做好船货衔接工作 (Do a Good Job in the Connection of the Vessel and Goods)

按FOB成交，由买方租船订舱，而卖方负责备妥货物装船，因此存在船货衔接问题。买方应及时租船订舱，并将船名、装货点和约定期限内的交货时间（如有）及时通知给卖方，以便卖方按时备货、装船。根据《2020通则》的规定，若买方未能按照规定给予卖方有关船名、装货点及约定期限内的交货时间的充分通知，或买方指定的船舶未准时到达，或未接收货物，或早于通知的时间停止装货，则买方承担自约定日期起或约定期限届满之时起的货物灭失或损坏的一切风险和任何额外费用。但以货物已清楚地确定为合同项下的货物为前提条件，如卖方可以采用约定方式对该批货物进行包装、刷唛等，将该批货物特定化为合同项下的货物。

Under the FOB term, the buyer is responsible for chartering and booking the vessel, while the seller is responsible for preparing the goods for shipment. Therefore, there is the issue of connection between the goods and the vessel. The buyer should promptly charter and book a vessel and notify the seller of the vessel name, loading point, and time of delivery within the agreed period (if any), so that the seller can prepare and load the goods on time. According to the provisions of the Incoterms® 2020, if the buyer fails to provide the seller with sufficient notice regarding the vessel name, loading point, and time of delivery within the agreed period, or if the vessel designated by the buyer does not arrive on time or accept the goods, or stops loading earlier than the notified time, then the buyer bears all risks of loss or damage to the goods and any additional expenses from the agreed date or the end of the agreed period. However, it is a prerequisite that the goods are clearly identified as the goods under the contract. For example, the seller can use the agreed method to package and mark the goods, specifying them as the goods under the contract.

在实践业务中，买卖双方应在合同中明确规定买方派船接货的时间和违约责任，并加强联系、及时沟通，或由卖方代办运输。如已约定由卖方代办运输，卖方必须按惯常条款订立运输合同，由买方承担风险和费用。

In practical business operations, the buyer and seller should clearly specify in the contract the time for the buyer to dispatch a vessel to pick up the goods and the liabilities associated with the breach of contract, and should enhance communication and timely coordinate with each other. Or alternatively, the seller can handle the carriage for the buyer. If it has been agreed that the seller will handle the carriage, the seller must enter into a contract of carriage on customary terms, with the buyer bearing the risks and expenses.

案例分析：中国A公司与非洲B公司签订了出口小麦的FOB合同，规定分四批交货。合同中的装运规定："买方接货船只须于装船前8日内到达装运港，否则由此引起卖方任何损失和费用由买方承担。"同时规定："买方必须于船只到达港口前5天将船名和预计到港时间通知卖方。"前三批货均按期执行，但最后一批，买方迟迟不派船。A公司反复催促，B公司称船源紧张，租不到船，要求推迟两个月交货。A公司立即回复指出："按照合同规定，你方必须派船接运，如确有困难，我方可例外同意你方延期转运，但你方应赔偿合计20万美元。"最后经双方协商，将赔偿金额降至15万美元，B公司得以延期两个月派船。试分析该案例中B公司向A公司做出赔偿的原因。

Case analysis: Chinese company A and African company B have signed a FOB contract for the export of wheat, specifying delivery in four batches. The contract stipulates that "the buyer's vessel must arrive at the port of shipment no later than 8 days before the loading date, otherwise any losses and expenses incurred thereby shall be borne by the buyer." It also states that "the buyer must inform the seller of the vessel name and the estimated time of arrival 5 days before the vessel arrives at the port." The first three batches were delivered on time, but the buyer delayed dispatching the vessel for the final batch. Company A repeatedly urged Company B, who claimed there was a shortage of available vessels and requested a two-month delivery extension. Company A promptly responded, stating, "According to the contract, your company must dispatch a vessel for the delivery of the goods. If there is indeed a difficulty, we can make an exception and agree to a delayed shipment, but your company will need to compensate a total of USD 200,000." After negotiations, the compensation amount was reduced to USD 150,000, and Company B was allowed to delay dispatching the vessel for two months. In the above case, why should Company B compensate Company A?

分析提示：按FOB签订合同，按时派船接货是买方的义务。若买方未按期派船接货，则应由买方承担自约定的交货期届满起货物灭失或损坏的一切风险，并支付因此发生的额外费用。中国A公司在合同中明确规定了买方派船接货的义务和违约责任，拟定合同考虑周全，体现出认真、细致的工作作风。事后得知，B公司因小麦价格大幅下跌，于是采用拖延战术，试图使A公司自行提出取消合同。但A公司采取得当措施，有理有据地运用FOB规则，使B公司预谋失败，成功维护了中国公司的利益。此案例也告诉我们，重合同、守信用乃营商之根本，诚信和遵守规则，将大大减少贸易纠纷的产生。为防患未然和保护自己，我们需要更好地学习和理解贸易规则。

Analysis prompts: Under a FOB contract, the buyer is obliged to timely dispatch a vessel to pick up the goods. If failing to do so, the buyer should bear all risks of loss or damage to the goods from the end of the agreed time of delivery and pay any additional expenses incurred therefrom. Chinese company A specified in the contract the buyer's obligation to dispatch a vessel for goods delivery as well as the liabilities for the breach of contract, demonstrating a thoughtful and meticulous work approach. Afterward, it was learned that Company B, due to a significant drop in the wheat price, resorted to stalling tactics in an attempt to compel Company A to voluntarily cancel the contract. However, Company A took appropriate measures and utilized the FOB rule rationally, thwarting Company B's scheme and successfully safeguarding the interests of the Chinese company. We learn from the case that respecting contracts and maintaining good faith are fundamental to doing business, and that upholding integrity and adhering to rules can significantly reduce trade disputes. To prevent potential risks and protect ourselves, it is important to improve our learning and understanding of trade rules.

3. FOB 的局限性 (Limitations of FOB)

FOB不适合内陆地区出口商使用，它会增加出口商承担的风险、责任和费用，推迟运输单据出单时间，延缓出口商交单收汇。因为卖方如果采用集装箱运输或多式联运，可以直接在内陆地区（卖方所在地或其他交货地点）将货物交给承运人，凭承运人签发的集装箱提单交单收汇。若采用FOB则要多承担从内陆地区仓库至港口装船的风险、责任和费用。在实践业务中，若采用其他运输方式或国际多式联运，应选用FCA，合同附加买方须指示承运人出具已装船批注提单给卖方的规定，或允许卖方提交收妥待运的提单。

The FOB rule is not suitable for exporters in inland areas, as it can increase the risks, responsibilities, and costs borne by the exporter, prolong the issuance of transport documents, and delay the exporter's submission of documents and receipt of payments. This is because, if the seller uses container freight transport or multimodal transport, it can directly hand over the goods to the carrier in the inland area (at the location of the seller or another place of delivery). It can then submit the container bill of lading issued by the carrier to receive payment. If FOB is used, the seller would bear additional risks, responsibilities, and expenses associated with transporting the goods from the inland warehouse to the port for loading. In practical business operations, if other modes of transportation or international multimodal transport are adopted, it is advisable to use the FCA rule instead. The contract should include provisions that require the buyer to instruct the carrier to issue a bill of lading with on board notation to the seller or allow the seller to submit a received-for-shipment bill of lading.

二、CFR
II. CFR

（一）CFR的含义 (Meaning of CFR)

CFR [Cost and Freight (insert named port of destination)，成本加运费（填入指定目的港）]，是指卖方以在指定装运港将货物装上船，或取得已经如此交付的货物即完成交货，货物灭失或损坏的风险在货物交到船上时转移给买方，卖方还需订立将货物运至指定目的港的运输合同并支付运费。

CFR [Cost and Freight (insert named port of destination)] means that the sellers complete delivery by loading the goods on board the vessel at the named port of shipment or taking possession of the goods already so delivered, and the risk of loss or damage to the goods passes to the buyers when the goods are delivered on board the vessel. The sellers are also required to enter into a contract of carriage and pay freight charges for the carriage of goods to the named port of destination.

该术语仅适用于海运或内河水运，不适合于货物在交到船上之前已经移交给承运人的情形，如在集装箱终端被交给承运人。此种情况下，双方应考虑采用CPT。

The FOB rule applies only to sea or inland waterway transportation and is not appropriate where goods are handed over to the carrier before they are on board the vessel, for example where goods are handed over to a carrier at a container terminal. In this case, both parties should consider CPT.

从商品的价格构成上看，CFR=FOB+主运费。

From the perspective of price composition, CFR = FOB + Main Freight.

在合同中正确使用CFR的方法是，将CFR订入合同的价格条款，如"USD 55.00 / CARTON CFR SOUTHAMPTON INCOTERMS® 2020"，CFR后应填入具体的目的港，并注明适用的规则及版本。特别建议双方尽可能精准地指定目的港的特定地点，因为卖方需承担将货物运往该地点的运费。

The correct way to use CFR in the contract is to include CFR in the price clause of the contract, such as "USD 55.00 /CARTON CFR SOUTHAMPTON INCOTERMS® 2020". The specific port of destination shall be filled in after CFR with applicable rules and versions indicated. In particular, it is recommended that both parties name a specific location of port of destination as precisely as possible since the sellers are responsible for freight charges to ship goods to this location.

（二）CFR对买卖双方主要义务的划分 (Main Obligations of Buyers and Sellers under CFR)

根据《2020通则》规定，CFR下买卖双方的主要义务如表3-5所示。

According to Incoterms® 2020, the main obligations of buyers and sellers under CFR are as follows (Table 3-5).

表3-5　CFR下买卖双方的主要义务
Table 3-5　Main Obligations of Buyers and Sellers under CFR

项目 Item	卖方 Seller	买方 Buyer
责任 Responsibilities	1. 必须提供符合销售合同约定的货物和商业发票，及合同可能要求的其他与合同相符的证据，以及运输单据 The sellers must provide goods and commercial invoice conforming to the provisions of the sales contract, other evidence that may be required by the contract to comply with the contract, as well as transport documents 2. 必须在约定日期或期限内，按照该港口的习惯方式，以将货物装上船，或以取得已经如此交付的货物的方式交货，并给予买方充分通知 The sellers must, on the agreed date or within the agreed time limit, complete delivery by loading the goods on board the vessel or taking possession of the goods already so delivered in accordance with the customary method of the port, and give adequate notices to the buyers	1. 必须按销售合同约定支付货款，提取货物，接受运输单据 The buyers must pay the price of goods, take delivery of goods and accept transport documents as agreed in the sales contract 2. 买方有权决定运输时间及/或指定目的港的收货点，买方必须给予卖方充分通知 The buyers shall have the right to determine the time of carriage and/or named port of destination, and must give adequate notices to the sellers

续表

项目 Item	卖方 Seller	买方 Buyer
责任 Responsibilities	3. 必须签订或取得运输合同，将货物自交货地送至指定目的港，并遵守运输过程中与运输有关的安全要求 The sellers must sign or obtain a contract of carriage to transport the goods from the place of delivery to the named port of destination, and comply with the relevant safety requirements during carriage 4. 必须提供其所拥有的买方获取保险所需的信息 The sellers must provide the information they have that the buyers need to obtain insurance 5. 如需要，必须办理出口国（地区）要求的所有清关手续并支付费用，如出口许可证、出口安检清关、装运前检验及任何其他官方授权 The sellers must complete all customs clearance formalities required by the exporting country (region), such as export licenses, export security clearance, pre-shipment inspection and any other official authorization and pay for them if necessary 6. 必须以适合该货物运输的方式对货物进行包装和标记 The sellers must pack and mark the goods in a manner appropriate to carriage	3. 如需要，必须办理任何过境国和进口国（地区）要求的所有手续并支付费用，如进口许可及过境所需的任何许可、进口及任何过境安检清关、装运前检验及任何其他官方授权 The buyer must complete and pay for all formalities required by any transit and importing country (region), if necessary, such as import licenses and any permits required for transit, import and any transit security clearance, pre-shipment inspection and any other official authorization
费用 Costs	1. 货物在装运港装上船之前的一切费用 All costs relating to the goods before they are on board the vessel at the named port of shipment 2. 货物运至指定目的港的运费和装船费、与运输相关的安全费用，以及根据运输合同由卖方承担的过境费和在约定卸货港的卸货费用 Freight and loading charges of the goods to the named port of destination, security charges related to the carriage, transit charges borne by the sellers under the contract of carriage and unloading charges at the agreed port of discharge 3. 如需要，办理出口清关的关税、税款和任何其他费用 Customs duty, tax and any other charges for export clearance if required	1. 货物在装运港装上船之后的一切费用 All costs relating to the goods after they are on board the vessel at the named port of shipment 2. 过境费用，除非根据运输合同该项费用由卖方承担 Transit charges, unless they are to be borne by the Sellers in accordance with the contract of carriage 3. 包括驳运费和码头费在内的卸货费用，除非根据运输合同该项费用由卖方承担 Unloading charges including lighterage and pierage, unless such charges are to be borne by the sellers in accordance with the contract of carriage

续表

项目 Item	卖方 Seller	买方 Buyer
费用 Costs		4. 如需要，办理过境或进口清关的关税、税款和任何其他费用 Customs duty, tax and any other charges for transit or import clearance if required
风险 Risks	承担货物在装运港装上船之前的一切风险 The seller bears all risks relating to the goods before they are on board the vessel at the named port of shipment	承担货物在装运港装上船之时起的一切风险 The buyer bears all risks relating to the goods from the time they are on board the vessel at the named port of shipment

（三）按CFR成交应注意的问题 (Precautions for CFR)

1. 装船通知的重要性 (Importance of Shipping Advice)

按CFR成交时，由卖方负责安排货物运至指定目的港的运输，而买方需要为其自身利益投买货运保险。货运保险主要是针对运输过程中可能出现的风险和损失，若卖方未及时发出装船通知，买方可能无法及时办理货运保险，甚至可能出现漏保货运险的情况。根据英国《货物买卖法》（1979年修订）第三十二条规定，"除非另有约定，卖方向买方运送货物的路线涉及海运时，在多数情形下货物通常要保险，卖方对买方负有告知义务，以使买方为海上运输期间的货物购买保险，如果卖方未能告知，则货物在海上的风险在于卖方。"各国法律、国际惯例和合同一般都支持上述英国《货物买卖法》的规定。因此，按CFR成交，卖方装船后务必及时向买方发出装船通知，以便买方及时给货物投保；否则，将由卖方继续承担货物风险，而不能以货物已装船、风险已经转移为由免除责任。

Carriage of goods to the named port of destination shall be arranged by the sellers on a CFR basis, while the buyers are required to insure the goods for their own benefit. Cargo insurance is mainly aimed at the risks and losses that may occur during the carriage of goods. If the sellers fail to issue shipping advice in time, the buyers may not be able to handle cargo insurance in a timely manner, and may even miss the coverage of cargo insurance. According to Article 32 of the Sale of Goods Act (as amended in 1979) of the United Kingdom, "Unless otherwise agreed, when the route from sellers to the buyers involves sea transportation, in most cases the goods are usually subject to insurance. The sellers have an obligation to inform the buyers so that the buyers can insure the goods during sea carriage. If the sellers fail to do so, the risk of the goods at sea lies with the sellers." The above-mentioned provisions of the Sale of Goods Act are generally supported by national laws, international practice and contracts. Therefore, on a CFR basis, the sellers must issue shipping advice to the buyers in time after shipment so that the buyers can insure the goods in a timely manner Otherwise, the seller will continue to bear the risk of the goods and cannot be exempted from liability on the ground that the goods have been loaded on board and the risk has passed.

案例分析：我国A公司从泰国B公司进口一批泰国香米，双方按CFR达成合同，因货物装船时正值周五，B公司业务员在货物装船后未及时向A公司发出装船通知，故A公司未能及时向保险公司投保。待周一上班后A公司收到船方消息，称载运该批大米的货轮因恶劣天气在海上倾覆，货物全部损失。该批大米的损失应由谁来承担？

Case study: Company A of China imported a batch of jasmine rice from Company B of Thailand, and both parties reached a contract on a CFR basis. As it was Friday, the salesperson of Company B failed to issue shipping advice to Company A in time after the goods were shipped, resulting in Company A not being able to assure with the insurance company in time. After starting work on Monday, Company A received a message from the shipowner stating that the cargo ship carrying the batch of rice capsized at sea due to bad weather, resulting in total loss of goods. Who shall bear the loss of this batch of rice?

分析提示：《2020 通则》规定，卖方对买方没有购买保险的义务，特别建议买方为其自身购买一定的保险。虽然卖方对买方没有订立保险合同的义务，但应买方要求并由其承担风险和费用，卖方必须向买方提供卖方所拥有的买方获取保险所需的信息。根据国际惯例和有关法律，若卖方未及时通知买方，则货物运输中的风险应由卖方承担。在该案例中，B 公司未及时向 A 公司发出装船通知，导致 A 公司未能及时向保险公司投保，故货物发生的损失应由 B 公司承担。

Analysis prompts: According to Incoterms® 2020, the sellers are not obliged to purchase insurance for the buyers. It is especially recommended that the buyers be properly insured for themselves. Although the Sellers are not obligated to enter into an insurance contract for the buyers, at the request of the buyers and at their own risk and expense, the sellers must provide the information they have that the buyers need to obtain insurance. According to international practice and relevant laws, if the sellers fail to timely notify the buyers, the risks in carriage of goods shall be borne by the sellers. In this case, Company B failed to issue shipping advice to Company A in time, resulting in Company A not being able to assure with the insurance company in time. Therefore, the losses of goods shall be borne by Company B.

2. 卖方租船订舱的责任 (Sellers' Responsibility for Charter and Booking)

"租船订舱"是在贸易实务中对办理海运货物运输的说法。若需要运输的货物数量多或无班轮通航，可采用租船运输；如果需要运输的货物数量不多又有班轮通航，可以预订舱位，采用班轮运输。CFR 术语要求卖方负责安排运输，但《2020 通则》规定，卖方按惯常条款订立运输合同，由卖方承担费用，经由通常航线，用通常运输该类货物的船舶运送货物。因此，卖方对买方提出的关于限制船籍、船型、船龄、船级及指定班轮公司船只或航线的要求，有权拒绝。但从维护双方良好合作关系的角度，在卖方办得到又不增加费用的情况下，可考虑接受。合同中另有规定的，则另当别论。

"Charter and Booking" is a term for handling the carriage of goods by sea in trade practice. If the quantity of goods required for carriage is large or no liner is available, charter can be adopted; if the quantity of goods required for carriage is small and liner is available, shipping space can be booked and Liner can be adopted. The CFR term requires sellers to be responsible for arranging the carriage, but Incoterms® 2020 stipulate that sellers enter into a contract of carriage on customary terms and at sellers' expense, carry the goods by vessel normally carrying such goods via customary routes. Therefore, the sellers shall have the right to refuse the buyers' request for restrictions on the registry, type, age and class of ships as well as the vessels or routes of named liner companies. However, from the perspective of maintaining a good cooperative relationship between both parties, it may be considered acceptable if the sellers can do so without increasing costs, unless otherwise specified in the contract.

3. 明确目的港卸货费用的负担问题 (Clarify the Bearing of Unloading Charges at Port of Destination)

按 CFR 成交，如货物采用班轮运输，运费由办理货物运输的卖方支付，在目的港的卸货费用实际上由卖方负担。而大宗商品通常采用租船运输，如船方按不负担装卸费的条件出租船舶，卸货费应由哪方承担呢？按《2020 通则》规定，包括驳船费和码头费在内的卸货费应由买方承担,除非运输合同规定该项费用由卖方承担。但如果卖方根据运输合同产生了目的港的卸货费用,除非双方另有约定,卖方无权向买方追偿该项费用。所以,目的港卸货费原则上应由买方承担,但建议买卖双方事先就卸货费用的负担问题达成一致。

If the goods are transported by liner, freight charges shall be paid by the sellers handling carriage of goods and unloading charges at port of destination shall actually be borne by the sellers. However, charter is usually adopted for carriage of bulk commodities. If the shipowner delivers the goods on an FIO basis, who shall bear the unloading charges? According to Incoterms® 2020, the unloading charges including lighterage and pierage shall be borne by the buyers, unless such charges are to be borne by the sellers in accordance with the contract of carriage. However, if the sellers incur unloading charges at port of destination according to the contract of carriage, unless otherwise agreed by both parties, the sellers shall not be entitled to recover such expenses from the buyers. Therefore, in principle, unloading charges at port of destination shall be borne by the buyers. However, it is suggested that both parties reach an agreement in advance on the bearing of unloading charges.

4. CFR合同属于装运合同 (CFR Contract Is a Shipment Contract)

《2020通则》规定CFR后填入的是指定目的港,且由卖方负责安排货物运至指定目的港的运输,这是否表示卖方需要在指定目的港完成交货?回答是否定的。CFR和FOB的交货点一样,都是在装运港货交船上时,在该点卖方完成交货,货物灭失或损坏的风险同时转移,而无论货物是否实际以良好的状态、约定的数量或是否确实到达目的地。在业务实践中,这种卖方只保证按时完成装运,即完成交货,而无须保证货物是否按时、完好抵达目的地的合同,被称为"装运合同",六种常用贸易术语都属于装运合同。

According to Incoterms® 2020, the named port of destination is filled in after CFR, and the sellers are responsible for arranging the carriage of goods to the named port of destination. Does this mean that the sellers need to complete delivery at the named port of destination? The answer is no. The delivery point for CFR and FOB is the same, where the Sellers complete the delivery of the goods at the port of shipment when they are delivered to the ship. The risk of loss or damage to the goods also passes, regardless of whether the goods actually arrive in good condition, in the agreed quantity or not. In business practice, this kind of contract in which the sellers only guarantee to complete shipment on time, i.e. delivery, without guaranteeing whether the goods arrive at the destination on time and in good condition is called "Shipment Contract". The six commonly used trade terms are all shipment contracts.

三、CIF
III. CIF

(一) CIF的含义 (Meaning of CIF)

CIF [Cost Insurance and Freight (insert named port of destination),成本、保险费加运费(填入指定目的港)],是指卖方以在指定装运港将货物装上船,或取得已经如此交付的货物即完成交货,货物灭失或损坏的风险在货物交到船上时转移给买方,卖方还需订立将货物运至指定目的港的运输合同并支付运费,订立货运保险合同并支付保险费。

CIF [Cost Insurance and Freight (insert named port of destination)] means that the sellers complete delivery by loading the goods on board the vessel at the named port of shipment or taking possession of the goods already so delivered, and the risk of loss or damage to the goods passes to the buyers when the goods are delivered on board the vessel. The sellers are also required to enter into a contract of carriage and pay freight charges for the carriage of goods to the named port of destination, as well as conclude a freight insurance contract and pay the premium.

该术语仅适用于海运或内河水运，不适合于货物在交到船上之前已经移交给承运人的情形，如在集装箱终端被交给承运人。在此种情况下，双方应考虑采用CIP。

The FOB rule applies only to sea or inland waterway transportation and is not appropriate where goods are handed over to the carrier before they are on board the vessel, for example where goods are handed over to a carrier at a container terminal. In this case, both parties should consider CIP.

从商品的价格构成上看，CIF=FOB+主运费+保险费。

From the perspective of price composition, CIF=FOB + Main Freight + Premium.

在合同中正确使用CIF的方法是，将CIF订入合同的价格条款，如"USD 58.00 /CARTON CIF SOUTHAMPTON INCOTERMS® 2020"，CIF后应填入具体的目的港，并注明适用的规则及版本。特别建议双方尽可能精准地指定目的港的特定地点，因为卖方需承担将货物运往该地点的运费和保险费。

The correct way to use CIF in the contract is to include CIF in the price clause of the contract, such as "USD 58.00 /CARTON CIF SOUTHAMPTON INCOTERMS® 2020". The specific port of destination shall be filled in after CIF with applicable rules and versions indicated. In particular, it is recommended that both parties name a specific location of port of destination as precisely as possible since the sellers are responsible for freight charges and premium to ship goods to this location.

（二）CIF对买卖双方主要义务的划分 (Main Obligations of Buyers and Sellers under CIF)

根据《2020通则》规定，CIF下买卖双方的主要义务如表3-6所示。

According to Incoterms® 2020, the main obligations of buyers and sellers under CIF are as follows (Table 3-6).

表3-6　CIF下买卖双方的主要义务
Table 3-6　Main Obligations of Buyers and Sellers under CIF

项目 Item	卖方 Seller	买方 Buyer
责任 Responsibilities	1. 必须提供符合销售合同约定的货物和商业发票，及合同可能要求的其他与合同相符的证据，以及运输单据和保险单据 The sellers must provide goods and commercial invoice conforming to the provisions of the sales contract, other evidence that may be required by the contract to comply with the contract, as well as transport documents and insurance policy 2. 必须在约定日期或期限内，按照该港口的习惯方式，以将货物装上船，或以取得已经如此交付的货物的方式交货，并给予买方充分通知 The sellers must, on the agreed date or within the agreed time limit, complete delivery by loading the goods on board the vessel or taking possession of the goods already so delivered in accordance with the customary method of the port, and give adequate notices to the buyers	1. 必须按销售合同约定支付货物价款，提取货物，接受运输单据 The buyers must pay the price of goods, take delivery of goods and accept transport documents as agreed in the sales contract 2. 买方有权决定运输时间及/或指定目的港的收货点，买方必须给予卖方充分通知 The buyers shall have the right to determine the time of carriage and/or named port of destination, and must give adequate notices to the sellers.

续表

项目 Item	卖方 Seller	买方 Buyer
责任 Responsibilities	3. 必须签订或取得运输合同，将货物自交货地运送至指定目的港，并遵守运输过程中与运输有关的安全要求 The sellers must sign or obtain a contract of carriage to transport the goods from the place of delivery to the named port of destination, and comply with the relevant safety requirements during carriage 4. 必须自付费用取得货物保险 The sellers must obtain cargo insurance at their own expense 5. 如需要，必须办理出口国（地区）要求的所有清关手续并支付费用，如出口许可证、出口安检清关、装运前检验及任何其他官方授权 The sellers must complete all customs clearance formalities required by the exporting country (region), such as export licenses, export security clearance, pre-shipment inspection and any other official authorization and pay for them if necessary 6. 必须以适合该货物运输的方式对货物进行包装和标记 The sellers must pack and mark the goods in a manner appropriate to carriage	3. 如需要，必须办理任何过境国和进口国（地区）要求的所有手续并支付费用，如进口许可及过境所需的任何许可、进口及任何过境安检清关、装运前检验及任何其他官方授权 The buyer must complete and pay for all formalities required by any transit and importing country (region), if necessary, such as import licenses and any permits required for transit, import and any transit security clearance, pre-shipment inspection and any other official authorization
费用 Costs	1. 货物在装运港装上船之前的一切费用 All costs relating to the goods before they are on board the vessel at the named port of shipment 2. 货物运至指定目的港的运费和装船费，与运输相关的安全费用，以及根据运输合同由卖方承担的过境费和在约定卸货港的卸货费用 Freight and loading charges of the goods to the named port of destination, security charges related to the carriage, transit charges borne by the sellers under the contract of carriage and unloading charges at the agreed port of discharge 3. 货物运输保险费 Cargo transportation insurance premiums 4. 如需要，办理出口清关的关税、税款和任何其他费用 Customs duty, tax and any other charges for export clearance if required	1. 货物在装运港装上船之后的一切费用 All costs relating to the goods after they are on board the vessel at the named port of shipment 2. 过境费用，除非根据运输合同该项费用由卖方承担 Transit charges, unless they are to be borne by the sellers in accordance with the contract of carriage 3. 包括驳运费和码头费在内的卸货费用，除非根据运输合同该项费用由卖方承担 Unloading charges including lighterage and pierage, unless such charges are to be borne by the sellers in accordance with the contract of carriage

续表

项目 Item	卖方 Seller	买方 Buyer
费用 Costs		4. 如需要，办理过境或进口清关的关税、税款和任何其他费用 Customs duty, tax and any other charges for transit or import clearance if required
风险 Risks	承担货物在装运港装上船之前的一切风险 The seller bears all risks relating to the goods before they are on board the vessel at the named port of shipment	承担货物在装运港装上船之时起的一切风险 The buyer bears all risks relating to the goods from the time they are on board the vessel at the named port of shipment

（三）按CIF成交应注意的问题 (Precautions for CIF)

1. 卖方办理保险的责任 (Sellers' Responsibility for Insurance)

按CIF成交，卖方必须签订保险合同，以对由买方承担的从装运港到目的港运输过程中货物灭失或损坏的风险投保。如果目的地要求在本地购买保险，则可能给卖方投保造成困难，双方应考虑使用CFR。买方还应注意，按《2020通则》规定，CIF下的卖方只需投保符合英国《协会货物保险条款》（C）或其他类似条款下的有限险别，而不是英国《协会货物保险条款》（A）款下的较高险别。最低保险金额应为合同规定价格另加10%（即110%），并采用合同货币。所以，如果买方有更高或额外的投保要求，应与卖方协商一致，并在销售合同中明确规定，或自行做出额外的保险安排。

Under CIF, the sellers must sign an insurance contract to insure the buyers against the risk of loss or damage of goods during the carriage process from port of shipment to port of destination. If the country (region) of destination requires insurance to be purchased locally, this may create difficulties for the sellers and both parties should consider CFR. The buyers should also note that under Incoterms® 2020 sellers on a CIF basis are only required to maintain limited coverage in accordance with ICC(C) or other similar provisions rather than higher coverage under ICC(A). The minimum Insured Amount shall be the Contract Price plus 10% (i.e. 110%) and denominated in the currencies of the contract. Therefore, if the buyers have higher or additional insurance requirements, they shall reach an agreement with the sellers through negotiation and explicitly specify them in the sales contract, or make additional insurance arrangements by themselves.

2. CIF属于象征性交货 (CIF Is a Symbolic Delivery)

从交货方式来看，CIF是一种典型的象征性交货（symbolic delivery）。所谓象征性交货，是针对实际交货（physical delivery）而言的。前者指卖方只要按期在约定地点完成装运，并向买方提交合同规定的包括物权凭证在内的有关单证，就算完成了交货义务，而无须保证到货。后者则是指卖方要在规定的时间和地点，将符合合同规定的货物提交给买方或其指定人，而不能以交单代替交货。在象征性交货方式下，卖方是凭单交货，买方是凭单付款，只要卖方按时向买方提交了符合合同规定的全套单据，即使货物在运输途中损坏或灭失，买方也必须履行付款义务。反之，如果卖方提交的单据不符合要求，即使货物完好无损地运达目的地，买方仍有权拒付货款。由此可见，CIF交易实际上是一种单据的买卖。所以，装运单据在CIF

交易中具有特别重要的意义。但必须指出，按CIF成交，卖方履行其交单义务，只是得到买方付款的前提条件，除此之外，卖方还必须履行交货义务。如果卖方提交的货物不符合要求，买方即使已经付款，仍然可以根据销售合同向卖方提出索赔。

From the perspective of delivery method, CIF is a typical symbolic delivery. Symbolic delivery refers to physical delivery. The former means that as long as the sellers complete shipment at the agreed place on schedule and submit to the buyers relevant documents (including documents of title) specified in the contract, they will be deemed to have fulfilled their delivery obligations without guaranteeing arrival. The latter means that the Sellers shall deliver the goods conforming to the provisions of the contract to the buyers or their nominees at the specified time and place, instead of replacing delivery with presentation of documents. Under symbolic delivery, the sellers deliver goods against documents and the buyers make payment against documents. As long as the sellers submit a full set of documents conforming to the provisions of the contract to the buyers on time, the buyers must fulfill the payment obligation even if the goods are damaged or lost in transit. On the contrary, if the documents submitted by the sellers do not meet the requirements, the buyers still have the right to refuse to pay for the goods even though they arrive at the destination in good condition. It can be seen that CIF transaction is actually a transaction of documents. Therefore, shipping documents are of particular importance in CIF transactions. However, it must be pointed out that under CIF, the sellers' performance of their obligation to present documents is only a prerequisite for obtaining payment from the buyers. In addition, they must also perform their delivery obligations. If the goods submitted by the sellers do not meet the requirements, the buyers can still lodge a claim against the sellers according to the sales contract even if payment has been made.

案例探讨：我国某公司与荷兰某客商以CIF条件达成一笔交易，合同规定以即期信用证为付款方式。卖方收到买方开来的信用证后，及时办理了装运手续，并制好了一整套结汇单据，准备交单议付。在卖方准备到银行办理议付手续时，收到买方来电，告知载货船只在运输途中遭遇意外事故，大部分货物受损。因此，买方表示将等到具体货损情况确定以后，才同意银行向卖方支付货款。你认为卖方可否及时收回货款，为什么？买方应如何处理此事？

Case study: A company in China has reached a transaction with a merchant in the Netherlands on CIF terms. The Contract stipulates that the payment method is L/C at sight. After receiving the L/C from the buyers, the Sellers have handled the shipping formalities in time and prepared a complete set of foreign exchange settlement documents ready for presentation by negotiation. When the sellers were about to go through available by negotiation formalities at the bank, they received a call from the buyers informing them that most of the goods had been damaged due to fortuitous accidents on the carrying vessel. Therefore, the buyers stated that they would not agree to pay the sellers for the goods until the specific damage had been determined. Do you think the sellers will be able to collect the payment in time? Why? What should the buyers do about it?

3. CIF并非"到岸价" (CIF is Not "Price of POD")

FOB常被称为"离岸价"，而CIF常被称为"到岸价"，实际上CIF并非到岸价。因为按《2020通则》对CIF的规定，卖方在装运港货交船上时即完成交货，货物灭失或损失的风险自卖方转移给买方，卖方既无须承担自装运港完成交货后的风险，也无须将货物按时、完好地交付到目的港。而且，卖方只需支付将货物运至指定目的港的正常运费和保险费，其他额外费用在卖方完成交货后应由买方承担。所以，按CIF成交，卖方承担的责任、费用和风险都没有"到岸"，也无须"到岸"交货，称CIF为到岸价，其实是不妥当的。

FOB is often referred to as "offshore price" and CIF is often referred to as "price of POD", which in fact is not "price of POD". According to the CIF provisions of Incoterms® 2020, the sellers shall complete the delivery at the port of shipment on board the ship, and the risk of loss or damage of the goods shall be transferred from the sellers to the buyers. The sellers are neither required to bear the risks after the completion of delivery from the port of shipment nor to deliver the goods to the port of destination in a timely and intact manner. In addition, the Sellers shall only pay the normal freight and premium for shipping the goods to the named port of destination. Other additional costs shall be borne by the buyers after the completion of delivery by the sellers. Therefore, it is inappropriate to refer to CIF the price of POD (port of destination) when a transaction is concluded on a CIF basis without any "CIF" responsibility, expense and risk borne by the sellers.

四、FCA
IV. FCA

（一）FCA的含义 (Meaning of FCA)

FCA [Free Carrier (insert named place of delivery)，货交承运人（填入指定交货地点）]，是指卖方在约定日期或期限内在指定地点（卖方所在地或其他地点）将货物交给买方指定的承运人时即完成交货，货物灭失或损坏的风险自该点起转移给买方。该术语可适用于任何或多种运输方式。

FCA [Free Carrier (insert named place of delivery)] means that the goods are delivered by the sellers to the carrier named by the buyers on the agreed date or within the agreed time limit (sellers' location or other places). From this point, the risk of loss or damage to the goods is transferred to the buyers. It is applicable to various transportation modes.

在合同中正确使用FCA的方法是，将FCA订入合同的价格条款，如"USD 50.00 / CARTON FCA HAIKOU MEILAN INTERNATIONAL AIRPORT INCOTERMS® 2020"，FCA后应填入尽可能具体的交货点，因为该地点是确定风险转移给买方且买方开始承担费用的地点。

The correct way to use FCA in the contract is to include FCA in the price clause of the contract, such as "USD 50.00 /CARTON FCA HAIKOU MEILAN INTERNATIONAL AIRPORT INCOTERMS® 2020", and insert the delivery point as specific as possible after FCA, because it is the place where the transfer of risks to the buyers is determined and the buyers begin to bear the expenses.

（二）FCA对买卖双方主要义务的划分 (Main Obligations of Buyers and Sellers under FCA)

根据《2020通则》规定，FCA下买卖双方的主要义务如表3-7所示。

According to Incoterms® 2020, the main obligations of buyers and sellers under FCA are as follows (Table 3-7).

表3-7　FCA下买卖双方的主要义务
Table 3-7　Main Obligations of Buyers and Sellers under FCA

项目 Item	卖方 Seller	买方 Buyer
责任 Responsibilities	1. 必须提供符合销售合同约定的货物和商业发票，及合同可能要求的其他与合同相符的证据，以及交货的通常证明 The seller must provide goods and commercial invoices conforming to the provisions of the sales contract and any other evidence of conformity that may be required by the contract, as well as general proof of delivery	1. 必须按销售合同约定支付货物价款，提取货物，接受交货证明 The buyer must pay the price of goods, take delivery of goods and accept proof of delivery as agreed in the sales contract

续表

项目 Item	卖方 Seller	买方 Buyer
责任 Responsibilities	2. 必须在约定日期或买方通知的约定期限内的交货时间在指定地或指定点（如有），向买方指定的承运人（或其他人）交付货物，或以取得已经如此交付的货物的方式交货，并给予买方充分通知 The sellers must deliver the goods to the carrier (or others) named by the buyers at the specified place or point (if any) on the agreed date or within the time limit agreed in the buyers' notices, or by taking delivery of the goods that have been so delivered, and shall give adequate Notices to the buyers 3. 必须提供其所拥有的买方安排运输和保险所需的信息，遵守与运输有关的安全要求 The seller must provide the buyer with any information in their possession that the buyer needs for arranging carriage and insurance and comply with any carriage-related security requirements 4. 如需要，必须办理出口国（地区）要求的所有清关手续并支付费用，如出口许可证、出口安检清关、装运前检验及任何其他官方授权 The seller must complete all customs clearance formalities required by the exporting country (region), such as export licenses, export security clearance, pre-shipment inspection and any other official authorization and pay for them if necessary 5. 必须以适合该货物运输的方式对货物进行包装和标记 The seller must pack and mark the goods in a manner appropriate to the carriage	2. 必须自付费用订立运输合同或安排从指定交货地开始的货物运输，并就指定承运人的名称、在约定交货期限内所选承运人收取货物的时间、指定承运人使用的运输方式（包括任何与运输有关的安全要求）、指定交货地的收货点，给予卖方充分通知 The buyers must conclude a contract of carriage or arrange the carriage of goods from the named place of delivery at their own expense and give the sellers adequate notices as to the name of the named carrier, the time within which the goods will be taken over by the selected carrier within the agreed time of delivery, the transportation mode used by the named carrier (including any safety requirements relating to the carriage), and the place of receipt at the named place of delivery 3. 如需要，必须办理任何过境国和进口国（地区）要求的所有手续并支付费用，如进口许可及过境所需的任何许可、进口及任何过境安检清关、装运前检验及任何其他官方授权 The buyer must complete and pay for all formalities required by any transit and importing country (region), if necessary, such as import licenses and any permits required for transit, import and any transit security clearance, pre-shipment inspection and any other official authorization
费用 Costs	1. 货物在指定交货点货交承运人处置之前的一切费用 All expenses before the goods are disposed of by the carrier at the named delivery point 2. 如需要，办理出口清关的关税、税款和任何其他费用 Customs duty, tax and any other charges for export clearance if required	1. 货物在指定交货点货交承运人处置之后的一切费用 All expenses after the goods are disposed of by the carrier at the named delivery point 2. 如需要，办理过境或进口清关的关税、税款和任何其他费用 Customs duty, tax and any other charges for transit or import clearance if required

项目 Item	卖方 Seller	买方 Buyer
风险 Risks	承担货物在指定交货点货交承运人处置之前的一切风险 Assume all risks before disposal by the carrier at the named delivery point of goods	承担货物在指定交货点货交承运人处置之时起的一切风险 Assume all risks from the time of disposal by the carrier at the named delivery point of goods

（三）按FCA成交应注意的问题 (Precautions for FCA)

1. 明确交货地内的交货点 (Specify the Delivery Point within the Place of Delivery)

按FCA成交，需填入指定交货地点，该交货地点将对买卖双方装卸货物的责任产生不同影响。按《2020通则》规定，若指定地点是卖方所在地，则卖方要将货物装上买方的运输工具；若指定地点是另一地点，则卖方要将货物装上卖方的运输工具并运抵该指定地点，且做好从卖方运输工具上卸载的准备，以完成交货义务。

If a transaction is concluded on an FCA basis, the named place of delivery shall be filled in. This place of delivery will have different impacts on the responsibility of buyers and sellers to load or unload goods. According to Incoterms® 2020, if the named place is where the sellers are located, the sellers shall load the goods on the buyers' means of conveyance; if the named place is another place, the sellers shall load the goods on the sellers' means of conveyance and deliver them to the named place, and be ready for unloading from the sellers' means of conveyance to complete the delivery obligation.

在实际业务中，建议买卖双方尽可能清楚地指明在指定交货地范围内的详细交货点。详细的交货点会让双方均可清楚货物交付的时间和风险转移至买方的时间，并可明确买方承担费用的地点。若双方未指明详细的交货点，根据《2020通则》规定，卖方有权选择"最适合卖方目的"的地点，该地点即成为交货点，风险和费用从该点起转移至买方。

In practice, it is recommended that both parties indicate as clearly as possible a detailed point of delivery within the specified place of delivery. The detailed delivery point will make it clear to either party when the goods are delivered and when risks are transferred to the buyers, as well as the place where the buyers bear the expenses. If neither party specifies a detailed delivery point, in accordance with Incoterms® 2020, the sellers shall have the right to choose the location "most suitable for sellers' purposes", which becomes the delivery point from which risk and expense pass to the buyers.

2. 卖方可取得已装船批注的提单 (Sellers may Obtain a B/L with on Board Notation)

海运提单具有物权凭证的性质，在银行托收或信用证支付会要求卖方凭已装船的提单取得付款。而FCA适用于任一或多种运输方式，如果货物是在陕西西安由买方的公路运输车接载，承运人是无法出具在陕西西安装运的已装船批注提单的，因为陕西西安不是海运港口，船舶无法抵达该地装运货物。为满足卖方使用FCA销售时对已装船提单的需求，FCA Incoterms® 2020首次提供以下可选机制。如果双方在销售合同中如此约定，则买方必须指示承运人出具已装船批注提单给卖方。如果双方已约定卖方将提交给买方一份仅声明货物已收妥待运的提单，则无须选择该方案。

Ocean B/L has the nature of documents of title. In bank collection or L/C payment, sellers are required to obtain payment against shipped B/L. However, FCA is applicable to any one or more transportation modes. If the goods are picked up by the buyers' road transport vehicle in Xi'an, Shaanxi Province, the carrier cannot issue a B/L with on board notation for shipment in Xi'an, Shaanxi Province, because Xi'an, Shaanxi Province is not a sea port and no ship cannot arrive there to load the goods. To meet the sellers' needs for shipped B/L when selling under FCA, FCA Incoterms® 2020 provides the following optional mechanisms for the first time. If both parties so agrees in the sales contract, the buyers must instruct the carrier to issue a B/L with on board notation to the sellers. This option is not required if both parties have agreed that the sellers will submit to the buyers a B/L which only states that the goods have been received for shipment.

五、CPT
V. CPT

(一) CPT的含义 (Meaning of CPT)

CPT [Carriage Paid to (insert named place of destination),运费付至(填入指定目的地)],是指卖方必须订立将货物运往指定目的地的运输合同并支付运费,并且在约定日期或期限内将货物交给与卖方签订运输合同的承运人,或取得已经如此交付的货物,即完成交货义务,货物灭失或损坏的风险自货物移交给承运人时起转移给买方。该术语可适用于任何或多种运输方式。

CPT [Carriage Paid to (insert named place of destination)] means that the sellers must enter into a contract of carriage and pay freight charges for carrying the goods to the named place of destination and deliver the goods to the carrier who has entered into a contract of carriage with the sellers on an agreed date or within an agreed time limit. The buyers shall be deemed to have fulfilled the delivery obligation by taking possession of the goods so delivered, and the risk of loss or damage to the goods shall be transferred to the buyers from the time when the goods are handed over to the carrier. It is applicable to various transportation modes.

在合同中正确使用CPT的方法是,将CPT订入合同的价格条款,如"USD 60.00 / CARTON CPT WINCHESTER RAILWAY STATION INCOTERMS® 2020",CPT后填入的是目的地的名称,卖方必须自费订立将货物运至该指定目的地的运输合同。

The correct way to use CPT in the contract is to include CPT in the price clause of the contract, such as "USD 60.00 /CARTON CPT WINCHESTER RAILWAY STATION INCOTERMS® 2020", followed by the name of the destination, and the sellers must conclude a contract of carriage at their own expense to transport the goods to the named destination.

(二) CPT对买卖双方主要义务的划分 (Main Obligations of Buyers and Sellers under CPT)

根据《2020通则》,CPT下买卖双方的主要义务如表3-8所示。

According to Incoterms® 2020, the main obligations of buyers and sellers under CPT are as follows (Table 3-8).

表3-8 CPT下买卖双方的主要义务
Table 3-8 Main Obligations of Buyers and Sellers under CPT

项目 Item	卖方 Seller	买方 Buyer
责任 Responsibilities	1. 必须提供符合销售合同约定的货物和商业发票,及合同可能要求的其他与合同相符的证据,以及运输单据 The sellers must provide goods and commercial invoice conforming to the provisions of the sales contract, other evidence that may be required by the contract to comply with the contract, as well as transport documents	1. 必须按销售合同约定支付货物价款,提取货物,接受运输单据 The buyers must pay the price of goods, take delivery of goods and accept transport documents as agreed in the sales contract

续表

项目 Item	卖方 Seller	买方 Buyer
责任 Responsibilities	2. 必须在约定日期或期限内在约定的交货地点将货物交给与卖方签订运输合同的承运人,或以取得已经如此交付的货物,并给予买方充分通知 The sellers must deliver the goods to the carrier who has signed a contract of carriage with them on the agreed date or within the agreed time limit at the agreed place of delivery, or take possession of the goods so delivered, and give adequate notices to the buyers 3. 必须签订或取得运输合同,将货物自交货地运送至指定目的地,并遵守与运输有关的安全要求 The sellers must sign or obtain a contract of carriage to transport the goods from the place of delivery to the named destination, and comply with the relevant safety requirements 4. 必须提供其所拥有的买方取得保险所需的信息 The sellers must provide the information they have that the buyers need to obtain insurance 5. 如需要,必须办理出口国(地区)要求的所有清关手续并支付费用,如出口许可证、出口安检清关、装运前检验及任何其他官方授权 The sellers must complete all customs clearance formalities required by the exporting country (region), such as export licenses, export security clearance, pre-shipment inspection and any other official authorization and pay for them if necessary 6. 必须以适合该货物运输的方式对货物进行包装和标记 The sellers must pack and mark the goods in a manner appropriate to carriage	2. 如需要,必须办理任何过境国和进口国(地区)要求的所有手续并支付费用,如进口许可及过境所需的任何许可、进口及任何过境安检清关、装运前检验及任何其他官方授权 The buyers must complete and pay for all formalities required by any transit and importing country (region), if necessary, such as import licences and any permits required for transit, import and any transit security clearance, pre-shipment inspection and any other official authorization
费用 Costs	1. 货物在约定交货点货交承运人处置之前的一切费用 All expenses before the goods are disposed of by the carrier at the agreed delivery point 2. 如需要,办理出口清关的关税、税款和任何其他费用 Customs duty, tax and any other charges for export clearance if required	1. 货物在指定交货点货交承运人处置之后的一切费用 All expenses after the goods are disposed of by the carrier at the named delivery point 2. 如需要,办理过境或进口清关的关税、税款和任何其他费用 Customs duty, tax and any other charges for transit or import clearance if required

续表

项目 Item	卖方 Seller	买方 Buyer
费用 Costs	3. 货物运至指定目的地的运费，包括装货费用及与运输有关的安全费用 Freight charges for delivery of the goods to the named destination, including loading and security costs associated with carriage	3. 过境费用，除非根据运输合同该项费用应由卖方承担 Transit charges, unless they are to be borne by the sellers in accordance with the contract of carriage 4. 卸货费用，除非根据运输合同该项费用应由卖方承担 Unloading charges, unless they are to be borne by the sellers in accordance with the contract of carriage
风险 Risks	承担货交承运人处置之前的一切风险 Assume all risks before disposal by the carrier	承担货交承运人处置之时起的一切风险 Assume all risks from the time of disposal by the carrier

（三）按CPT成交应注意的问题 (Precautions for CPT)

1. 交货地和目的地 (Place of Delivery and Destination)

在CPT规则中，有两个地点非常重要：一个是货物的交货地或交货点（如有），另一个是约定为货物终点的目的地或目的点。需要特别注意的是，CPT后填入的是指定目的地，卖方需要自费订立将货物运至该目的地的运输合同，但卖方并不保证货物以良好的状态、约定的数量或是否确实到达该目的地，因为卖方在约定的交货地将货物交给承运人时就已经完成了交货，风险自该交货点起转移给买方。所以，交货点用于确定风险转移，目的地作为卖方承诺签订运输合同运至的地点，需要区别开来。

Under CPT, two places are very important: one is the place or point of delivery (if any) for the goods and the other is the place or point of destination for the goods. It should be noted that the named destination is filled in after CPT, and the sellers need to conclude a contract of carriage for transporting the goods to this destination at their own expense. However, they do not guarantee that the goods will arrive at the destination in good condition, in the agreed quantity, or indeed, because the goods have been delivered when they are handed over to the carrier at the agreed delivery place, and the risk passes to the buyers from this delivery point. Therefore, the delivery point is used to determine the transfer of risks, while the destination serves as the place the sellers promise to transport to in the contract of carriage, and the two need to be distinguished.

在实践业务中，建议双方在销售合同中尽可能精准地确定交货地和目的地，或交货地和目的地内的具体地点。对于多个承运人各自负责自交货地到目的地之间不同运输路程的情况，若双方未约定具体的交货地或交货点，则默认当卖方将货物交给第一个承运人时，风险即发生转移。在销售合同中尽可能精准地确定约定目的地内的具体地点，因为该地点是卖方必须签订运输合同运至的地点，并且是卖方承担运费直到该地点为止的地点。

In practice, it is recommended that the delivery place and destination or a specific location within the delivery place and destination be determined as precisely as possible by both parties in the sales contract. Where more than one carrier is responsible for different routes of carriage from the place of delivery to the destination, if no specific place or point of delivery has been agreed upon by both parties, it will be assumed that risk passes when the sellers hand over the goods to the first carrier. The place within the agreed destination is specified as precisely as possible in the sales contract, for it is the place the sellers must sign a contract of carriage to transport to and where they bear freight charges until that point.

2. 目的地卸货费用的负担 (Bearing of Unloading Charges at Destination)

根据《2020通则》，CPT下目的地卸货费用由买方承担，但运输合同规定由卖方承担的除外。如果卖方在其运输合同项下承担了在指定目的地的相关卸货费用，除非双方另有约定，卖方无权另行向买方追偿该费用。所以，如果按卖方订立的运输合同，运费中已包含了目的地卸货费用，则卸货费由卖方承担；如果目的地卸货费用是货到目的地后另外收取的，则卸货费由买方承担。

According to Incoterms® 2020, the unloading charges at destination under CPT shall be borne by the buyers, except for those specified in the contract of carriage which shall be borne by the sellers. If the sellers bear relevant unloading charges at the named destination under their contract of carriage, the sellers shall not be entitled to recover such expenses from the buyers unless otherwise agreed by both parties. Therefore, according to the contract of carriage concluded by the sellers, if the unloading charges at destination have been included in the freight charges, the unloading charges shall be borne by the sellers; if the unloading charges at destination are additionally charged after the goods arrive at the destination, the unloading charges shall be borne by the buyers.

六、CIP
VI. CIP

（一）CIP的含义 (Meaning of CIP)

CIP [Carriage and Insurance Paid to (insert named place of destination)，运费和保险费付至（填入指定目的地）]，是指卖方必须订立将货物运往指定目的地的运输合同并支付运费，订立货物运输保险合同并支付保险费，并且在约定日期或期限内将货物交给与卖方签订运输合同的承运人，或取得已经如此交付的货物，即完成交货义务，货物灭失或损坏的风险自货物移交给承运人时起转移给买方。该术语可适用于任何或多种运输方式。

CIP [Carriage and Insurance Paid to (insert named place of destination)] means that sellers must enter into a contract of carriage to transport the goods to the named destination and pay freight charges, enter into a cargo insurance contract and pay the premium. The buyers shall complete the delivery obligation by delivering the goods to the carrier who has signed the contract of carriage with the sellers on the agreed date or within the agreed period, or taking possession of the goods that have been so delivered. The risk of loss or damage to the goods shall be transferred to the buyers from the time when the goods are handed over to the carrier. It is applicable to various transportation modes.

在合同中正确使用CIP的方法是，将CIP订入合同的价格条款，如"USD 65.00 /CARTON CIP WINCHESTER RAILWAY STATION INCOTERMS® 2020"，CIP后填入的是目的地的名称，卖方必须自费订立将货物运至该指定目的地的运输合同和货物运输保险合同。

The correct way to use CIP in the contract is to include CIP in the price clause of the contract, such as "USD 65.00 /CARTON CIP WINCHESTER RAILWAY STATION INCOTERMS® 2020", followed by the name of the destination, and the sellers must conclude a contract of carriage and cargo insurance contract for transporting the goods to the named destination at their own expense.

（二）CIP对买卖双方主要义务的划分 (Main Obligations of Buyers and Sellers under CIP)

根据《2020通则》，CIP下买卖双方的主要义务如表3-9所示。

According to Incoterms® 2020, the main obligations of buyers and sellers under CIP are as follows (Table 3-9).

表3-9　CIP下买卖双方的主要义务

Table 3-9　Main Obligations of Buyers and Sellers under CIP

项目 Item	卖方 Seller	买方 Buyer
责任 Responsibilities	1. 必须提供符合销售合同约定的货物和商业发票，及合同可能要求的其他与合同相符的证据，以及运输单据和保险单据 The sellers must provide goods and commercial invoice conforming to the provisions of the sales contract, other evidence that may be required by the contract to comply with the contract, as well as transport documents and insurance policy 2. 必须在约定日期或期限内在约定的交货地点将货物交给与卖方签订运输合同的承运人，或以取得已经如此交付的货物，并给予买方充分通知 The sellers must deliver the goods to the carrier who has signed a contract of carriage with them on the agreed date or within the agreed time limit at the agreed place of delivery, or take possession of the goods so delivered, and give adequate notices to the buyers 3. 必须签订或取得运输合同，将货物自交货地运送至指定目的地，并遵守与运输有关的安全要求 The sellers must sign or obtain a contract of carriage to transport the goods from the place of delivery to the named destination, and comply with the relevant safety requirements 4. 必须自负费用取得货物保险 The sellers must obtain cargo insurance at their own expense 5. 如需要，必须办理出口国（地区）要求的所有清关手续并支付费用，如出口许可证、出口安检清关、装运前检验及任何其他官方授权 The sellers must complete all customs clearance formalities required by the exporting country, such as export licenses, export security clearance (region), pre-shipment inspection and any other official authorization and pay for them if necessary 6. 必须以适合该货物运输的方式对货物进行包装和标记 The sellers must pack and mark the goods in a manner appropriate to carriage	1. 必须按销售合同约定支付货物价款，提取货物，接受运输单据 The buyers must pay the price of goods, take delivery of goods and accept transport documents as agreed in the sales contract 2. 如需要，必须办理任何过境国和进口国（地区）要求的所有手续并支付费用，如进口许可及过境所需的任何许可、进口及任何过境安检清关、装运前检验及任何其他官方授权 The buyers must complete and pay for all formalities required by any transit and importing country (region), if necessary, such as import licences and any permits required for transit, import and any transit security clearance, pre-shipment inspection and any other official authorization

续表

项目 Item	卖方 Seller	买方 Buyer
费用 Costs	1. 货物在约定交货点货交承运人处置之前的一切费用 All expenses before the goods are disposed of by the carrier at the agreed delivery point 2. 如需要，办理出口清关的关税、税款和任何其他费用 Customs duty, tax and any other charges for export clearance if required 3. 货物运至指定目的地的运费，包括装货费用及与运输有关的安全费用 Freight charges for delivery of the goods to the named destination, including loading and security costs associated with carriage 4. 货物运输保险费 Cargo transportation insurance premiums	1. 货物在指定交货点货交承运人处置之后的一切费用 All expenses after the goods are disposed of by the carrier at the named delivery point 2. 如需要，办理过境或进口清关的关税、税款和任何其他费用 Customs duty, tax and any other charges for transit or import clearance if required 3. 过境费用，除非根据运输合同该项费用应由卖方承担 Transit charges, unless they are to be borne by the sellers in accordance with the contract of carriage 4. 卸货费用，除非根据运输合同该项费用应由卖方承担 Unloading charges, unless they are to be borne by the sellers in accordance with the contract of carriage
风险 Risks	承担货交承运人处置之前的一切风险 Assume all risks before disposal by the carrier	承担货交承运人处置之时起的一切风险 Assume all risks from the time of disposal by the carrier

（三）按 CIP 成交应注意的问题 (Precautions for CIP)

1. 卖方投保的义务 (Sellers' Obligation to Insure)

根据《2020 通则》，按 CIP 成交，卖方还必须签订从交货点起至少到目的点的货物运输保险合同。虽然自交货点到目的点的货物运输保险是由卖方负责办理的，但自交货点起货物灭失或损坏的风险却应由买方承担。所以，卖方的投保具有代办性质，即为买方的利益投保，保险单的投保人是卖方，在买方付款后，卖方可将保险单以背书的方式转让给买方，让买方取得保单上的权利。

The sellers must also enter into a cargo insurance contract from the delivery point to at least the destination point on a CIP basis as per Incoterms® 2020. Although the insurance for carriage of goods from delivery point to destination point is the responsibility of the sellers, the risk of loss or damage to the goods from delivery point shall be borne by the buyers. Therefore, the sellers' insurance is of an agency nature, that is, to insure the interests of the buyers. The policy holder of the insurance policy is the sellers. After the buyers' payment, the sellers can transfer the insurance policy to the buyers by endorsement, so that the buyers can obtain the rights on the insurance policy.

还需要特别注意的是，在 CIP Incoterms® 2020 规则下，卖方需要投保符合英国《协会货物保险条款》（A）或其他类似条款下的范围广泛的险别，而不是符合英国《协会货物保险条款》（C）下的范围较为有限的险别。但是，双方仍然可以自行约定更低的险别。这点是《2020通则》相比之前版本对CIP做出的较大修改，之前版本都规定CIP下的卖方与CIF下一样，只需投保最低险别，但现行版本则要求CIP下的卖方必须投保最高险别，而CIF下的卖方仍只需投保最低险别。最低保险金额应为合同规定价格另加10%（即110%），并采用合同货币。

It is also important to note that under the CIP Incoterms® 2020, the sellers are required to insure a wide range of coverage in accordance with ICC(A) or other similar provisions rather than more limited coverage in accordance with ICC(C). However, the buyers and sellers are still free to agree on less coverage. This is a major modification to CIP compared with previous versions of Incoterms® 2020. Previous versions stipulated that sellers under CIP only need to insure the minimum coverage as under CIF, but the current version requires sellers under CIP to insure the maximum coverage, while sellers under CIF still only need to insure the minimum coverage. The minimum insured amount shall be the contract price plus 10% (i.e. 110%) and denominated in the currencies of the contract.

2. 两个"分界点"的问题 (Two "Cut-off Points")

CIP存在两个"分界点"：一个是风险分界点，它划分了买卖双方承担的货物灭失或损坏的风险；一个是费用分界点，它划分了买卖双方承担的主运费和保险费。CIP的风险分界点应该是在交货地，即在约定的交货地卖方将货物交给承运人时，风险从卖方转移至买方，所以货物自交货地到指定目的地的风险是由买方承担的。CIP的主运费和保险费的分界点在指定目的地，因为卖方必须支付将货物运至指定目的地的运费和保险费。但需要明确的是，卖方只需支付通常的运费和保险费，其他额外费用除合同另有规定外，在卖方完成交货义务后应由买方承担。

There are two "cut-off points" in CIP: one is the risk cut-off point, which divides the risk of loss or damage to goods borne by both parties; the other is the cost cut-off point, which divides the main freight and premium borne by both parties. The risk cut-off point of CIP shall be at the delivery place, that is, when the sellers hand over the goods to the carrier at the agreed delivery place, the risks are transferred from the sellers to the buyers. Therefore, the risks of the goods from the delivery place to the named destination shall be borne by the buyers. The cut-off point of CIP's main freight and premium is at the named destination as sellers have to pay the freight charges and premium for shipping goods to the named destination. However, it should be made clear that the sellers only need to pay the usual freight charges and premium. Unless otherwise specified in the contract, other additional expenses shall be borne by the buyers after the sellers complete their delivery obligations.

实际上，六种主要贸易术语中，只有FOB和FCA两种贸易术语的风险分界点和费用分界点是重合的，CFR、CIF、CPT和CIP四种贸易术语都存在两个分界点的问题。很多人误以为贸易术语后填入的港口或地点就是交货地点，实际上，只有FOB和FCA等F组的术语可以这样理解，C组的术语（即首字母为C的贸易术语）后面填入的港口或地点并非交货地点，而是卖方需要办理至该地点的货物运输和保险，但卖方并不保证在该地点将货物按时、完好、安全地交给买方，因为卖方在交货地将货物交给承运人时即完成了交货，按这些贸易术语签订的合同都为术语装运合同。

In fact, among the six main trade terms, only FOB and FCA have overlapping risk and cost cut-off points, while CFR, CIF, CPT and CIP have two cut-off points. Many people mistakenly think that the port or place filled in after the trade terms is the place of delivery. In fact, only the terms in Group F such as FOB and FCA can be understood in this way. The port or place filled in after the terms in group C (i.e. Trade Terms with the initial letter of C) does not mean the place of delivery, but that the sellers need to handle the carriage and insurance of goods to this place, but they do not guarantee that the goods will be delivered to the buyers on time, in good condition and safely at this place. Since the sellers complete delivery when they hand over the goods to the carrier at the place of delivery, all contracts concluded under these trade terms are shipment contracts.

第三节　其他五种贸易术语
Section 3　Five Other Trade Terms

除了六种主要贸易术语以外，《2020 通则》还规定了其他五种贸易术语。虽然这五种贸易术语并不常用，但在某些情况下，可以满足买方或卖方的特定要求。因此，也需要了解并掌握其他五种贸易术语。

In addition to the six main trade terms, five others are specified in Incoterms® 2020. Although these five trade terms are not commonly used, they can meet the specific requirements of the buyers or sellers in some cases. Therefore, it is also necessary to understand and master the other five trade terms.

一、EXW
I. EXW

EXW [Ex Works (insert named place of delivery)，工厂交货（填入指定交货地点）]，是指卖方在约定的日期或期限内，在指定地点（如工厂或仓库）将货物交给买方处置时，即完成交货。卖方不需要将货物装上任何前来接收货物的运输工具，需要清关时，卖方也无须办理出口清关手续。该术语可适用于任何或多种运输方式。

EXW [Ex Works (insert named place of delivery)] refers to the time when the sellers deliver the goods to the buyers for disposal at a named place (such as factory or warehouse) on an agreed date or within an agreed time limit. The sellers are not required to load the goods on any means of conveyance to receive them, nor are they required to clear customs for export. It is applicable to various transportation modes.

EXW 是卖方承担的义务最少，而买方承担的义务最多的贸易术语。因此，从买方角度出发，基于以下原因，应谨慎使用该术语。若买方希望规避在卖方场所装载货物期间的风险，应考虑选择 FCA（在 FCA 下，若货物在卖方场所交付，则卖方负有装载货物的义务并承担货物装载中的风险）。若买方预计办理出口清关会有困难时，建议买方最好选择 FCA（在 FCA 下，办理出口清关的义务和费用由卖方承担）。

EXW is a trade term in which the sellers have the least obligation and the buyers the most. Therefore, from the perspective of the buyers, this term should be used with caution for the following reasons. If the buyers wish to avoid risks during loading of the goods at sellers' premises, they should consider FCA (under which if the goods are delivered at sellers' premises, the sellers have an obligation to load and bear the risk in loading the goods). If the buyers anticipate difficulties in handling export customs clearance, it is suggested that the buyers choose FCA (under which the obligations and expenses of handling export customs clearance shall be borne by the sellers).

二、FAS
II. FAS

FAS [Free Alongside Ship (insert named port of shipment)，船边交货（填入指定装运港）]，

是指卖方在约定的日期或按买方通知的约定期限内的交货时间，将符合合同规定的货物交到指定装运港船边（如置于码头或驳船上），该船舶由买方指定，或取得已经如此交付的货物，即完成交货义务。货物灭失或损坏的风险在货物交到船边时发生转移，同时，买方承担自那时起的一切费用。该术语仅适用于海运或内河水运。

FAS [Free Alongside Ship (insert named port of shipment)] refers to that the sellers deliver the goods conforming to the provisions of the contract to the ship's side (such as the yard or barge) of the named port of shipment on the agreed date or within the delivery time agreed in the buyers' Notices. The buyers shall be deemed to have fulfilled the obligation of delivery if they nominate the vessel or take possession of the goods so delivered. The risk of loss or damage to the goods shall be transferred when they are delivered to the ship's side, and all expenses incurred therefrom shall be borne by the buyers. It applies only to sea or inland water transport.

在实践业务中，FAS一般适用于大宗货物的交易，因为大宗货物通常采用租船运输，若按照船方不负责装卸费用的条件签订租船合同，则装船费用应由买卖双方中的一方承担。如果按FOB成交，因为卖方需要将货物装上船以完成交货，所以装船费用应由卖方承担，不仅如此，卖方还须承担货物装船的风险和责任。而如果按FAS成交，则装船的风险、责任和费用均由买方承担，因为卖方只需在船边完成交货。所以，FAS和FOB就货物装船义务给出了不同的划分，由此给买卖双方不同的选择。此外，当买方所派船只不能靠岸时，卖方要负责用驳船把货物运至买方指派船只的船边，仍在船边交货。

In practice, FAS is generally applicable to the trading of bulk cargoes, because the charter is usually adopted for bulk cargoes. If a charter contract is signed on an FIO basis, the loading expenses shall be borne by either the buyers or the sellers. If the transaction is concluded on an FOB basis, the loading cost shall be borne by the sellers because they need to load the goods on board to complete the delivery. Moreover, the sellers must also bear the risk and responsibility of loading the goods on board. However, if the transaction is concluded on an FAS basis, all risks, responsibilities and expenses of shipment shall be borne by the buyers, because the sellers only need to complete delivery alongside the vessel. Therefore, FAS and FOB have given different divisions to the obligation of loading goods, thus offering buyers and sellers a different choice. In addition, when the ship dispatched by the buyers cannot dock, the sellers shall be responsible for transporting the goods to the ship's side by barge for FAS.

三、DAP
III. DAP

DAP [Delivered at Place (insert named place of destination)，目的地交货（填入指定目的地）]，是指卖方在指定目的地将处于抵达运输工具上已做好卸货准备的货物交由买方处置时，完成交货并转移风险。卖方承担将货物运送到指定目的地或该指定目的地内的约定交货点的一切风险。卖方不需要将货物从抵达的运输工具上卸载。DAP可适用于任何或多种运输方式。

DAP [Delivered at Place (insert named place of destination)] means that the sellers complete delivery and transfer risks when the goods ready for unloading on the means of conveyance are placed at the buyers' disposal at the named destination. The sellers assume all risks in delivering the goods to the named destination or agreed delivery point within such named destination. The sellers are not required to unload the goods from the means of conveyance upon arrival. DAP is applicable to various transportation modes.

在DAP下，交货地和目的地是相同的，也就是说卖方是在目的地完成交货的，所以按

DAP 成交的合同属于到达合同，卖方必须将货物按时、完好、安全地交付到买方才能完成交货。在实践业务中，建议买卖双方尽可能清楚地约定目的地或目的点，因为以下几个原因：第一，货物灭失或损坏的风险在该目的地或目的点转移至买方；第二，该目的地或目的点之前的费用由卖方承担，该目的地或目的点之后的费用由买方承担；第三，卖方必须签订运输合同或安排货物运输至该目的地或目的点。若卖方未履行上述义务，卖方即违反了 DAP Incoterms® 2020 规则中的义务，并将对买方任何随之产生的损失承担责任。

Under DAP, the place of delivery and destination are the same, that is to say, the sellers complete the delivery at the destination. Therefore, the contract concluded under DAP is an arrival contract, and the sellers must deliver the goods to the buyers on time, in good condition and safely before completing the delivery. In practice, it is recommended that both parties agree on a place or point of destination as precisely as possible for several reasons: First, the risk of loss or damage to the goods is transferred to the buyers at that destination; Second, the expenses before such place or point of destination shall be borne by the sellers and the expenses after such place or point of destination shall be borne by the buyers; Third, the sellers must enter into a contract of carriage or arrange for the goods to be transported to such place or point of destination. If the sellers fail to fulfill the above obligations, the sellers are in breach of their obligations under DAP Incoterms® 2020 and will be liable for any consequential losses incurred by the buyers.

四、DPU
IV. DPU

DPU [Delivered at Place Unloaded (insert named place of destination)，目的地卸货后交货（填入指定目的地）]，是指卖方在指定目的地将已从抵达运输工具上卸载的货物交由买方处置时，完成交货并转移风险。卖方承担将货物运送到指定目的地以及卸载货物的一切风险。DPU 可适用于任何或多种运输方式。

DPU [Delivered at Place Unloaded (insert named place of destination)] means that the sellers complete delivery and transfer risks when the goods unloaded from the means of conveyance are placed at the buyers' disposal at the named destination. The sellers bear all the risks of transporting the goods to their named destination and unloading them. DPU is applicable to various transportation modes.

DPU 是唯一要求卖方在目的地卸货的贸易术语。因此，卖方应确保其可以在指定地组织卸货。

DPU is the only trade term that requires the sellers to unload at destination. Therefore, the sellers shall ensure that they can organize unloading at the named place.

五、DDP
V. DDP

DDP [Delivered Duty Paid (insert named place of destination)，完税后交货（填入指定目的地）]，是指卖方在指定目的地将已办理进口清关并处于抵达运输工具上已做好卸货准备的货物交由买方处置时，完成交货并转移风险。卖方承担将货物运送到指定目的地或该指定目的地内的约定交货点的一切风险。DDP 可适用于任何或多种运输方式。

DDP [Delivered Duty Paid (insert named place of destination)] means that the sellers complete delivery and transfer risks when the goods that have been cleared for import and are ready for unloading on the means of conveyance are placed at the buyers' disposal at the named destination. The sellers assume all risks in delivering the goods to the named destination or agreed delivery point within such named destination. DDP is applicable to various transportation modes.

DDP 是《2020 通则》规定的全部 11 个贸易术语中卖方承担的风险、责任最大和费用最多的贸易术语。在 DDP 下，交货发生在目的地，并且由卖方负责进口清关，并支付任何进口关税或办理任何海关手续。因此，如果卖方无法办理进口清关，应考虑选择 DAP 或 DPU。

It is the trade term with the greatest risk, liability and cost borne by sellers of all 11 trade terms under Incoterms® 2020. Under DDP, delivery takes place at the destination and sellers are responsible for import clearance and payment of any import duties or customs formalities. Therefore, DAP or DPU should be considered if the sellers are unable to clear imports.

第三章拓展知识、专业词汇和练习

第四章　商品的名称和质量
Chapter 4　Name and Quality of Commodity

导　读
Introduction

在国际货物买卖中，从签订合同到交付货物往往需要相隔较长的时间。另外，交易双方在磋商交易和签订买卖合同时，通常很少见到具体商品，一般只是凭借对将要买卖的商品做必要的描述来确定交易的标的。

In the international trade of goods, it often takes a long time from signing the contract to delivering the goods. In addition, when negotiating a transaction and signing a sales contract, the buyers and sellers rarely see specific commodities, and generally only rely on the necessary description of the commodities to be sold to determine the subject matter of the transaction.

进入国际市场的货物种类繁多，即使是同一种商品，其品种、花色、质量、产地、外观等也会有所不同，因此标的物及其品质的不同，不仅会影响商品的用途、运输方式，而且会造成价格上的差异。可见，明确规定标的物及其品质要求，是买卖双方商订国际贸易合同时需要首先达成一致的条款。

As there are many kinds of goods entering the international market, even the same commodity will have different varieties, designs and colors, quality, place of origin, appearance, etc. Therefore, the difference in subject matter and its quality will not only affect the purpose and transportation mode of the commodity, but also cause price differences. It can be seen that defining the subject matter and its quality requirements is the first clause that needs to be agreed upon by both parties when negotiating an international trade contract.

第一节　品名、品质的含义
Section 1　Meaning of Commodity and Quality

一、品名的含义
I. Meaning of Commodity

商品名称或品名（name of commodity），是指能使某种商品区别于其他商品的一种称呼或概念。商品的名称在一定程度上体现了商品的自然属性、用途及主要的性能特征。

Name of commodity refers to a name or concept that can distinguish a certain commodity from other commodities. To some extent, the name of a commodity reflects its natural attributes, purpose, and main performance characteristics.

二、品质的含义
II. Meaning of Quality

商品的品质（quality of goods）是指商品的外观形态和内在质量的综合指标。商品的外观形态是通过人们的感觉器官可以直接获得的商品的外形特征，如商品的大小、长短、造型、款式、色泽、味觉等。商品的内在质量则是指商品的物理性能、机械性能、化学成分、生物特征、技术指标和要求等，如纺织品的色牢度、防水性能，机械商品的精密度，肉禽类商品的各种菌类含量等。

Quality of goods (QOG) refers to a comprehensive indicator of the appearance and internal quality of goods. Appearance of goods is the appearance characteristics of goods that can be directly obtained through people's sensory organs, such as size, length, shape, style, color, taste, etc. The internal quality of commodities refers to the physical properties, mechanical properties, chemical compositions, biological characteristics, technical indicators and requirements of commodities, such as color fastness, waterproof performance, precision of machinery commodities, various fungi contents of meat and poultry commodities, etc.

第二节　品质的表示方法
Section 2　Representation of Quality

国际贸易中所交易的商品种类繁多，特点各异，通常根据商品特性和交易习惯，有两大类表示商品品质的方法，即凭实物表示和凭说明表示。

There are many kinds of commodities traded in international trade with different characteristics. Usually, based on the characteristics and trading practice of the goods, there are two main methods to represent the QOG, namely physical representation and description.

一、凭实物表示商品品质
I. Representation of QOG with Physical Objects

凭实物表示品质，包括凭成交商品的实际品质和凭样品两种表示方法。前者指看货买卖，后者指凭样品买卖。

Representation of QOG with includes the actual quality of traded goods and samples. The former refers Sale by Actual Quality, while the latter refers to Sale by Sample.

（一）看货买卖 (Sale by Actual Quality)

当买卖双方采用看货成交时，则买方或其代理人通常先在卖方存放货物的场所验看货物，一旦达成交易，卖方就应按对方验看过的商品交货。只要卖方交货是买方验看过的货物，买方就不得对品质提出异议。采用看货成交有很大的局限性，一般只适用于一些具有独特性质的商品，如特殊的工艺品、古玩、首饰、名人字画等，通常是在拍卖、寄售或展卖时采用。

When both parties conclude the transaction based on actual quality, the buyers or their agents usually inspect the goods first at the place where the sellers store them. Once the transaction is concluded, the sellers shall deliver the goods according to the goods inspected by the other party. As long as the goods delivered by the sellers are those inspected by the buyers, the buyers shall not raise any objection to the quality. There are great limitations in the use of sale by actual quality, which is generally only applicable to some commodities with unique properties, such as special handicrafts, antiques, jewelry, paintings of celebrities, etc. It is usually used at auction, consignment or exhibition.

（二）凭样品买卖 (Based on Samples)

样品是指从一批商品中抽出来的或由生产使用部门设计加工出来的，足以反映和代表整批商品品质的少量实物。凡以样品表示商品品质，并以样品作为交货依据的买卖，称为"凭样品买卖"。样品有标准样品和参考样品之分，标准样品是卖方交货的品质依据，而参考样品是供买方了解品质状况、促进成交使用。故为避免误解，在寄送参考样品时应注明"仅供参考"（For reference only）字样。

Samples refer to a small number of physical objects drawn from a batch of goods or designed and processed by the production and use department, which are sufficient to reflect and represent the quality of the whole batch. A sale with QOG represented by samples and delivery on the basis of samples is called "Sale by Sample". Samples are divided into type sample and reference sample. Type sample is the quality basis for sellers to deliver goods, while reference sample is used by the buyers to understand the quality status and promote transaction. To avoid misunderstandings, the words "For reference only" should be indicated when sending reference samples.

按照提供样品者的不同，凭样品买卖可分为凭卖方样品买卖、凭买方样品买卖和凭对等样品买卖三种。

According to different sample providers, sale by sample can be divided into three types: sale by seller's sample, sale by buyer's sample and sale by counter sample.

1. 凭卖方样品买卖 (Sale by Seller's Sample)

凡凭卖方样品作为交货依据的，称为凭卖方样品买卖，应在合同中列明："Quality as per Seller's sample"。

Where the seller's sample is used as the basis for delivery, it is sale by seller's sample and "Quality as per Seller's sample" shall be specified in the contract.

采用凭卖方样品买卖时应注意以下几个问题。

The following issues should be noted when using sale by seller's sample.

（1）卖方所提供的样品应具有代表性。代表性样品应从有关商品中抽取并足以代表将来交货的品质。样品品质偏高会给卖方日后交货履约带来困难，偏低则会使卖方在价格上吃亏。

(1) The samples provided by the sellers shall be representative. A representative sample shall be taken from the commodity concerned and sufficient to represent the quality of future deliveries. High sample quality will make it difficult for sellers to fulfill their obligations in the future, while low sample quality will disadvantage sellers in price.

（2）卖方向买方提供样品时，都应留存复样（duplicate sample），并注明相同编号及送交买方的日期，以备日后交货或处理品质纠纷时核对之用。留存的复样应妥善保管，以保证样品品质的稳定。为避免买卖双方在履约过程中发生质量争议，必要时还可使用封样（sealed sample），即由第三方或由公证机关在一批商品中抽取并封存同样质量的样品若干份，由第三方或公证机关留存一份备案，其余供当事人使用。

(2) When the sellers provide samples to the buyers, they shall keep duplicate sample and indicate the same number and date of delivery to the buyers for future delivery or verification when handling quality disputes. Duplicate samples retained shall be properly kept to ensure the stability of sample quality. To avoid a quality dispute between the buyers and the sellers during the performance of the contract, sealed sample may also be used when necessary, that is, several samples with the same quality shall be taken and sealed by a third party or notary organ from a batch of commodities, one of which shall be kept by the third party or notary organ for filing, and the rest shall be used by the parties.

（3）要注意区分标准样品和参考样品。标准样品（type sample）为卖方日后交货的品质依据，而参考样品（reference sample）仅用作业务参考而不作为买卖双方交货的品质依据。所以，如果卖方寄送的样品若为参考样品，最好在寄送该样品时注明"仅供参考（For reference only)"字样，若没有注明，根据国际贸易惯例，买方可以将该样品当作标准样品。

(3) Pay attention to distinguish type sample from reference sample. Type sample is the quality basis for future delivery by sellers, while reference sample is only used as business reference and not as the quality basis for delivery by buyers and sellers. Therefore, if the sample sent by sellers is reference sample, it is better to indicate "For reference only" when sending the sample. If not indicated, the buyers may regard this sample as a type sample according to international trade customs.

2. 凭买方样品买卖 (Sale by Buyer's Sample)

买方为了使其订购的商品符合自身要求，有时也提供样品由卖方依样承制，如卖方同意按买方提供的样品成交，称为凭买方样品买卖。在我国出口业务中，习惯将其称为"来样成交"。采用这种方式时，卖方应核实自己在原材料、生产工艺、加工技术、设备和安排生产方面能否落实，是否有能力生产；并注意买方样品有无涉及第三者工业产权，并在合同中规定一切侵权责任概由买方负责。

In order to make the goods ordered meet their own requirements, sometimes the buyers also provide samples for the sellers to manufacture. If the sellers agree to conclude a transaction according to the samples provided by the buyers, it is sale by buyer's sample. In China's export business, it is customary to call it a "Sale by Buyer's Sample". When adopting this method, the sellers shall verify whether they can implement raw materials, production process, processing technology, equipment and arrangement of production, and whether they have the ability to produce; pay attention to whether the buyers' samples involve industrial property rights of a third party, and stipulate that all infringement liabilities shall be borne by the buyers in the contract.

在实际交易中，谨慎的卖方往往不愿意承接凭买方样品交货的交易，以免因交货品质与买方样品稍有不符就招致买方索赔、退货的危险。基于此，双方可采用凭对等样品买卖，这是一种折中的做法。

In actual transactions, prudent sellers are often unwilling to accept sale by buyer's sample, so as to avoid the risk of claim and return due to slight discrepancies in delivery quality with the buyers' samples. Under this consideration, both parties can adopt sale by counter sample, which is a compromise.

3. 凭对等样品买卖 (Sale by Counter Sample)

卖方可根据买方提供的样品，加工复制出一个类似的样品交买方确认，这种经确认后的样品称为对等样品（counter sample）或回样（return sample），也有称之为确认样品（confirming sample）。这种做法实际上是变凭买方样品买卖为凭卖方样品买卖，以避免由于实物与样品不符造成的交货困难或纠纷。

According to the samples provided by the buyers, the sellers can process and copy a similar sample for the buyers to confirm. This confirmed sample is called counter sample or return sample, also known as confirming sample. This practice is actually to change sale by buyer's sample into sale by seller's sample, so as to avoid delivery difficulties or disputes caused by inconsistency between the physical object and the sample.

在国际贸易实务中有时使用凭样品成交。在采用凭样品买卖时，应注意以下事项。

Sale by sample is used in the practice of international trade. When using sale by sample, attention shall be paid to the following matters.

（1）注意选择适于凭样品成交的商品。一般来说，凡不能用具体的质量指标和科学方法表示其品质的，或在色、香、味和造型等方面有特殊要求的商品，才适于凭样品成交，如工艺品、服装样式、部分轻工业品与农副土特产品。

(1) Pay attention to selecting commodities suitable for sale by sample. Generally speaking, goods whose

quality cannot be expressed by specific quality indicators and scientific methods or for which there are special requirements in color, fragrance, taste and shape are applicable to sale by sample, such as handicrafts, clothing styles, some light industrial products and agricultural and sideline local products.

（2）应了解和掌握有关法律对凭样品买卖的具体规定。按照有关法律和惯例，凡凭样品进行的买卖，卖方交付的货物品质必须与样品完全一致，否则，买方有权要求损害赔偿，甚至拒收货物、撤销合同。

(2) Understand and master the specific provisions of relevant laws on sale by sample. QOG delivered by the sellers must be exactly consistent with that of samples. Otherwise, the buyers shall have the right to claim damages or even reject the goods or cancel the contract.

（3）若使用凭样品买卖，为便于履约，双方可在合同中订立一些弹性品质条款，以防因交货品质与样品略有差异而导致买方拒收货物。例如：

(3) For sale by sample, in order to facilitate the performance of the contract, both parties may make some flexible quality clauses in the contract, so as to prevent the buyers from rejecting the goods due to slight differences in quality between delivered goods and the sample. Example:

Quality shall be about equal to the sample.
Shipment shall be similar to the sample.
Quality is to be nearly the same as the sample.

二、凭说明表示商品品质
II. Representation of QOG by Description

凭说明表示商品品质，是指用文字、图表、照片等方式来说明成交商品的品质。在国际货物买卖中，大部分商品采用这种方法表示其品质，但根据商品的特性不同，其具体方法又可分为以下几种。

QOG expressed by description refers to the quality of traded goods explained in words, charts and photos. Quality is expressed in this way for most commodities in international trade of goods. However, according to different characteristics of commodities, the specific methods can be divided into.

1. 凭规格买卖 (Sale by Specifications)

商品的规格是指一些足以反映商品品质的主要指标，如化学成分、含量、纯度、性能、容量、长短、粗细等。用它来表示商品品质，简明、方便、准确，所以在国际贸易中应用很广。

Specification of goods refers to some main indicators that can fully reflect the QOG, such as chemical composition, content, purity, performance, capacity, length and thickness. It is used to express QOG, which is concise, convenient and accurate, so it is widely used in international trade.

如Printed Shirting "Jumping Fish", 30 s×36 s（纱支），72×69（经纬密度），35"/36"（幅阔）× 42 yds（长度）

For example, Printed Shirting "Jumping Fish", 30 s×36 s (yarn count), 72×69 (warp count), 35"/36" (width) × 42 yds (length).

凭规格买卖时，说明商品品质的指标因商品不同而异。即使是同一商品，也会因用途不同而要求用不同的规格指标表示其品质。如同是大豆，榨油用的大豆须列明含油量，食用大豆则不一定要求列明含油量，而是把蛋白质含量作为重要指标。

For sale by specifications, the indicators demonstrating QOG vary from commodity to commodity. Even for the same commodity, different specification indicators will be required to express its quality according to different purposes. As in the case of soybeans, oil content must be stated for soybeans used for oil pressing, while it is not necessarily required for soybeans to be consumed. Protein content is an important indicator.

2. 凭等级买卖 (Sale by Grade)

商品的等级是指同一类商品按其规格上的差异，分为品质优劣各不相同的若干等级。如大中小、重中轻、一二三、甲乙丙、ABC等用文字、数码、符号来表示商品的品质。如我国出口的冻带骨兔（去皮、头、爪、内脏）肉可分为：特级，每只净重不低于1500克；大级，每只净重不低于1000克；中级，每只净重不低于600克；小级，每只净重不低于400克，每一级都规定了相对固定的规格。故等级是相对固定了的规格。

The grade of commodities refers to the classification of the same type of commodities into several grades with different quality according to their differences in specification. For example, "Big, Medium and Small", "Heavy, Medium and Light", "One, Two and Three", and "ABC" are used to represent the QOG by words, numbers and symbols. For example, frozen bone-free rabbit meat (without skin, head, claws, viscera) exported from China can be divided into: Special Grade, with a net weight of not less than 1500 g; Large Grade, with a net weight of not less than 1000 g; Medium Grade, with a net weight of not less than 600 g; Small Grade, with a net weight of not less than 400 g. Specification for each grade is relatively fixed. Therefore, the grade is a relatively fixed specification.

如Chinese Green Tea, Special Chunmee Grade 1 Art. No. 9318。

e.g. Chinese Green Tea, Special Chunmee Grade 1 Art. No. 9318.

在一般情况下，凭等级交易时，只要说明等级即可了解商品规格。但是为了便于履行合同和避免争议，在列明等级的同时，最好一并规定每一等级的具体规格。这种表示品质的方法，对简化手续、促进成交和体现按质论价等方面都有一定的作用。

In general, the commodity specification can be understood by simply stating the grade in sale by grade. However, in order to facilitate the performance of the contract and avoid disputes, it is advisable to provide the specific specification for each grade while listing the grades. This method of expressing quality is helpful in simplifying procedures, promoting transaction and embodying pricing according to quality.

3. 凭标准买卖 (Sale by Standard)

商品的标准是指将商品的规格和等级予以标准化。它一般由标准化组织、政府机关、行业团体、工商组织及商品交易所等制定、公布，并在一定范围内实施。各国都有自己的标准，如英国为BS，美国为ANSI，法国为NF，德国为DIN，日本为JIS等。另外，还有国际标准，如国际标准化组织ISO标准，国际电工委员会（IEC）制定的标准等。各国的标准常常随着生产技术的发展和情况的变化进行修改和变动，所以某个国家或某个部门颁布的某类产品的标准往往会有不同年份的版本。版本不同，质量标准的内容也不尽相同。因此，在买卖货物采用标准时，应当注明采用标准的版本年份。

Standard for a commodity means standardizing the specification and grade of the commodity. It is generally formulated and promulgated by standardization organizations, government agencies, industry groups, industrial and commercial organizations and commodity exchanges, and implemented within a certain range. Each country has its own standards, such as BS for the United Kingdom, ANSI for the United States, NF for France, DIN for Germany and JIS for Japan. In addition, there are also international standards, such as ISO standards and IEC standards. Since the standards of various countries are often modified and changed with the development of production technology and changes in circumstances, the standards for a certain type of products promulgated by a certain country or department often have different versions in different years. The content of quality standards varies with versions. Therefore, when a standard is adopted for the sale of goods, the year in which the standard was adopted shall be indicated.

如 Tetracycline HOI Tablets (Sugar Coated), 250mg, B.P. (British Pharmacopoeia, 1973) 盐酸四环素糖衣片，250毫克，1973年版英国药典。

e.g. Tetracycline HOI Tablets (Sugar Coated), 250mg, B.P. (British Pharmacopoeia, 1973).

对于某些品质变化较大而难以规定统一标准的农副产品，往往采用以下两种标准。

For some agricultural and sideline products whose quality changes greatly and it is difficult to specify a unified standard, the following two standards are often adopted.

（1）"良好品均品质"（fair average quality, FAQ）：是指一定时期内某地出口货物的平均品质水平，一般是对中等货或大路货而言。良好品均品质的确定方法有二：一是农产品的每个生产年度的中等货；二是某一季度或某一装船月份在装运地发运的同一种商品的平均品质。为了在执行合同时不发生争执，双方应在合同中订明是何季度或何年的FAQ，或同时列明具体的规格指标。

(1) "Fair Average Quality" (FAQ): It refers to the average quality level of exported goods from a certain place within a certain period of time, usually for medium or staple goods. FAQ is determined as the average quantity of an agricultural commodity in each production year or as the average quality of the same commodity shipped at the place of shipment during a quarter or month of shipment. To avoid disputes during the execution of the contract, both parties shall specify in the contract for which quarter or year the FAQ is, or list specific specification indicators at the same time.

如 Chinese Sweet Potato Slices, FAQ 2022 Crop. Moisture 16% max。

e.g. Chinese Sweet Potato Slices, FAQ 2022 Crop. Moisture 16% max.

（2）"上好可销品质"（good merchantable quality, GMQ）：是指卖方必须保证其交付的货物品质良好，合乎销售条件，在成交时无须以其他方式证明产品的品质。但是，这种方法比较抽象笼统，容易引起争议，应尽量少用。它主要适应于木材和冷冻产品的买卖。

(2) "Good Merchantable Quality" (GMQ): means that the sellers must ensure that the goods delivered by them are of good quality and meet the sales conditions. There is no need to prove the product quality in other ways at the time of transaction. However, this method is abstract and general, which is easy to cause dispute and should be reduced in use. It is mainly suitable for trading in timber and frozen products.

4. 凭品牌或商标买卖 (Sale by Brand or Trade Mark)

牌名或品牌是指工商企业给其制造或销售的商品所冠的名称，以便与其他企业生产的同类产品区别开来，如耐克运动鞋、佳能相机、大众汽车等。商标则是品牌的图案化，是由一些有特色的单词、字母、数字、文字、图形或图片组成的标志。商标经过国内或国际注册后便成为注册商标，是一种工业产权，受法律保护。

Brand name or brand refers to the name given by an industrial and commercial enterprise to the goods it manufactures or sells, so as to distinguish them from similar products produced by other enterprises, such as Nike sneakers, Canon cameras, Volkswagen cars. A trademark is a pictorial representation of the brand and consists of distinctive words, letters, numbers, texts, graphics or pictures. Trademarks become registered after domestic or international registration, which is an industrial property right and protected by law.

®是"注册商标"的标记，意思是该商标已在国家商标局进行注册申请并已经商标局审查通过，成为注册商标。圆圈里的R是英文register（注册）的开头字母。注册商标具有排他性、独占性、唯一性等特点，属于注册商标所有人所独占，受法律保护，任何企业或个人未经注册商标所有权人许可或授权，均不可自行使用，否则将承担侵权责任。TM是英文trademark的缩写。TM表示该商标已经向国家商标局提出申请，并且国家商标局也已经下发了《受理通知书》，进入了异议期，这样就可以防止其他人提出重复申请，也表示现有商标持有人有优先使用权。

® is the mark of "registered trademark", which means that the trademark has been registered with the Chinese Trademark Office (CTMO) and has been examined and approved by CTMO as a registered trademark. The R in the circle is the initial letter of "register". A registered trademark has the characteristics of exclusivity, monopoly and uniqueness. It is exclusively owned by the owner of the registered trademark and protected by law. No enterprise or individual may use it without the permission or authorization of the owner of the registered trademark, otherwise it will bear the liability for infringement. TM is an abbreviation of trademark. TM stated that the trademark has been applied to CTMO, which has also issued Notices of Acceptance and entered the opposition period, so as to prevent other people from filing repeated applications and indicate that existing trademark holders have priority of use.

在国际上行销已久、品质稳定、信誉良好，并为买方或消费者所熟知的商品可凭品牌或商标交易。因为其品牌或商标本身就是一种品质的象征。这种品质表示方法一般适用于一些品质稳定的日用消费品、加工食品、耐用消费品等工业制成品。同一品牌产品同时有多种不同型号或规格时，为了明确起见，还应列明型号或规格。在接受和采用定牌生产时，即外方要求我方在产品上打上由其提供的商标和牌号，应检查是否侵权，并要求在合同中规定："商标牌号由外方提供，如有侵权，应由外方负责。"

Commodities that have been marketed internationally for a long time, with stable quality and good reputation and are well-known to the buyers or consumers can be traded by brand or trademark. Because the brand or trademark itself is a symbol of quality. This quality representation method is generally applicable to some manufactured products with stable quality, such as daily consumer goods, processed foods and durable consumer goods. When there are different models or specifications of the same brand, they shall also be listed for clarity. When accepting and adopting the designated brand for production, i.e. the foreign party requires us to have a dozen trademarks and brands provided by it on the products, we shall check whether there is any infringement, and require that "the trademark and brand are provided by the foreign party, and if there is any infringement, the foreign party shall be responsible" in the contract.

如 Wujiang Brand Preserved Sichuan Fuling pickle。

e.g. Wujiang Brand Preserved Sichuan Fuling pickle.

5. 凭产地名称或地理标志买卖 (Sale by Name of Origin or Geographical Indication)

在国际货物买卖中，有些农副土特产品因产区的自然条件、加工工艺等因素的影响，在品质方面具有其他产区产品所不具有的独特风格和特色，在国际上享有盛誉。对于这类产品，一般可用产地名称表示其品质，如长白山人参、北京烤鸭、张家口绿豆、龙口粉丝、镇江香醋、贵州茅台、金华火腿等。

In international trade of goods, the quality of some local agricultural and sideline products has a unique style and characteristics, which are not found in other production areas. Quality of such products can generally be expressed by the name of origin. Examples include Changbaishan ginseng, Beijing roast duck, Zhangjiakou mung bean, Longkou vermicelli, Zhenjiang aromatic vinegar, Guizhou Moutai, Jinhua ham and so on.

6. 凭说明书和图样买卖 (Sale by Description and Illustration)

有些技术密集型产品，如机器、仪器、仪表等，由于构造复杂，对材料、设计、性能要求严格，无法简单地用几项指标来表示其品质的全貌，通常以说明书并附以图样、照片、设计图纸、分析表及各种数据作为品质的完整说明。按此品质表示方法成交时，卖方所交货物必须符合说明书和图样的要求。但由于对这类产品的技术要求较高，同说明书和图样相符的产品，在使用时不一定能发挥设计所要求的性能，买方为了维护自身利益，往往要求在合同中加订卖方品质保证条款和技术服务条款。

For some technology-intensive products, such as machines, instruments and meters, due to their complex structures and strict requirements for materials, design and performance, it is impossible to simply express the full picture of their quality with several indicators. Description is usually used together with illustration, photos, design drawings, analysis sheets and various data as a complete description of product quality. When the transaction is concluded according to this quality expression method, the goods delivered by the sellers must meet the requirements of description and illustration. However, due to the high technical requirements for such products, the products conforming to the description and illustration may not have the performance required by the design during use. In order to safeguard their own interests, the buyers often require that the sellers' quality assurance clause and technical service clause be added to the contract.

第三节　合同中的品名、品质条款
Section 3　Commodity and Quality Clause in the Contract

一、品名条款
I. Commodity Clause

（一）品名条款的意义 (Significance of Commodity Clause)

品名条款是买卖合同中不可缺少的一项主要交易条款。按照有关的法律和惯例，对成交商品的描述，是构成商品说明的一个主要组成部分，是买卖双方交接货物的一项基本依据，它关系到买卖双方的权利和义务。若卖方交付的货物不符合约定的品名，买方有权提出损害赔偿要求，直至拒收货物或撤销合同。因此，在国际货物买卖合同中列明具体的商品名称，具有重要的法律和实践意义。

Commodity clause is an indispensable part of the sales contract. According to relevant laws and practices, the description of the contracted goods is an important part of the commodity description and a basis for the delivery of goods between buyers and sellers. It is related to the rights and obligations of buyers and sellers. If the goods delivered by the sellers do not conform to the agreed commodity, the buyers shall have the right to claim damages until rejection of the goods or revocation of the contract. Therefore, it is of great legal and practical significance to specify the specific commodity name in the contract for international sale of goods.

（二）品名条款的主要内容 (Main Contents of Commodity Clause)

国际货物买卖合同中的品名条款并无统一格式，通常在"货物描述（description of goods）"或"商品名称/品名（name of commodity）"栏内具体列明交易双方成交商品的名称即可。但有的商品往往具有不同的品种、等级和型号。因此，为了明确起见，也可把有关具体品种、等级和型号的概括描述包括进去，作为进一步的限定。此外，有的甚至把商品的品质规格也包括进去，这实际上是把品名条款与品质条款合并在一起。

There is no uniform format for the commodity clause in contract for international sale of goods, and it is usually sufficient to specify the names of the goods traded by both parties in the "Description of Goods" or "Name of Commodity" columns. However, some commodities often have different varieties, grades and models. For the sake of clarity, a general description of specific varieties, grades and models may also be included as a further qualification. In addition, some even include the quality and specification of commodities, which actually merges the commodity clause with the quality clause.

（1）只列明品名。

(1) Commodity only.

Name of Commodity: Northeast Soybeans

（2）不仅包括品名，还包括有关具体品种、等级、型号的概括性描述。

(2) It includes not only commodity, but also a general description of specific variety, grade and model.

Name of Commodity: "Hair" Brand Air Conditioners

Name of Commodity: Pongee Silk Art. No. 6234

（三）规定品名条款的注意事项 (Precautions for Commodity Clause)

在国际货物买卖合同中，品名条款是合同的主要条款。因此，在规定此项条款时，应注意下列事项。

In the contract for international sale of goods, commodity clause is the main clause in the contract. Therefore, attention shall be paid to the following matters when specifying this clause.

（1）品名必须能够确切反映交易标的物的特点，明确、具体，避免空泛、笼统的规定。如应避免使用诸如果品、花卉等笼统的商品名称。

(1) Commodity must accurately reflect the characteristics of the subject matter of transaction, be explicit and specific, and avoid vague and general provisions. For example, the use of general commodity such as food and flowers should be avoided.

（2）尽可能使用国际上通用的名称，若使用地方性的名称，交易双方应事先就其含义取得共识。对于某些新商品的定名及其译名，应力求准确、易懂，并符合国际上的习惯称呼。目前各国的海关统计、普惠制待遇都按《商品名称及编码协调制度》进行，我国在采用品名时，应与《商品名称及编码协调制度》规定的品名相适应。

(2) Try to use internationally recognized names as much as possible. If local names are used, both parties to the transaction should reach a consensus on their meanings in advance. The designation and translation of some new commodities should be accurate, easy to understand and in line with international customary names. At present, the customs statistics and GSP treatment of all countries are carried out according to the Harmonized Commodity Description and Coding System. The commodity adopted in our country shall be compatible with that specified by the Harmonized Commodity Description and Coding System.

（3）条款中规定的品名，必须是卖方能够提供且买方所需要的商品，凡做不到或不必要的描述性的词句都不应列入。我国某公司在广交会期间，与日本A会社签订一项出口"手工制造书写纸"的合同，并约定看样成交。合同签订后，买方又将该合同转让给另一家日本公司B会社。我方公司按样品备齐货物后，依合同约定将货物发运至目的地。货物抵达日本横滨后，经开箱检验，B会社以货物部分工序为机械操作为由，向我方提出异议和索赔。

(3) Commodity specified in the clause must be those that can be provided by the sellers and required by the buyers. Any descriptive words that are impossible or unnecessary shall not be included. During the Canton Fair, a company in China signed a contract with Japanese company A Co. Ltd. to export "Handmade Writing

Paper" and agreed on sale by sample. After the contract was signed, the buyers transferred the contract to another Japanese company B Co. Ltd. After preparing all the goods according to the samples, Chinese company shipped them to the destination as agreed in the contract. After the goods arrived in Yokohama, Japan, company B lodged an objection and claim against us on the grounds that some processes of the goods were mechanically operated.

（4）注意选用合适的品名，以便于降低关税、方便进出口和节省运费开支。有些国家的海关税则和进出口限制的规定与品名有关。如向美国出口铁链（chain），若用于闸门开关滚辘，进口关税税率只有5%，若用作自行车链条，进口关税税率则高达30%。现时国际上班轮运费是按商品等级确定收费标准的，同一商品的名称不同，其收费费率可能不同。在班轮运输中，按运费吨计价的货物，一般分为20个等级，等级越高则运费越高。如棉织品的运费率为10级，毛巾为9级，尿布为8级。选用合适的名称，可以节省运费、降低成本。

(4) Commodity should be properly selected to reduce duties, facilitate import and export and save freight charges. Customs tariff and import/export restrictions are related to commodity in some countries. For example, when the chain is exported to the United States, the import tariff rate is only 5% for gate switch rollers and as high as 30% for bicycle chains. Freight charges for international liners are based on commodity grade. For the same commodity, different names may lead to different rates. In liner, the goods priced by freight ton are generally divided into 20 grades. The higher the grade is, the higher the freight charges will be. For example, the rate of freight is 10 for cotton fabrics, 9 for towels and 8 for diapers. Freight charges and costs can be saved by choosing the right name.

（5）同一份合同的同一种商品的品名前后要一致。若同一份合同的同一种商品品名前后条款中的称谓不一致，将可能导致合同无效；另外，该合同涉及的单据也应与合同中的品名一致，否则可能导致进口商的拒付，引发纠纷。

(5) The name of the same commodity in the same contract shall be consistent. Any inconsistency between the terms and conditions of the same commodity under the contract may invalidate the contract. In addition, the documents involved in the contract shall also be consistent with the commodity under the contract, otherwise it may lead to non-payment by the importer and cause disputes.

二、品质条款
II. Quality Clause

（一）品质条款的意义 (Significance of Quality Clause)

品质条款是国际货物买卖合同中不可缺少的一项主要交易条件，是买卖双方交接货物的基本依据。作为合同中的一项主要条款，品质条款是买卖双方对商品质量、规格、等级、标准、商标、牌号等的具体规定。卖方以约定品质交货，否则买方有权提出索赔或拒收货物，以至撤销合同。合同中的品质条款也是商检机构进行品质检验、仲裁机构进行仲裁和法院解决品质纠纷案件的依据。

Quality clause is an indispensable part of contract for international sale of goods, which serves as a basis for goods delivery between buyers and sellers. As one of the main clauses in the contract, quality clause refers to the specific provision on quality and quantity, specification, grade, standard, trademark and brand made by buyers and sellers. The sellers shall deliver the goods in accordance with the agreed quality standards; otherwise, the buyers have the right to lodge a claim or reject the goods and even cancel the contract. Quality clause in the contract is also the basis for commodity inspection authorities to carry out quality inspection, arbitration institutions to carry out arbitration and courts to settle quality dispute cases.

合同中的品质条件是构成商品说明的重要组成部分，是买卖双方交接货物的依据。英国

《货物买卖法》把品质条件作为合同的要件。《公约》规定卖方交货必须符合约定的质量条件，如卖方交货不符合约定的品质条件，买方有权要求损害赔偿，也可要求修理或交付替代物，甚至拒收货物和撤销合同。这就进一步说明了品质的重要性。

Quality conditions in the contract are an important part of commodity description and the basis for goods delivery between buyers and sellers. The sale of goods act makes the conditions of quality an essential part of a contract. The Convention stipulates that the sellers' delivery must conform to the agreed quality conditions. If the sellers' delivery does not conform to the agreed quality conditions, the buyers have the right to claim damages, repair or delivery of substitutes, and even reject the goods and cancel the contract. This further illustrates the importance of quality assurance.

（二）品质条款的主要内容 (Main Contents of Quality Clause)

品质条款的基本内容是商品的品质、规格、等级、标准和商标、牌号等。商品品种不同，表示品质的方法也不一，故品质条款的内容及其繁简应视商品特性而定。在凭样品买卖时，应列明样品的编号和寄送日期，有时还加列交货品质与样品一致或相符的说明。在凭标准买卖时，一般应列明所采用的标准及标准版本的年份。在凭图样和说明书买卖时，还应列明图样、说明书的名称、份数。

The basic contents of the quality clause are quality, specification, grade, standard, trademark, brand, etc. of the product. Due to different varieties of commodities, the methods for expressing quality are also different. Therefore, the content and complexity of quality clause shall be determined according to the characteristics of commodities. For sale by sample, the sample number and delivery date shall be stated. Sometimes a statement that the quality of delivery is consistent with or conforms to the sample shall also be added. For sale by standard, the standard adopted and the year of its version shall generally be listed. For sale by description and illustration, the name and number of copies of the illustration and description shall be specified.

（三）规定品质条款的注意事项 (Precautions for Quality Clause)

1. 正确选择表示商品品质的方法 (Correct Method of Expressing QOG)

品质条款的内容必然涉及品质的表示方法，究竟采用何种表示品质的方法又应视商品的特性而定。首先，描述商品品质的方法要得当。一般来讲，凡能用科学指标说明品质的商品，适用于凭规格、等级或标准买卖；难以规格化和标准化的商品，如工艺品等，适用于凭样品买卖；具有名优特色的商品，适用于凭品牌或商标买卖；复杂的机器、电器和仪表等商品，适用于凭说明书和图样交易；具有地方风味和特色的产品，可凭产地名称买卖。此外，上述表示品质的方法，凡能采用一种表示商品品质的，就不宜采用两种或两种以上方法表示，以免卖方受制太多而给交货带来困难。

The content of quality clause necessarily involves the expression method of quality, and which expression method should be adopted depends on the characteristics of commodities. First of all, describe the QOG in a proper way. Generally speaking, commodities whose quality can be demonstrated by scientific indicators are suitable for sale by specification, grade or standard; commodities that are difficult to standardize, such as handicrafts, are applicable to sale by sample; commodities with famous and distinctive features are suitable for sale by brand or trade mark; commodities such as complex machines, electrical appliances and instruments are suitable for sale by description and illustration; commodities with local flavor and characteristics can be bought and sold by the name of origin. In addition, if one of the above-mentioned methods can be used to express the QOG, it is not advisable to use two or more methods, so as to avoid difficulties in delivery caused by too much control on the part of sellers.

2. 科学合理、实事求是地规定品质条件 (Scientific, Reasonable and Practical Quality Conditions)

订立品质指标要从实际出发，要符合买卖双方的具体要求和能力。指标既不能定得过高，给今后履约带来困难；也不宜定得过低，以免使卖方在价格上吃亏或引起纠纷。

Setting quality indicators should start from reality and meet the specific requirements and capabilities of buyers and sellers. It should not be too high to cause difficulties in future performance, nor should it be too low to avoid causing losses or disputes for sellers in terms of price.

3. 注意品质条款的灵活性 (Flexibility of Quality Clause)

品质条款应力求明确、具体、完整、简洁，不宜使用诸如"大约""左右""合理误差"之类笼统、模糊字眼，以免在交易中引起争议。但也不宜将品质条款规定得过死，给卖方履行交货义务带来困难。对某些制成品和初级产品，应根据货物特性和实际需要规定品质机动幅度和品质公差，必要时订立品质增减价条款。

Quality clause shall be explicit, specific, complete and concise. General and vague words such as "about", "approximate" and "reasonable allowance" should not be used to avoid disputes in transactions. However, it is inappropriate to stipulate the quality clause too rigidly, which will make it difficult for sellers to fulfill their delivery obligations. For some finished products and primary products, quality latitude and quality tolerance shall be specified according to the characteristics of goods and actual needs, and a price adjustment clause for quality shall be concluded when necessary.

（1）品质机动幅度（quality latitude）。某些初级产品，如农副产品等的质量不甚稳定，为了交易的顺利履行，在规定其品质指标的同时，可订立一定的品质机动幅度，即允许卖方所交货物的品质指标在一定幅度内有灵活性。只要卖方交货品质没有超出机动幅度范围，买方就无权拒收货物。品质机动幅度的规定方法主要有以下三种。

(1) The quality of some primary products, such as agricultural and sideline products, is not very stable. In order to smoothly fulfill the transaction, a certain Quality Latitude can be established while specifying their quality indicators, that is, the Sellers are allowed to have certain flexibility in the quality indicators of the goods delivered. The buyers have no right to reject the goods as long as the sellers' delivery quality does not exceed the latitude. There are three main methods for specifying quality latitude.

①规定范围。规定某项品质指标允许有差异的范围，如 35"/36"。

①Specify the range. Specify the allowable deviation range of a quality indicator. For example, 35"/36".

②规定极限。对品质规格规定上下极限，如最大、最高、最多（maximum, max.），最小、最低、最少（minimum, min.）。如 Feeding Horsebean, moisture (max.) 15%, admixture (max.) 2%。

②Specify the limits. Specify the upper and lower limits in the quality specification, such as Maximum (max.), minimum, (min.). For example, Feeding Horsebean, moisture (max.) 15%, admixture (max.) 2%.

③规定上下差异。即在规定某一具体质量指标时，允许浮动一定的百分比。例如灰鸭毛，含绒量 18%，允许上下 1%。

③Specify the upper and lower differences. That is, when a specific quality indicator is specified, it is allowed to fluctuate by a certain percentage. For example, the down content of gray duck feather is 18%, and it is allowed to rise or fall by 1%.

（2）品质公差（quality tolerance）。品质公差是指国际上公认的产品品质的误差，即允许交付货物的特定质量指标有公认的差异。在工业品生产过程中，产品的质量指标产生一定的误差有时是难以避免的，如手表走时一段时间内误差若干秒。这种误差若为某一国际同行业所公认，即为"品质公差"。卖方交货品质在此范围内，即可认为与合同相符，买方不得拒收或要求调整价格。品质公差适用于对精度要求较高的工业制成品的交易中。

(2) Quality tolerance refers to internationally recognized errors in the quality of products, i.e. accepted differences are allowed for specific quality indicators of deliverables. In the production process of industrial products, it is sometimes difficult to avoid certain errors in product quality indicators, such as the error of several seconds during a certain period of time when a watch is running. This error, if recognized by an international industry, is called "Quality Tolerance". QOG delivered by the Sellers within this range can be deemed as conforming to the contract, and the buyers shall not reject or require price adjustment. Quality tolerance is applicable to the transaction of manufactured products requiring high accuracy.

卖方交货在品质机动幅度或品质公差允许的范围内,买方无权拒收货物,且一般均按合同价格计收货款,不再按品质高低另做调整。在采用品质机动幅度的情况下,有时为体现按质论价的原则,有些货物也可按交货品质情况调整价格,即订立品质增减价条款。

The buyers shall not have the right to reject the goods if the sellers deliver the goods within the allowable range of quality latitude or quality tolerance, and shall generally calculate and collect the payment according to the contract price without further adjustment according to the quality level. In the case of quality latitude, sometimes in order to reflect the principle of pricing according to quality, the price of some goods can also be adjusted according to the delivery quality, that is, to conclude a price adjustment clause for quality.

For example,
Northeast Soybeans, moisture per unit ± 1, price $\mp 1\%$
admixture per unit $\pm 1\%$, price $\mp 1\%$
oil content per unit $\pm 1\%$, price $\pm 1\%$

第四章拓展知识、专业词汇和练习

第五章　商品的数量
Chapter 5　Quantity of Goods

导　读
Introduction

商品的数量是国际贸易中不可缺少的主要条件之一。有了一定数量的商品，再有了一定金额的货款，便有了一笔买卖。数量条款是合同的重要条款之一，也是合同履行的重要基础。按合同约定的数量交货是卖方的一项基本义务。

Quantity of goods is one of the indispensable main conditions in international trade. With a certain quantity of goods and a certain amount of payment, there is a transaction. Quantity clause is one of the important clauses in the contract and also an essential support for the performance of contract. Quantity delivery as agreed in the contract is a basic obligation of the sellers.

第一节　商品数量的含义
Section 1　Meaning of Commodity Quantity

商品的数量（quantity of goods）是指用度、量、衡单位来表示一定商品的重量、数量、长度、面积、体积、容积等。

Quantity of goods refers to the weight, quantity, length, area, volume and capacity of a certain commodity expressed in units of measurement.

商品的数量是进出口交易双方进行磋商的主要内容，在国际货物买卖合同中约定商品的数量具有十分重要的实践意义和法律意义。

Quantity of goods is the main content of negotiation between import and export transaction parties. It is of great practical and legal significance to agree on quantity of goods in contract for international sale of goods.

第二节　计量单位与计重方法
Section 2　Unit and Method of Measurement

一、计量制度
I. Measurement System

目前国际贸易中常用的度量衡制度有国际单位制（international system of unit）、公制（metric system）、英制（British system）和美制（US system）。国际单位制是 1960 年国际标准计量组织在公制基础上颁布的。由于各国的度量衡制度不同，所使用的计量单位各异，甚至同一计量单位所表示的实际数量有时会有很大不同。例如重量单位吨有公吨、长吨和短吨之分，它们分别等于 1000 千克、1016 千克和 907.2 千克。再如棉花通常用"包"计量，在美国 1 包=480 磅，巴西为 396.8 磅，埃及为 730 磅。1 加仑=4.546 升（美）=3.785 升（英）。

At present, the commonly used weights and measures in international trade include international system of unit, metric system, British system and U.S. system. The international system of unit was issued by ISO in 1960 on the basis of the metric system. Quantity expressed in the same unit of measurement can sometimes vary considerably due to differences in national systems of weights and measures. For example, the weight unit of a ton can be divided into m/t, l/t and s/t, which are equal to 1000 kg, 1016 kg and 907.2 kg respectively. For another example, cotton is usually measured in "bale", 1 bale=480 lb in the United States, 396.8 lb in Brazil and 730 lb in Egypt. 1 gallon = 4.546 litre (USA) = 3.785 litre (UK).

根据《中华人民共和国计量法》："国家实行法定计量单位制度。国际单位制计量单位和国家选定的其他计量单位，为国家法定计量单位。"在我国对外贸易业务中，出口商品除合同规定需用公制、英制或美制计量单位外，应使用法定计量单位。

According to the Law on Metrology of the People's Republic of China, "China implements a legal system of measurement units. The measurement units of the International System of Unit and others selected by the state shall be the national legal units of measurement." In China's Foreign Trade Business, the exporter shall use legal units of measurement except for those required by the Contract to be measured in the metric system, British system or US system.

在国际贸易中，通常使用的数量计算方法有六种，不同的计算方法有不同的计量单位。具体交易时采用何种计算方法和计量单位，要视商品的性质、包装、运输、市场习惯等而定。

In international trade, there are six commonly used methods of quantity calculation, and different calculation methods have different units of measurement. The calculation method and unit of measurement used in the specific transaction depend on the nature, packing, carriage of the goods, market practice, etc.

（一）重量单位 (Weight Unit)

农副产品、矿产品及部分工业制成品都按重量计算。主要计量单位有：公吨(metric ton, m/t)、长吨(long ton, l/t)、短吨(short ton, s/t)、千克(kilogram, kg)、克(gram, g)、盎司(ounce, oz)、磅(pound, lb)等。

Agricultural and sideline products, minerals and some manufactured goods are all calculated by weight. The main units of measurement include: metric ton (m/t), long ton (l/t), short ton (s/t), kilogram (kg), gram (g), ounce (oz), pound (lb), etc.

1 磅＝16 盎司＝0.454 千克

1 lb ＝ 16 oz ＝ 0.454 kg

（二）个数单位 (Number Unit)

大多数工业制成品，尤其是日用消费品、工业品、机械产品，以及一部分土特产品按数量进行买卖。主要计量单位有：件(piece, pc)、双(pair)、套(set)、打(dozen, doz)、卷(roll)、令(ream, rm)、罗(gross, gr)、辆(unit)、头(head)。有些商品也可按包装单位，如件(package, pkg)、袋(bag)、包(bale)、箱(case, carton, crate)、桶(barrel, drum)等。

Most manufactured products, especially consumer goods, industrial products, machinery products and some local specialties are sold in quantity. The main units of measurement include: piece (pc), pair, set, dozen (doz), roll, ream (rm), gross (gr), unit and head. Packing units can also be used for some commodities, such as package (pkg), bag, bale, case (carton/crate) and barrel (drum).

（三）长度单位 (Length Unit)

在绳索、布匹、电线电缆等商品的交易中通常采用。长度的主要计量单位有：码(yard)、米(meter)、英尺(foot)、厘米(centimeter, cm)等。其中：

It is commonly used in the trading of goods such as ropes, cloth, wires and cables. The main units of measurement include yard, meter, foot and cm. Where:

1 码=3 英尺=0.914 米，1 英尺=12 英寸=30.48 厘米，1 英寸=2.54 厘米

1 yard = 3 foot = 0.914 meter, 1 foot = 12 inches = 30.48 cm, 1 inch = 2.54 cm

（四）面积单位 (Area Unit)

面积单位在玻璃板、地毯、皮革、塑料制品等商品的交易中使用。主要计量单位有：平方码(square yard)、平方米(square meter)、平方英尺(square foot)等。

It is used in the trading of goods such as glass plates, carpets, leather and plastic products. The main units of measurement include: square yard, square meter and square foot.

（五）体积单位 (Volume Unit)

体积单位仅用于木材、天然气和化学气体等。主要计量单位有：立方码(cubic yard)、立方米(cubic meter)、立方英尺(cubic foot)等。

For wood, natural gas and chemical gases only. The main units of measurement include: cubic yard, cubic meter and cubic foot.

（六）容积单位 (Capacity Unit)

容积单位适用于各种谷物和流体货物。主要计量单位有：升(litre)、加仑(gallon)、蒲式耳(bushel)等。

It is applicable to all kinds of grain and fluid goods. The main units of measurement are: litre, gallon and bushel.

1 蒲式耳 = 35.24 升(美玉米)

1 bushel = 35.24 litre (American corn)

二、重量的计算方法
II. Calculation Method of Weight

在国际贸易中，按重量计量的商品很多。根据一般商业习惯，通常计算重量的方法有以下几种。

In international trade, there are many goods measured by weight. According to general business practice, there are several common methods for calculating weight.

（一）毛重 (Gross Weight)

毛重是指商品本身的重量加包装物的重量。包装物的重量称皮重。低值商品可按毛重计量，即以毛重作为计算价格和交付货物的基础。这种做法在贸易实践中被称为"以毛作净"（gross for net），实际上就是以毛重当作净重计价，适用于有些价值较低的农产品或其他商品。注意订立合同时，不仅要在数量条款，还应在价格条款中注明。

Gross weight is the weight of the commodity itself plus the weight of the packing. The weight of the packing is tare. Low-value commodities can be measured by gross weight, which serves as the basis for calculating prices and delivering goods. This is called "Gross for Net" in trade practice, which actually means that gross weight is used as net weight. It applies to some agricultural products or other commodities with low value. Note that when concluding the contract, it shall be indicated not only in the quantity clause but also in the price clause.

（二）净重 (Net Weight)

净重是指商品本身的重量，即除去包装物后的商品实际重量。净重是国际贸易中最常见的计重方法。可以理解为：毛重＝净重＋皮重。

Net weight refers to the weight of the commodity itself, i.e. the actual weight of the commodity after packing is removed. Net weight is the most common method in international trade. It can be understood as: gross weight = net weight + tare weight.

国际贸易中，计算皮重的方法有实际皮重、平均皮重、习惯皮重和约定皮重四种。按何种方法计算皮重，应根据交易商品的特点及商业习惯的不同，由买卖双方事先商定并在合同中订明。

In the international trade, there are four methods to calculate tare weight: actual tare weight, average tare weight, customary tare weight and agreed tare weight. The method for calculating the tare weight shall be agreed upon in advance by both parties according to the characteristics of the traded goods and different business practice, and specified in the contract.

（三）公量 (Conditioned Weight)

有些商品如棉花、羊毛、生丝等有较强的吸湿性，其所含水分受客观环境的影响较大，故其重量很不稳定，国际上采用按公量计算的方法，即以商品的干净重加上国际标准含水量所得出的重量。

Some commodities such as cotton, wool and raw silk have strong hygroscopicity. Moisture contained in them is greatly affected by the objective environment, so their weight is very unstable. The international calculation method of conditioned weight is adopted, that is, the weight obtained by adding dry net weight of commodities to international standard moisture content.

公量＝干量＋标准含水量＝商品净重×（1+标准回潮率）/（1+实际回潮率）

Conditioned Weight = Dry Weight + Standard Moisture Content = Net Weight of Commodity × (1+Standard Moisture Regain)/(1+Actual Moisture Regain)

（四）理论重量 (Theoretical Weight)

理论重量是指某些有固定规格形状和尺寸的商品（如马口铁、钢板等），只要规格一致，每件重量大体上相同，故可以从其件数推算出总量。这种计重方法称为理论重量。

It refers to some commodities (such as tinplate and steel plate) with fixed specification, shape and size. As long as the specifications are consistent and the weight of each piece is roughly the same, the total amount can be calculated from its number. This method is called theoretical weight.

（五）法定重量和实物净重 (Legal Weight and Physical Net Weight)

法定重量是商品重量加上直接接触商品的包装物料的重量。海关征收从量税时，常以法定重量作为征税基础。而扣除这部分内包装重量及其他包含杂物的纯商品重量则称为实物净重或净净重。

Legal weight is the weight of the commodity plus packing material in direct contact with the commodity. Legal Weight is often used as the basis for levying specific duty. The net commodity weight after deducting the weight of the inner packing and other impurities is physical net weight or net net weight.

在国际货物买卖合同中，若货物是按重量计量和计价的，但未明确规定采用何种方法计算重量和价格，根据《公约》第五十六条的规定，应按净重计量和计价。

In the contract for international sale of goods, if the goods are measured and priced by weight but there is no specified method to calculate the weight and price, they shall be measured and priced by net weight according to Article 56 of the Convention.

第三节　合同中的数量条款
Section 3　Quantity Clause in the Contract

一、数量条款的意义
I. Significance of Quantity Clause

商品的数量是国际贸易中不可缺少的主要条件之一，数量条款是买卖双方交接货物的依据。《联合国国际货物销售合同公约》规定：按约定的数量交付货物是卖方的一项基本义务。如果卖方交付货物数量大于合同规定的数量，买方可以拒收多交的部分、也可以收取多交部分中的一部分或全部，但应按合同价格付款；如果卖方交货数量少于合同规定，卖方应在规定的交货期内补交不足部分，但不得给买方造成不合理的不便或承担不合理的开支，即便如此，买方也保留要求损害赔偿的权利。按照某些国家的法律规定，卖方交货数量必须与合同规定相符，否则，买方有权提出索赔，甚至拒收货物。

Quantity of goods is one of the indispensable main conditions in international trade, and quantity clause is the basis for goods delivery between buyers and sellers. the Convention stipulates that it is a basic obligation of the sellers to deliver the goods in accordance with the agreed quantity. If the quantity of goods delivered by the sellers is greater than the quantity specified in the contract, the buyers may reject the overdelivery or accept part or all of the overdelivery. Payment shall be made according to the contract price; If the sellers' delivery quantity is less than that specified in the contract, the sellers shall make up the deficiency within the stipulated time of delivery, but shall not cause unreasonable inconvenience or incur unreasonable expenses to the buyers. Even so, the buyers reserve the right to claim damages. According to the laws and regulations of some countries, the Sellers' delivery quantity must be consistent with the provisions of the contract. Otherwise, the buyers have the right to lodge a claim or even reject the goods.

二、数量条款的主要内容
II. Main Contents of Quantity Clause

（一）数量条款的基本内容 (Basic Contents of Quantity Clause)

买卖合同中的数量条款，主要包括成交商品的数量和计量单位。按重量成交的商品，还需订明计算重量的方法。如：中国大米 1000 公吨，麻袋装，以毛作净。5%溢短装，由卖方选择，按合同价格计算。

Quantity clause in the sales contract mainly includes the quantity and unit of measurement of traded goods. For goods traded by weight, the method of calculating the weight shall also be indicated. For example: Chinese rice 1000 m/t, gunny bag, Gross for Net. 5% More or Less, at the sellers' option, at the contract price.

（二）数量机动幅度条款 (More or Less Clause)

在国际贸易中，理论上讲任何商品都是可以约定精确计量的。但在实际业务中，许多商品受本身特性、生产、运输或包装及计量工具的限制，在交货时不易精确计算，如散装谷物、油类、水果、粮食、矿产品、钢材及一般的工业制成品等。为了便于合同的顺利履行，减少争议，买卖双方通常要在合同中规定数量机动幅度条款，允许卖方交货数量可以在一定范围内灵活掌握。合同中的数量机动幅度条款常有以下几种规定方法。

In international trade, theoretically, any commodity can be precisely measured by agreement. However, in actual business, many commodities are limited by their own characteristics, production, carriage or packing and measuring tools, so it is not easy to calculate accurately at the time of delivery, such as bulk cereals, oils, fruits, grains, mineral products, steel and general manufactured goods. In order to facilitate the smooth performance of the Contract and reduce disputes, both parties shall specify the more or less clause in the contract, allowing the sellers to flexibly control the delivery quantity within a certain range. More or less clause in the contract is often specified as follows:

1. 溢短装条款 (More or Less Clause)

溢短装条款即合同明文规定卖方交货时可多装或少装合同规定数量一定百分比的条款。卖方交货数量只要在允许增减的范围内，即为符合合同数量条款的规定。如 5000 M/T, with 5% more or less at the Seller's option.

That is, the contract expressly provides that the sellers may deliver more or less than a certain percentage of the quantity specified in the contract. As long as the sellers' delivery quantity is within the allowable range of more or less, it shall be deemed to comply with the quantity clause in the contract. e.g. 5000 M/T, with 5% more or less at the seller's option.

溢短装条款由三部分组成，即数量机动幅度的范围、溢短装的选择权与溢短装部分的作价办法。数量机动幅度范围通常用百分比表示。在机动幅度范围中是多交货物还是少交货物，该选择权一般由卖方决定。但在采用海洋运输情况下，因为交货的数量与载货船舶的舱容有着非常密切的关系，所以溢短装的选择权应由安排货物运输的一方掌握。至于溢短装部分的作价办法，如果合同中没有做特别的规定，大多按合同价格计算。但也有的合同规定按装船日或卸货日市场价格计算，其目的是防止有权选择溢短装一方，为获取额外利益而有意多交或少交货物。若合同交易双方对装船时或货到时的市价不能达成协议，则可交由仲裁解决。

The more or less clause consists of three parts, i.e. the range of more or less, the option of more or less, and the pricing method for more or less. The range of more or less is usually expressed as a percentage. It is up to the sellers in the range of more or less. However, in the case of ocean transportation, since the quantity of goods to be delivered is closely related to the capacity of the carrying vessel, the option of more or less shall be held by the party arranging the carriage. Regarding the pricing method for more or less, unless otherwise specified in the contract, it is mostly calculated according to the contract price. However, some contract stipulate that the price shall be calculated according to the market price on the date of shipment or discharge. The purpose is to prevent the party entitled to the option of more or less from intentionally delivering more or less goods for additional benefits. If the parties to the contract cannot reach an agreement on the market price at the time of shipment or arrival, it may be referred to Arbitration.

2. 规定"约"量 (Specify the "About" Quantity)

规定"约"量即在合同规定的交易数量前加一个"约"字（about, circa, approximate, Appr.）。因为"约"的含义在国际上解释不一，所以双方当事人应事先明确对允许增减的幅度进行约定，以免引起纠纷。

That is, add the word "about/circa/approximate/Appr." before the transaction quantity specified in the contract. As the meaning of "About" differs in international interpretation, both parties should agree on the allowable range of more or less in advance to avoid disputes.

但在采用信用证支付方式时，按照 UCP600 的解释，凡"约""大约"或此类意义的词语用于信用证金额或信用证所列的数量或单价时，应理解为允许对有关金额、数量或单价有不超过 10% 的增减幅度。

However, in the case of payment by L/C, as construed under UCP600, wherever "about", "approximate" or words to that effect are used for the purposes of L/C amount or quantity or unit price listed therein, it shall be understood that an increase or decrease of not more than 10% in such amount, quantity or unit price is permitted.

3. 默认的溢短装条款 (Default More or Less Clause)

若在合同中未明确规定数量机动幅度，则卖方应严格按照合同中规定的数量交货。但是，买方若采用信用证方式付款，根据UCP600第30条b款的规定：在信用证未以包装单位或货物自身件数的方式规定货物数量时，货物数量允许有5%的增减幅度，只要总支取金额不超过信用证金额。按照UCP600的上述解释，凡是散装货物的买卖，即使信用证中未规定数量机动幅度，但只要支取金额不超过信用证规定的金额且信用证中未规定数量不得增减，那么卖方交货的数量就可以与信用证规定的数量有不超过5%的差异。但以包装单位或个数计数的商品交易，卖方交货的数量必须与合同规定的数量完全一致。

If the more or less clause is not specified in the contract, sellers shall deliver the goods strictly in accordance with the quantity stipulated in the contract. However, if the buyers make payment by L/C, according to Article 30b of UCP600: If the L/C does not specify the quantity of goods in terms of packing unit or number of goods, an increase or decrease of 5% is allowed for the quantity of goods as long as the total withdrawal amount does not exceed the L/C amount. In accordance with the above interpretation of UCP600, for any trading of Bulk Cargo, even if there is no more or less specified in L/C, as long as the withdrawal amount does not exceed the L/C amount and there is no regulation in the L/C that the quantity cannot be increased or decreased, then the quantity delivered by sellers may differ from the quantity specified in L/C by not more than 5%. However, for commodity trade counted by packing unit or number, the quantity delivered by the sellers must be exactly consistent with the quantity specified in the contract.

第五章拓展知识、专业词汇和练习

第六章　商品的包装
Chapter 6　Packing of Goods

导　读
Introduction

国际贸易中的货物，除了少数不必包装、可直接装入运输工具的散装货（bulk cargo）和在形态上自然成件、无须包装或略加捆扎即可成件的裸装货（nude cargo）以外，绝大多数商品都是需要有适当包装的包装货（packed cargo）。

In international trade, the vast majority of goods are packed cargo requiring proper packing except for a few bulk cargo that can be directly loaded into means of conveyance and nude cargo that is naturally finished in form and ready to be finished without packing or with slight bundling.

商品的包装是保护商品在流通过程中品质完好和数量完整的重要条件，是实现商品使用价值和增加价值的重要手段之一。适当的包装对保护、保存商品，美化、宣传商品以及方便商品的贮存、运输、销售和使用都起着重要作用。且包装的好坏直接影响到商品售价的高低。因此，交易双方在磋商时，应对包装做出具体、明确的规定。包装条款是合同的重要条款之一。

Packing of goods is an important condition to protect the integrity of quality and quantity in circulation, as well as one of the important means to realize the use value and add value of goods. Proper packing plays an important role in protecting, preserving, beautifying and advertising commodities as well as facilitating the storage, carriage, sale and use of them. Packing quality directly affects the price of goods. Packing should therefore be specifically and explicitly defined by the parties to a transaction during negotiations. Packing clause is one of the important clauses in the contract.

第一节　商品包装的含义与意义
Section 1　Meaning and Significance of Commodity Packing

商品的包装（packing of goods），是指为了有效保护商品品质的完好和数量的完整，采用一定的方法将商品置于合适容器中的一种措施。

Packing of Goods refers to a measure to put goods into suitable containers by certain means, so as to effectively protect the integrity of quality and quantity.

我国国家标准《包装通用术语》（GB/T 4122.1—2008）中，对现代商品包装做了明确定义："为在流通过程中保护产品，方便储存，促进销售，按一定技术方法而采用的容器、材料及辅助物等的总体名称。"

China's national standard General Packaging Terms (GB/T 4122.1—2008) clearly defines modern packing of commodity: "The general name of containers, materials and accessories used according to certain technical methods in order to protect products, facilitate storage and promote sales during circulation."

在国际贸易中，除一些货物因其本身特点不需要包装或难以包装外，如钢铁、木材、汽车等，大多数货物都需要有一定的包装。包装在国际贸易中具有特殊意义，包装是说明货物的重要组成部分，而且包装可以保护商品便于流通，方便消费，促进销售，提高商品价值，促进商品使用价值的实现。

Packing is required for most of the goods in international trade, except that some goods do not need packing or are difficult to pack due to their own characteristics, such as steel, wood and automobiles. Packing plays a significant role in international trade. It is an important part of the description of goods, and it can protect commodities for easy circulation, consumption, promotion of sales, improvement of value and realization of use value.

第二节 包装的种类
Section 2　Types of Packing

按包装在流通过程中所起的作用不同，可将包装分为运输包装和销售包装。

Packing can be divided into transport packing and sales packing according to its different roles in circulation.

一、运输包装
I. Transport Packing

运输包装（transport packing）习惯上称为大包装或外包装，是将货物装入特定容器，或以特定方式成件或成箱包装。它的作用主要在于保护货物在长时间和远距离的运输过程中不被损坏和散失，同时也起到便于储存、检验、计数、分拨及节省运费的作用。根据包装方式不同，运输包装可分为单件运输包装和集合运输包装。

Transport packing, commonly known as large packing or outer packing, refers to the packing of goods into specific containers or in individual pieces or cases in specific ways. It is mainly used to protect the goods from damage and loss during long-distance carriage, as well as facilitate storage, inspection, counting, distribution and saving of freight charges. According to different packing methods, transport packing can be divided into single packing and collective packing.

（一）单件运输包装 (Single Packing)

（1）箱（case）。按材料不同，箱子有木箱、板条箱、纸箱、瓦楞纸箱（corrugated carton）、漏孔箱（skeleton case）等。

(1) Case. According to different materials, case includes wooden case, batten case, carton, corrugated carton, skeleton case, etc.

（2）桶（drum, cask）。桶有木桶、铁桶、塑料桶等。

(2) Drum (cask). Drum includes wooden drum, iron drum and plastic drum.

（3）袋（bag）。袋有麻袋（gunny bag）、布袋、纸袋、塑料袋等。

(3) Bag. Bag includes gunny bag, cloth bag, paper bag and plastic bag.

（4）包（bundle, bale）。

（二）集合运输包装 (Collective Packing)

除上述单件运输包装外，还可将一定数量的单件运输包装组合成一件大的包装或装入一个大的包装容器内的集合运输包装。国际贸易中，常见的集合运输包装有集装箱、集装袋/包和托盘。在实际交易中，买卖双方应根据商品特性、形状、运输方式、贸易习惯的要求及相关国家的法律法规选择恰当的运输包装，并在保证包装牢固的前提下尽可能节省运输费用。

In addition, a quantity of single packings may be combined into one large packing or a collective packing in one large packing container. In international trade, the common collective packing includes container, flexible container and pallet. In actual transactions, the buyers and sellers shall select appropriate transport packing according to the characteristics, shape, transportation mode, requirements of trade practice and laws and regulations of relevant countries, and save carriage expenses as much as possible on the premise of ensuring reliable packing.

1. 集装箱 (Container)

集装箱是一种运输货物的容器，它是运输工具的组成部分，可以使用机械直接装卸、搬运，还可以从一种运输工具直接换装到另一种运输工具上，而不需要碰触箱内的货物。实际上集装箱本身起到一个强度很大的外包装作用，因而箱内的货物可以大大简化外包装，有些商品甚至无须包装。

Container is a container for the carriage of goods. It is an integral part of means of conveyance, which can be loaded, unloaded and transported by machinery, or transferred from one means of conveyance to another without touching the goods inside. In fact, the container itself plays a significant role in outer packing. Therefore, the outer packing can be greatly simplified for goods inside, and some goods even do not need to be packed.

2. 托盘（Pallet）

托盘是按一定规格制成的一种平板载货工具，一定数量的单件货物叠放于平板上并捆扎加固，组成一个运输单位，便于运输过程中使用机械进行装卸、搬运和堆放。适宜用托盘运输的货物是箱装罐头食品、硬纸盒装消费品等比较小的包装商品。而比较大、形状不一的商品如机械或散装冷冻货物等，不适用于采用托盘进行运输。

Pallet is a kind of flat carrier made according to a certain specification. A certain number of individual goods are stacked on a flat plate and bundled for reinforcement, forming a carriage unit, which is convenient for loading/unloading, handling and stacking by machinery during carriage. Carriage by pallet is suitable for small packaged goods such as canned food in cases and consumer goods in cartons. Carriage by pallet is not suitable for large and differently shaped commodities such as machinery or bulk frozen goods.

3. 集装袋/包（Flexible Container）

集装袋/包是一种用合成纤维或复合材料编织成的圆形大口袋或方形大包，其容量一般在 1～4 吨，最高可达 13 吨左右。它一般适于装载粉粒状货物，如化工原料、矿产品、农产品、水泥等散装货。

Flexible container is a circular or square large bale woven with synthetic fibers or composite materials. Its capacity is generally 1~4 tons, up to about 13 tons. It is generally suitable for loading powdery and granular cargoes, such as chemical raw materials, mineral products, agricultural products, cement and other bulk cargo.

二、销售包装
II. Sales Packing

销售包装又称小包装、内包装或直接包装，它是指直接接触商品，随着商品进入零售环节和消费者直接见面的包装。这类包装除具有保护商品的作用外，还能起到提供商品信息、美化商品和促销的作用。

Sales packing, also known as small packing, inner packing or direct packing, refers to the packing that comes into direct contact with the commodity and meets consumers directly as it enters the retail process. It can not only protect goods, but also provide information, beautify goods and promote sales.

（一）出口商品销售包装的设计 (Design of Sales Packing for Export Goods)

出口商品销售包装在材料、造型、文字说明等方面都有较高要求，应按商品性质、形态、数量和所销售的不同国家和地区的特点设计出科学的结构和造型，不但要保护商品在储运中的安全，还要便于在国际市场中陈列展销、方便消费者携带和使用。

Sales packing for export goods has high requirements in terms of material, shape and text description. Scientific structure and shape shall be designed according to the nature, form and quantity of goods and characteristics of different countries and regions where goods are sold, so as to protect the safety of goods during storage and transportation, facilitate display and sales in the international market and make it easy for consumers to carry and use.

（1）要起到保护商品的功能。商品的性能不同，因此选用包装材料首先必须考虑到对商品是否起到保护作用。就食品而言，水分达到一定含量时，细菌、酵母霉等微生物就会生长繁殖。因此，选用食品包装材料时，要起到防腐、防霉、防异味、防毒的功能。当今密封性能比较好的材料是高密度聚乙烯和聚丙烯，可制作真空复合包装和充惰气包装。

(1) Protect the goods. The performance of goods varies, therefore, it is necessary to first consider whether it can protect the goods when selecting packing materials. Moisture content reaches a certain level in food, and microorganisms such as bacteria and yeast will grow and reproduce. Therefore, when choosing food packing materials, it should play the role of anti-corrosion, mildew prevention, odor prevention and gas defense. At present, the materials with good sealing performance are HDPE and PP, which can be used to make vacuum composite packing and inert gas filled packing.

（2）要适应陈列展销的要求。销售包装不但要起到保护商品的功能，同时还要具有美化商品、适应市场陈列展销的要求。因此，选用包装材料时，必须考虑美化商品的功能。国际市场上的透明包装和开天窗包装较为流行，因为它能有效地展示商品的质感和形象。我国北方某进出口公司出口到日本的"乳黄瓜"原用泥坛，每坛装10公斤，既不美观又不便于陈列展销，销路一直打不开，后改为300克造型别致的玻璃瓶，标贴精致，乳黄瓜的实感展示在消费者面前，给人一种清洁、卫生、高档商品的感觉，受到消费者青睐，销路很快打开，销售额成倍增长。

(2) Meet the requirements of display and sales. Sales packing should not only protect the goods, but also beautify them to meet the requirements of display and sales. Therefore, packing material selection must take into account the function of beautifying goods. Transparent packing and skylight packing are popular in the international market because they can effectively display the texture and image of goods. A pickled cucumber exported to Japan by an import and export company in northern China was originally packed in clay jars. Each jar contains 10 kg, which is neither beautiful nor convenient for display and sales, resulting in dull sales. Later, it was changed into 300 g glass bottles with unique design and exquisite labels. The actual display of pickled cucumber in front of consumers gave a feeling of hygiene and quality, which was favored by consumers. Sales soon increased and prices doubled.

（3）要考虑包装成本的核算。有些人认为出口的商品，都要设计高档华贵的包装，其实并不都是如此，不同类型和不同档次的商品，选用包装材料的档次应该有所不同，即使同一种商品，销售国家和地区不一样，由于经济水平和地理气候不同，选用包装材料也应该有所区别。

(3) Packing cost shall be considered. Some people believe that exported goods should be designed with high-grade and luxurious packaging. In fact, this is not always the case. Packing materials should be selected for different types and grades of goods; even if the same goods are sold in different countries and regions, due to differences in economic level and geographical climate, the selection of packing materials should also be different.

（4）要注意回收利用，保护环境。包装材料的使用和处理，与环境保护有密切关系。纸可以回收，基本上不会污染环境；玻璃瓶、罐头盒较难处理；塑料烧毁时则会对空气造成污染。法国通过一项包装法规，实施瓦楞纸箱包装使用无钉箱黏合，同时还规定：①塑料包装绝不可用PVC（聚氯乙烯）制作，在塑料袋上必须注明质地，显示成分。②不得使用有毒油墨颜料印刷标记。③打包带要用PE（聚乙烯）质地。因此，选用包装材料时，要考虑到国际市场不同国家（地区）对材料使用的具体规定和要求。

(4) Pay attention to recycling and environmental protection. The use and disposal of packing materials are closely related to environmental protection. Paper can be recycled and basically does not pollute the environment; glass bottles and cans are difficult to dispose of; when plastic is burnt, it will cause air pollution. Packing regulations in France provide that corrugated carton packing shall be bonded with nailless carton. At the same time, it also stipulates: ① Plastic packing must never be made of PVC, and texture and composition must be indicated on plastic bag. ② Toxic ink pigments shall not be used for printing. ③ The packing tape shall be made of PE. Therefore, when selecting packing materials, the specific regulations and requirements of international market different countries (regions) for material use shall be taken into account.

（二）销售包装的装潢和文字说明 (Decoration and Text Description of Sales Packing)

商品销售包装上的装潢和文字说明，是美化、宣传商品，吸引消费者，便于消费者了解商品特性和妥善使用商品的必要手段。装潢图案和文字说明通常直接印刷在商品包装上，也有在商品上粘贴、加标签、挂吊牌等方式。

Decoration and text description on sales packing are necessary means to beautify and publicize commodities, attract consumers, facilitate consumers' understanding of their characteristics and proper use of commodities. Decorative patterns and text descriptions are usually printed on the packing of goods, or pasted, labeled, or hung on the goods.

销售包装的装潢通常包括图案与色彩，应美观大方、富于艺术吸引力，并突出商品特征；同时还应适应进口国或销售地区的民族习惯和爱好。全球最大的饮料品牌可口可乐在风靡全球的同时，在不同的地区、文化背景和种族中采取分而治之，因地制宜的策略。可口可乐的包装——世界范围的红白颜色到了阿拉伯（中东）却要改在当地象征生命与吉祥的绿色。在中国，可口可乐每年的春节都会推出以中国农历的12生肖年为主题的贺岁包装，充分挖掘中国民俗文化，提高品牌亲和力从而吸引消费者。因此，在采用各种图案来进行包装设计时，销售企业一定要弄清商品进口国（地区）消费者的禁忌，避免产生误会甚至引起纠纷从而影响销售。

The decoration of sales packing usually consists of patterns and colors, which should be beautiful, artistic and highlight the characteristics of the commodity; meanwhile, it should also adapt to the national customs and preferences of the importing country or sales region. Coca Cola, the world's largest beverage brand, adopting a divide-and-rule strategy in different regions, cultural backgrounds, and ethnicities. Packing of Coca Cola—the red and white colors worldwide—has to be changed to green, which symbolizes life and auspiciousness in the Arab region (Middle East). In China, Coca Cola will launch New Year's Eve Packing with the theme of 12

Chinese zodiac years on the lunar calendar every year to fully explore China's folk culture and improve brand affinity so as to attract consumers. Therefore, when using various patterns for packing design, it is necessary to find out the consumer taboos of importing countries (regions), so as to avoid misunderstanding and even disputes that affect sales.

文字说明通常包括商品名称、商品品牌、数量规格、成分构成与使用说明的内容。这些文字说明不仅应与装潢画面和谐统一,还应注意符合有关国家标签管理条例规定。准确的文字翻译将表达的内容翻译成目标市场国的语言是建立信任感、正确传递信息的关键之一。梧州市某肉食制品厂猪肉腊肠包装上,"名师制作"的"名师"曾被译为excellent cooker(名锅)。产品标签日益成为各国(地区)关注的焦点,不同国家(地区)对各行业产品不断有新的标签要求,具备清晰、完整的标签内容是未来产品畅通出口的关键因素之一。为了减少能源消耗,能效标识的应用已成全球发展趋势,各国(地区)都在强制执行能耗标准。美国颁布的家电标签法规最终修订案规定从2008年2月29日开始,在美销售的大多数新家电须加贴黄色的"能源指南"标签,并用规定的格式和式样提供能耗信息。

The text description usually includes the commodity, brand, quantity specification, components and instructions for use. These text descriptions shall be harmonious and unified with the decoration picture, and attention shall also be paid to complying with relevant national label management regulations. Accurate translation of text into the language of the target market is critical to building trust and communicating properly. On the packing of pork sausages at a meat product factory in Wuzhou City, "excellent chef" was translated into "excellent cooker". Product labels have increasingly become the focus of attention in various countries (regions). Different countries (regions) continuously have new labeling requirements for products in various industries, and clear and complete label content is one of the key factors for smooth export of products in the future. In order to reduce energy consumption, the application of energy efficiency labels has become a global trend, and countries (regions) are enforcing energy consumption standards. The final amendment to the Appliance Labeling Rule (ALR) issued by the United States requires that newest appliances sold in the United States be labeled with yellow "Energy Guide" and provide energy consumption information in the prescribed format and style from February 29, 2008.

(三)**物品条码标志 (Marking of Bar Code)**

物品条码标志又称条形码标志,它是由一组配有数字的黑白及粗细间隔不等的平行条纹所组成,它是一种利用光电扫描阅读设备为计算机输入数据的特殊代码语言。国际上通用的包装上的条形码有两种:一种是美国、加拿大组织的统一编码委员会编制,其使用的物品标识符号为UPC码;一种是国际物品编码协会编制,其使用的物品标示符号为EAN·UCC码。1994年4月我国正式加入国际物品编码协会,该会分配给我国的国别号为690~695。目前,许多国家(地区)的超级市场和连锁店,都使用条形码标志技术来实现自动扫描结算、库存管理,如果商品销售包装上没有条形码,就不能进入超市或连锁店销售。所以,我国的出口商品都应在销售包装上刷印条形码标志。

Marking of bar code also known as barcode, it is composed of a group of black and white parallel stripes with numbers and varying thickness. It is a special code language that uses photoelectric scanning and reading devices to input data for computers. There are two types of barcodes commonly used on packing in the world: one is prepared by UCC organized by the United States and Canada, and its identification symbol is UPC; the other is prepared by EAN, and its identification symbol is EAN·UCC. In April 1994, China officially joined EAN, which assigned country codes of 690~695 to China. At present, supermarkets and chain stores in many countries (regions) use the barcode technology to realize automatic scanning settlement and inventory management. If there is no barcode on the sales packing of goods, they cannot enter the supermarket or chain store for sales. Therefore, China's exporters should print the barcode on the Sales Packing.

第三节 运输包装的标志
Section 3　Transport Packing Marks

运输包装的标志是指印刷在包装上的文字、符号或图案。按其用途可分为运输标志、指示性标志和警告性标志三种，以便人们识别货物和操作时注意。

Transport packing mark means a word, symbol or pattern printed on the packing. According to its purpose, it can be divided into three types: shipping mark, indicative mark and warning mark for people to identify goods and pay attention to during operation.

一、运输标志
I. Shipping Mark

运输标志又称唛头，通常是由一个简单的几何图形和一些字母、数字及简单的文字组成，印刷在运输包装的明显位置。它是国际货物买卖合同、货运单据中有关货物标志事项的基本内容。给出口商品刷唛的目的是使货物运输途中的有关人员辨认货物、核对单证。

Shipping mark, also known as shipping marks, is usually composed of a simple geometric figure and some letters, numbers and simple texts printed in a prominent position on the transport packing. It is the basic content related to the marking of goods in contract for international sale of goods and shipping documents. Export goods are marked to enable relevant personnel during carriage to identify the goods and check the documents.

按照国际标准化组织的建议，一个标准运输标志应由以下4个部分按顺序构成。

As recommended by ISO, a standard Shipping Mark shall consist of the following 4 parts in sequence.

（1）收货人或买方名称的英文缩写字母或简称。

(1) Abbreviations or acronyms of the consignees' or the buyers' names.

（2）参考文件号码：如运单号、订单号、发票号、合同号、信用证号等。

(2) Reference document number: such as waybill number, order number, invoice number, contract number and L/C number.

（3）目的地：货物最终目的地或目的港的名称。

(3) Destination: the name of final destination or port of destination.

（4）件号：包装货物的每件货物的顺序号和总件数均需标上，如："NO.1/100"。

(4) Packing number: the serial number and total number of packages of packed cargo shall be marked, such as "NO.1/100".

在我国的外贸实践中，外贸企业应参照该运输标志设计和制作唛头，还可根据需要增加重量、体积标志及生产国别等作为运输标志的一部分。

In China's foreign trade practice, foreign trade enterprises shall design and make shipping marks with reference to the shipping mark, and may also add weight, volume marks and country of manufacture as part of the shipping mark according to needs.

二、指示性标志
II. Indicative Mark

指示性标志是根据商品特征，对一些易碎、易损、容易变质的商品，在搬运装卸和存放保管条件方面所提出的要求和注意事项，用图形或文字表示。

Indicative mark refers to the requirements and precautions proposed for handling, loading/unloading and storage conditions of some fragile, vulnerable and perishable commodities according to their characteristics, which are expressed in graphics or words.

三、警告性标志
III. Warning Mark

警告性标志又称危险品标志，是在装有危险货物的运输包装上用图形或文字，其作用是警告有关装卸、运输和保管人员按货物特性采取相应措施，以保障人身和物资安全。为方便运输，我国在出口危险货物时，应在运输包装上同时刷制我国的危险品标志和国际海运危险品标志。

Warning mark (also known as dangerous cargo mark) is a graphic or text used on the transport packing containing dangerous goods. Its function is to warn relevant loading, unloading, carriage and storage personnel to take corresponding measures according to the characteristics of the goods to ensure personal and material safety. For the convenience of carriage, when exporting dangerous goods in China, both Chinese and international shipping marks on dangerous goods shall be printed on the transport packing.

第四节　合同中的包装条款
Section 4　Packing Clause in the Contract

一、包装条款的意义
I. Significance of Packing Clause

包装条款是合同的主要条款之一，是货物说明的组成部分。《联合国国际货物销售合同公约》第三十五条规定，卖方交付的货物必须与合同所规定的数量、质量和规格相符，并须按合同所规定的方式装箱或包装。如果卖方不按照合同规定的方式装箱或包装，即构成违约。买方有权索赔损失，甚至拒收货物。因此，买卖双方必须在合同中明确规定包装条款。

The packing clause is one of the main clauses of the contract and an integral part of the description of goods. Article 35 of the United Nations Convention on Contracts of International Sales of Goods (CISG) provides that the goods delivered by the sellers must conform to the quantity, quality and specification specified in the contract and shall be packed as agreed in the contract. If the sellers fail to pack as agreed in the contract, it shall constitute a breach of contract. The buyers have the right to claim for damages and even reject the goods. Packing clause must therefore be specified by the both parties in the contract.

二、包装条款的主要内容
II. Main Contents of Packing Clause

由于商品的品种、特性不一，运输方法以及运输距离又不相同，包装条款的内容及繁简也不尽相同。包装条款一般包括包装材料、包装方式、包装规格、包装标志和包装费用的负担等内容。

Due to different varieties and characteristics of commodities, as well as different carriage methods and distances, the contents and complexity of packing clause are also different. Packing clause generally includes packing material, packing method, packing specification, packing mark and bearing of packing costs.

包装材料和包装方式应按合同中订立的内容进行包装，若合同中没有规定，卖方应按同种商品的惯常方式进行包装。

Packing materials and packing methods shall be in accordance with the contents agreed in the contract. If there is no provision in the contract, the sellers shall pack according to the customary method of the same commodity.

运输包装的方式与包装用料、辅料由不同商品的特性决定。与运输包装有关的内容，如费用、包装标志以及包装提供者的责任与义务等有时也必须在合同中明确规定。

Transport packing mode, packing materials and accessories are determined by the characteristics of different commodities. Contents related to transport packing, such as cost, packing mark and responsibilities and obligations of packing provider must also be specified in the contract from time to time.

三、规定包装条款的注意事项
III. Precautions for Packing Clause

在商定包装条款时，应注意以下事项。

When negotiating the Packing Clause, attention shall be paid to the following.

1. 要考虑商品特性、运输方式及有关国家的法律的要求 (Characteristics of Goods, Transportation Mode and Legal Requirements of Relevant Countries)

每种商品都有其特性，如水泥怕湿、玻璃制品易碎、流体货物易渗漏和流失等，这就相应地要求包装有相应的防潮、防震、防渗、防锈和防毒的性能。不同的运输方式对包装也有不同要求，如海运包装要牢固，并有防止挤压和碰撞的功能；铁路运输要求包装有抗震的功能；航空运输包装要求轻便且不宜过大。

Each commodity has its own characteristics, such as moisture-proof cement, fragile glass products and easy leakage and loss of fluid goods. Packing materials shall have moisture-proof, shock-proof, anti-seepage, rust-proof and gas-proof properties accordingly. Different transportation modes have different requirements for packing. For example, seaworthy packing shall be strong and have the function of preventing extrusion and collision; packing for railway transportation shall be anti-seismic; packing for air transportation shall be lightweight and not too large.

2. 对包装的规定要明确具体 (Provisions on Packing shall be Explicit and Specific)

在合同中要明确规定包装材料、包装方式和规格，如纸箱包装，每箱6块。约定包装时，应明确具体，不宜笼统规定。在国际贸易中，有时也使用"适合海运的包装（seaworthy packing）"或"习惯包装（customary packing）"等术语。但这种术语含义模糊，各国（地区）理解不一，应避免使用。包装条款举例：

Packing material, packing method and specification shall be specified in the contract, such as carton packing, 6 pieces per carton. Provisions on packing shall be explicit and specific, rather than general. Terms such as "seaworthy packing" or "customary packing" are sometimes used in international trade. However, such terms are ambiguous and differ from country (region) to country (region) in understanding and should be avoided. Examples of packing clause:

In wooden cases containing 30 pcs. of 40 yds. each.

Peanuts to be packed in poly-bags of 1 kg. each, 10 bags to a box, 10 boxes to a carton.

3. 明确包装费用由谁负担 (Clarify Who will Bear the Packing Costs)

关于包装费用，一般包括在货价之内，不另计收。但也有不计在货价之内，而规定由买方另外支付。究竟由何方负担，应在包装条款中订明。包装由谁提供，通常有下列三种做法。

Packing costs are generally included in the price of goods and will not be charged separately. Sometimes they are not included in the price of goods and are to be paid by the buyers separately. The exact party responsible shall be specified in the packing clause. There are usually three ways to provide packing.

（1）由卖方提供包装，包装连同商品一块交付买方。

(1) Packing shall be provided by the sellers and delivered to the buyers together with the commodities.

（2）由卖方提供包装，但交货后，卖方将原包装收回。关于原包装返回给卖方的运费由哪方负担，应做具体规定。

(2) Packing shall be provided by the sellers, but after delivery, the sellers will take back the original packing. The bearing of freight charges for return of original packing to the sellers shall be specified.

（3）由买方提供包装或包装物料。但应同时在合同中订明买方提供包装物料的期限，若逾期则卖方不对交货延迟负责。

(3) Packing or packing materials shall be provided by the buyers. However, the time limit for the buyers to provide packing materials shall be specified in the contract. If it is overdue, the sellers will not be responsible for the delay of delivery.

4. 明确规定运输标志 (Specify the Shipping Mark)

根据贸易惯例，运输标志一般由卖方设计确定和刷制，这种做法习惯称为"卖方唛头"；若由买方指定运输标志并提交给卖方刷制，习惯上称为"买方唛头"。在采用买方唛头时，应在合同中明确规定买方提出唛头式样的时限。考虑到买方有可能提供唛头的时间过晚而影响卖方装运货物，可在合同中规定"如果货物在装运前……天未收到买方有关唛头的通知，卖方可自行设计和刷制唛头"。

According to trade practices, shipping marks are generally designed, determined and painted by the sellers, which is customarily called "Sellers' Shipping Marks". If the buyers designate shipping marks and submit them to the sellers for painting, it is customarily called "Buyers' Shipping Marks". When the buyers' shipping marks are used, the time limit for the buyers to propose the style of shipping marks shall be specified in the contract. Considering that the buyers may provide shipping marks too late, which may affect the sellers' shipment of goods, it can be specified in the contract that "if the Buyers' notice regarding Shipping Marks is not received... days before the shipment of goods, the Sellers may design and print Shipping Marks by themselves".

第七章　商品的价格
Chapter 7　Price of Goods

导　读
Introduction

一名合格的外贸业务员，在面对客户询盘时，必须能够熟练地核算并报出自己产品的价格；在面对客户讨价还价时，必须能够熟练地核算盈亏并正确判断是否可以按客户的还价成交。这是外贸业务员必须掌握的技能之一。商品的价格一般由成本、费用和利润三部分构成。在进出口业务中，采用不同的贸易术语成交，买卖双方承担的风险、责任和费用不同，最终报价也不同。另外，核算商品的出口价格还需要考虑选择采用何种外币计价，并进行本币和外币间的转换。

A qualified foreign trade salesperson must be able to skillfully calculate and quote the price of his own products when facing customers' inquiry; he must be able to skillfully calculate the profit and loss and correctly judge whether the transaction can be concluded at the customer's counter-offer when facing customers' bargaining. This is one of the skills that foreign trade salesperson must have. The price of goods is generally composed of three parts: cost, expense and profit. In the import and export business, when a transaction is concluded under different trade terms, the buyers and sellers will bear different risks, responsibilities and expenses, and the final price will also be different. When calculating the export price of goods, we also need to consider the choice of foreign currency for pricing and conversion between local and foreign currencies.

第一节　出口商品的价格构成与计算
Section 1　Price Composition and Calculation of Export Goods

一、了解出口商品的价格构成
I. Understand the Price Composition of Export Goods

出口商品的价格主要包括商品本身的成本、国内经营总费用、国外经营总费用和利润。

The price of export goods mainly includes the cost of the goods themselves, total domestic operating expenses, total foreign operating expenses and profit.

（一）商品本身的成本 (Cost of the Goods Themselves)

根据出口商类型的不同，商品本身的成本分为生产成本、加工成本和采购成本三种类型。生产成本是指制造商生产某一产品所需的投入。加工成本是指加工商对成品或半成品进行加工所需的投入。采购成本是指贸易商向供应商采购的价格。

According to the type of exporter, there are three types of costs: production cost, processing cost and procurement cost. Production cost refers to the input required by a manufacturer to produce a product. Processing cost is the input required by a processor to process finished or semi-finished products. Procurement cost refers to the price at which a trader purchases from a supplier.

（二）国内经营总费用 (Total Domestic Operating Expenses)

国内经营总费用主要包括认证费、包装费、仓储费、国内运输费、商检费、税费、港区港杂费、贷款利息、业务费用、银行费用等。

The total domestic operating expenses mainly include certification fee, packing fee, storage fee, domestic carriage fee, commodity inspection fee, taxes, port surcharges, loan interest, business expenses and bank charges.

（三）国外经营总费用 (Total Foreign Operating Expenses)

国外运费：指货物出口时支付的海运、陆运、空运或多式联运的费用。

Foreign Freight: refers to the fees paid for sea, land, air or multimodal transportation when goods are exported.

国外保险费：指出口商向保险公司购买货运保险所支付的费用。

Foreign Premium: refers to the expenses paid by the exporter for purchasing cargo insurance from the insurance company.

佣金：指出口商向中间商支付的酬金。

Commission: refers to the remuneration paid by the exporter to the broker.

（四）利润 (Profit)

因为进出口报价时，商品尚未销售出去，因此这里的利润一般指预期利润。

Since the goods have not been sold when quoting for import and export, profit here generally refers to expected profit.

二、掌握实际采购成本的计算方法
II. Master the Calculation Method of Actual Procurement Cost

对于从事贸易的出口商而言，商品成本即为采购成本，是贸易商向供货商购买货物的支出。一般来讲，供货厂商所报的价格就是贸易商的采购成本。然而，供货商报出的价格一般包含税收，即增值税。增值税是以商品进入流通环节所发生的增值额为课税对象的一种流转税。由于出口商品是进入国外流通领域的，为了增加产品在售价上的竞争力，要将含税的采购成本中的出口退税部分予以扣除，从而得出实际采购成本。我国实行出口退税制，对不同的商品实施不同的退税率。出口商品是否享受退税及退税率可以在通关网、中国出口退税咨询网等网站查询。我国现行增值税属于比例税率，根据应税行为分为 13%、9%、6% 三档税率。

For an exporter engaged in trade, the cost of goods is the procurement cost and is the expenditure incurred by a trader to purchase goods from a supplier. Generally speaking, the price quoted by the supplier is the procurement cost of the trader. The prices quoted by suppliers generally include taxes, i.e. VAT. Value-added tax is a type of turnover tax levied on the value-added amount of goods entering the circulation process. Due to the fact that export goods enter the field of foreign circulation, in order to increase the competitiveness of the product on selling price, the export refund in the procurement cost including tax shall be deducted to obtain the actual procurement cost. China implements a system of refunding export taxes with different refund rates for different commodities. Whether export goods enjoy tax refund and the tax refund rate can be checked on websites such as hscode.net and taxrefund.com.cn. The current VAT in China shall be taxed at a flat rate, which is divided into three levels: 13%, 9% and 6% according to the taxable behavior.

实际采购成本＝采购成本－出口退税额

Actual Procurement Cost ＝ Procurement Cost－Export Refund Amount

$$出口退税额 = \frac{出口采购成本}{1+增值税率} \times 出口退税率$$

$$\text{Export Refund Amount} = \frac{\text{Procurement Cost}}{1+\text{VAT Rate}} \times \text{Export Refund Rate}$$

$$实际采购成本 = 采购成本 \times \frac{1+增值税率 - 出口退税率}{1+增值税率}$$

$$\text{Actual Procurement Cost} = \text{Procurement Cost} \times \frac{1+\text{VAT Rate} - \text{Export Refund Rate}}{1+\text{VAT Rate}}$$

例1,某公司采购一批足球,每只足球购货成本为80元人民币(含13%增值税),若足球出口退税率为13%,求每只足球的实际采购成本?

Example 1: A company purchases a batch of footballs, and the procurement cost of each football is RMB 80 (including 13% VAT). If the export tax rebate rate of footballs is 13%, what is the actual procurement cost of each football?

$$实际采购成本 = 80 \times \frac{1+13\% - 13\%}{1+13\%} = 70.80 \text{(元/只)}$$

$$\text{Actual Procurement Cost} = 80 \times \frac{1+13\% - 13\%}{1+13\%} = 70.80 \text{ (yuan/PC)}$$

三、了解国内费用的名目与计算
III. Understand the Items and Calculation of Domestic Expenses

国内费用是指卖方为完成出口商品交货所发生的各项费用。主要包括:①包装费;②仓储费;③国内运输费;④国内保险费;⑤证书费;⑥商检费;⑦出口关税;⑧出口报关费;⑨港口费;⑩装船/货费;⑪银行费用;⑫邮寄费;⑬经营管理费用等。

Domestic Expenses refer to the expenses incurred by sellers in completing the delivery of export goods. Mainly including: ① packing charges; ② warehousing charges; ③ domestic carriage charges; ④ domestic premium; ⑤ certificate fees; ⑥ commodity inspection fees; ⑦ export duties; ⑧ customs declaration fees for export; ⑨ port dues; ⑩ loading charges; ⑪ bank charges; ⑫ postal charges; ⑬ operation and management expenses, etc.

出口货物涉及的各种国内费用在报价时大部分还没有发生,因此该费用的预算实际是一种估算。其方法有以下两种。

Most of the domestic expenses involved in exporting goods have not been incurred in the quotation, so the budget for such costs is actually an estimate. There are two methods.

(一)加总求和法(Summation)

加总求和法是将货物装运前的各项费用根据以往的经验进行估算并叠加,然后除以出口商品数量获得单位商品装运前的费用,即

Summation is to estimate and superimpose the expenses before shipment of goods based on previous experience, and then divide them by the quantity of export goods to obtain the expenses before shipment per unit, i.e.

$$单位出口商品国内费用 = \frac{国内总费用}{出口商品数量}$$

$$\text{Domestic Expense Per Unit of Exported Commodities} = \frac{\text{Total Domestic Expense}}{\text{Quantity of Exported Commodities}}$$

（二）定额费用率的做法（Fixed-rate Approach）

所谓定额费用率是指贸易公司在业务操作中对货物装运前发生的费用按公司年度支出规定一个百分比，一般为公司购货成本的3%～10%。实际业务中，该费率由贸易公司按不同的商品、交易额大小、竞争的激烈程度自行确定。

The so-called fixed rate refers to a percentage specified by the trading company for the expenses incurred before shipment of goods in business operations according to the annual expenditure of the company, which is generally 3%~10% of the procurement cost of the company. In actual business, the rate is determined by trading companies according to commodities, turnover and competition.

$$国内费用 = 采购成本 \times 定额费率$$

$$\text{Domestic Expense} = \text{Procurement Cost} \times \text{Fixed Rate}$$

例2，某出口公司出口冻虾17公吨，每公吨进货价格为5600元人民币，估计该批货物国内运杂费1200元，出口商检费300元，报关费100元，港口费用950元，其他各种费用共计1200元，银行手续费800元，求该商品的国内费用是多少？

Example 2: An export company exports 17 m/t of frozen shrimp. The purchase price per m/t is RMB 5600. It is estimated that the domestic freight and miscellaneous charges for this batch of goods are RMB 1200, the export inspection fee is RMB 300, the customs declaration fee is RMB 100, the port due is RMB 950, other various expenses are RMB 1200 in total, and the bank charge is RMB 800. Please calculate the domestic expenses of this commodity?

$$每吨冻虾国内费用 = \frac{1200+300+100+950+1500+800}{17}$$
$$= 285.2941（元/公吨）$$

$$\text{Domestic Expense Per Ton of Frozen Shrimp} = \frac{1200+300+100+950+1500+800}{17}$$
$$= 285.2941 \text{ (yuan/metric ton)}$$

接上题背景，若定额费率为进货价的5.5%，则该商品的国内费用为多少？

In the above scenario, if the fixed rate is 5.5% of the purchase price, what will be the domestic expenses of this commodity?

$$每吨冻虾国内费用 = 5600 \times 5.5\% = 308（元/公吨）$$

$$\text{Domestic expenses of frozen shrimp per ton} = 5600 \times 5.5\% = 308 \text{ (yuan/metric ton)}$$

究竟采用何种方法确定单位产品的国内费用，应结合收集数据的准确性、价格的竞争性及定价策略等综合考虑决定。在实践中，因出口费用涉及项目繁杂、单位众多、各项费用不易精确估算，所以常采用定额费率的方法加以预算。

The method to determine the domestic expenses per unit product should be determined by comprehensively considering the accuracy of collected data, price competitiveness and pricing strategy. In practice, the fixed-rate approach is often used for budgeting because export costs involve complex items and numerous units, and it is difficult to accurately estimate various costs.

四、了解国外费用的项目与计算
IV. Understand the Items and Calculation of Foreign Expenses

出口价格中是否需要核算国外费用，取决于采用的贸易术语，以及对方的要求（要包含佣金或净价）。

Whether foreign expenses need to be accounted for in the export price depends on the trade terms adopted and the requirements of the other party (CIFC or net price).

（一）出口运费预算 (Budget of Export Freight)

进出口货物的运输通常采用的是海运运输方式，在采用CFR、CIF价格术语时，办理运输并支付运费是出口商的责任。这时，运费就构成货价的要素之一。

Import and export goods are usually transported by sea. When CFR or CIF Terms are adopted, it is the responsibility of the exporter to handle the carriage and pay freight charges. Freight then constitutes one element of the price.

在海运方式中，根据承运货物船舶的营运方式不同，可以分为班轮运输和租船运输两种。除大宗初级产品外，多数商品采用班轮运输方式。在班轮运输中，根据托运货物是否装入集装箱又可分为散装货物与集装箱货物两类。

According to the different operation methods of cargo-carrying ships, sea transportation can be divided into two types: liner and charter. Liner is used for most commodities except bulk primary products. In liner, the consignment can be divided into bulk cargo and container cargo according to whether it is stuffed in a container.

1. 散装货（件杂货）运费预算 [Budget of Freight Charges for Bulk Cargo (General Cargo)]

（1）海运运费的构成：主要由基本运费和附加运费两部分构成。附加运费主要有燃油附加费、货币贬值附加费、港口拥挤费、转船附加费等。

(1) Composition of ocean freight: It is mainly composed of basic freight and additional freight. Additional freight mainly includes fuel additional, currency depreciation additional, port congestion charge and transshipment additional.

（2）海运运费计算标准：包括W、M、W/M、Ad Val.等计收基本运费的标准。

(2) Calculation standard of ocean freight: It includes the standards for calculating basic freight such as W, M, W/M and Ad Val.

（3）海运运费计算公式：

(3) Calculation formula of ocean freight:

$$海运运费＝（1+附加费率）\times 基本费率\times 货运量$$

$$\text{Ocean Freight} = (1+\text{Surcharge Rate}) \times \text{Basic Rate} \times \text{Freight Volume}$$

（4）海运运费的计算步骤：

(4) Calculation steps of ocean freight:

①根据货物名称，在运价表中的货物分级表上查到货物的等级和运费计算标准；

①According to the name of goods, find out the grade of goods and the calculation standard of freight charges on the classification of commodities in freight tariff;

②根据货物的装运港、目的港，找到相应航线，按货物的等级查到基本运价；

②Find the corresponding route according to the port of shipment and port of destination of the goods, and find out the basic rate according to the grade of the goods;

③查出该航线和港口所要收取的附加费项目和数额（百分比）及货币种类；

③Find out the items and amount (percentage) of additional to be charged for the route and port, as well as the types of currencies;

④根据基本运价和附加费算出实际运价（单位运价）；

④Calculate the actual rate (unit rate) based on base rate and additional;

⑤根据货物的托运数量算出应付的运费总额。

⑤Calculate the freight payable according to the consigned quantity of goods.

例3，某公司出口一批蛋制品，毛重10公吨，体积11立方米，从上海装运，直航至英国普利茅斯港，求海运运费是多少？

Example 3: A company exports a batch of egg products with gross weight of 10 m/t and volume of 11 cubic meters. They are shipped from Shanghai directly to Plymouth Port in the United Kingdom. How much is the ocean freight?

①查货物分级表知：蛋制品为12级，W/M。
① According to the classification of commodities, egg products are classified as Grade 12, W/M.
②查航线费率表知：基本费率为USD 116/F.T.。
② According to the route rate table, the basic rate is USD 116/F.T.
③查附加费率表知：直航附加费为USD 18/F.T.；燃油附加费是基本运费的35%。
③ According to the additional rate table, the direct additional is USD 18/F.T.; the fuel surcharge is 35% of the basic freight.

$$海运运费 = [116×(1+35\%)+18]×11 = 1920.60（美元）$$
$$Ocean\ Freight = [116×(1+35\%)+18]×11 = USD\ 1920.60$$

2. 集装箱货物海运运费预算 (Budget of Ocean Freight for Container Goods)

对于集装箱货物运费的计收有两种：拼箱货按散装货的方法计算运费；整箱货按包箱价计算。计算公式为：

Freight charges for container cargo can be calculated and collected in two ways: LCL freight is calculated using the method of bulk cargo; FCL freight is charged on a container basis. The calculation formula is as follows:

$$海运运费 = 包箱价 × 集装箱个数$$
$$Ocean\ Freight = Box\ Rate × Number\ of\ Containers$$

例4，从上海出口女式套头衫9110件至纽约，用2个20'集装箱装或用1个40'集装箱装的海运费分别是多少？通过"航线及运费查询"查得上海至纽约海运费为：20'集装箱USD 3702，40'集装箱USD 4674。

Example 4: What is the ocean freight for exporting 9110 pieces of women's pullover from Shanghai to New York in two 20' containers or one 40' container? Ocean freight from Shanghai to New York Sea is USD 3702 for a 20' container and USD 4674 for a 40' container through "Route and Freight Inquiry".

装2个20'集装箱：海运费 = 3702×2 = 7404（美元）
In two 20' containers: Ocean Freight = 3702×2 = USD 7404

装1个40'集装箱：海运费 = 4674×1 = 4674（美元）
In one 40' container: Ocean Freight = 4674×1 = USD 4674

（二）保险费、佣金的预算 (Budget of Premium and Commission)

1. 保险费预算 (Premium Budget)

在出口交易中，在以CIF或CIP术语成交的情况下，出口方就需要进行保险费的预算。保险费是按照货物的保险金额乘以一定的百分比（保险费率）来计算的。

Premium budgeting is required for export transactions in the case of CIF or CIP terms. Premium is calculated by multiplying the insured amount of goods by a certain percentage (premium rate).

$$保险费 = 保险金额 × 保险费率$$
$$Premium = Insured\ Amount × Premium\ Rate$$
$$保险金额 = CIF或CIP价格 × (1+投保加成率)$$

$$\text{Insured Amount} = \text{CIF or CIP Price} \times (1+\text{Percentage of Addition})$$

其中，投保加成率由买卖合同确定，一般为 10%，不超过 30%。

The percentage of addition is determined by the sales contract, generally 10% and not more than 30%.

$$\text{保险费} = \text{CIF 或 CIP 价格} \times (1+\text{投保加成率}) \times \text{保险费率}$$

$$\text{Premium} = \text{CIF or CIP Price} \times (1+\text{Percentage of Addition}) \times \text{Premium Rate}$$

由于保险金额一般是以 CIF 或 CIP 价格为基础加成确定的，若已知 CFR 或 CPT 价格，可按下述公式换算：

Since the insured amount is generally an addition to the CIF or CIP price, if CFR or CPT price is known, it can be converted according to the following formula:

$$\text{CIF 或 CIP 价} = \frac{\text{CFR 或 CPT 价}}{1-(1+\text{投保加成率}) \times \text{保险费率}}$$

$$\text{CIF or CIP Price} = \frac{\text{CFR or CPT Price}}{1-(1+\text{Percentage of Addition}) \times \text{Premium Rate}}$$

例 5，向日本出口钢材，已知 CFR 价格为每公吨 520 美元，现改报 CIF 价，投保一切险，投保加成率为 10%，保险费率为 0.55%，试计算 CIF 价和每公吨的保险费是多少？

Example 5: For the export of steel to Japan, it is known that the CFR price is USD 520 per m/t. Now we change the quotation to CIF price and insure all risks with a percentage of addition of 10% and a premium rate of 0.55%. Please calculate the CIF price and the premium per m/t?

$$\text{CIF 价格} = \frac{520}{1-(1+10\%) \times 0.55\%} = 523.165 \text{（美元/公吨）}$$

$$\text{CIF Price} = \frac{520}{1-(1+10\%) \times 0.55\%} = \text{USD } 523.165/\text{metric ton}$$

$$\text{每公吨保险费} = 523.165 \times (1+10\%) \times 0.55\% = 3.165 \text{（美元/公吨）}$$

$$\text{Premium Per Metric Ton} = 523.165 \times (1+10\%) \times 0.55\% = \text{USD } 3.165/\text{metric ton}$$

2. 佣金预算 (Budget of the Commission)

佣金是买方或卖方付给中间商的报酬，包含佣金的价格称含佣价，价格中不包含佣金的称为净价，净价与含佣价之间的换算关系是：

Commission is the remuneration paid by the buyers or sellers to the intermediary. The price including commission is called CIFC, and the price excluding commission is called net price. The conversion between net price and CIFC is as follows:

$$\text{净价} = \text{含佣价} - \text{佣金}$$

$$\text{Net Price} = \text{CIFC} - \text{Commission}$$

$$\text{佣金} = \text{含佣价} \times \text{佣金率}$$

$$\text{Commission} = \text{CIFC} \times \text{Commission Rate}$$

$$\text{含佣价} = \frac{\text{净价}}{1-\text{佣金率}}$$

$$\text{CIFC} = \frac{\text{Net Price}}{1-\text{Commission Rate}}$$

例 6，买卖双方以每公吨 1000 美元 CIF 含佣 3% 的价格达成交易，每公吨的佣金为多少？

Example 6: If the buyers and sellers conclude a transaction at a CIFC of USD 1000 (3% commission) per m/t, what is the commission per m/t?

佣金=1000×3%=30（美元/公吨）

Commission=1000×3%=USD 30/metric ton

例7，某商品的CFR价为840美元，加成10%投保，保险费率为1.2%，佣金率为3%，若客户要求改报CIFC3价，试求其含佣价？

Example 7: The CFR price of a commodity is USD 840, with a percentage of addition of 10% for insurance. The premium rate is 1.2% and the commission rate is 3%. If the customer requests to quote a CIFC, what is the price?

$$CIFC3 = \frac{CFR}{1-佣金率-(1+投保加成率)\times 保险费率}$$

$$= \frac{840}{1-3\%-(1+10\%)\times 1.2\%} = 877.93（美元）$$

$$CIFC3 = \frac{CFR}{1-\text{Commission Rate}-(1+\text{Percentage of Addition})\times \text{Premium Rate}}$$

$$= \frac{840}{1-3\%-(1+10\%)\times 1.2\%} = USD\ 877.93$$

五、掌握利润的预算方法
V. Master the Budgeting Method for Profits

价格中所包含的利润根据商品价格与商品出口成本之差来决定，在实践中，公司决定利润的预算方法有两种：一是根据出口成本利润率计算利润；二是根据出口销售价格利润率计算利润。

Profit included in the price is determined by the difference between the price of the goods and the export cost of the goods. In practice, there are two budgeting methods for companies to determine profits: one is to calculate profits based on the profit margin of export costs; the other is to calculate profits based on the profit margin of export sales prices.

例8，某公司单位产品的出口成本为100美元，假设预期出口成本利润率为20%，出口销售价格利润率为20%，分别计算出口价格和利润额是多少？

Example 8: The export cost per unit product of a company is USD 100. Assuming that the expected profit margin of export cost is 20% and the profit margin of export sales price is 20%, calculate the export price and profit respectively.

①出口价格＝100×(1+20%)＝120（美元）

①Export Price＝100×(1+20%)＝USD 120

　出口利润额＝100×20%＝20（美元）

　Export Profit＝100×20%＝USD 20

②出口价格＝100÷(1－20%)＝125（美元）

②Export Price＝100÷(1－20%)＝USD 125

　出口利润额＝125×20%＝25（美元）

　Export Profit＝125×20%＝USD 25

由此可见，计算利润的基础不同，出口报价和利润大小也不同。因此，公司在进行价格预算时，应特别注意本公司利润预算的依据，以免报价失误，造成损失。

It can be seen that the basis for calculating profits is different, so are the export quotation and profit.

Therefore, the company shall pay special attention to the basis of its profit budget when making price budget, so as to avoid losses caused by quotation errors.

第二节　六种贸易术语价格的构成及换算
Section 2　Price Composition and Conversion of Six Trade Terms

一、六种贸易术语价格的构成
I. Price Composition of Six Trade Terms

FOB价格＝实际采购成本＋国内费用＋预期利润

FOB Price = Actual Procurement Cost + Domestic Expenses + Expected Profit

FCA价格＝实际采购成本＋国内费用＋预期利润

FCA Price = Actual Procurement Cost + Domestic Expenses + Expected Profit

CFR价格＝实际采购成本＋国内费用＋海运运费＋预期利润

CFR Price = Actual Procurement Cost + Domestic Expenses + Ocean Freight + Expected Profit

CPT价格＝实际采购成本＋国内费用＋国外运费＋预期利润

CPT Price = Actual Procurement Cost + Domestic Expenses + Foreign Freight + Expected Profit

CIF价格＝实际采购成本＋国内费用＋海运运费＋海运保险费＋预期利润

CIF Price = Actual Procurement Cost + Domestic Expenses + Ocean Freight + Ocean Premium + Expected Profit

CIP价格＝实际采购成本＋国内费用＋国外运费＋国外保险费＋预期利润

CIP Price = Actual procurement cost + Domestic Expenses + Foreign Freight + Foreign Premium + Expected Profit

二、不同贸易的价格换算
II. Price Conversion of Different Trades

CFR价=FOB价+海运运费（F）

CFR = FOB + Ocean Freight (F)

CIF价=FOB价+海运运费（F）+海运保险费（I）

CIF = FOB + Ocean Freight (F) + Ocean Premium (I)

因为，保险费=CIF或CIP价格×(1+投保加成率)×保险费率，将保险费的计算公式代入上式，移项合并同类项后，得到如下公式：

Since Premium = CIF or CIP × (1 + percentage of addition) × Premium Rate, the calculation formula of Premium is substituted into the above formula. After moving items and merging similar items, the following formula is obtained:

$$CIF价 = \frac{FOB价 + F}{1 - (1 + 投保加成率) \times 保险费率}$$

$$CIF\ Price = \frac{FOB\ Price + F}{1 - (1 + Percentage\ of\ Addition) \times Premium\ Rate}$$

上述公式的分子也就是CFR价，所以上述公式可以作为将FOB、CFR和CIF三种价格进行换算的万能公式。

The numerator of the above formula is a CFR, so the above formula can be used as a universal formula for converting FOB, CFR and CIF.

例9，某公司业务员参加广交会，对其负责的某种商品计算后得出该商品可报每桶150美元FOB厦门，但他认为只准备一种报价是不够的，该商品销往北美比较多，他准备再计算CIF洛杉矶价（经查：该商品每桶海运费15美元，加成10%投保，保险费率0.5%），请帮他计算报价。

Example 9: A salesperson of a company participated in the Canton Fair and calculated that a price of 150 USD FOB Xiamen per barrel could be quoted for certain goods under his charge. However, he thought it was not enough to prepare only one quotation. The goods were sold more often to North America, so he planned to calculate the CIF Los Angeles price also: ocean freight USD 15 per barrel, plus 10% premium and 0.5% premium rate). Please help him calculate the price.

$$CIF 价 = \frac{150+15}{1-(1+10\%) \times 0.5\%} = \frac{165}{0.9945} \approx 165.91（美元/桶）$$

$$CIF\ Price = \frac{150+15}{1-(1+10\%) \times 0.5\%} = \frac{165}{0.9945} \approx USD\ 165.91/barrel$$

FOB、CFR和CIF换算公式可以适用于FCA、CPT和CIP，因为前三种贸易术语与后三种贸易术语在价格构成上是一一对应的关系。

FOB, CFR and CIF conversion formulas can be applied to FCA, CPT and CIP, because the first three trade terms correspond to the latter three trade terms in terms of price composition.

第三节　定价原则和报价时应考虑的因素
Section 3　Pricing Principles and Factors to be Considered in Quotation

一、定价原则
I. Pricing Principles

我国进出口商品的作价原则是，在贯彻平等互利的基础上，根据国际市场价格水平，结合国别或地区政策，并按照我方的购销意图确定适当的价格。国际市场价格通常是指商品在国际集散中心的市场价格，主要出口国或地区当地市场的出口价格或主要进口国或地区当地市场的进口价格。由于价格构成因素不同，影响价格变化的因素也是多种多样的，因此在确定进出口商品价格时，必须充分考虑影响价格的各种因素，并注意同一商品在不同情况下应有合理差价，防止不分情况、采用全球同一价格的错误做法。

The pricing principle of imports and exports in China is to determine the appropriate price on the basis of equality and mutual benefit, referring to the international market price level, combined with national or regional policies and in accordance with our purchase and sale intentions. International market price usually refers to the market price of goods in international distribution centers, export prices in local markets of major exporting countries or regions, or import prices in local markets of major importing countries or regions. Due to the different price components, there are also many factors affecting price changes. Therefore, when determining the prices of import and export goods, it is necessary to fully consider all factors affecting prices and allow reasonable price difference in different circumstances for the same commodity to prevent the wrong practice of adopting the same global price regardless of circumstances.

二、报价应考虑的因素
II. Factors to be Considered in Quotation

为了正确掌握进出口商品价格，除遵循上述作价原则外，还必须考虑下列因素。

In order to properly obtain the prices of import and export goods, the following factors must be considered in addition to following the pricing principles mentioned above.

（一）商品的质量和档次 (Quality and Grade of Goods)

在国际市场上，一般都贯彻按质论价的原则，即优质高价，劣质低价。商品质量的优劣、档次的高低、包装装潢的好坏、式样的新旧、商标或品牌的知名度，都会影响到商品的价格。

In the international market, we generally implement the principle of pricing according to quality, that is, high price for good quality and low price for inferior quality. The quality, grade, packing and style of a product, as well as the recognition of a trademark or brand will affect the price of goods.

（二）运输距离 (Carriage Distance)

国际贸易中的商品一般要经过长途运输，运输距离的远近会影响运费和保费的开支，从而影响商品的价格。因此，确定商品价格时，必须核算运输成本，做好比价工作，以体现地区差价。例如，在其他交易条件都相同的情况下，我国出口商报CIF BUSAN价肯定要低于CIF LOS ANGELES价，因为前者是从我国运到韩国釜山港，后者是从我国运到美国洛杉矶港，运输距离不同。

Carriage of goods in international trade generally involves long-distance transportation. Freight charges and premiums will be affected by the distance of carriage, thus affecting the price of goods. Therefore, when determining the price of goods, it is necessary to calculate the cost of carriage and compare prices to reflect regional differences. For example, CIF BUSAN quoted by our exporter is definitely lower than CIF LOS ANGELES under the same other trading conditions. Carriage distances of the former from China to Busan Port in Korea and the latter from China to Los Angeles Port in United States are different.

（三）交货地点和交货条件 (Place of Delivery and Delivery Conditions)

国际贸易中，由于交货地点和交货条件不同，买卖双方承担的责任、费用和风险就有区别，在确定进出口商品价格时，必须考虑这些因素。例如，在其他交易条件都相同的情况下，按EXW条件和按DDP条件成交，EXW报价肯定要低于DDP报价。

In international trade, the responsibilities, expenses and risks borne by buyers and sellers are different due to the difference in place of delivery and delivery conditions. These factors must be taken into account when determining the price of import and export goods. For example, if a transaction is concluded on EXW and DDP with all other things being equal, the price quoted by EXW will certainly be lower than that quoted by DDP.

（四）季节性需求的变化 (Changes in Seasonal Demand)

在国际市场上，某些节令性的商品，如赶在节令前到货，抢先应市，就能卖上好价。过了节令的商品，其售价往往很低，甚至以低于成本价的"跳楼价"出售。因此，应充分利用季节性需求的变化，切实掌握好季节性差价，争取按对我方有利的价格成交。

In the international market, some seasonal goods can be sold at good prices if they arrive before the holidays. After the holidays, their selling prices are often very low, even at a "flop price" below cost. Therefore, we should make full use of the changes in seasonal demand, effectively grasp the seasonal price difference and strive to conclude business at a price favorable to us.

（五）成交数量 (Volume of Business)

按国际贸易的习惯做法，成交量的大小会影响价格。即成交量大时在价格上应给予适当优惠，或者采用数量折扣的办法；反之，如成交量过少，甚至低于起订量时，可以适当提高售价。因此，无论成交数量多少，都采取同样价格成交的做法是不恰当的，外贸业务员应当掌握好数量差价。

According to international trade practices, the volume of business affects prices. That is, when the volume of business is large, an appropriate discount shall be given on the price, or the method of quantity discount shall be adopted; On the contrary, if the volume of business is too small or even lower than the minimum order quantity, the selling price can be appropriately increased. Therefore, it is inappropriate to adopt the same price regardless of the volume of business. Quantity difference shall be well controlled by foreign trade salespersons.

（六）支付条件和汇率变动的风险 (Risks of Changes in Payment Terms and Exchange Rates)

支付条件是否有利和汇率变动风险的大小，都会影响商品的价格。例如，同一商品在其他交易条件相同的情况下，采用预付货款和货到付款时，其价格应当有所区别，同时，确定商品价格时，一般应争取采用对自身有利的货币成交，如采用不利的货币成交，应当把汇率变动的风险考虑到货价中去，即出口时适当提高售价，进口时适当压低购买价格。

Payment conditions and exchange rate fluctuations will affect the price of goods. For example, when payment in advance and payment after arrival of goods are used for the same commodity under the same other trading conditions, their prices shall be different. At the same time, when determining the commodity price, it is necessary to strive to use the favorable currency for transaction. If unfavorable currencies are used for transaction, the risk of exchange rate changes shall be taken into account, that is, the selling price shall be appropriately increased during export and the purchase price shall be appropriately lowered during import.

（七）国际市场商品供求变化和价格走势 (Changes in Supply and Demand of Commodities and Price Trends in the International Market)

国际市场价格因受供求变化的影响而上下波动，有时甚至出现瞬息万变的情况。因此，在确定成交价格时，必须考虑供求状况和价格变动的趋势。当市场上的商品供不应求时，价格会呈上涨趋势；反之，商品供过于求，价格就会呈下降趋势。由此可见，切实了解国际市场供求变化状况，有利于对国际市场价格的走势做出正确判断，也有利于合理地确定进出口商品的成交价格，避免价格掌握上的盲目性。

Prices fluctuate up and down in international market due to changes in supply and demand, sometimes even rapidly. Therefore, when determining the transaction price, it is necessary to consider the supply and demand and the trend of price changes. When the supply of goods in the market exceeds demand, prices will tend to rise; conversely, when the supply of goods exceeds demand, prices will tend to fall. It can be seen that an effective understanding of the changes in supply and demand in the international market is conducive to making a correct judgment on the trend of international market prices, as well as reasonably determining the transaction price of import and export goods, so as to enhance the control of price.

此外，交货期的远近、市场销售习惯和消费者的偏好等因素，对确定价格也有不同影响，必须通盘考虑、权衡得失，在此基础上确定合适的价格。

In addition, factors such as time of delivery, sales practice and consumer preferences also have different impacts on pricing. Therefore, the appropriate price must be determined based on overall consideration and trade-off.

第四节　合同中的价格条款
Section 4　Price Clause in the Contract

商品的价格涉及买卖双方的经济利益，是交易磋商的焦点，价格条款是合同中的核心条款之一。所以，必须正确掌握进出口商品价格的表示方法，学会拟定合同中的价格条款。

The price of goods involves the economic interests of buyers and sellers, and is the focus of business negotiation. Price clause is one of the core clauses in the contract. Therefore, it is necessary to correctly grasp the price expression of import and export goods and learn to draw up price clause in the contract.

一、合同中的价格条款
I. Price Clause in the Contract

国际货物买卖合同中的价格条款包括商品的单价和总值两项基本内容。

The price clause in the contract for international sale of goods includes two basic aspects, i.e. unit price and total amount.

（一）单价 (Unit Price)

国际贸易中的商品单价比国内贸易中的商品单价复杂，通常由计量单位、单位价格金额、计价货币和贸易术语四个基本要素构成。例如：

The Unit price of goods in international trade is more complex than that in domestic trade. It usually consists of four basic elements: unit of measurement, unit price, quote currency and trade terms. Example:

美元	100	每公吨	FOB海口
USD		per metric ton	FOB Haikou
（计价货币）	（单位价格金额）	（计量单位）	（贸易术语）
(Quote Currency)	(Unit Price)	(Unit of Measurement)	(Trade Terms)

合同中的单价条款由四个要素构成：计价货币、单位价格金额、计量单位和贸易术语。例如，GBP100.00/DOZEN CIF LONDON INCOTERMS® 2020。

The unit price clause in the contract consists of four elements: quote currency, unit price, unit of measurement and trade terms. For example, GBP100.00/DOZEN CIF LONDON INCOTERMS® 2020.

在制定单价条款时应注意以下几点。

Please note the following when formulating unit price clause.

（1）要正确写明计价货币的名称。世界上有很多国家和地区的货币单位名称是相同的，而币值差别却很大，所以必须清楚写明是何国或地区的货币，在简写时应尤其注意这一点。如"元"有人民币元、日元、美元、欧元、加拿大元、港元、新加坡元等，应用货币的英文缩写或中文全称说明具体货币名称（见表7-1）。

(1) The name of the quote currency shall be properly indicated. There are many countries and regions in the world with the same name of currency unit, but there are significant differences in currency values. Therefore, it is necessary to indicate which country or region's currency it is. When abbreviating, special attention shall be paid to this. For example, "yuan" may refer to RMB, JPY, USD, EUR, CAD, HKD and SGD. The currency name shall be indicated by the English abbreviation or full Chinese name of the currency (see Table 7-1).

表7-1 世界主要货币名称及其英文缩写

Table 7-1 Names and English Abbreviations of Major Currencies in the World

货币英文代码 English Abbreviations of Currency	货币英文全称 Full Name of Currency in English	中文名称 Chinese
CNY	Chinese Yuan	人民币
HKD	Hong Kong Dollar	港元
EUR	Euro	欧元
CHF	Chweizer Franken（德文）	瑞士法郎
USD	United States Dollar	美元
CAD	Canadian Dollar	加拿大元
GBP	Great Britain Pound	英镑
JPY	Japanese Yen	日元
AUD	Australian Dollar	澳大利亚元

（2）明确计量单位采用何种度量衡制度。由于国际贸易中各国和地区使用的度量衡制度不一，不同度量衡制度下的计量单位表示的商品实际数量差别很大，如以"吨"为单位，应明确是公吨、长吨或短吨，否则容易引起争议。

(2) Clarify the system of weights and measures adopted by units of measurement. Due to the different systems of weights and measures used by countries and regions in international trade, there are great differences in the actual quantity of goods indicated by units of measurement under different systems of weights and measures. If the unit is "ton", it shall be defined as m/t, l/t or s/t; otherwise, disputes may easily arise.

（3）贸易术语的表述要准确、完整，不能省略港口和适用惯例版本年份。世界上同名港或城市不少，例如美国和英国都有港口Boston，牙买加、加拿大和澳大利亚都有港口Kingston。若遇上同名港，一定要在港口后加注国名，以示区别。

(3) The expression of trade terms shall be accurate and complete, and the port and year of the applicable version cannot be omitted. There are many ports or cities of the same name in the world, such as Boston, a port in the United States and the United Kingdom, and Kingston, a port in Jamaica, Canada and Australia. For a port with the same name, be sure to add the country name after the port to distinguish it.

（4）佣金与折扣的表示方法要正确、清楚。

(4) The expressions of commission and discount shall be correct and clear.

(二) 总值 (Total Amount)

总值也称总价，是单价与成交商品数量的乘积，即一笔交易的货款总金额。总值使用的货币应与单价使用的货币一致，并要用大小写同时表示。

Total amount, also known as total value, is the product of unit price and transaction quantity, i.e. the total amount of payment for a transaction. The total amount shall be expressed in the same currency as that used for the unit price, both in words and figures.

(三) 合同中价格条款举例 (Examples of Price Clause in the Contract)

HKD 5.00 per dozen CIF Hong Kong Incoterms® 2020.

USD 21.00 per set FOBC5% Shanghai Incoterms® 2020.

二、佣金和折扣
II. Commission and Discount

在磋商交易和计算价格时，有时会涉及佣金和折扣。正确掌握与运用佣金和折扣，可以达到扩大销售和增加经济效益的目的。与之相适应，在合同的价格条款中，有时也会涉及佣金和折扣。价格条款中规定的价格，可分为包含有佣金或折扣的价格和不包含此类因素的净价（net price）。在业务实践中，除非事先另有约定，若有关价格条款未对佣金或折扣做出表示，通常理解为合同价格是不含佣金或折扣的价格。

Commission and discount are sometimes involved in negotiating transactions and calculating prices. Properly grasping and using commission and discount can achieve the purpose of expanding sales and increasing economic benefits. Accordingly, commission and discount are sometimes involved in the price clause of the contract. The price specified in the price clause can be divided into price that includes commission or discount and net price that does not include such factors. In business practice, unless otherwise agreed in advance, if the relevant price clause does not indicate commission or discount, it is generally understood that the contract price is exclusive of commission or discount.

（一）佣金和折扣的含义 (Meaning of Commission and Discount)

在国际贸易中，有些交易是通过中间商（包括代理商、经纪人等）进行的。佣金（commission）就是中间商介绍生意或代买代卖而收取的酬金。包含佣金的价格被称为含佣价。我国某些外贸公司在代理国内企业开展进出口业务时，通常由双方签订协议规定佣金率，而在对外报价时，佣金率则不明示在价格中，这种做法被称为"暗佣"。若在价格条款中，明确表示佣金多少，这种做法被称为"明佣"，常出现在我国出口企业向国外中间商的报价中。正确运用佣金，有利于调动中间商的积极性和扩大交易，合理的佣金比率应控制在商品售价的1%～5%之间。佣金的支付方法有两种：一种是由中间商直接从货价中扣除；另一种是卖方收妥货款后，按事先约定的期限和佣金率，另外支付给中间商。

In International trade, some transactions are carried out through intermediaries (bale agents, brokers etc.). A commission is a fee charged by an intermediary for introducing business or buying or selling on behalf of others. The price including commission is called CIFC. When some foreign trade companies in China carry out import and export business on behalf of domestic enterprises, they usually sign an agreement to specify the commission rate, while when making an offer, the commission rate is not expressly indicated in the price. This practice is known as "Commission not Shown on Invoice". If the commission is clearly stated in the price clause, it is called "Commission Shown on Invoice", which often appears in the quotes from Chinese export enterprises to foreign intermediaries. The proper use of commission is conducive to mobilizing the enthusiasm of intermediaries and expanding transactions. The reasonable commission rate shall be controlled between 1% and 5% of the selling price of goods. Commission can be paid in two ways: One is that the broker deducts directly from the price of the goods, and the other is that the sellers pay the broker separately according to the pre-agreed time limit and commission rate after receiving the payment.

佣金的支付方式有三种：①直接从货价中扣除，即合同中规定的价格为含佣价，而买方实际支付的价格为扣除佣金之后的价格；②待出口商收妥货款后，再按事先约定的期限和佣金率，将佣金汇付给中间商；③如采用信用证付款，则在信用证中规定佣金在议付时直接从信用证款项中扣除，称为"议扣"。

There are three ways to pay for the commission: ① Deduct directly from the price of goods, i.e. the price specified in the contract is CIFC, while the actual price paid by the buyers is the price after deducting the commission; ② Remit commission to the intermediary at a pre-agreed time limit and commission rate after receipt of payment by the exporter; ③ If L/C payment is adopted, it shall be specified in the L/C that the commission will be directly deducted from the payment of L/C when available by negotiation, which is called "negotiation deduction".

折扣（discount /allowance）是卖方按原价给予买方一定百分比的价格减让，即在价格上给予适当的优惠。使用折扣的方式减让价格，而不直接降低报价，使卖方既保持了商品的价位，又明确表示了其能给予买方价格优惠，是一种促销手段，如数量折扣、季节折扣、特别折扣、现金折扣等。

Discount refers to a certain percentage of price concession given by the sellers to the buyers based on the original price, that is, appropriate discount on price. Discount is used to reduce the price without directly reducing the quotation, so that the sellers can not only maintain the price of goods but also make it clear that they can give preferential prices to the buyers. It is a promotion means, such as quantity discount, seasonal discount, special discount and cash discount.

（二）佣金和折扣的表示方法 (Representation of Commission and Discount)

在合同的价格条款中，佣金和折扣有不同的表示方法。

Commission and discount have different expressions in the price clause of the contract.

（1）用文字来说明，例如：

(1) In words, e.g.

① USD 200 per M/T CIF New York including 2% commission.

② GBP 200 per M/T CIF London including 3% discount，或 GBP 200 per M/T CIF London less 3% discount。

（2）用C表示佣金。在贸易术语后面加上大写的字母C和佣金率来表示含佣价，折扣一般不使用此法。例如：

(2) C for commission. Add the capital letter C and commission rate after trade terms to indicate CIFC, which is generally not used for discount. Example:

HKD 50 per dozen CFRC2% Hong Kong.

USD 200 per case CIFC5 San Francisco.

（3）用绝对数表示，例如

(3) In absolute numbers, e.g.

Pay ABC Company USD 50 as commission per M/T.

Discount USD 10 per M/T.

三、计价货币的选择
III. Selection of Quote Currency

计价货币指合同中规定用来计算价格的货币，而支付货币是实际支付给卖方的货币。通常计价货币与支付货币为同一货币，但也可以不是同一种货币。计价货币首先要选择可自由兑换的货币（自由外汇，free convertible currency），以便调拨与运用，以及在必要时转移货币的汇率风险。在国际金融市场普遍实行浮动汇率制的情况下，不同货币的汇率在市场上不断变动，有"硬币"（hard currency）和"软币"（soft currency）之分。在选择计价和支付货币时的总体原则是：出口尽量选用硬币，进口尽量选用软币。当然，最后买卖双方采用何种货币成交，是双方在平等互利的基础上协商一致的结果。如果无法按照符合自己利益的货币成交，买卖合同的当事人应当做到以下几点：

Quote currency means the currency in which the price is to be calculated as specified in the contract, and payment currency shall be the currency actually paid to the sellers. Usually, quote currency is the same as that of payment, but it may not be. Free convertible currency is the first choice of quote currency to facilitate allocation and application, as well as transfer of exchange rate risk when necessary. In the context of the widespread implementation of a floating exchange rate system in the international financial market, the exchange rates of different currencies are constantly changing in the market, including "hard currency" and "soft currency". The general principle for the selection of quote and payment currency is: Hard currency shall be selected as far as possible for exports, while soft currency shall be selected as far as possible for imports. Negotiation on the basis of equality and mutual benefit between buyers and sellers is, of course, an unanimous result. If the transaction cannot be concluded in a currency that meets its own interests, the parties to the sales contract shall:

（1）尽量缩短交货和结汇时间，以减少汇率变化带来的损失；

(1) Minimize the delivery and settlement time to reduce losses caused by exchange rate changes;

（2）若成交金额较大，可在合同中订立"汇率保值条款"；

(2) If the transaction amount is large, an "exchange rate proviso clause" can be concluded in the contract;

（3）对于成交金额大、履约期长的合同，还可采用单一货币计价、一篮子货币支付的方法，以防计价货币汇率变动给合同双方带来损失。

(3) For a contract with large transaction amount and long performance period, a single currency can be used for pricing and a basket of currencies can be used for payment to prevent losses caused by changes in the exchange rate of the quote currency to either party of the contract.

四、作价方法
IV. Pricing Method

（一）固定作价 (Fixed Pricing)

固定作价是最常见的作价方法，即在交易磋商时就把价格确定下来，事后无论发生什么情况都按确定的价格结算应付货款。固定作价具有明确、肯定、便于结算的优点，我国对外贸易多采用这种方法。但采用固定作价，意味着买卖双方要承担从订约到结算期间商品的市场价格变动的风险。所以，固定作价主要适用于价格波动不大的商品，不适用于价格敏感性商品或远期交货的买卖。

Fixed pricing is the most common method of pricing, that is to say, the price is fixed at the time of business negotiation and the payables are settled according to the fixed price no matter what happens afterwards. Fixed pricing has the advantages of definiteness, certainty and convenience for settlement, and is commonly used in China's foreign trade. However, fixed pricing means that the both parties bear the risk of changes in the market price of the commodity from contracting to settlement. Therefore, it is mainly applicable to commodities with little price fluctuations and not applicable to the sale of price-sensitive commodities or future delivery.

例如，合同中的价格条款明确规定"USD 280.00 per carton FOB Haikou Incoterms® 2020"，此价格即为固定价格，若合同中无其他规定，双方必须按此价格结算货款，即使订约后商品的市场价格发生重大变化，任何一方也不得要求变更原定价格。

For example, the price clause in the contract is specified as "USD 280.00 per carton FOB Haikou Incoterms® 2020", which is a fixed price. Unless otherwise specified in the contract, either party must settle the payment according to this price. Even if the market price of the contracted goods changes significantly, neither party shall request to change the original price.

（二）非固定作价 (Non-fixed Pricing)

1. 暂不固定价格（后定价格）[Flexible price for the time being (price to be determined later)]

某些商品价格变动频繁且波动幅度较大或交货期较长，买卖双方对市场趋势难以预测但又有订约意图，则可以采用这种定价方法，只约定将来确定价格的时间或方法，其具体做法又有以下两种。

If the price of some commodities fluctuates frequently and greatly or the time of delivery is long, and it is difficult for both parties to predict the market trend but they have contract intention, this pricing method can be adopted, and only the time or method of determining the price in the future can be agreed. The specific practices are as follows.

（1）在价格条款中明确规定定价时间和定价方法，如"以××年××月××日纽约商品交易所该商品的收盘价为基础加 3 美元作价"，按此作价方法，双方可以规避商品市场价格变动的风险；

(1) Specify the pricing time and method in the price clause, e.g. "the closing price of the commodity on the New York Mercantile Exchange on MM/DD/YY plus USD 3". By using this pricing method, both parties can avoid the risk of price fluctuations in the commodity market;

（2）只规定作价时间而不规定作价方法，如"由双方在××年××月××日协商确定价格"。但这种方式作价方式未做出规定，执行时易产生争执，一般只适用于双方有长期交往并已形成比较固定的交易习惯的合同。

(2) Only specify the pricing time without specifying the pricing method, e.g. "the price shall be determined through negotiation between both parties on MM/DD/YY". However, there are no regulations on the pricing method in this way, which is prone to disputes during implementation. Generally, it is only applicable to the contract where both parties have long-term connection and have formed more fixed trading practice.

2. 暂定价格 (Tentative Price)

对于某些价格变动较大、交货期较长的商品，买卖双方可以在合同中先订立一个初步价格，作为开立信用证和初步付款的依据，待双方确定最后价格后再进行最后清算，多退少补。如"单价暂定每公吨 1000 英镑CIF神户（备注：上述价格为暂定价格，买方按本合同规定的暂定价开立信用证，于装船月份前 15 天再由买卖双方协商确定价格）"。

For some commodities with large price changes and long time of delivery, the buyers and sellers may first establish a preliminary price in the contract as the basis for L/C issuance and preliminary payment. After the final price is determined, the final settlement will be carried out to refund any overpayment or make up any deficiency. For example, "The Unit Price is tentatively set at GBP 1000 per M/T CIF Kobe (Note: The above prices are tentative, the buyers shall issue an L/C according to the tentative price specified in the contract, and the price will be determined through negotiation between both parties 15 days before the shipment month)".

3. 部分固定价格和部分非固定价格 (Partly Fixed and Partly Non-fixed)

对于大量分批装运的商品买卖，在订约时将近期交货的部分采用固定作价，远期交货的部分暂不作价，而在交货前一定期限内由双方议定价格，以兼顾买卖双方的利益。

For the sale of a large number of partial shipments, a fixed price is adopted for the near delivery and not for the future delivery at the time of contracting. The price shall be negotiated by both parties within a certain period before delivery to take into account the interests of the buyers and sellers.

（三）滑动作价 (Sliding Pricing)

滑动作价指签订合同时先规定一个基础价，交货时再按工资、原材料价格变动指数对基础价做出调整，确定最后价格。某些生产周期长的机器设备和原材料商品，买卖双方为了避免承担价格变动的风险，往往采用滑动价格的规定方法。在合同中订有价格调整系数，具体规定有关价格调整的办法。例如，"以上基础价格将按下列调整公式根据×××（机构）公布的××年××月的工资指数和物价指数予以调整。"

  Sliding pricing refers to specifying a basic price when signing the contract, and then adjusting the basic price according to the wage and raw material price change indicator at the time of delivery to determine the final price. In order to avoid the risk of price change, the buyers and sellers often adopt the sliding price method for some machinery equipment and raw material commodities with long production cycle. A price adjustment factor is specified in the contract, specifying the method of price adjustment. For example, "The above basic price will be adjusted according to the following adjustment formula based on the wage indicator and price indicator published by ××× (institution) in MM/YY."

第七章拓展知识、专业词汇和练习

第八章 国际货物运输
Chapter 8　International Carriage of Goods

导　读
Introduction

　　在国际贸易中，买卖双方分隔两地，甚至远隔重洋，双方成交的货物一般都需要经过长途运输才能从卖方所在地抵达买方所在地。在国际货物运输中，涉及的运输方式种类很多，其中包括海洋运输、铁路运输、公路运输、航空运输、邮政运输、江河运输、管道运输以及由各种运输方式组合而成的国际多式联运。在一笔进出口业务中采用何种运输方式，应由买卖双方在磋商交易时做出具体约定。

　　In international trade, the buyers and sellers are separated from each other, even across the ocean. Goods traded by them generally require long-distance transportation to arrive at the buyers' place from the sellers' place. In the international carriage of goods, there are many transportation modes involved, including ocean transportation, railway transportation, road transportation, air transportation, postal transportation, river transportation, pipeline transportation and international multimodal transport combined by various transportation modes. Transportation mode in an import and export business shall be specifically agreed upon by both parties when negotiating a transaction.

第一节　国际货物运输方式
Section 1　International Transportation Mode of Goods

一、国际海洋运输
I. International Ocean Transportation

　　海洋运输（ocean transportation）不受道路和轨道的限制，通过能力很大，万吨至数十万吨的巨轮都可以在海洋中航行。由于海洋运输的运量很大，且运输成本较低，许多国家（地区）特别是沿海国家（地区）货物的进出口，大部分都采用海洋运输的方式。在国际贸易总量中，通过海洋运输的货物占80%以上。因此，海洋运输是国际贸易中最主要的运输方式。

　　Ocean transportation is not limited by roads and tracks, and has a large carrying capacity. Large ships of over ten thousand tons to hundreds of thousands of tons can sail in the ocean. Due to the large traffic volume and low cost of ocean transportation, most countries (regions), especially coastal countries (regions), import and export goods by ocean transportation. Transportation of goods through the ocean accounts for more than 80% of total international trade. It is the most important transportation mode in international trade.

　　海洋运输虽有上述优点，但也存在一些不足之处，例如：船舶航行速度较慢；有些港口冬季可能会结冰，有些港口枯水期水位会较低，难以保证全年通航；海洋运输距离较长，易受气候影响，面临的货损风险较大等。

　　Despite the above advantages, ocean transportation also has some deficiencies, such as: slow sailing speed of ships; some ports may freeze in winter, and the water level of some ports will be low in dry season, making it difficult to ensure navigation throughout the year; Ocean transportation has a long distance, which is vulnerable to climate influence and faces a high risk of cargo damage.

按照船舶经营方式的不同，海洋运输可分为班轮运输（regular shipping liner/liner）和租船运输（charter）。

According to the shipping operation mode, ocean transportation can be divided into liner and charter.

（一）班轮运输 (Liner)

班轮运输又称定期船运输，是指船舶按照规定的时间，在固定的航线上和固定的停靠港口之间，从事客货运输业务，并按事先公布的运费率或协议运费率收取运费的一种船舶经营方式。

Liner, also known as regular shipping liner, refers to a shipping operation mode in which ships engage in passenger and freight carriage business on fixed routes and between fixed ports of call at specified time and charge freight according to the pre-announced or negotiated rate of freight.

1. 班轮运输的特点 (Characteristics of Liner)

班轮运输具有以下四个特点。

Liner has the following four characteristics.

（1）"四固定"。班轮公司有固定的船期表，有固定的航线，每条航线有固定的停靠港口，并按照相对固定的运费率收取运费。

(1) "Four fixations". Liner companies have fixed shipping schedules and routes, each of which has a fixed port of call. Freight is charged at a relatively fixed rate of freight.

（2）"一负责"。在班轮运输中，由船方负责货物的配载、装卸，相关的装卸费包括在运费中，货方无须在运费之外支付装卸费。船货双方不约定装卸时间，因而也不计算滞期费和速遣费。

(2) "One responsibility". In liner, the shipowner is responsible for stowage and loading/unloading of goods. The relevant handling charges are included in freight charges, and the cargo owner does not need to pay handling charges in addition to freight charges. Laytime is not agreed by the shipowner and cargo owner and therefore demurrage charges and dispatch money are not calculated.

（3）船货双方的权利、义务与责任豁免的规定，以船方签发的提单条款为依据。

(3) The provisions on the rights, obligations and liability exemption of the shipowner and cargo owner shall be based on the B/L clause issued by the shipowner.

（4）班轮承运的货物品种、数量比较灵活，货运质量有保证，且一般采取在码头堆场或仓库交接货物的方式，货物交接比较便利。

(4) Quantity and varieties of goods carried by liners are relatively flexible, with guaranteed freight quality. Generally, the goods are delivered and received at the yard or warehouse, which is convenient.

2. 班轮运输运费 (Freight of Liner)

班轮运输有杂货班轮运输和集装箱班轮运输两种。杂货班轮运输的特点是运输的货物不装在集装箱内，以件杂货为主，也可以是一些散货、重大件货物等，这种运输方式特别适合小批量零星件杂货的海上运输。集装箱班轮运输是以集装箱为运输单元的班轮运输。集装箱班轮运输具有货运质量高、运送速度快、装卸方便、机械化程度高、作业效率高、便于开展联运、能降低货运成本等优点，它正逐步取代传统的杂货班轮运输。

Liner includes general cargo liner and container liner. General cargo liner is characterized in that the goods are not packed in a container, mainly general cargoes, or bulk and heavy cargoes. This transportation mode is especially suitable for sea carriage of small batches of general cargo. Container liner is a liner with container as the unit of carriage. Container liner has the advantages of high shipping quality, fast transportation, convenient loading and unloading, high degree of mechanization, high operation efficiency, easy combined transport and reduced cost. It is gradually replacing the traditional liner for general cargo.

（1）杂货班轮运费的计算。

(1) Calculation of freight charges for general cargo liner.

杂货班轮运费包括基本运费和附加费两部分。前者是指将货物从装运港运到目的港所应收取的基本运费，它是构成全程运费的主要部分；后者是指对一些需要特殊处理的货物或者由于突发事件或客观情况变化等原因而需另外收取的费用（部分附加费种类见表8.3）。杂货班轮运费的计算公式如下：

Freight charges of general cargo liner include basic freight and additional. The former refers to the basic freight that shall be charged for transporting goods from port of shipment to port of destination, which constitutes the main part of the whole-process freight charges; the latter refers to the additional charges required for some goods requiring special handling or due to emergencies or changes in objective circumstances (see Table 8.3 for some types of additional). Freight charges for general cargo liner are calculated as follows:

基本运费＝基本运费率×货运量

Basic Freight = Basic Rate of Freight × Freight Volume

附加费＝基本运费×∑附加费率

Additional = Basic Freight × ∑ Additional Rate

班轮运费＝基本运费+附加费＝基本运费率×货运量×(1+∑附加费率)

Liner Freight Charges = Basic Freight + Additional= Basic Rate of Freight × Freight Volume × (1+∑ Additional Rate)

基本运费率和附加费率按班轮公司公布的班轮运价表（freight tariff）的规定收取，船公司一般会定期公布自己的运价表。运价表一般包括货物分级表（部分货物等级分类见表8-1）、各航线运费率表（航线基本运费率示例见表8-2）、附加费率表（部分附加费种类见表8-3）以及计算运费的规则和规定。货物分级表将货物分为20个等级，不同等级有不同的运费率，其中1级运费率最低，20级运费率最高。

The basic rate of freight and surcharge rates are charged according to the freight tariff published by the liner company, which generally publishes its own freight tariff on a regular basis. The freight tariff generally includes the classification of commodities (see Table 8-1 for classification of some commodities), the freight tariff for each route (see Table 8-2 for examples of basic rates of freight on routes), the additional rate table (see Table 8-3 for some types of surcharges) and the rules and regulations for calculating freight charges. The classification of commodities divides the goods into 20 grades. Different grades have different rate of freight, among which grade 1 has the lowest rate of freight and grade 20 has the highest rate of freight.

表8-1 部分货物等级分类

Table 8-1　Classification of Some Commodities

货名	COMMODITIES	级别 CLASS	计费标准 BASIS
人造革及制品	ARTIFICIAL LEATHER & GOODS	11	M
棉布及棉纱	COTTON GOODS & PIECE GOODS	10	M
玩具(木制、铁制、长毛绒制)	TOY (WOODEN, METAL, PLUSH)	8	M
各种豆类	BEANS, ALL KINDS	5	W/M

续表

货名	COMMODITIES	级别 CLASS	计费标准 BASIS
自行车及零件	BICYCLES&PARTS	9	W/M
纸（捆、卷）	PAPER (IN BALES & REELS)	12	W
瓷砖、瓷器	TILES, PROCELAIN	7	W
各种毛巾	COTTON TOWELS, ALL KINDS	9	M
卫生洁具	SANITARY WEAR	8	M

表8-2　中国—美国航线基本运价
Table 8-2　Basic Rate for China-US Route

Scale of class rates for China-America service（in USD）				
CLASS	SEATTLE, PORTLAND SAN FRANCISCO	LOS ANGELES LONG BEACH	MIAMI CHARLESTON	PHILADELPHIA NEW YORK, BOSTON
1	95	100	115	120
2	100	105	120	125
…	…	…	…	…
7	130	135	142	145
8	136	140	146	150
9	143	147	153	156
10	150	155	160	165

表8-3　国际海运的部分附加费
Table 8-3　Some Additionals for International Shipping

附加费名称及缩写 Name and Abbreviation of Additional	解释 Interpretation
燃油附加费（BAF/BAC/FAF） Bunker Adjustment Factor (Charge)/ Fuel Adjustment Fee	由于燃油价格上涨，船舶的燃油费用支出超过原核定的运输成本中的燃油费用，承运人在不调整运价的前提下增加的附加费 Additional added by the carrier on the premise of no adjustment to rate due to the increase in fuel price, which causes the ship's fuel expenditure to exceed the fuel cost included in the original approved carriage cost
超重附加费（OWS/HLA） Over Weight Surcharge /Heavy Lift Additional	由于单件货物重量超过一定限度而加收的一种附加费 An additional due to the weight of a single piece of goods exceeding a certain limit
超长附加费（LLA） Long Length Additional	由于单件货物长度超过一定限度而加收的一种附加费 An additional due to the length of a single piece of goods exceeding a certain limit
港口拥挤附加费（PCS） Port Congestion Surcharge	由于港口拥挤，船舶抵港后需要长时间等泊而产生额外费用，为补偿船期延误损失而增加的临时附加费。一般在以色列、印度某些港口及中南美航线中使用 It refers to the interim additional added to compensate for the loss of delay in shipping due to additional costs incurred by long-time waiting after arrival of ships due to port congestion. It is generally used in some ports of Israel, India and Central and South American routes.

续表

附加费名称及缩写 Name and Abbreviation of Additional	解释 Interpretation
直航附加费 Direct Additional	一批货物达到规定的数量，托运人要求将其直接运抵非基本港卸货，船公司为此而加收的费用 Additional charges by the shipping company for a batch of goods reaching the specified quantity and requested to be directly delivered to non-base port for unloading
转船附加费 Transshipment Additional	如果货物需要转船运输，公司必须在转船港口办理换装和转船的手续而增加的费用 If the goods need to be transshipped for carriage, the company must go through the formalities of transshipment and reloading at the port of transshipment
货币贬值附加费（CAF） Currency Adjustment Factor	由于国际外汇市场汇率发生较大的变化，计收运费的货币贬值，承运人的实际收入减少，为弥补这种损失而加收的附加费 Additional charged to cover losses resulting from significant changes in exchange rates on the international foreign exchange market, depreciation of the currency in which freight charges are collected and reduction in the carrier's actual revenue
码头操作费（THC） Terminal Handling Charge	船公司在运费之外，向货代企业额外收取的一项费用，是随着国际海上集装箱班轮运输的发展而产生的 Freight charges are additionally charged by shipping companies to freight forwarding enterprises, which is generated with the development of international sea container regular shipping liner.
美国仓单费（AMS） American Manifest System	自动舱单系统录入费，用于美加线，根据美国"反恐"的需要，规定船公司必须于装货前24小时将货物资料通过AMS系统报美国海关 Automated Manifest System (AMS) is used for the America-Canada line. According to the "anti-terrorism" needs of the United States, shipping companies must report cargo data to the US Customs through the AMS system 24 hours before loading
直接收货附加费（ORC） Origin Receiving Charge	也称本地出口附加费，一般在我国华南地区使用 Also known as local export additional, commonly used in southern China

班轮运费的计费标准，是指货运量的确定方法。根据货物的不同，通常采用下列几种标准确定货运量的计算方式。

The charging standard of liner freight refers to the determination method of freight volume. According to different goods, the following standards are used to determine the calculation method of freight volume.

①按货物的实际毛重计收，一般称"重量吨"（weight ton）。1重量吨按1公吨或1长吨计算，在运价表内用字母"W"表示。

①It is calculated and collected according to the actual gross weight of goods, generally called "weight ton". 1 weight ton shall be calculated as per 1 m/t or 1 l/t and indicated by letter "W" in the freight tariff.

②按货物的体积或容积计收，一般称"尺码吨"（measurement ton）。1尺码吨按1立方米

或40立方英尺（1.13立方米）计算，在运价表内用字母"M"表示。

②It is calculated and collected according to the volume or capacity of goods, generally called "measurement ton". 1 measurement ton shall be calculated on the basis of 1 cubic meter or 40 cubic foot (1.13 cubic meters) and indicated by the letter "M" in the freight tariff.

③按重量或体积计收，统称"运费吨"（freight ton），即指班轮公司按货物的重量或体积较高者确定货运量，在运价表内以"W/M"表示。

③It is calculated and collected by weight or volume, collectively referred to as "freight ton", i.e. the freight volume determined by the liner company according to the higher of the weight or volume of the goods, which is expressed as "W/M" in the freight tariff.

④按货物的FOB总值计收，即从价运费。班轮公司在承运黄金、白银、精密仪器、手工艺品等贵重货物或高价货物时，由于在积载、保管方面需要采取特别措施，并承担较大的责任，所以对这类货物收取从价运费，其费率占FOB货价的百分之零点几到5%不等，在运价表上用"A.V."表示。

④It is calculated and collected according to the FOB total amount of goods, i.e. ad valorem freight. Liner companies charge ad valorem freight on precious or high value goods such as gold, silver, precision instruments and handicrafts due to the need for special measures in stowage and custody and greater responsibility. The rate varies from a few tenths of a percent to five percent of the FOB price, which is indicated by "A.V." on the freight tariff.

⑤按货物重量、体积和价值中最高者计收（W/M or A.V.），船公司从托运货物的重量、体积和价值中选择计收运费最高者作为计收标准。

⑤It is calculated and collected according to the weight, volume or value of goods, whichever is highest (W/M or A.V.). The shipping company selects the highest of the weight, volume and value of consigned goods as the charging standard.

⑥按货物重量或尺码选择较高者，再加上从价运费计收，运价表中用"W/M plus A.V."表示。

⑥It is calculated and collected according to the weight or measurement of goods, whichever is higher, plus ad valorem freight. The freight tariff shall be expressed as "W/M plus A.V.".

⑦按个数计收（per unit）。适用于车辆、活牲畜等特殊商品。

⑦It is calculated and collected by unit (per unit). Applicable to special commodities such as vehicles and live animals.

⑧按议价计费（open rate）。适用于托运人的货物特别多的情况，由货主和船公司临时协调议定，在运价表中用"Open"表示。

⑧Open rate. It is applicable to the situation where there are too many cargoes for the shipper, which shall be temporarily negotiated and agreed by the cargo owner and the shipping company and expressed as "Open" in the freight tariff.

⑨起码运费（minimum rate）。如果单笔托运货物的重量、体积太小，价值太低，没有达到运价表中规定的最低计费标准，承运人就按照最低的运费水平计收。

⑨Minimum rate. If the weight, volume and value of a single consignment are too low to meet the minimum charging standards specified in the freight tariff, the carrier will charge at the lowest freight.

（2）集装箱班轮运费的计算。

(2) Calculation of freight charges for container liner.

集装箱班轮运费与杂货班轮运费一样，也由基本运费和附加费组成。基本运费的计算方法有两种：第一种是采用与普通杂货班轮运输基本运费相同的计算方法，对具体的航线按货物的等级和不同的计费标准来计算基本运费，一般适用于拼箱货；第二种是采用包箱费率，即以一个集装箱为计费单位计算基本运费，常用于集装箱整箱交货的情况。表 8-4 为深圳—美国航线的普通干货集装箱海运包箱费率。常见的包箱费率有以下三种形式。

Freight charges for container liners, like freight charges for general cargo liners, also consist of basic freight and additional. There are two calculation methods for basic freight: The first is to calculate the basic freight according to the grade of goods and different charging standards for specific routes, which is generally applicable to LCL; the second is to use box rate, which calculates the basic freight with one container as the charging unit, and is commonly used in the case of FCL. Table 8-4 shows the box rate of general dry container shipping on the route from Shenzhen to the United States. Common box rates come in the following three forms.

①FAK 包箱费率（freight for all kinds），即对每一个集装箱不分货类，按统一标准收取费用的费率。

①FAK (freight for all kinds), i.e. the rate at which each container is charged according to a uniform standard regardless of cargo type.

②FCS 包箱费率（freight for class），即按不同货物等级制定的包箱费率。货物等级也是 1～20 级，但级差较小。一般低价货费率高于传统运输费率，高价货费率则低于传统运输费率；同一等级货物，重量货运价高于体积货运价。

②FCS (freight for class), i.e. box rates based on classification of commodities. Commodities are classified into 1~20 grades, but the difference is small. Generally, the low-price cargo rate is higher than the traditional carriage rate, and the high-price cargo rate is lower than the traditional carriage rate. For goods of the same grade, the weight cargo rate is higher than the volume cargo rate.

③FCB 包箱费率（freight for class or basic），是既按不同货物等级或货类制定包箱费率，又按计费标准制定包箱费率。

③FCB (freight for class or basic) is not only based on different grades or categories, but also based on charging standards.

表8-4　深圳—美国航线普通干货集装箱海运包箱费率
Table 8-4　Box rates of general dry container shipping on routes from Shenzhen to the United States

单位：美元（Unit: USD）

FINIAL DESTINATION	FCL 20GP	FCL 40GP	FCL 40HQ
SEATTLE, PORTLAND, SAN FRANCISCO	5100	6600	6650
LOS ANGELES LONG BEACH	4000	6000	6000
MIAMI, CHARLESTON	8250	10700	10900
PHILADELPHIA, NEW YORK, BOSTON	6800	9900	9900

说明：需另收取美国仓单费（AMS）USD 35/set；
Note: An additional AMS of USD 35/set is required;
直接收货附加费（ORC）USD 141/20GP，USD 269/40GP，USD 269/40HQ
Origin Receiving Charge (ORC) USD 141/20GP, USD 269/40GP, USD 269/40HQ
集装箱整箱货按包箱价计算运费，计算公式为：
FCL freight shall be calculated on a container basis. The calculation formula is as follows:
海运运费＝包箱价×集装箱个数
Ocean Freight ＝ Box Rate×Number of Containers

(二)租船运输 (Charter)

租船运输又称不定期船运输，是指租船人向船方租赁船舶用于运输货物的一种运输方式。

Charter, also known as tramp shipping, refers to a transportation mode in which the charterer leases a ship from the shipowner for the carriage of goods.

1. 租船运输的特点 (Characteristics of Charter)

租船运输与班轮运输相比，没有"四固定"的特点，具体的区别体现在以下几个方面。

Compared with liner, charter does not have the characteristics of "four fixations". The specific differences are reflected in the following aspects.

（1）属于不定期船，无固定的航线、挂靠港和船期，一切由租船双方在装运前协商确定。

(1) It is a non-scheduled ship without fixed route, port of call and shipping schedule. All matters shall be negotiated by both parties before shipment.

（2）运价不固定，受市场供求的约束，随租船市场行情的变化而变化。

(2) The rate is not fixed, subject to market supply and demand, and varies with the change of chartering market.

（3）租船运输中的港口使用费、装卸费及船期延误等责任费用的划分由双方协定。

(3) The division of liability expenses such as port use charges, handling fees and shipping delay in the charter shall be agreed by both parties.

（4）租船运输主要适用于粮谷、煤炭、石油、木材等大宗货物的运输。

(4) Charter is mainly applicable to the carriage of bulk goods such as grain, coal, petroleum and timber.

（5）租船人和出租人双方之间的权利、义务和责任以签订的租船合同为准。

(5) The rights, obligations and responsibilities between the charterer and the owner shall be subject to the signed charter contract.

2. 租船运输的方式 (Charter Methods)

租船运输的方式包括定程租船、定期租船、光船租船等。

Charter methods includes voyage charter, time charter and bareboat charter.

（1）定程租船（voyage charter）是指按航程（包括单程、来回程和连续单航次）租赁船舶，故又称程租船或航次租船。在定程租船方式下，船方必须按租船合同规定的航程完成货物运输任务，并负责经营管理船舶和承担船舶在航行中的一切开支。

(1) Voyage charter refers to the chartering of ships by voyage (including one-way, round-trip and continuous single voyage), so it is also called trip charter. Under voyage charter, the shipowner must complete the carriage of goods according to the voyage specified in the charter contract, and be responsible for operating and managing the ship and bearing all expenses incurred by the ship during the voyage.

（2）定期租船（time charter）是指按一定期限租赁船舶。在租赁期间，租船人在租船合同规定的航行区域内可自行使用和调度船舶。一般来说，定期租船方式下，各航次中所产生的燃料费、港口费、装卸费、垫舱物料费等各项费用均由租船人负担，而船方仅对船舶的维护、修理、机器的正常运转和船员工资与给养负责。定期租船方式下的租金一般按租期每月每吨若干金额计算，租船双方不规定装卸率和滞期费、速遣费。

(2) Time charter refers to the chartering of ships for a certain period. During the charter period, the charterer may use and dispatch the vessel within the navigation area specified in the charter contract. Generally speaking, under time charter, all expenses incurred in each voyage such as fuel charges, port fees, handling fees and dunnage materials shall be borne by the charterer, while the owner is only responsible for the maintenance,

repair, normal operation of machines and crew wages and supplies. The hire under time charter is generally calculated at a certain amount per ton per month during the charter period, and there are no stipulations on loading rate, demurrage charges and dispatch money for each party.

（3）光船租船（bareboat charter）是指船舶所有人将船舶出租给承租人使用一段时期，船舶所有人所提供的船舶是一艘空船，既无船长，又未配备船员，承租人自己要任命船长、配备船员，并负责船员的给养和船舶营运管理所需的一切费用。船舶所有人除了在租期内收取租金外，对船舶本身和船舶运营均不负责。这种光船租船方式，实际上属于单纯的财产租赁，与上述定期租船有所不同。

(3) Bareboat charter means that the shipowner leases the ship to the charterer for a period of time, and the ship provided by the shipowner is an empty ship without master or crew. The charterer shall appoint the master and crew, and be responsible for the supply of the crew and all expenses required for the operation and management of the ship. The shipowner shall not be responsible for the ship or its operation except to collect hire payments during the charter period. Bareboat charter is actually a simple lease of property, which differs from the above time charter.

（三）定程租船运费 (Voyage Charter Freight)

定程租船是租船市场上使用得较多的一种方式，且对运费的波动最为敏感。其运费构成包括基本运费、装卸费（船方不负装卸，或不负责装货，或不负责卸货时产生）及滞期费或速遣费。

Voyage charter is one of the more widely used methods in the charter market and is most sensitive to fluctuations in freight charges. The freight composition includes basic freight, handling charges (incurred when the shipowner is not responsible for handling or loading or unloading) and demurrage charges or dispatch money.

1. 基本运费 (Basic Freight)

定程租船的基本运费是指从装运港到目的港的海上运费。其计算方式有两种：一种是按运费率（rate of freight）计算，即规定每单位重量或每单位体积的运费额，同时规定按装船时的货物重量（in taken quantity）或按卸船时的货物重量（delivered Quantity）来计算总运费；另一种是整船包价（lump sum freight），即不管租方实际装货多少，一律按包价支付。

Voyage charter basic Freight means the ocean freight from port of shipment to port of destination. There are two calculation methods: one is to calculate by rate of freight, i.e. specifying the freight charges per unit weight or volume and calculating the total freight by in taken quantity or delivered quantity; the other is lump sum freight, which means payment will be made at the lump sum price regardless of the Charterer's actual shipment.

2. 装卸费 (Handling Charges)

有关货物的装卸费用由租船人和船方协商确定，并在定程租船合同中做出具体的规定。主要有下列四种不同的规定。

The handling charges of the relevant goods shall be determined by the charterer and the shipowner through negotiation, and specifically provided in the voyage charter contract. There are mainly four different provisions as follows.

（1）船方不负担装卸费（F.I.O.）或船方不负责装卸、理舱和平舱（F.I.O.S.T.），采用此法的情况较为普遍。

(1) Free in and out (F.I.O.) or free in, out, stowed and trimmed (F.I.O.S.T.), which is a common practice.

（2）船方负担装卸费（Gross Terms /Liner Terms）。

(2) Gross terms.

（3）船方只负担装货费，不负担卸货费（F.O.）。

(3) Free out (F.O.).

（4）船方只负担卸货费，不负担装货费（F.I.）。

(4) Free in (F.I.).

3. 滞期费和速遣费 (Demurrage Charges and Dispatch Money)

在定程租船运输中，装卸货时间的长短会影响船舶的使用周期和在港费用，这直接关系船方的经营效益。因而，为了节省船期，定程租船合同中一般都有规定租船人在一定时间内完成装卸作业的条款，即装卸时间条款，或称装卸期限条款。如果在约定的允许装卸时间内未能将货物装卸完，致使船舶在港内停泊时间延长，给船方造成经济损失，则延迟期间的损失，应按每天若干金额补偿给船方，这项补偿金称为滞期费（demurrage charges）；反之，如果提前完成装卸任务，使船方节省了船舶在港的费用支出，船方将其获取的利益的一部分给租船人作为奖励，这部分费用称为速遣费（dispatch money）。

Under voyage charter, the length of laytime will affect the life cycle and port charges of ships, which is directly related to the operating benefits of shipowners. Therefore, in order to save the shipping time, there are generally provisions in the voyage charter contract stating that the charterer shall complete the loading and unloading operations within a certain period of time, i.e. laytime clause. If the goods are not loaded and unloaded within the agreed allowable laytime, resulting in prolonged berthing time of the ship in the port and economic losses to the shipowner, the loss during the delay period shall be compensated to the shipowner at a rate per day, which is called demurrage charges; on the contrary, if the loading and unloading tasks are completed in advance so that the shipowner can save the expenses of the ship at the port, the shipowner will reward the charterer with a portion of the benefits it obtains, which is called dispatch money.

二、国际铁路货物运输
II. International Railway Cargo Transportation

在国际货物运输中，铁路运输（railway transportation）是一种仅次于海洋运输的主要运输方式。铁路运输具有许多优点，例如，火车运行速度较快，载运量较大，一般不易受气候条件的影响，能终年正常运行，而且在运输途中遭受的风险较小，所以铁路运输具有高度的连续性。办理铁路货运手续要比办理海洋运输手续简单，并且发货人和收货人可以在就近的始发站（装运站）和目的站办理托运和提货手续。

In the international carriage of goods, railway transportation is a major transportation mode second only to ocean transportation. Railway transportation has many advantages. For example, trains run faster and have a larger carrying capacity. Generally, they are not susceptible to climatic conditions, can operate normally all year round, and suffer less risks on the way. Therefore, railway transportation is highly continuous. It is easier to handle railway transportation than ocean transportation, and the consignor and consignee can handle consignment and pick-up procedures at the nearest departure station (shipping station) and destination station.

进出口货物采用铁路运输，称国际铁路货物联运（international railway transportation），是指两个或两个以上国家（地区）按照协定，利用各自的铁路，联合起来完成一票货物的全程运输的方式。它使用统一的国际联运单据，在一国（地区）铁路向另一国（地区）铁路移交货物时，无须发货人、收货人参加，由铁路部门对全程运输负连带责任。

Import and export goods are transported by railway, also known as international railway transportation, which refers to the method in which two or more countries (regions), in accordance with an agreement, use their respective railways to jointly complete the entire transportation of a single shipment of goods. It uses unified international through waybill. When transferring goods from one country's (region's) railway to another country's (region's) railway, there is no need for the consignor and consignee to participate, and the railway department is jointly and severally responsible for the entire transportation.

国际铁路货物联运的有关当事国事先必须有书面约定，才能协作进行货物的联运工作。相关的国际条约主要有《国际铁路货物运送公约》(简称《国际货约》)和《国际铁路货物联运协定》(简称《国际货协》)两个。1954年1月，中国加入了《国际货协》，开办了国际铁路联运。目前，中国和邻近的中亚国家、南亚国家以及和欧洲国家运送进出口货物，采用铁路联运的货运量日渐增长。

The relevant parties to international railway transportation must have a prior written agreement before they can cooperate in the through transport of goods. The relevant international treaties mainly include the Convention Concerning International Carriage of Goods by Rail ("CIM") and the Agreement on International Railroad Through Transport of Goods ("CMIC"). In January 1954, China joined CMIC and launched international railway through transport. At present, China and neighboring Central Asian countries, South Asian countries and Central and European countries are transporting import and export goods. The freight volume through railway through transport is increasing day by day.

中欧班列（China Railway Express）是由中国铁路总公司组织，按照固定车次、线路、班期和全程运行时刻开行，运行于中国与欧洲以及共建"一带一路"国家间的集装箱等铁路国际联运列车。中欧班列作为往来于中国与欧洲及共建"一带一路"国家的集装箱国际铁路联运班列，铺划了西、中、东3条通道中欧班列运行线：西部通道由我国中西部经阿拉山口（霍尔果斯）出境，中部通道由我国华北地区经二连浩特出境，东部通道由中国东北地区经满洲里（绥芬河）出境。从2011年3月19日，首列中欧班列（重庆—杜伊斯堡）成功开行以来，中欧班列联通的国家和城市，以及每年开出的班列数量都在快速增加。2011年开行仅17列，2016—2023年，中欧班列年开行数量由1702列增加到超1.7万列，增长近10倍，年均增长39.5%。开行万列所需时间由开行之初的90个月缩短至2024年的7个月。截至2024年，中欧班列已铺画了91条运行线路，通达欧洲25个国家224个城市，逐步"连点成线""织线成网"，运输服务网络覆盖欧洲全境，运输货物品类涉及衣服鞋帽、汽车及配件、粮食、木材等53大门类、5万多种品类。中欧班列以比海运的时间短、比空运的价格低的优势，吸引了大量进出口公司采用铁路方式运送货物，受到了国际市场的青睐。

China Railway Express, organized by China State Railway Group Co., Ltd., is the container and other international railway intermodal trains running between China and Europe and countries along Belt and Road partner countries according to fixed train numbers, routes, schedules and whole-journey operation timetables. As a container international railway intermodal train between China and Europe as well as countries along the Belt and Road partner countries, China Railway Express has laid out three corridors in the West and Middle East: The western corridor leaves China through Alataw Pass (Horgos), the central corridor leaves China through north China via Erenhot, and the eastern corridor leaves China through Manzhouli (Suifen River) from northeast China. Since the first China Railway Express (Chongqing-Duisburg) was successfully put into operation on March 19, 2011, the number of countries and cities connected by China Railway Express and the number of trains dispatched every year have been increasing rapidly. Only 17 trains in 2011, from 2016 to 2023, the annual number of China-EV trains increased from 1702 to more than 17000, an increase of nearly 10 times, with an average annual growth rate of 39.5%. The time needed to start 10000 trains has been shortened from 90 months at the beginning to 7 months in 2024. As of 2024, China Railway Express has launched 91 running routes to 224 cities in 25 countries in Europe, gradually "connecting points into lines" and "forming a network with lines". Carriage service networks cover the whole of Europe, and cargo categories include more than 50,000 types in 53 major categories such as clothing, shoes and hats, automobiles and accessories, grain and wood. China Railway Express has attracted a large number of import and export companies to transport goods by railway due to its advantages over ocean transportation in shorter time and lower price than air transportation, which is favored by the international market.

国际铁路货物联运所使用的运单和运单副本，是铁路部门与发货人间缔结的运送契约。在发货人提交全部货物和付清其所负担的一切费用后，始发站有关人员在运单和运单副本上加盖始发站日期戳记，证明货物已经承运，运送契约即告缔结。按照我国同参加《国际货协》的各国所签订的贸易交货共同条件的规定，运单副本是卖方通过有关银行向买方结算货款的主要文件之一。但铁路运单并非物权凭证，不能通过背书转让和作为抵押品向银行融通资金。

Waybill and copies of the waybill used in international railway transportation is the transportation contract concluded between railway department and consignor. After the consignor submits all goods and pays off all expenses borne by him, the relevant personnel of the departure station shall stamp the date of departure on the waybill and copy of waybill to prove that the goods have been carried and the contract of carriage is concluded. Based on the common terms of trade delivery signed between China and countries participating in CIM, copy of waybill is one of the main documents for the sellers to settle with the buyers through relevant banks. However, the railway bill is not documents of title and cannot be transferred by endorsement and used as collateral for bank financing.

三、国际航空货物运输
III. International Airline Cargo Transportation

航空运输（air transportation）是一种现代化的运输方式，它与海洋运输、铁路运输相比，具有运输速度快、货运质量高，且不受地面条件的限制等优点。因此，它最适宜运送急需物资、鲜活商品、精密仪器和贵重物品。近年来，随着国际贸易的迅速发展以及国际货物运输技术的不断现代化，采用空运方式日趋普遍。国际航空货物运输（international airline cargo transportation）是指以航空器作为运输工具，根据当事人订立的航空运输合同，无论运输有无间断或者有无转运，运输的出发地点、目的地点或者约定的经停地点之一在一国境外，而将运送货物至目的地并收取报酬或提供免费服务的运输方式的统称。

Air transportation is a modern transportation mode. Compared with ocean transportation and railway Transportation, it has the advantages of fast carriage, high quality and no restriction by ground conditions. Therefore, it is most suitable for transporting urgently needed materials, fresh commodities, precision instruments and valuables. In recent years, with the rapid development of international trade and the continuous modernization of international cargo transportation technology, air transportation has become increasingly popular. International airline cargo transportation (IACT) is a general term for the carriage of goods to the destination with payment or free service according to the air transportation contract concluded by the parties, regardless of whether the carriage is interrupted or not and whether the departure point, destination point or one of the agreed stopover points of the carriage is outside a country.

我国通过航空运输进口的货物，主要是贵重货物、稀有金属、精密仪器仪表、电脑、手表、钻石、种禽、种畜和技术资料等。我国航空运输出口的货物，主要是鲜活货物（如鱼、蟹）、生丝、绸缎、服装、裘皮和羊绒等。

The goods imported by China through air transportation mainly include valuables, rare metals, precision instruments and meters, computers, watches, diamonds, breeding poultry, breeding livestock and technical data. The goods exported by China through air transportation mainly include fresh and live goods (such as fish and crab), raw silk, satin, clothing, fur and cashmere.

（一）航空运输的主要类型 (Main Types of Air Transportation)

航空运输包括班机运输、包机运输、集中托运和急件快递四种方式。

Air transportation includes four modes: scheduled airline, chartered carrier, consolidation and air express.

（1）班机运输（scheduled airline）是指航班在固定航线上飞行的运输方式，它有固定的始发站、途经站和目的站。一般航空公司都采用客货混合型飞机。

(1) Scheduled airline refers to the transportation mode of a flight on a fixed route, which has a fixed airport of departure, airport of stopover and airport of destination. Generally, airlines use combination carrier.

（2）包机运输（chartered carrier）是指包租整架飞机或由几个发货人（或航空货运代理人）联合包租一架飞机来运送货物的运输方式，分为整包机和部分包机两种。前者适合运送大批量货物，后者适用于有多个发货人且他们的货物到达同一个目的站的情况。

(2) Chartered carrier refers to the transportation mode in which the whole aircraft is chartered or several consignors (or air freight forwarders) jointly charter an aircraft to carry goods. It can be divided into two types: full charter and partial charter. The former is suitable for transporting large quantities of goods, while the latter applies when there are multiple consignors and their goods arrive at the same destination.

（3）集中托运（consolidation）是指由航空货运代理公司将若干单独发货人的货物集中起来，组成一整批货，由其向航空公司申请托运到同一目的站，货到后由目的站的空运代理办理收货、报关并分拨给各个实际收货人的运输方式。此种方式运费较低，在外贸业务中使用较多。

(3) Consolidation refers to the transportation mode in which several individual consignors' goods are collected by an air freight forwarder to form a whole batch, which applies to the airline for consignment to the same airport of destination. After the goods arrive, the air freight forwarder at the airport of destination handles the receipt, customs declaration and distribution to each actual consignee. Freight charges in this way are relatively low, and it is widely used in foreign trade business.

（4）急件快递（air express）是由专门经营这项业务的公司与航空公司合作，设专人用最快的速度将急件在发货人、机场、收货人之间进行传递的运输方式。

(4) Air express is a transportation mode in which the company specializing in this business cooperates with airlines to assign special personnel to transfer urgent cargo between consignor, airport and consignee at the fastest speed.

（二）航空运输的运费与运单 (Freight Charges and Waybills for Air Transportation)

航空运输货物的运价是指从起运机场至目的机场的运价，不包括其他额外费用（如提货、仓储费等）。运价一般是按重量（kg）或体积重量（6000 cm³米折合1 kg）计算的，以两者中高者为准。空运货物按照普通物流价、指定商品运价和等级货物规定运价标准。

Rate for air transportation of cargo means the charge from departure airport to destination airport, excluding other additional charges (e.g. pick-up, warehousing etc.). Rate is generally calculated by weight (kg) or volumetric weight (6000 cm³ equivalent to 1 kg), whichever is higher. Air cargo charges are based on the standard freight rates for General Cargo Rate (GCR), Specific Commodity Rate (SCR), and Commodity

Classifcation Rate (CCR).

航空货运单（airway bill）是航空运输的正式凭证，它是承运人与托运人之间订立的运输契约，也是承运人或其代理人签发的货物收据。货物运抵目的地后，收货人凭航空公司的到货通知及有关证明领取货物，并在航空货运单上签收。因此，航空货运单并非物权凭证，是不可转让的，卖方只可凭此向银行办理结汇。若合同约定采用航空运输方式，建议使用信用证方式支付或100%前T/T方式支付货款（即卖方在办理货物托运手续前买方必须电汇支付100%货款），以防个别不法商人钻航空货运单不是物权凭证的空子，在未向卖方支付货款的情况下将货物提走。

Airway bill is the official voucher of air transportation. It is the contract of carriage concluded between the carrier and the shipper, as well as the receipt for the goods issued by the carrier or its agent. After the goods arrive at the destination, the consignee shall collect the goods by presenting the airline's notices of arrival and relevant certificates, and sign on the airway bill. Therefore, the airway bill is not documents of title and is non-negotiable. The sellers can only settle foreign exchange with banks on this basis. If the contract specifies the use of air transportation, it is recommended to pay by L/C or 100% T/T (i.e. the buyers must make 100% payment by telegraphic transfer before the sellers go through the consignment procedures), so as to prevent some illegal businessmen from taking advantage of the fact that the airway bill is not a document of title and picking up the goods without paying the sellers.

（三）航空运输货物的运作程序 (Operation Procedures for Air Transportation of Cargo)

采用航空运输需要办理一定的货运手续，航空公司一般只负责空中运输，货物在始发机场交给航空公司之前的揽货、接货、报关、订舱，以及在目的站机场从航空公司手中接货、报关、交付或送货上门等业务则由航空货运代理公司办理。以下是航空货运代理公司对出口货物的航空运输操作的一般流程：市场销售→委托运输→审核单证→预配舱→预订舱→接单→制单→接货→标签→配舱→订舱→出口报关→出仓单→提板箱→货物装箱装板→签单→交接发运→航班跟踪→信息服务→费用结算。

Carriage by air transportation requires certain freight formalities. Generally, airlines are only responsible for the carriage of goods by air. Solicitation, receipt, customs declaration and booking of goods before they are handed over to airlines at the departure airport, as well as receipt, customs declaration, delivery or door-to-door delivery from airlines at the destination airport, shall be handled by air freight forwarders. The following is the general process of air transportation operation for export goods by air freight forwarder: market sales → entrusted carriage → document review → pre-allocation of space → pre-booking → order receiving → bill making → goods receipt → labeling → space allocation → booking → export customs declaration → warehouse-out note → case/carton/crate requisition → packing → signing → delivery and shipment → flight tracking → information service → expense settlement.

四、其他运输方式
IV. Other Transportation Modes

（一）国际公路货物运输 (International Road Cargo Transportation)

国际公路货物运输是指国际货物借助一定的运载工具，沿着公路做跨越两个或两个以上国家或地区的移动过程，在国际货物运输中起重要的衔接作用。公路货物运输与其他运输方式相比较，具有机动灵活、应急性强，能深入其他运输工具到达不了的地方等优点，也存在汽车的载重量小，车辆运输时震动较大，易造成货损事故，费用和成本也比海运和铁路运输高等缺点。国际公路货物运输的作用主要体现在以下方面。

International road cargo transportation (IRCT) refers to the movement process of international goods across two or more countries or regions along highways with the help of certain means of conveyance, which plays an important role in connection. Compared with other means of conveyance, road cargo transportation has the advantages of flexibility, emergency response and being able to go deep into places that cannot be reached by other means of conveyance. It also has the disadvantages of small loading capacity and high vibration during carriage, which are easy to cause cargo damage, as well as higher expenses and costs than ocean transportation and railway transportation. The role of IRCT is mainly reflected in the following aspects.

（1）公路运输的特点决定了它最适合于短途运输。它可以将两种或多种运输方式衔接起来，实现多种运输方式联合运输，做到进出口货物运输的"门到门"服务；

(1) The characteristics of road transportation make it most suitable for short-distance carriage. It can connect two or more transportation modes to realize multimodal transport and achieve "DOOR TO DOOR" service of import and export goods.

（2）公路运输可以配合船舶、火车、飞机等运输工具完成运输的全过程，是港口、车站、机场集散货物的重要手段。尤其是在鲜活商品、货物集港和疏港抢运方面，往往能够起到其他运输方式难以起到的作用。可以说，其他运输方式往往要依赖汽车运输来最终完成两端的运输任务。

(2) Road transportation can cooperate with ships, trains, aircraft and other means of conveyance to complete the whole process of carriage. It is an important means of collecting and distributing goods at ports, stations and airports. Especially fresh and live goods, cargo concentration and port evacuation can often play a role that other transportation modes cannot. It can be said that other transportation modes rely on motor transportation to finally complete the carriage tasks at both ends.

（3）公路运输也是一种独立的运输体系，可以独立完成进出口货物运输的全过程。公路运输是欧洲大陆国家之间进出口货物运输的最重要的方式之一。我国的边境贸易运输、港澳货物运输，其中有相当一部分也是靠公路运输独立完成的。

(3) Road transportation is also an independent transport system, which can independently complete the entire carriage of import and export goods. Road transportation is one of the most important transportation modes for import and export goods between continental European countries. A considerable portion of China's border trade carriage and Hong Kong-Macao carriage of goods is independently completed by road transportation.

（4）集装箱货物通过公路运输实现国际多式联运。集装箱由交货点通过公路运到港口装船，或者相反。美国陆桥运输，我国内地通过香港的多式联运都可以通过公路运输来实现。

(4) Container goods are transported by road to achieve international multimodal transport. The container is transported by road from the delivery point to the port for shipment, or vice versa. Land bridge transport in the United States and multimodal transport through Hong Kong in the Chinese mainland can be realized by road transportation.

（二）内河运输 (Inland Water Transportation)

内河运输是指使用船舶通过国际内江湖河川等天然或人工水道，运送货物和旅客的一种运输方式。它是水上运输的一个组成部分，是内陆腹地和沿海地区的纽带，也是边疆地区与邻国边境河流的连接线，在现代化的运输中起着重要的辅助作用。

Inland water transportation refers to a transportation mode of goods and passengers by ships through natural or artificial waterways such as international rivers and lakes. It is an integral part of water transportation, a link between the inland hinterland and areas along Haiti, as well as a connecting line between frontier areas and border rivers of neighboring countries. It plays an important supporting role in modern transportation.

我国拥有四通八达的内河航运网,长江、珠江等主要河流中的一些港口已对外开放,同一些邻国还有国际河流相通(如黑龙江、澜沧江等),为我国进出口货物通过河流运输和集散提供了十分有利的条件。

China has an inland shipping network extending in all directions. Some ports of major rivers such as the Yangtze River and Pearl River have been opened to the outside world, and are connected with some neighboring countries and international rivers (such as Heilongjiang and Lancang River), providing very favorable conditions for the transportation and distribution of import and export goods through rivers in China.

近几年,西北欧内河运输发展迅速,特别是荷兰,欧洲内河船队有一半是荷兰籍。在荷兰,超过一半的货物和40%的集装箱使用内河水运。干货船运输最为普遍,但近年来油轮和集装箱船增长较快。西北欧地区有超过50个内河集装箱码头在运营,其中荷兰、德国各20个。所有码头都开设了内河集装箱定期班轮服务。除此之外,还有5个内河集装箱码头已经宣布要开工建设。在此基础上,欧洲正在逐步建立内河集装箱班轮运输网,密集的集装箱水运网络可以提供到西北欧全部地区的运输服务,今后这个网络甚至要发展为涵盖50公里以内的极短距离的运输线路。

Inland water transportation in Northwest Europe has developed rapidly in recent years, especially in the Netherlands. Half of the European inland water fleet is from the Netherlands. In the Netherlands, more than half of cargo and 40% of containers are transported by inland waterways. Carriage by dry cargo ships is the most common, but tankers and container carriers have grown rapidly in recent years. There are more than 50 inland container yards in operation in Northwest Europe, including 20 each in the Netherlands and Germany. Inland container liner services are available at all yards. In addition, 5 inland container yards have been announced for construction. On this basis, Europe is gradually establishing the inland container shipping liner network. The dense container water transportation network can provide transportation services to all regions of Northwest Europe. In the future, this network will even develop into an extremely short-distance shipping line covering less than 50 km.

(三)邮包运输 (Parcel Post Transportation)

邮包运输是指利用邮局办理货物运输的方式。这种方式具有手续简便、费用低等特点,但只适用于重量轻、体积小的商品,如精密仪器、配件、药品和样品、材料等零星物品的运输。

Parcel post transportation refers to the way of handling transportation of goods by post office. This method is characterized by simple procedures and low cost, but it is only suitable for the transportation of lightweight and small volume goods, such as precision instruments, accessories, medicines, samples, materials and other sporadic items.

各国(地区)邮政部门之间订有协定和公约,通过这些协定和公约,各国(地区)的邮件包裹可以互相传递,从而形成国际邮包运输网。国际邮政运输具有国际多式联运和"门到门"运输的性质,托运人只需按邮局章程一次托运、一次付清足额邮资,取得邮政包裹收据(parcel post receipt),交货手续即告完成。邮件在国(地区)与国(地区)之间的传递由各国(地区)的邮政部门负责办理,邮件到达目的地后,收件人可凭邮局到件通知向邮局提取。

There are agreements and conventions between postal departments of various countries (regions), through which mail packages from different countries (regions) can be transmitted to each other, thus forming an international parcel post transportation network. International postal carriage features international multimodal transport and "DOOR TO DOOR". The shipper only needs to consign in one time, pay full postage in one time according to the regulations of the post office, and obtain parcel post receipt to complete the delivery formalities. The international delivery of mail is handled by the postal departments of various countries (regions). After the mail arrives at the destination, the recipient can collect it from the post office with a notice of arrival.

邮包收据是邮包运输的主要凭证。它既是邮局收到寄件人邮包后所签发的凭证，也是收件人凭以提取邮件的凭证，又是当邮包发生灭失或损坏时索赔和理赔的依据，但邮包收据也不是物权凭证。

Parcel post receipt is the main voucher for parcel post transportation. It is not only a voucher issued by the post office after receiving the parcel post from the sender, but also a voucher for the recipient to pick up the post. It is also the basis for claim and claim settlement when the parcel post is lost or damaged. However, the receipt of parcel post is not documents of title.

近年来，网上跨境电子商务发展，针对消费者的小额国际贸易开始出现，使得特快专递业务迅速发展。国际快递（International Express Service）是指在两个或两个以上国家（地区）之间所进行的快递、物流业务。目前，国际快递业务的主要承运人有EMS（International Express Mail Service，国际特快专递业务）、DHL（敦豪航空货运公司）、FedEx（联邦快递）、UPS（United Parcel Service，联合包裹服务公司）、TNT（Thomas National Transport，天地物流）等。

In recent years, with the development of cross-border e-commerce and small international trade for consumers, special delivery has developed rapidly. International express service refers to the express and logistics business carried out between two or more countries (regions). At present, the main carrier of international express service business includes EMS (International Express Mail Service), DHL, FedEx, UPS (United Parcel Service) and TNT (Thomas National Transport).

（四）管道运输 (Pipeline Transportation)

管道运输是用管道作为运输工具的一种长距离输送液体和气体物资的输方式，是一种专门由生产地向市场输送石油、煤和化学产品的运输方式，是统一运输网中干线运输的特殊组成部分。许多盛产石油和天然气的国家（地区）都积极发展管道运输，因为管道运输速度快，流量大，中途装卸环节少，运费低廉。

Pipeline transportation is a long-distance transportation mode that uses pipelines as means of conveyance to transport liquid and gas materials. It is a special way to transport petroleum, coal and chemical products from the production site to the market, and is a special component of the trunk line transportation in the united transportation network. Many countries (regions) rich in oil and gas are actively developing pipeline transportation because of its high speed, large flow, few midway loading and unloading links and low freight.

（五）集装箱运输 (Container Freight Transport)

集装箱运输，是指以集装箱这种大型容器为载体，将货物集合组装成集装单元，以便在现代流通领域内运用大型装卸机械和大型载运车辆进行装卸、搬运作业和完成运输任务的一种新型、高效率和高效益的运输方式。在现代海洋、内河、铁路、航空和公路运输中，都广泛采用集装箱运输货物，集装箱运输可以将不同运输方式有机结合起来，从而更好地实现货物的"门到门"运输。

Container freight transport (CFT) is a new, high-efficiency and cost-effective transportation mode in which large containers are used as carriers to assemble goods into container units so that large handling machinery and vehicles can be used for loading/unloading and handling operations and completion of carriage tasks in the modern logistics system. CFT is widely used in modern ocean, inland waterway, railway, air and road transportation. It can organically combine different transportation modes to better realize the "DOOR TO DOOR" transport of goods.

集装箱（container）是指具有一定强度、刚度和规格，专供周转使用并便于机械操作的大型装货容器。使用集装箱装运货物，可直接在发货人的仓库装货，运到收货人的仓库卸货，中途更换车、船时，无须将货物从箱内取出换装。图8-1是常见的通用集装箱。

Container refers to a large cargo container with certain strength, rigidity and specification, which is specially used for turnover and convenient for mechanical operation. If the goods are transported by container, they can be directly loaded in the Consignor's warehouse and unloaded in the Consignee's warehouse. When changing vehicles or ships midway, there is no need to take out the goods from the container for replacement. Figure 8-1 shows a commonly used container.

图 8-1　集装箱
Figure 8-1　Container

集装箱有多种类型，根据国际标准化组织的规定，集装箱的规格有三个系列，仅第一个系列就有15种之多。在国际货运中使用的集装箱规格主要有20英尺（1英尺=0.3048米）和40英尺两种，常用的有1CC型20英尺×8英尺×8英尺6英寸与1AA型40英尺×8英尺×8英尺6英寸。集装箱箱体上都有一个11位字符的编号，前四位是字母，后七位是数字，此编号是统一的。关于四个英文字母，前三个字母是箱主（船公司、租箱公司）代码，如CCL是中远海运集装箱运输有限公司的代码，CBH、FBL都是租箱公司佛罗伦萨的代码；第四个字母U代表集装箱。第5～10位数字是箱主对此集装箱的编号，第11位为校验码。

There are many types of container. According to ISO, there are three series of container specifications, and the first series alone has as many as 15. Specification of container used in international freight mainly includes 20 foot (1 foot = 0.3048 meter) and 40 foot. Commonly used containers include 1CC type 20′×8′×8′6″ and 1AA type 40′×8′×8′6″. There is an 11-digit code on the container body, with the first four digits being letters and the last seven digits being numbers. This code is uniformly numbered. Regarding the four English letters, the first three letters are owner code (shipping company, leasing company). For example, CCL is the code of Cosco Container Lines Co., Ltd., CBH and FBL are the codes of container leasing companies in Florence; the fourth letter U represents container. The 5th~10th digits are registration code of this container, and the 11th digit is the check digit.

1. 集装箱的种类 (Types of Container)

集装箱按用途分类可分为通用集装箱（干货箱）（general-purpose container/dry cargo container）、冷冻集装箱（reefer container）、挂衣集装箱（dress hanger container）、开顶集装箱（open-top container）、框架集装箱（flat-rack container）、罐式集装箱（tank container）、平台集装箱（platform container）等。

According to the purpose, the container can be divided into general-purpose container/dry cargo container, reefer container, dress hanger container, open-top container, flat-rack container, tank container and platform container.

2. 集装箱的规格及载重说明 (Specification and Load Description of Container)

表 8-5 为通用集装箱的规格及载重说明。

Table 8-5 shows the specification and load description of general-purpose container.

表8-5 通用集装箱的规格及载重说明
Table 8-5 Specification and Load Description of General-purpose Container

集装箱箱型 Container specifications	箱内尺寸/长×宽×高 Inner dimensions / L×W×H	最大载重/千克 Maximum load / kg	内容积/立方米 Internal volume / cubic meter
20 英尺货柜（20GP）（20′×8′×8′6″） 20-foot Container (20GP) (20′×8′×8′6″)	5.898×2.352×2.391	28270	33.2
40 英尺货柜（40GP）（40′×8′×8′6″） 40-foot Container (40GP) (40′×8′×8′6″)	12.031×2.352×2.391	26650	67.7
40 英尺加高货柜（40HQ）（40′×8′×9′6″） 40-foot High Cube (40HQ) (40′×8′×9′6″)	12.031×2.352×2.698	26500	76.3
45 英尺加高货柜（45HQ）（45′×8′×9′6″） 45-foot High Cube (45HQ) (45′×8′×9′6″)	13.544×2.352×2.698	28680	86.0

说明：表 8-5 中技术参数只供参考，并不具有普遍性，因为即使是同一规格的集装箱，因结构和制造材料的不同，其技术参数也会略有差异。

Note: The technical parameters in Table 8-5 are for reference only and not universal, because even a container of the same specification may have slightly different technical parameters due to differences in structure and manufacturing materials.

3. 集装箱的装箱方式 (Loading Mode of Container)

采用集装箱运输货物时，集装箱的装箱方式有整箱货（full container load, FCL）和拼箱货（less than container load, LCL）之分。凡装货量达到每个集装箱容积的 75% 或达到每个集装箱负荷量的 95% 都为整箱货，由发货人负责装箱、计数、积载并加铅封（shipper count, load and seal），以箱为单位向承运人进行托运。凡装货量达不到上述整箱标准的，则选择拼箱托运，通常由发货人或货运代理公司将货物从工厂送交集装箱货运站（container freight station, CFS），运输部门按货物的性质、目的地分类整理，然后将运往同一目的地的货物拼装成整箱后再发运。

In container freight transport of goods, the loading modes of containers include full container load (FCL) and less than container load (LCL). If the loading capacity reaches 75% of the volume of each container or 95% of the load capacity of each container, it shall be deemed as FCL. The shipment shall be made with shipper count, load and seal to the carrier on a container basis. If the loading volume fails to meet the above standards of

FCL, the consignor or freight forwarder shall usually deliver the goods from the factory to CFS (container freight station). The carriage department shall classify and sort out the goods according to their nature and destination, and then assemble the goods transported to the same destination into FCL before shipment.

4. 集装箱的处置场所 (Disposal Site of Container)

集装箱的处置场所主要是集装箱堆场和集装箱货运站。

The container disposal sites are mainly container yard and container freight station.

（1）集装箱堆场（container yard, CY），是专门用来保管和堆放集装箱（重箱和空箱）的场所，是整箱货办理交接的地方，一般设在港口的装卸区内。

(1) Container yard (CY) is a place specially used for storing and stacking containers (F and E). It is the place where FCL is delivered. Generally, it is located in the handling area of the port.

（2）集装箱货运站，又叫中转站或拼装货站，是拼箱货办理交接的地方，一般设在港口、车站附近，或内陆城市交通方便的场所。

(2) Container Freight station (CFS), also known as container depot or LCL station, is the place where LCL is delivered. It is generally located near ports, stations, or in places with convenient transportation in inland cities.

5. 集装箱的交接方式 (Delivery Mode of Container)

集装箱的装箱方式有整箱货和拼箱货之分，整箱货和拼箱货的交接方式有所不同。集装箱的交接方式可以分为以下几种。

The packing modes of containers include FCL and LCL. The delivery mode of FCL and LCL is different. Containers can be delivered in the following ways.

（1）整箱交、整箱收（FCL-FCL），适用于"场到场"运输（CY TO CY）、"门到门"运输（DOOR TO DOOR）、"场到门"运输（CY TO DOOR）、"门到场"运输（DOOR TO CY）;

(1) FCL-FCL, for "CY TO CY", "DOOR TO DOOR", "CY TO DOOR" and "DOOR TO CY";

（2）整箱交、拆箱收（FCL-LCL），适用于"场到站"运输（CY TO CFS）、"门到站"运输（DOOR TO CFS）;

(2) FCL-LCL, for "CY TO CFS" and "DOOR TO CFS";

（3）拼箱交、整箱收（LCL-FCL），适用于"站到场"运输（CFS TO CY）、"站到门"运输（CFS TO DOOR）;

(3) LCL-FCL, for "CFS TO CY" and "CFS TO DOOR";

（4）拼箱交、拆箱收（LCL-LCL），适用于"站到站"运输（CFS TO CFS）。

(4) LCL-LCL, for "CFS TO CFS".

由发货人进行装箱，然后其自行将货物运至集装箱堆场等待装运，货到目的港（地）后，收货人可以直接在目的港（地）的集装箱堆场提货，此方式为"场到场"运输；由发货人进行装箱，并在其货仓或工厂仓库将货物交承运人验收后，由承运人负责全程运输，直到收货人的货仓或工厂仓库交接为止，这种全程连续运输为"门到门"运输；承运人在集装箱货运站负责将不同发货人的运往同一目的地的货物拼装在一个集装箱内，货到目的港（地）后，再由承运人在集装箱货运站拆箱分拨给不同的收货人，此方式为"站到站"运输。

The consignor shall load the goods into containers, and then transport them to CY for shipment. After they arrive at port of destination, the consignee can directly pick up the goods in CY of port of destination. This mode is "CY TO CY"; the shipper shall pack the goods and deliver them to the carrier for acceptance in its warehouse or factory warehouse, and the carrier shall be responsible for the whole process of carriage until delivery by the consignee's warehouse or factory warehouse. This kind of continuous carriage is called "DOOR TO DOOR"; the carrier is responsible for assembling goods from different shippers to the same destination into one container at CFS. After the goods arrive at the port (place) of destination, the carrier unpacks and distributes them to different consignees at CFS. This mode is "CFS TO CFS".

（六）国际多式联运 (International Multimodal Transport)

国际多式联运简称多式联运，是在集装箱运输的基础上产生和发展起来的一种综合性的连贯运输方式，是指按照国际多式联运合同，以至少两种不同的运输方式，由多式联运经营人将货物从一国（地区）接管地点运至另一国（地区）指定交付地点的运输组织形式。

International multimodal transport (hereinafter referred to as "multimodal transport") is a comprehensive and coherent transportation mode based on CFT. It refers to the organization form in which goods are transported by multimodal transport operators from the place of receipt in one country (region) to the named place of delivery (region) in another country in at least two different transportation modes according to the contract for international multimodal transport.

班轮运输和集装箱运输的发展促进了国际货物多式联运的发展。这种联运方式将不同的运输方式组合成综合性的一体化运输，通过一次托运、一次计费、一张单证、一次保险，由各运输区段的承运人共同完成货物的全程运输。构成国际多式联运必须具备以下条件。

The development of liner and container freight transport has promoted the development of international multimodal freight transport. This through transport combines different transportation modes into a comprehensive integrated transportation. Through one-time consignment, one-time billing, one-time document and one-time Insurance, the carrier in each carriage section jointly completes the entire transportation. The following conditions must be met to constitute an international multimodal transport system.

（1）必须具有一份多式联运合同，明确规定多式联运经营人（承运人）和托运人之间的权利、义务、责任、豁免的合同关系和多式联运的性质。

(1) There must be a multimodal transport contract that defines the rights, obligations, responsibilities, contractual relationship of exemptions and nature of multimodal transport between the multimodal transport operator (carrier) and the shipper.

（2）必须使用一份全程多式联运单据（multimodal transport documents，M.T.D.），证明多式联运合同已经成立，多式联运经营人已经接管货物并负责按照合同条款交付货物。

(2) Multimodal transport documents (M.T.D.) must be used to prove that the multimodal transport contract has been concluded and that the multimodal transport operator has received the goods and is responsible for delivering them in accordance with the terms of the contract.

（3）必须是至少两种不同运输方式的连贯运输，这是确定一票货运是否属于多式联运的最重要的特征，为履行单一方式运输合同而进行的货物接送，则不应视为多式联运。

(3) Carriage must be consecutive in at least two different transportation modes, which is the most important characteristic for determining whether a single shipment of goods belongs to multimodal transport. The receipt and delivery of goods for the purpose of performing the contract of carriage by single mode shall not be considered as multimodal transport.

（4）必须执行全程单一运费费率。多式联运经营人在对货主负全程运输责任的基础上，还需制定一个货物从发运地至目的地的全程单一费率，并以包干形式一次向货主收取。

(4) Freight must be charged at a single rate throughout the process. On the basis of being responsible for the entire transportation of the goods to the shipper, the multimodal transport operator shall establish a single rate

for the entire process of the goods from place of shipment to place of destination, and collect it from the shipper in a lump sum manner.

（5）必须由一个多式联运经营人对全程运输负总的责任。

(5) A multimodal transport operator must take overall responsibility for the entire transportation process.

（6）必须是跨越国境的国与国之间的货物运输。

(6) It must be an international transportation of goods that crosses national borders.

第二节　国际货物运输单据
Section 2　International Goods Transport Documents

一、海运提单
I. Ocean Bill of Lading

海运提单（ocean bill of lading, B/L），简称提单，根据《中华人民共和国海商法》第七十一条："提单，是指用以证明海上货物运输合同和货物已经由承运人接收或者装船，以及承运人保证据以交付货物的单证。"提单所涉及的当事人主要有承运人、托运人、收货人等。其中，承运人通常是指与托运人签订运输合同或承担运输任务的船公司；托运人是指与承运人签订运输合同或将货物交给承运人的人；收货人是指有权提取货物的人。

According to Article 71 of the Maritime Code of the People's Republic of China, Ocean B/L refers to a document used to prove that the contract for carriage of goods by sea and the goods have been received or loaded by the carrier and that the carrier guarantees to deliver the goods. The parties involved in the B/L mainly include carrier, shipper and consignee. Among them, the carrier refers to the shipping company that has signed the contract of carriage with the shipper or undertaken the task of carriage; the shipper refers to the person who has signed the contract of carriage with the carrier or delivered the goods to the carrier; the consignee refers to the person who has the right to take delivery of the goods.

（一）海运提单的性质和作用 (Nature and Function of Ocean B/L)

提单的性质与作用主要表现在以下三个方面。

The nature and function of B/L are mainly reflected in the following three aspects.

1. 货物收据 (Receipt for the Goods)

提单是承运人（或其代理人）签发给托运人的货物收据（receipt for the goods），用来证实已按提单记载的事项收到货物，承运人应凭提单所列内容向收货人交货。

B/L is the receipt for the goods issued by the carrier (or its agent) to the shipper, which is used to certify that the goods have been received according to the items recorded in the B/L. The carrier shall deliver the goods to the consignee against the contents listed in the B/L.

2. 物权凭证 (Documents of Title)

提单是一种货物所有权的凭证（documents of title），因此拥有提单就拥有支配货物的权利，就等于占有货物。卖方凭提单向银行结算货款，提单的合法持有人凭提单可以在目的港向船公司提取货物，也可以在载货船舶抵达目的港交货前，通过转让提单来转移货物的所有权，也可以凭提单向银行抵押以取得贷款。

B/L is a kind of documents of title. Therefore, possession of B/L means the right to dispose of goods, which is equivalent to possession of goods. The sellers shall settle the payment to the bank with B/L, and the legal holder of B/L may take delivery of the goods from the shipping company at port of destination with B/L, or transfer the ownership of the goods by transferring B/L before the carrying vessel arrives at port of destination for delivery, or mortgage the goods to the bank with B/L to obtain a loan.

3. 运输契约的证明 (Evidence of Contract of Carriage)

运输契约是在装货前签订的，而提单是在装货后才签发的，因此提单本身并不是运输契约，而只是运输契约的证明（evidence of contract of carriage）。在提单背面照例印有各项运输条款和条件，规定了承运人和托运人双方的权利与免责事项，提单的合法持有人有权向承运人索取违约赔偿。

The contract of carriage is signed before loading, while the B/L is issued after loading. Therefore, the B/L itself is not a contract of carriage, but rather an evidence of contract of carriage. The clauses and conditions of carriage are routinely printed on the reverse side of the B/L, providing the rights and exemptions of the carrier and shipper, and the rightful holder of the B/L is entitled to claim compensation from the carrier for breach of contract.

（二）海运提单的内容 (Contents of Ocean B/L)

提单的格式有很多，每个船公司都有自己的提单格式，但基本内容大致相同，一般包括提单正面记载的事项和提单背面印有的运输条款。提单的样式见图 8-2 海运提单样本。

B/L has many formats. Each shipping company has its own B/L format, but the basic contents are roughly the same, including the items specified on the front of B/L and the carriage clauses printed on the back of B/L. See Figure 8-2 Ocean B/L Sample for the style of B/L.

1. 提单的正面内容 (Content on the Front of B/L)

提单正面记载的事项，分别由托运人和承运人或其代理人填写，通常包括下列事项。

The items specified on the front of B/L shall be filled in by the shipper and the carrier or their agents, usually including the following.

（1）托运人（shipper）。

（2）收货人（consignee）。

（3）被通知人（notify party）。

（4）前程运输（pre-carriage by）。

（5）收货地点（place of receipt）。

（6）装运港（port of loading）。

（7）船名及航次（vessel's name and voyage number）。

（8）卸货港（port of discharge）。

（9）最后交货地点（place of delivery）。

（10）唛头及件号（marks and numbers）。

（11）集装箱数或包装件数、包装种类和货物的描述（No. of containers or packages, kind of packages and description of goods）。

（12）毛重（gross weight）。

（13）尺码（measurement）。

（14）运费和费用（freight and charges）。

（15）正本提单份数（number of original B/L）。

（16）签单地点和日期（place and date of issue）。

（17）签署人及身份（signature）。

BILL OF LADING — GOREEFERS TIANJIN LOGISTICS CO., LTD.

Shipper (full style and address)
CHINA AUTO CAIEC LTD
NR. 265 BEISIHUAN ZHONGLU,
HAIDIAN DISTRICT, BEIJING 100083, CHINA

GOREEFERS TIANJIN LOGISTICS CO., LTD.
Bill of Lading for Port-To-Port or Combined Transport

Consignee (full style and address) or Order
TO ORDER OF ALIMPORT

B/L Number: 597597443G
Reference Number: BJSSE160719

Vessel And Voyage No.: SOROE MAERSK 1607

Notify Party (full style and address)
ALIMPORT
HAVANA
CUBA

Port of Loading: NINGBO PORT, CHINA
Port of Discharge: MARIEL PORT, CUBA

PARTICULARS DECLARED BY THE SHIPPER BUT NOT ACKNOWLEDGED BY THE CARRIER

Container Numbers, Seal Numbers and Marks	Number and kind of packages - description of cargo	Gross weight - kg	Measurement - m³
NOMBRE DE PRODUCTO: ATUN EN ACEITE VEGETAL 12X1000G NOMBRE DE LA PLANTA: NINGBO TODAY FOOD CO.,LTD. PAIS DE ORIGEN: CHINA FECHA DE PRODUCCION: FECHA DE VENCIMIENTO: LOT: NOMBRE DE PRODUCTO: ATUN EN ACEITE VEGETAL 48X170G NOMBRE DE LA PLANTA: NINGBO TODAY FOOD CO.,LTD. PAIS DE ORIGEN: CHINA FECHA DE PRODUCCION: FECHA DE VENCIMIENTO: MSKU8760662/CN6500406/1617CARTONS/20755.000KGS/29.130CBM/20GP MSKU3079494/CN6831541/1852CARTONS/20920.260KGS/29.500CBM/20GP MSKU3755182/CN6500405/1440CARTONS/20692.800KGS/29.060CBM/20GP MSKU7106704/CN6831542/1852CARTONS/20920.260KGS/29.500CBM/20GP	6761 CARTONS SHIPPER'S LOAD, COUNT & SEAL SAID TO CONTAIN: PRESERVES OF TUNA TRANSSHIPMENT AND/OR STOPOVERS IN U.S PORTS AND/OR TERRITORIES UNDER USA CONTROL ARE FORBIDDEN. CLEAN ON BOARD THC AT DESTINATION PREPAID FREIGHT PREPAID SAY: SIX THOUSAND SEVEN HUNDRED AND SIXTY ONE CARTONS ONLY.	83288.320 KGS 4*20'GP	117.190 CBM CY-CY

SHIPPED on board in apparent good order and condition, unless otherwise stated and to be discharged at the aforesaid port of discharge or so near thereto as the Vessel may safely get and be always safe afloat. This Bill of Lading is a receipt only for the number of packages shown herein. Weight, measurements, marks and numbers, quality, quantity, contents and value shown above are furnished by the Merchant and have not been checked and are to be considered unknown unless expressly acknowledged and agreed to. The signing of this Bill of Lading is not to be considered as such acknowledgement or agreement. In accepting this Bill of Lading the Merchant expressly accepts and agrees to all its stipulations, exceptions and conditions, on both pages, whether printed, written, stamped or otherwise incorporated, as fully as if they were all signed by the Merchant. One of the Bills of Lading must be surrendered duly endorsed in exchange for the Goods or delivery order.
Full freight and charges are payable as per agreement, but always deemed earned latest on signing Bills of Lading, discountless and non returnable, Ship and/or Goods lost or not.

Total number of Containers / Packages or Units received by the carrier

Shipper's declared value | Declared value charge

Freight details and charges

Carrier's name / principal place of business
Delivery Agent:
EXPEDIMAR S.A.
CALLE 1RA # 1404 E/ 14 & 16, MIRAMAR,
LA HABANA, CUBA.
TEL: 53 7 204 2440 / 1481 / 0158
FAX: 53 7 204 0080
EMAIL: EXPEDIMAR@EXPEDIMAR.CU

Date shipped on board: 2016-08-07
Place and date of issue: BEIJING, CHINA 2016-08-07
Number of original Bills of Lading: THREE
Pre-carriage by:

Signature
天津瑞鲜国际物流有限公司
Goreefers Tianjin Logistics Co., Ltd
Authorized Signature as Agents
THE CARRIER: MAERSK LINE

Place of receipt by pre-carrier:
Place of delivery by on-carrier:

图 8-2 海运提单样本
Figure 8-2 Ocean B/L Sample

2. 提单的背面条款 (Clauses on the Back of B/L)

在班轮提单背面，通常都印有运输条款，这些条款是确定承托双方以及承运人、收货人和提单持有人之间的权利与义务的主要依据。为了缓解船货双方的矛盾并照顾双方的利益，各国为了统一提单背面条款的内容，曾先后签署了四个有关提单的国际公约，分别如下。

On the reverse side of a liner B/L, there are usually printed clauses of carriage which are the primary basis for determining rights and obligations between the shipper and the carrier, as well as between the carrier, consignee and holder of B/L. In order to address conflicts between the shipowner and cargo owner and take into account the interests of both parties, various countries have signed four international conventions on B/L in order to unify the content of the clauses on the back of B/L, as follows.

（1）1924年签署的《统一提单的若干法律规则的国际公约》，简称《海牙规则》（Hague Rules）。

(1) The International Convention for the Unification of Certain Rules of Law Relating to Bill of Lading, signed in 1924, referred to as *Hague Rules*.

（2）1968年签署的《布鲁塞尔议定书》，简称《维斯比规则》（Visby Rules）。

(2) The Brussels Protocol, signed in 1968, referred to as *Visby Rules*.

（3）1978年签署的《联合国海上货物运输公约》，简称《汉堡规则》（Hamburger Rules）。

(3) The United Nations Convention on Carriage of Goods by Sea, signed in 1978, referred to as Hamburg Rules.

（4）2008年签署的《联合国全程或部分海上国际货物运输合同公约》，简称《鹿特丹规则》（The Rotterdam Rules 2008）。

(4) The United Nations Convention on Contract for the International Carriage of Goods Wholly or Partly by Sea, signed in 2008, referred to as The Rotterdam Rules 2008.

由于上述四个公约签署的历史背景不同、内容不一，各国对这些公约的态度也不尽相同。因此，各国船公司签发的提单的背面条款也就互有差异。

Due to different historical backgrounds and contents of the signing of the above-mentioned four conventions, countries' attitudes towards these conventions also vary. Therefore, the clauses on the back of B/L issued by shipping companies in different countries are also different.

（三）海运提单的种类 (Types of Ocean B/L)

在国际贸易业务中，可以从各种不同的角度对提单加以分类，主要有以下几种分类方式。

In international trade business, B/L can be classified from various perspectives. There are mainly the following classification methods.

1. 按货物是否已装船分类 (Classification by Whether the Goods Have Been Shipped or Not)

按货物是否已装船分类，提单可分为已装船提单和备运提单。

According to whether the goods have been shipped or not, B/L can be divided into shipped B/L and received for shipment B/L.

（1）已装船提单（shipped/on board B/L），是指货物装船后，由承运人签发给托运人的提单，它必须载明装货船名和装船日期。提单上记载的装船日期表明了装货完毕的日期，该日期应完全符合买卖合同规定的装运时间。已装船提单对收货人按时收货有了保障，因此在买卖合同中一般都规定卖方须提供已装船提单。

(1) Shipped B/L refers to the B/L issued by the carrier to the shipper after the goods are loaded on board, which must specify the name and date of loading. The date of shipment specified on the B/L indicates the date

when loading is completed, which shall fully conform to the time of shipment specified in the sales contract. Since shipped B/L can guarantee the consignee to receive goods on time, it is generally stipulated in the sales contract that the sellers must provide shipped B/L.

（2）备运提单（received for shipment B/L），又称收讫待运提单，是承运人在收到托运货物等待装船期间，向托运人签发的提单。

(2) Received for shipment B/L, is a B/L issued by the carrier to the shipper during the period when the consignment is received and waiting for shipment.

2. 按提单有无不良批注分类 (Classification by B/L with or without Bad Comments)

按提单上有无不良批注分类，提单可分为清洁提单和不清洁提单。

B/L can be classified into clean B/L and unclean B/L or foul B/L according to whether there are bad comments on the B/L.

（1）清洁提单（clean B/L），是指交运货物的"外表状况良好"（in apparent good order and condition），承运人在提单上未加任何有关货损或包装不良之类批注的提单。在买卖合同中，一般都明确规定卖方提供的已装船提单必须是清洁提单，银行也只接受清洁提单，所以卖方只有提交了清洁提单，才能取得货款。

(1) Clean B/L refers to "in apparent good order and condition" of the consigned goods. The carrier does not add any comments such as damage or poor packing on the B/L. In the sales contract, it is generally specified that shipped B/L provided by sellers must be clean B/L, and banks only accept clean B/L. Therefore, sellers can obtain payment only after submitting clean B/L.

（2）不清洁提单（unclean B/L or foul B/L）。承运人为了保护自身利益，在托运货物的外表状况不良或件数、重量与提单记载不符时，在提单上加注批语，如"铁条松散"（iron-strap loose or missing）、"×件损坏"（… packages in damaged condition）等。凡承运人加注了这类表明货物外表状况不良或存在缺陷等批语的提单，称为不清洁提单。银行为了自身的安全，对不清洁提单，除信用证明确规定可接受外，一般都拒绝接受。因此，在实际业务中，有些托运人为了便于向银行结汇，当遇到货物外表状况不良或存在缺陷时，便要求承运人不加批注，仍给予签发清洁提单。在这种情况下，托运人必须向承运人出具保函（letter of indemnity），保证如因货物破残短损及因承运人签发清洁提单而引起的一切损失，概由托运人负责。在国际贸易业务中，一般认为，包含下列三种批注的提单，不应被视为不清洁提单：①不明确表示货物或包装不能令人满意的条款，如"旧箱""旧桶"等；②强调承运人对货物或包装品质所引起的风险不负责任的条款；③否认承运人知道货物内容、重量、容积、质量或技术规格的条款。

(2) Unclean B/L or Foul B/L. In order to protect its own interests, the carrier shall add comments such as "iron-strap loose or missing" and "… packages in damaged condition" on the B/L when the appearance of the consigned goods is poor or the number and weight are inconsistent with those specified in the B/L. A B/L to which the carrier has added such remarks indicating that the goods are in poor apparent condition or defective is called unclean B/L or foul B/L. For the sake of their own safety, banks generally refuse to accept foul B/L unless expressly stipulated as acceptable by L/C. Therefore, in order to facilitate the settlement of foreign exchange with the bank, some shippers will require the carrier to issue a clean B/L without comments when encountering poor appearance or defects. In this case, the shipper must issue a letter of indemnity to the carrier to ensure that all losses caused by damage or shortage of goods and issuance of clean B/L by the carrier will be borne by the shipper. In international trade business, it is generally believed that B/L with the following three comments shall

not be regarded as unclean B/L or foul B/L: ① Clauses which do not make it clear that the goods or packing are unsatisfactory, such as "old carton", "old drum", etc.; ② Clauses which emphasize that the carrier is not responsible for the risks arising from the quality of the goods or packing; ③ Clauses which deny that the carrier knows the contents, weight, volume, quality or technical specification of the goods.

3. 按提单收货人抬头分类 (Classification by B/L Consignee)

按提单收货人抬头的不同分类，提单可分为记名提单、不记名提单和指示提单三种。

B/L can be divided into straight B/L, bearer B/L and order B/L according to different filling in the Consignee.

（1）记名提单（straight B/L），是指在提单收货人栏内填写特定收货人名称的提单。此种提单不能背书（endorsement）转让，货物只能交给提单上填写的特定收货人。根据某些国家（地区）的习惯，承运人签发记名提单，记名收货人可以只凭身份证明而无须出示正本提单即可提货，此时该提单就失去了物权凭证的作用。记名提单一般用于买方预付货款的情况中。

(1) Straight B/L refers to a B/L in which a specific consignee's name is filled in the Consignee. Such B/L cannot be negotiated by endorsement and the goods can only be delivered to the specific consignee named on the B/L. According to the custom of some countries (regions), the carrier issues a straight B/L, and the named consignee can take delivery of the goods only by presenting the identity certificate without showing the original B/L. At this time, the B/L loses its function of documents of title. A straight B/L is generally used when the buyers pay in advance.

（2）不记名提单（bearer B/L），是指在提单收货人栏内不填写收货人或指示人的名称而留空，或只写明"货交来人（to bearer）"的提单。提单持有人不做任何背书，就能凭提单转让货物所有权或提取货物，承运人只凭提单交货。这种提单风险较大，故国际贸易业务中一般极少使用。

(2) Bearer B/L refers to a B/L in which the consignee is left blank without indicating the name of consignee or order, or only "to bearer" is indicated. The holder of the B/L can transfer title to or take delivery of the goods against the B/L without any endorsement, and the carrier can only deliver the goods against the B/L. Due to the high risk of such B/L, it is rarely used in international trade business.

（3）指示提单（order B/L），是指在提单收货人栏内只填写"凭指定"（to order）或"凭某人指定"（to order of）字样的一种提单。这种提单经过背书才可以转让，通过转让可以买卖仍在运输途中的货物。这种提单有利于资金周转，故在国际贸易业务中使用较多。

(3) Order B/L refers to a B/L in which only the words "to order" or "to order of" are filled in the consignee. Such B/L is negotiable only by endorsement, which enables the sale and purchase of goods still in transit. This kind of B/L is conducive to capital turnover, so it is commonly used in international trade business.

背书的方法有两种：单纯由背书人（提单转让人）签字盖章的，称为空白背书；除背书人签字盖章以外，还列有被背书人（受让人）的名称的，称为记名背书。注明"凭指定"且托运人注明是卖方的提单，在卖方未背书转让之前，卖方仍拥有货物的所有权。在我国出口贸易中，大多是采用这种"凭指定"、空白背书的提单，习惯上称为"空白抬头、空白背书"提单（ocean marine bill of lading made out to order and blank endorsed）。

Endorsement can be carried out in two ways: if it is signed and stamped by the endorser (B/L assignor), it is called blank endorsement; if it also lists the name of the endorser (assignee) in addition to the signature and stamp of the endorser, it is called endorsement in full. For B/L marked "to order" and noted by the shipper as sellers' B/L, title to the goods shall remain with the sellers until such time as the sellers have given their endorsement. In China's export trade, this kind of B/L with "to order" and blank endorsement is mostly adopted, which is customarily called ocean or marine B/L "made out to order" and "blank endorsed".

4. 按运输方式分类 (Classification by Transportation Mode)

按运输方式的不同分类，提单可分为直达提单、转船提单和联运提单。

B/L can be classified into direct B/L, transshipment B/L and through B/L according to different transportation modes.

（1）直达提单（direct B/L），是指从装运港将货物直接运抵目的港所签发的提单。如合同和信用证规定了不准转运，托运人就必须在取得直达提单后，才可向银行结汇。

(1) Direct B/L refers to the B/L issued when goods are shipped directly from port of shipment to port of destination. If the contract and L/C set forth that transshipment is not allowed, the shipper must obtain direct B/L before settlement with the bank.

（2）转船提单（transshipment B/L），是指载货船舶不直接驶往目的港，需在途中某港换装另一艘船舶时所签发的包括全程运输的提单。转船提单中一般会注明"在某港转船"（with transshipment at）字样。

(2) Transshipment B/L refers to a B/L issued when a carrying vessel does not directly sail to the port of destination and needs to be loaded into another ship at a port on the way, including the whole carriage. The words "with transshipment at" will generally be indicated in the transshipment B/L.

（3）联运提单（through B/L），是指货物需经两种或两种以上的运输方式才能运抵目的港，而其中第一程为海运时由第一程承运人所签发的提单。联运提单用于海陆联运、海空联运或海海联运。

(3) Through B/L means that the goods need to be transported to the port of destination by two or more transportation modes, and the first carriage is the B/L issued by the first carrier during ocean transportation. Through B/L is used for sea-land combined transport, air-sea combined transport or sea-sea combined transport.

5. 按提单内容的繁简分类 (Classification by Content of B/L)

按提单内容的繁简分类，提单可分为全式提单和略式提单。

According to the content of B/L, it can be divided into long form B/L and short form B/L.

（1）全式提单（long form B/L），是指通常应用的带有背面条款的提单。这种提单除在其正面列明必要的项目外，在其背面还列有各项有关装运的条款，以表明承运人和托运人的权利与义务。

(1) Long form B/L refers to a commonly used B/L with clauses on the back. In addition to the necessary items listed on the front, such B/L also includes various shipping clauses on the back to indicate the rights and obligations of the carrier and the shipper.

（2）略式提单（short form B/L），是指不带背面条款，仅保留其正面的必要项目的提单。这种提单上一般都印有"本提单货物的收受、保管、运输和运费等项，均按本公司全式提单上的条款办理"的字样。

(2) Short form B/L refers to a B/L without clauses on the back and with only necessary items on the front. Such B/L is generally printed with the words "Receipt, safekeeping, carriage and freight charges of the goods shall be subject to the terms on our long form B/L".

6. 按提单使用的效力分类 (Classification by Effectiveness of B/L)

按提单使用的效力分类，提单可分为正本提单和副本提单。

B/L can be divided into original B/L and copy B/L according to the effectiveness.

（1）正本提单（original B/L），是指经承运人、船长或他们的代理人签字盖章，注明签发日期并标明"正本"（original）字样的提单。正本提单在法律上和商业上都是公认的物权凭证，是提货的依据，可流通转让。

(1) Original B/L refers to a B/L signed and stamped by the carrier, master or their agents, indicating the date of issue and marked with "Original". Original B/L is legally and commercially recognized documents of title, the basis for delivery, and negotiable.

全套正本海运提单（full set original ocean B/L），是指承运人签发的全部份数的正本提单。提单正面注明已签发三份正本，三份即构成全套，如注明只签发一份正本，一份也构成全套。大多数船公司都会签发三份正本，凭其中一份提货后，其余各份均告失效。

Full set original ocean B/L refers to the original B/L of all copies issued by the carrier. The B/L is marked on its face as having been issued in three originals, which shall constitute a complete set or if it is stated that only one original has been issued, one shall also constitute a complete set. Most shipping companies will issue three originals. Invalidation of the remaining copies is subject to delivery of one.

（2）副本提单（non-negotiable /copy B/L），是指没有承运人、船长或他们的代理人签字盖章，一般都标明"Copy"或"Non-Negotiable"字样的提单。副本提单仅供内部流转、业务工作参考及企业确认装船信息使用。

(2) Copy B/L refers to a B/L without the signature and stamp of the carrier, master or their agents and generally marked with "Copy" or "Non-Negotiable". Copy B/L is only used for internal circulation, business work reference and enterprises to confirm shipping information.

7. 其他分类 (Other Classifications)

在国际贸易实际业务中，除了上述几类提单外，还有一些具有特殊性质的提单。

In the actual business of international trade, in addition to the above-mentioned types of B/L, there are also some B/L with special properties.

（1）舱面提单（on deck B/L），是指承运人对装在船舶甲板上的货物签发给托运人的提单，故又称甲板货提单。承运人在这种提单上打印或书写"装舱面"（On Deck）字样，以表明提单所列的货物装在甲板上。由于货物装在甲板上风险比较大，托运人一般需向保险公司加保甲板险。

(1) On deck B/L refers to a B/L issued by the carrier to the shipper for the goods loaded on the deck of the ship, so it is also called on deck B/L. The words "On Deck" are printed or written by the carrier on such B/L to indicate that the goods listed in the B/L have been loaded on deck. Due to the high risk of cargo on deck, the shipper is generally required to add the coverage of on deck risks.

（2）过期提单（stale B/L），是指错过规定的交单日期或晚于货物到达目的港的提单。前者是指超过信用证规定的交单期或信用证未规定交单期时在装运日后21天才交到银行兑用的提单，根据UCP600的规定，银行可拒绝接受此类提单；后者是近洋短程运输所致，在近洋短程运输情况下，很难避免出现过期提单的情况，所以卖方为了维护自身的利益，一般都要求买方在申请开证时，须列入可以接受过期提单的条款，以免引起争议。

(2) Stale B/L refers to a B/L that misses the specified date of presentation or is later than the arrival of goods at port of destination. The former means a B/L which exceeds the period for presentation specified in the L/C or is delivered to the bank for availability 21 days after the date of shipment when the L/C does not specify a period for presentation. It may be rejected by the bank under UCP600; the latter is caused by offshore short-distance carriage. In the case of offshore short-distance carriage, it is difficult to avoid stale B/L. Therefore, in order to safeguard their own interests, the sellers generally require the buyers to include a clause accepting stale B/L when applying for L/C to avoid disputes.

（3）倒签提单（anti-dated B/L），是指货物装船后，应托运人要求，承运人在签发提单时，倒签已装船日期的一种提单。例如，实际装船日期是8月5日，而合同或信用证规定的装运时间是7月31日前，为了符合合同或信用证的规定，将提单日期倒签为7月31日，此为倒签提单。

(3) Anti-dated B/L refers to a B/L in which the carrier backdates the date of shipment when issuing the B/L at the request of the shipper after the goods are loaded on board. For example, if the actual date of shipment is August 5 and the time of shipment specified in contract or L/C is before July 31, to comply with the provisions of contract or L/C, the B/L shall be backdated to July 31, which is called anti-dated B/L.

（4）预借提单（advanced B/L），是指货物尚未装船，承运人预先签发给托运人的已装船提单。按规定，提单须在货物装船完毕时签发。不管是倒签提单还是预借提单，提单日期都不是真正的装船日期。这种行为侵犯了收货人的合法权益，故应杜绝使用。上述两种提单均需托运人提供保函才能获得，英、美、法等国对保函不予承认，亚洲、欧洲的一些国家认为只要未损害第三者利益，便不属违法，不过仍应严加控制。

(4) Advanced B/L refers to a shipped B/L issued by the carrier to the shipper in advance before the goods are loaded on board. It is stipulated that the B/L shall be issued when the goods have been loaded on board. The B/L date is not a true shipment date for either anti-dated B/L or advanced B/L. Such acts violate the legitimate rights and interests of the consignee, so they shall be prohibited. Both types of B/L can only be obtained after the shipper provides letter of indemnity. Countries such as the United Kingdom, the United States and France do not recognize letter of indemnity. Some Asian and European countries believe that it is not illegal as long as the interests of the third party are not harmed, but it should still be strictly controlled.

（5）第三方提单（third party B/L），是指提单上注明的托运人为与买卖双方或信用证的受益人无关的第三方的提单。有时，中间商为了防止买方与真正的供货商接洽，或是代理商、批发商为了利用业务或经营上的优势推销商品、出售或转让他人商品，会使用背书方式转让提单，要求出口商（真正的供货商）在提单上不列出其名称或国别，而以第三方作为托运人，其目的就是不想把真正的供货商暴露给买方，以防买方绕开中间商直接找供货商订货。采用这种提单时，必须在合同或信用证中做出相应的规定，如规定"第三方提单可接受"（third party B/L is acceptable）。

(5) Third party B/L refers to the B/L indicating that the shipper is a third party irrelevant to either party or the beneficiary of L/C. Sometimes, endorsement method will be used to transfer B/L for intermediaries to prevent the buyers from contacting with real suppliers, or for agents and wholesalers to promote commodities, sell or transfer others' commodities by taking advantage of business or operation, requiring the exporter (real supplier) not to list its name or country on the B/L. The purpose of using a third party as the shipper is to avoid exposing the real supplier to the buyer, in case the buyer skips the intermediaries and directly places an order with the supplier. When such B/L is adopted, corresponding provisions must be made in the contract or L/C, for example, "Third party B/L is acceptable".

（四）海运出口货物的运作程序 (Operating Procedures for Seaborne Exports)

海运出口货物的运作程序，根据贸易条件的不同而有所差异。按照FOB条件成交，卖方无须办理租船订舱手续；按照CFR条件成交，卖方无须办理保险手续；按照CIF条件成交，卖方既要租船订舱，又要办理保险手续。这里仅以CFR成交条件下的班轮装运程序为例加以说明。

The operational procedures for seaborne exports vary according to trade conditions. Sellers do not need to go through charter and booking formalities if the transaction is concluded on an FOB basis; sellers do not need to go through insurance formalities if the transaction is concluded on a CFR basis; sellers need to go through both charter and booking and insurance formalities if the transaction is concluded a CIF basis. The liner shipping procedure under CFR is taken as an example only.

备货报检→托运订舱→货物集港→报关→装船→换取提单。
Stocking for inspection → Consignment booking → Concentration of goods in port → Customs declaration → Shipment → Exchange of B/L.

（1）备货报检。出口商根据出口合同或信用证中有关货物的品种、规格、数量、包装等规定，按时、按质、按量准备好应交的出口货物，并做好申报检验和领证工作。在我国，凡列入海关实施检验的进出口商品目录的商品属于需要进行法定检验的商品，进出口商必须向海关申报检验。若信用证或出口合同规定在装船前需由有关商品检验机构出具货物品质、数量、重量检验证书的，出口商应在出口报关前向有关的具备资质的商品检验机构报检，并取得合格的检验证书。在做好出运前的准备工作，货证都已齐全之后，出口商即可办理托运工作。

(1) Stocking for inspection. The exporter shall prepare the export goods to be delivered on time in accordance with the provisions of the export contract or L/C on variety, specification, quantity and packing of goods, and do a good job in declaration, inspection, and certification. In China, all goods listed in the catalogue of import and export commodities for inspection at the customs are goods that require legal inspection, and importers and exporters must declare inspection to the customs. If the L/C or export contract stipulates that the quality, quantity and inspection certificate of weight of the goods shall be issued by the relevant commodity inspection agency before shipment, the exporter shall apply for inspection to the relevant qualified commodity inspection agency before export customs declaration and obtain a qualified inspection certificate. After the preparations before shipment are made and the goods and certificates are complete, the consignment can be handled.

（2）托运订舱。出口商（托运人）编制出口托运单（shipping note, S/N; booking note, B/N），向货运代理公司办理委托订舱手续。货运代理公司根据托运人的具体要求按航线分类整理后，及时向船公司或其代理订舱。托运人也可直接向船公司或其代理订舱。当船公司或其代理签发了装货单（shipping order, S/O）后，订舱工作即告完成，也意味着托运人和承运人之间的运输合同已经缔结。

(2) Consignment booking. The exporter (shipper) prepares shipping note (S/N) and handles the entrusted booking formalities with the freight forwarder. The freight forwarder shall, according to the specific requirements of the shipper, classify and sort out the routes, and then make a booking with the shipping company or its agent in time. Booking may also be made directly to the shipping company or its agents. Booking is completed when the Shipping Order (S/O) is issued by the shipping company or its agent, which also means that the contract of carriage between the shipper and the carrier has been concluded.

（3）货物集港。当船舶到装运港装货的计划确定后，按照港区进货通知在规定的期限内，由托运人办妥集运手续，将出口货物及时运至港区集中，等待装船，货物集港要做到批次清、件数清、标志清。

(3) Concentration of goods in port. After the ship arrives at the port of shipment plan is determined, the shipper shall complete the consolidation procedures within the specified time limit according to the purchase notices of the port area, and transport the exported goods to the port area in a timely manner for concentration

and waiting for loading. The cargoes shall be clear in batches, number of packages and marks.

（4）报关。进出口货物的收发货人经与直属海关、第三方认证机构（中国电子口岸数据中心）签订电子数据应用协议后，可在全国海关适用"通关作业无纸化"的方式，通过"中国国际贸易单一窗口"或"互联网+海关"平台向海关发送报关单数据。海关直接对电子报关单及随附单据的电子数据进行无纸化审核。无纸化审核完成后，符合放行条件的，海关就会发送电子放行指令。

(4) Customs declaration. After signing an electronic data application agreement with the directly affiliated customs and a third-party certification agency (China Electronic Port Data Center), the consignee or consignor of import and export goods can send the customs declaration form data to the customs through the "China International Trade Single Window" or "Internet + Customs" platform in the way of "paperless customs clearance". The customs directly reviews the electronic data of the electronic customs declaration and accompanying documents in a paperless manner. After the paperless review is completed, if the release conditions are met, the customs will send an electronic release instruction.

（5）装船。凭海关电子放行指令或打印的"通关无纸化查验放行通知书"，托运人即可通知船公司装船。在装船过程中，应有托运人委托的货运代理在现场监ავ，随时掌握装船进度并处理临时发生的问题。装货完毕后，理货组长要与船方大副共同签署收货单（mate receipt, M/R），并交与托运人。理货员如发现某批货物有缺陷或包装不良，应在收货单上做批注，并由大副签署，以确定船货双方的责任。作为托运人，应尽量争取收货单上没有不良批注，以便取得清洁提单。

(5) Shipment. The shipper can notify the shipping company of shipment based on the customs electronic release instructions or the printed "Notices on Paperless Inspection and Release for Customs Clearance". In the process of shipment, a freight forwarder entrusted by the shipper shall supervise the loading on site to grasp the progress at any time and deal with temporary problems. After loading, the tally leader shall jointly sign mate receipt (M/R) with the chief officer and hand it over to the shipper. If the tally clerk finds that a shipment is defective or has poor packing, he shall make comments on M/R and have it signed by chief officer to determine the responsibility of the shipowner and cargo owner. The shipper shall strive for no bad comments on the M/R in order to get Clean B/L.

（6）换取提单。在装船完毕后，托运人除向收货人发出装船通知外，还应仔细审核船公司或货运代理公司签发的提单样本是否与实际情况及信用证的要求一致。如相符，托运人应及时凭收货单向船公司或其代理交纳运费和港杂费，换取已装船清洁提单。

(6) Exchange of B/L. After completion of shipment, the shipper shall not only issue shipping advice to the consignee, but also carefully review whether the sample B/L issued by the shipping company or freight forwarder is consistent with the actual situation and the requirements of L/C. If it is consistent, the shipper shall pay freight charges and port surcharges to the shipping company or its agent in time with M/R in exchange for clean B/L on board.

二、其他运输单据
II. Other Transport Documents

（一）航空货运单 [Airway Bill (AWB)]

1. 航空货运单的性质与作用 (Nature and Function of AWB)

航空货运单（airway bill, AWB）是由承运货物的航空公司制定、由托运人（或以托运人的名义）按照航空公司的要求填制并由航空公司确认的，用以表明托运人和承运人之间所订立的运输契约。航空货运单与海运提单不同，它不具备物权凭证的特性，不可转让，在空运单上都会有"Not Negotiable"字样。

Airway Bill (AWB) is formulated by the airline carrying goods, filled in by the shipper (or in the name of the shipper) according to the requirements of the airline and confirmed by the airline to indicate the contract of carriage between the shipper and the carrier. Different from ocean B/L, AWB does not have the characteristics of documents of title. They are non-negotiable and will be marked with "Not Negotiable".

航空货运单主要有以下作用。

The main functions of AWB are as follows.

（1）承运人与托运人之间的运输合同证明。

(1) Proof of contract of carriage between the carrier and the shipper.

（2）承运人已接收货物的证明文件。

(2) Documentary evidence that the carrier has received the goods.

（3）承运人据以核收运费的凭证及运费收据。

(3) Voucher and receipt based on which the carrier collects freight charges.

（4）承运人内部业务的依据。

(4) Basis for carrier's internal business.

（5）进出口货物办理清关手续的必需单证。

(5) Documents necessary for customs clearance of import and export goods.

（6）航空公司业务操作的依据。航空运单随货机同行，承运人会根据运单上的相关信息对货物做出相应的组织安排。

(6) Basis for airline business operation. AWB accompany the freighter, and the carrier will organize and arrange for the cargo according to relevant information on the waybill.

（7）当承运人承办保险或托运人要求承运人代办保险时，航空货运单也可以作为保险证明（载有保险条款的航空货运单又被称为红色航空运单）。

(7) When the carrier undertakes insurance or the shipper requires the carrier to undertake insurance, AWB can also be used as an insurance certificate (AWB containing insurance clause is also known as Red AWB).

2. 航空货运单的构成 (Composition of AWB)

我国国际航空货运单由一式十二联组成，包括三联正本、六联副本和三联额外副本。航空货运单的每一份正本都印有背面条款，涉及航空货物运输的相关法律问题，如索赔、保险、运输更改等。航空货运单的构成及各联的功能如表 8-6 所示。

The international airway bill of China is made in twelve copies, including three originals, six copies and three additional copies. Each original airway bill is printed with clauses on the back covering legal issues related to carriage of goods by air such as claim, insurance, change of carriage etc. The composition of airway bill and the functions of each copy are shown in Table 8.6.

表8-6 航空货运单构成表

Table 8-6　Composition of Airway Bill

序号 S/N	名称 Description	分发对象及用途 Object and Purpose	颜色 Color
1	Original 3	交托运人，作为承托双方运输合同及承运人收运货物的证明 To the shipper, as proof of contract of carriage between the carrier and the shipper, as well as the carrier's receipt of the goods	浅蓝色 Light blue

续表

序号 S/N	名称 Description	分发对象及用途 Object and Purpose	颜色 Color
2	Copy 9	交代理人,供代理人留存 To the agent for his retention	白色 White
3	Original 1	交出票航空公司,作为承托双方运输合同证明及运费结算凭证 To the issue carrier, as proof of contract of carriage between the carrier and the shipper and settlement voucher of freight charges	浅绿色 Light green
4	Original 2	随航班货物交收货人,以备进口报关、提货之用 To the consignee along with the flight cargo, for import customs clearance and pick-up purposes	粉红色 Pink
5	Copy 4	提货收据,收货人提货时签字,并由承运人留存以证明妥善交货 Delivery receipt, signed by the consignee at the time of delivery and retained by the carrier to certify proper delivery	浅黄色 Light yellow
6	Copy 5	目的地机场 Airport of destination	白色 White
7	Copy 6	第三承运人 Third carrier	白色 White
8	Copy 7	第二承运人 Second carrier	白色 White
9	Copy 8	第一承运人 First carrier	白色 White
10	Extra copy	供承运人使用 For carrier	白色 White
11	Extra copy	供承运人使用 For carrier	白色 White
12	Extra copy	供承运人使用 For carrier	白色 White

3. 航空货运单分类 (Classification of Airway Bill)

航空货运单按不同的角度可以划分为不同类别。

The airway bill can be divided into different categories from different perspectives.

(1) 按空运单有无出票人的标志,可分为航空公司运单和中性运单。

(1) Air waybills can be divided into airline waybills and neutral waybills according to whether there is a drawer or not.

航空公司运单上面有航空公司的标志(logo)等,而中性运单上面则没有。

The airline waybill has the airline's logo and other signs, while the neutral waybill does not.

(2) 按空运单的出票人,可分为主运单和分运单。

(2) According to the drawer of airway bill, it can be divided into master airway bill (MAWB) and house airway bill (HAWB).

主运单(master air waybill, MAWB)由航空公司签发,每一票货物的出运都必须出具主运单。分运单(house air waybill, HAWB)是在集中托运业务(consolidation)中,由空运代理人在办理货物出运时签发给各发货人的运单。集中托运业务中的空运代理即体现为集中托运人

（consolidator）的身份。

Master airway bill (MAWB) is issued by the airline and must be provided for each shipment of goods. House airway bill (HAWB) is a waybill issued by the air freight agent to each consignor when handling the shipment of goods in consolidation. The air freight forwarder in the consolidation is embodied as a consolidator.

在集拼业务中，航空运输公司向始发机场的集拼商（货运代理）签发航空公司的主运单（MAWB），集拼商再向每一个托运人（货主）签发自己的空运单——分运单（HAWB）；在目的地机场，航空公司凭主运单向分拨商（break bulk agent）（集中托运在目的地的代理或分支机构）交货，分拨商再凭分运单向每一个收货人交货。两者的主要区别如下。

In consolidation business, the airline issues its MAWB to the consolidator (freight forwarder) at the airport of departure, and the consolidator issues its own air HAWB to each shipper (cargo owner); at the airport of destination, the airline delivers to break bulk agent (consolidation agent or branch at destination) by MAWB and the break bulk agent delivers to each consignee by HAWB. The main differences are as follows.

分运单是发货人与集拼商（空运代理人）之间的航空货物运输契约，合同的双方当事人分别是发货人和集拼商（空运代理人）；而主运单则是集拼商（空运代理人）与航空公司之间的航空货物运输契约，合同的双方当事人分别是集拼商（空运代理人）与航空公司集中托运中，货主与航空公司之间没有直接的运输合同关系。

HAWB is the contract of carriage for air cargo between consignor and consolidator (air freight agent), with contracting parties being consignor and consolidator (air freight agent) respectively; while MAWB is the contract of carriage for air cargo between the consolidator (air freight agent) and the airline, with contracting parties being the consolidator (air freight agent) and the airline. In the consolidation, there is no direct contractual relationship of carriage between the cargo owner and the airline.

主运单的托运人栏（shipper）填写集拼商（空运代理人），收货人栏（consignee）填写分拨商，两者均是空运代理人；而分运单中的托运人栏和收货人栏均是实际货主。

Fill in the shipper of MAWB with consolidator (air freight agent) and the consignee with break bulk agent, both of which are air freight agents; while the shipper and consignee of HAWB are actual cargo owners.

在非集拼业务中，有时托运人会为了达到某种商业目的，方便业务操作，特向集拼商（空运代理人）提出签发分运单的请求。

In non-consolidated business, sometimes the shipper will make a request to the consolidator (air freight agent) for issuing HAWB in order to achieve certain commercial purpose and facilitate business operation.

（二）铁路运单 (Railway Bill)

铁路运单（railway bill）是国际铁路货物联运所使用的运单和运单副本，是铁路与货主间缔结的运送契约。运单副本是卖方通过有关银行向买方结算货款的主要文件之一。铁路运单与航空运单相同，并非物权凭证，是不可转让的。

Railway bill (RB) is a waybill and a copy of the waybill used in international railway transportation, which is a transportation contract concluded between railways and cargo owners. Copy of waybill is one of the main documents for the sellers to settle payment to the buyers through relevant banks. Like RB, AWB is not documents of title and is non-negotiable.

第三节　合同中的装运条款
Section 3　Shipment Clause in the Contract

在进出口合同中，涉及装运方面的条款，除规定运输方式外，还必须规定装运期、装运港（地）和目的港（地）、分批装运和转运等各项内容。明确、合理地规定装运条款是保证进出口合同顺利履行的重要条件之一。

In the import and export contract, in addition to transportation mode, the clauses related to shipment must also specify such contents as date of shipment, port (place) of shipment and port (place) of destination, partial shipments and transshipment. Clear and reasonable stipulation of shipment clause is one of the important conditions to ensure smooth performance of the import and export contract.

一、装运时间
I. Time of Shipment

装运时间（time of shipment）又称装运期（date of shipment），是卖方完成货物装运的期限。装运期和交货期（time of delivery），在象征性交货条件下，两者的意思是一致的，这是因为卖方完成货物装运即完成了交货义务；但在实际交货条件下，如在DAP、DPU、DDP条件下，两者的含义就不一样了，这时的装运期是指货物装运的时间，交货期则是指货物到达目的地交货的时间，它们之间相差一个运输航程。

Time of shipment, also known as date of shipment, is the time limit for sellers to complete shipment of goods. Date of shipment and time of delivery, under symbolic delivery conditions, mean the same because the sellers fulfill their delivery obligations by completing shipment; under physical delivery conditions, such as DAP, DPU and DDP, the meanings of the two are different. In this case, date of shipment refers to the time when the goods are shipped, while time of delivery refers to the time when the goods arrive at the destination for delivery, with a difference of one voyage between them.

（一）装运时间的规定方法 (Provisions on Time of Shipment)

在国际货物买卖合同中，买卖双方必须对装运时间做出具体的规定。常用的规定方法有以下几种。

In the contract for international sale of goods, both parties must make specific provisions on time of shipment. The following methods are commonly used.

（1）规定在某月或跨月装运。例如，

(1) Specify shipment within a certain month or across months. Example:

Shipment during March, 2022.

Shipment during Feb. /Mar., 2022.

（2）规定在某月底或某日前装运。例如，

(2) Provide for shipment on or before the end of a month. Example:

Shipment at or before the end of May, 2022.

Shipment on or before July 15th, 2022.

Shipment not later than Sept. 15th., 2022.

（3）规定在收到信用证后一定期限内装运。例如，

(3) Provide that shipment shall be made within a certain period after receipt of L/C. Example:

Shipment within 45 days after receipt of L/C.

在对买方资信了解不够或为防止买方可能因某些原因不按时履行合同的情况下,可采用这种方法规定装运时间,以保障卖方的利益。注意,在采用这种方式规定装运时间时,为防止出现因买方拖延或拒绝开证而造成卖方不能及时安排生产及耽误装运进程的被动局面,合同中必须同时规定有关信用证开立或送达的期限。例如,

This method can be used to specify the time of shipment to protect the interests of the sellers in case of insufficient understanding of the buyers' credit or in order to prevent the buyers from failing to perform the contract on time for some reasons. Note that when time of shipment is provided in this way, the contract must also specify the time limit for issuance or delivery of L/C to prevent the sellers from being unable to arrange production and delay the shipment in a timely manner due to the buyers' delay or refusal to issue an L/C. Example:

> The buyer must open the relevant L/C to reach seller not later than June 15th. 2022.

(4)近期装运术语(recent shipping terms),表示这类规定的词语有"立即装运"(immediate shipment)、"即期装运"(prompt shipment)、"尽速装运"(shipment as soon as possible)等。应尽量避免使用这类规定方法,因为各国对此解释不一,有的理解为一个月,有的理解为两周,容易引起争议和纠纷。国际商会制定的UCP600中明确规定,不应使用如"迅速""立即""尽速"和类似词语,如使用这类词语,银行将不予受理。

(4) Recent shipping terms, words expressing such provisions include "immediate shipment", "prompt shipment" and "shipment as soon as possible". Dispute and controversy shall be avoided as far as possible, since the interpretation varies from one month to two weeks. The UCP600 issued by ICC specifies that words such as "promptly", "immediately", "as soon as possible" and similar words shall not be used. If such words are used, the bank will ignore them.

(二)规定装运时间应注意的问题 (Precautions for Time of Shipment)

规定装运时间时,一般应考虑货源情况,如生产周期、库存情况、交货数量、商品本身的特点、包装及市场情况;还应考虑运输情况,如航线、航班和国内运输情况;也应特别注意开证日期与装运时间的衔接等情况。

When providing time of shipment, the source of goods shall generally be considered, such as production cycle, inventory, delivery quantity, characteristics of goods themselves, packing and market conditions; carriage conditions shall also be considered, such as air routes, flights and domestic carriage conditions; special attention shall also be paid to the connection between date of issue and time of shipment.

(1)应考虑货源和船源的实际情况。从货源和船源的实际情况出发来确定装运期或交货期,有利于卖方按期装运和履行约定的交货义务。如货源无把握就盲目成交,很有可能出现到时交不了货,造成有船无货的情况。在按CFR或CIF条件出口和按FOB条件进口时,还应考虑船源情况。如对船源无把握就盲目成交,或者没有留出安排船位的合理时间,规定在成交的当月交货或装运,则可能出现到时租不到船或订不到舱位,而形成有货无船的情况。

(1) Source of goods and ships. Determining date of shipment or time of delivery based on the source of goods and ships is conducive to sellers' shipment on schedule and performance of agreed delivery obligations. If the source of goods is uncertain and the transaction is blindly concluded, it is very likely that there will be no delivery on time, resulting in a situation where there are ships but no goods. When exporting on a CFR or CIF basis and importing on an FOB basis, the ship source shall also be considered. If the source of ships is uncertain and the transaction is blindly concluded, or a reasonable time is not set aside to arrange the shipping space and stipulate that delivery or shipment should be made in the same month as the transaction, it may occur that no ship

can be chartered or booked, resulting in the situation where there are goods but no ships.

（2）应考虑市场情况。要考虑市场需求情况，特别是季节性商品，其装运时间与客户安排销售密切相关，要为客户着想。

(2) Market conditions. It is necessary to consider the market demand, especially seasonal goods. The time of shipment is closely related to sales arrangements and it is important to consider the customer's interests.

（3）应考虑开证日期的规定是否明确、合理。装运期与开证日期是相互关联的。为了保证按期装运和及时交货，在规定装运期的同时，还应明确、合理地规定开证日期，并使两者互相衔接。一般来说，信用证至少应在装运期开始前 15 天送达卖方，以便卖方有充足的时间安排装货。

(3) Whether the provisions on date of issue are clear and reasonable. Date of shipment and date of issue are interrelated. In order to ensure on-time shipment and timely delivery, the date of issue shall be clearly and reasonably provided while specifying the date of shipment. In general, the L/C shall reach sellers at least 15 days prior to date of shipment so that the sellers have sufficient time to arrange shipment.

二、装运港（地）和目的港（地）
II. Port of Shipment and Port of Destination

装运港（port of shipment /loading）是指货物起始装运的港口，目的港（port of destination / discharge）是指最终卸货的港口。

Port of Shipment refers to the port where goods are initially shipped, and port of destination refers to the port where goods are finally discharged.

（一）装运港和目的港的规定方法 (Method of Specifying Port of Shipment and Port of Destination)

在国际货物买卖合同中，买卖双方必须对装运港和目的港做出明确的规定。为了便于卖方安排装运和适应买方接收货物或转售货物的需要，装运港通常由卖方提出，经买方同意后确定；目的港通常由买方提出，经卖方同意后确定。常用的规定方法有以下几种。

In the contract for international sale of goods, both parties must make specific provisions on port of shipment and port of destination. In order to facilitate the sellers' arrangement for shipment and meet the buyers' needs for receiving or reselling goods, Port of shipment is usually proposed by the sellers and determined with the consent of the buyers; port of destination is usually proposed by the buyers and determined with the consent of the sellers. The following methods are commonly used.

（1）在一般情况下，只规定一个装运港和一个目的港，并列明港口名称。例如：

(1) In general, only one port of shipment and one port of destination are provided, and the name of the port is indicated. Example:

Port of Shipment: Shanghai.
Port of Destination: London.

（2）在大宗交易的情况下，有时需要规定两个或两个以上的装运港或目的港，并分别列明港口名称。例如：

(2) In the case of large transactions, it is sometimes necessary to provide for two or more ports of shipment or ports of destination with names indicated. Example:

Port of Shipment: Qingdao and Shanghai.
Port of Destination: London and Liverpool.

（3）在磋商交易时，如明确规定一个或几个装卸港有困难，可以采用选择港（optional

ports）的办法，即允许收货人在预先提出的两个或两个以上的卸货港，在货轮抵达第一个备选港口前，按船公司规定的时间，将最后确定的卸货港通知船公司或其代理人，船方负责按通知的卸货港卸货。按一般航运惯例，如果货方未在规定时间将选定的卸货港通知船方，船方有权在任何一个备选港口卸货。例如：

(3) When negotiating a transaction, if it is difficult to specify one or more ports of shipment/discharge, the method of optional ports may be adopted, that is, the consignee shall be allowed to notify the shipping company or its agent of the finalized port of discharge before the arrival of the cargo ship at the first optional port according to the time specified by the shipping company, and the shipowner shall be responsible for unloading according to the notified port of discharge. According to general shipping practice, if the cargo owner fails to notify the shipowner of the selected port of discharge within the specified time, the shipowner shall have the right to discharge the cargo at any optional port. Example:

CIF London /Hamburg /Rotterdam.
CIF London, optional Hamburg /Rotterdam, optional addition for buyer's account.

（4）笼统规定某一航区为装运港或目的港。例如，

(4) A certain service area is generally defined as port of shipment or port of destination. Example:

Port of Shipment: China ports.
Port of Destination: U.K. ports.

（二）规定国外装运港和目的港应注意的问题 (Precautions for Foreign Port of Shipment and Port of Destination)

在进口合同中规定国外的装运港，以及在出口合同中规定国外的目的港时，应注意以下事项。

When specifying a foreign port of shipment in the import contract and a foreign port of destination in the export contract, please note the following.

（1）力求具体、明确。国外港口应明确、具体，最好只有一个港口名称。在磋商交易中，如国外商人笼统地提出以"欧洲主要港口"或"非洲主要港口"为装运港或目的港时，不宜轻易接受。因为欧洲或非洲港口很多，究竟哪些港口是主要港口，并无统一的解释。而且到达各港的距离不同，港口条件不一，运费和附加费相差很大，所以我们应避免采用此种规定方法。

(1) Be specific. Foreign ports shall be specified, preferably with only one port name. In negotiation, if foreign merchants propose to use "European main ports" or "African main ports" as port of shipment or port of destination, it should not be acceptable. Because there are many ports in europe or africa, there is no unified explanation for which ports are the main ones. Freight and surcharges vary greatly from port to port, so we should avoid this method.

（2）合理使用"选择港"。采用"选择港"时应注意：①合同中规定的选择港的数目一般不超过3个；②备选港口要在同一条班轮航线上，而且是班轮公司的船只都能停靠的港口；③在核定价格和计算运费时，应按备选港口中最高的运费率加上选卸港附加费计算；④在合同中应明确规定买方确定目的港的时间，以及因选择港而增加的运费、附加费均由买方负担。

(2) Reasonably use "optional ports". When "optional ports" are used, attention shall be paid to: ① The number of optional ports specified in the contract is generally not more than 3; ② Optional ports shall be on the same liner route, and all ships of the liner company can call; ③ In determining prices and calculating freight charges, the highest rate of freight among optional ports plus optional surcharge shall be used; ④ The

contract shall specify that the time when the buyers determine the port of destination, and the freight charges and surcharges increased due to optional ports shall be borne by the buyers.

（3）注意装卸港的具体条件。关于装卸港的具体条件，主要是考虑有无直达班轮航线、港口装卸条件以及运费和附加费用水平等。如果采用租船运输，还应进一步考虑码头泊位水的深度、有无冰封期、冰封的具体时间以及港口对船舶国籍有无限制等因素。

(3) Pay attention to the specific conditions of port of shipment/discharge. As for the specific conditions of port of shipment/discharge, the main considerations include availability of direct liner routes, port loading and unloading conditions, as well as the level of freight and additional. For Charter, further consideration shall be given to such factors as water depth of dock berth, whether there is an icebound season, specific icebound time and whether the port has restrictions on ship nationality.

（4）注意港口有无重名。世界各国港口重名的很多，例如，维多利亚（Victoria）港，世界上有12个之多，波特兰（Portland）港、波士顿（Boston）港在美国、英国等其他国家都有同名港。为了防止发生差错、引起纠纷，在买卖合同中应明确注明装卸港所在国家和地区的名称。

(4) Be careful of ports with the same names. There are many ports in the world with the same names. For example, there are 12 Victoria ports in the world, and there are ports of Portland and Boston in countries such as the United States and the United Kingdom. To prevent errors and disputes, the name of the country or region where the port of shipment/discharge is located shall be indicated in the sales contract.

（三）规定国内装运港和目的港应注意的问题 (Precautions for Domestic Port of Shipment and Port of Destination)

在出口业务中，对国内装运港的规定，一般以选择接近货源地的对外贸易港口为宜，同时应考虑港口和国内运输的条件及费用水平。如果进出口公司对某一出口商品采取集中成交、分口岸交货的方式，由于在成交时还不能确定具体装运口岸，在这种情况下，也可规定两个或两个以上的港口或规定"中国口岸"为装运港，这样可以处于主动位置。

In the export business, it is generally advisable to choose a foreign trade port close to the source of goods as the domestic port of shipment, while considering the conditions and cost level of the port and domestic transportation. If an import and export company adopts the method of centralized transaction and delivery at different ports for certain export goods, and cannot determine the specific port of shipment at the time of transaction, in this case, two or more ports or "China port" can be specified as port of shipment, so that it can be in an active position.

在进口业务中，对国内目的港的规定，原则上应选择接近用货单位或消费地区的对外贸易港口最为合理。

In the import business, in principle, it is most reasonable to choose a foreign trade port close to the user or consumption area as the domestic port of destination.

三、分批装运和转运
III. Partial Shipments and Transshipment

分批装运（partial shipments）是指一个合同项下的货物在成交数量较大时先后分若干批或若干期装运的方式。在国际贸易中，有的交易因为数量较大，或由于备货、运输条件、市场需要或资金的限制，有必要分期、分批交货的时候，可在合同中规定分批装运条款。

Partial shipments refers to the shipment of goods under a contract in several batches or periods when the volume of business is large. Details of partial shipments may be specified in the contract when it is necessary to deliver goods in installments or batches due to large quantity, stocking, conditions of carriage, market needs or financial restrictions in international trade.

转船或转运（transshipment）是指货物自装运港运至目的港的过程中，从一个运输工具转移到另一个运输工具上，或是由一种运输方式转为另一种运输方式的行为。如果到目的港或目的地无直达班轮或班列等，或者合同规定集装箱装运，而出口口岸缺乏装卸设备要集中到其他口岸装箱时，都需要在合同中规定允许转运。

Transshipment refers to the behavior that goods are transferred from one means of conveyance to another, or from one transportation mode to another during transportation from port of shipment to port of destination. If there is no direct liner or train to the port/place of destination, or if the contract requires container shipment but there is a lack of loading and unloading equipment at the port of export and it is necessary to at other ports for packing, transshipment shall be allowed in the contract.

（一）合同中的分批装运和转运条款 (Partial Shipments and Transshipment in the Contract)

是否允许分批装运和转运，直接关系到买卖双方的经济利益。因此，能否分批装运和转运，合同双方当事人应该达成一致意见，并在合同中做出相应的规定。一般来说，允许分批装运和转运，能使卖方处于主动地位。

Whether partial shipments and Transshipment are allowed directly affects the economic interests of both parties. Therefore, the parties to the contract should reach an agreement on the possibility of partial shipments and transshipment, and make corresponding provisions in the contract. Generally, allowing partial shipments and transshipment puts the Sellers in an active position.

（1）规定允许分批装运和转运。例如：

(1) Provisions allowing for partial shipments and transshipment. Example:

Partial shipments and transshipment is to be allowed.

（2）规定不允许分批装运和转运。例如：

(2) Provisions not allowing for partial shipments and transshipment. Example:

Partial shipments and transshipment is not to be allowed.

（3）既规定允许分批装运，又规定分批的具体时间、批次及数量。例如：

(3) Provisions allowing for partial shipments, with the time, batch and quantity specified. Example:

Shipments are to be effected during April, May, June, July, 2022 in four equal monthly lots.

（二）国际惯例对分批装运和转运的规定 (Provisions of International Practice on Partial Shipments and Transshipment)

在实际业务中，我们应注意UCP600中关于分批装运和转运的相关规定。

In practice, we should pay attention to the relevant provisions of UCP600 on Partial Shipments and Transshipment.

（1）UCP600第三十一条a款规定：允许分批支款或分批装运。第三十一条b款规定：①表明使用同一运输工具并经由同次航程运输的数套运输单据在同一次提交时，只要显示相同目的地，将不被视为分批装运，即使运输单据上标明的发运日期不同或装卸港、接管地或发送地点不同。如果交单由数套运输单据构成，其中最晚的一个发运日将被视为发运日。②含有一套或数套运输单据的交单，如果表明在同一种运输方式下经由数件运输工具运输，即使运输工具在同一天出发运往同一目的地，仍将被视为分批装运。

(1) Article 31a of UCP600 provides that partial payments or shipments are allowed. According to Article

31b: ① A set of transport documents indicating the use of the same means of conveyance and carriage by the same voyage, when presented at the same time, will not be considered as partial shipments provided they show the same destination, even if the date of shipment or port of shipment/discharge, place of receipt or place of delivery indicated on the transport documents is different. If the presentation is made up of several set of transport documents, the latest one of them will be considered as date of shipment. ② Presentation of documents containing one or more set(s) of transport documents indicating carriage by several means of conveyance under the same transportation mode will be considered as partial shipments even if they are destined for the same destination on the same day.

（2）UCP600第三十二条规定：如信用证规定在指定的时间段内分期支款或分期发运，任何一期未按信用证规定期限支取或发运时，信用证对该期及以后各期均告失效。

(2) According to Article 32 of UCP600, if the L/C stipulates payment or shipment by installments within the specified time period, and any installment is not paid or shipped according to the time limit stipulated in the L/C, the L/C shall become invalid for this installment and subsequent installments.

（3）UCP600第二十条c款规定：i. 只要同一提单包括运输全程，则提单可以注明货物将被转运或可被转运。ii. 银行可以接受注明将要发生或可能发生转运的提单。即使信用证禁止转运，只要提单上证实有关货物已由集装箱、拖车或子母船运输，银行仍可接受注明将要发生或可能发生转运的提单。

(3) According to Article 20c of UCP600: i. A B/L may indicate that the goods are to be transshipped or may be transshipped, provided that the same B/L covers the entire transportation. ii. A B/L indicating that Transshipment will or may occur is acceptable to the bank. Notwithstanding the L/C prohibiting transshipment, banks may accept B/L indicating that transshipment will or may occur as long as the goods have been shipped in a container, trailer or LASH as evidenced by the B/L.

由此可知，UCP600中的禁止转运，实际上仅是禁止海运港至港除集装箱以外的货物（散货）运输的转运。UCP600对转运做了以上淡化和从宽的规定，主要是为了适应现代运输业的发展，有利于减少转运引起的纠纷。但该解释仅适用于信用证业务的处理而不涉及买卖合同条款的解释。在实际业务中，买卖双方还应在合同中明确规定允许转运条款。

It can be seen that the transshipment prohibition in UCP600 actually only prohibits the carriage of goods (in bulk) other than containers from seaports to ports. UCP600 has weakened provisions on transshipment, which is mainly to adapt to the development of modern transportation and help reduce disputes caused by transshipment. Such interpretation is only applicable to the handling of L/C business and does not involve the terms of the sales contract. In actual business, the buyers and sellers shall specify in the contract that transhipment is allowed.

四、装运通知
IV. Shipping Advice

装运通知是买卖合同中必不可少的一项条款。无论按哪种贸易术语成交，交易双方都要承担相互通知的义务。规定这项条款的目的在于，明确买卖双方的责任，促使买卖双方互相配合，共同做好船货衔接工作。

Shipping advice is an indispensable clause of the sales contract. Regardless of the trade term under which a transaction is concluded, the obligation to notify each other shall remain with both parties. The purpose is to clarify the responsibilities of both parties, so as to urge them to cooperate with each other and jointly do a good job in the schedule between ship and goods.

按照国际贸易的一般做法，按FOB条件成交时，卖方应在约定的装运期开始以前（一般为 30 天），向买方发出货物备妥准备装船的通知，以便买方及时派船接货。买方接到卖方发出的通知后，应按约定时间，将船名、船舶到港受载日期通知卖方，以便卖方及时安排货物出运和准备装船。

According to the general practice of international trade, when a transaction is concluded on an FOB basis, the sellers shall send notices that the goods are ready for shipment to the buyers before the agreed date of shipment (generally 30 days), so that the buyers can dispatch ships to receive the goods in time. After receiving the notices from the sellers, the buyers shall inform the sellers of the vessel name, date of arrival and laydays of the vessel at the agreed time so that the sellers can arrange shipment and prepare for loading in a timely manner.

按 CIF、CFR 或 FOB 条件成交时，卖方应于货物装船后，立即将合同号、货物的品名、件数、重量、发票金额、船名及装船日期等各项内容告知买方，以便买方在目的港做好接货和卸货的准备，并及时办理进口清关等手续。如按 FOB 或 CFR 条件成交，买方接到此项装运通知后，还需办理货物运输保险的投保手续。按照国际贸易惯例，如因卖方漏发或未及时发出此项装运通知，致使买方漏保或未及时投保，则卖方应负担买方因此而遭受的有关损失装货单如图 8-3 所示。

When the transaction is concluded under CIF, CFR or FOB, the sellers shall immediately inform the buyers of the contract No., commodity, number of packages, weight, invoice value, vessel name and shipment date of the goods after they are loaded, so that the buyers can prepare for receiving and unloading the goods at the port of destination and go through import clearance procedures in a timely manner. If the transaction is concluded under FOB or CFR, the buyers shall insure for carriage of goods after receiving this Shipping Advice. According to international trade customs, if the buyers fail to buy insurance in time due to the sellers' omission or failure to issue such shipping advice, the sellers shall bear the relevant losses suffered by the buyers. Shipping order is shows in Figure 8-3.

第八章拓展知识、专业词汇和练习

▽

委托号：

Forwarding agents

B/L No.（编号）

第二联 Second Copy

装货单
Shipping Order
场站收据副本
Copy of Dock Receipt

Shipper（发货人）：

Consignee（收货人）

Notify Party（通知人）

Received by the Carrier the Total number of containers or other packages or units stated below to be transported subject to the terms and conditions of the Carrier's regular form of Bill of Lading (for Combined Transport or port to Port Shipment) which shall be deemed to be incorporated herein..

Date(日期)：

场站章
Seal of Terminal

Pre carriage by（前程运输）		Place of Receipt（收货地点）
Ocean Vessel（船名）	Voy. No.（航次）	Port of Loading（装货港）
Port of Discharge（卸货港）	Place of Delivery（交货地点）	Final Destination for Merchant's Reference（目的地）

Container No.（集装箱号）	Seal No.（封志号） Marks & Nos.（标记与号码）	No. of containers Or P'kgs. 箱数或件数	Kind Packages: Description of Goods（包装种类与货名）	Gross Weight 毛重（公斤）	Measurement 尺码（立方米）

TOTAL NUMBER OF CONTAINERS OR PACKAGES (IN WORDS) 集装箱数或件数合计（大写）	

Container No.（箱号）	Seal No.（封志号）	Pkgs.（件数）	Container No.（箱号）	Seal No.（封志号）	Pkgs.（件数）

Received（实收）	By Terminal clerk/Tally clerk（场站员/理货员签字）

FREIGHT & CHARGES	Prepaid at（预付地点）	Payable at（到付地点）	Place of Issue（签发地点）	BOOKING（订舱确认） APPROVED BY
	Total Prepaid（预付总额）	No.of Original B(s)/L（正本提单份数）	货值金额：Value of Goods:	

Service Type on Receiving	Service Type on Delivery	Reeter Temperature Required（冷藏温度）	°F	℃
□-CY, □-CFS, □-DOOR	□-CY, □-CFS, □-DOORS			

TYPE OF GOODS（种类）	□Ordinary,（普通）	□Reefer,（冷藏）	□Dangerous,（危险品）	□Auto.（裸装车辆）	危险品 Dangerous Goods	Glass:
						Property:
	□Liquid,（液体）	□Live Animal,（活动物）	□Bulk,（散货）	□ ______		IMDG Code Page:
						UN NO.

发货人或代理人名称地址：Name and Address of Consigner or Agent:			联系人：Contact:	电话：Tel.:
可否转船：Transhipment:	可否分批 Partial Shipment:	装期：Latest Shipment Date:	备注 Remarks	装箱场站名称：Name of Container Terminal:
效期：Expiry Date:		制单日期：Prepared on:		
运费由 Freight to be paid by	支付，如预付运费托收承兑，请填准银行帐号 In the case of a Prepaid Freight Collection Acceptance, please fill in the bank account number accurately			

图 8-3　装货单

Figure 8-3　Shipping Order (S/O)

第九章　国际货物运输保险
Chapter 9　International Cargo Insurance

导　读
Introduction

　　保险是一种经济补偿制度。从法律角度来看，它是一种补偿性契约行为，被保险人（insured）向保险人（insurer）提供一定的对价（保险费），保险人则对被保险人将来可能遭受的承保范围内的损失负赔偿责任。

　　Insurance is an economic compensation system. From the legal point of view, it is a compensatory contractual act. The insured provides certain consideration (premium) to the insurer, and the insurer shall be liable for the losses that the insured may suffer within the coverage in the future.

　　保险的种类有很多，国际货物运输保险属于财产保险的范畴。货物运输保险已经成为国际贸易中不可缺少的组成部分。国际货物运输保险是指被保险人（卖方或买方）对一批或若干批货物向保险公司按照一定金额投保一定险别并交纳保险费，保险公司承保后，如果所保货物在运输途中发生承保范围内的损失，保险公司按保单的规定给予被保险人经济上的补偿。

　　There are many kinds of insurance, and the international cargo insurance falls under the category of property insurance. Cargo insurance has become an indispensable part of international trade. International cargo insurance refers to that the insured (sellers or buyers) insures one or more batches of goods with a certain amount of insurance and pays a premium. After being covered by the insurance company, if the insured goods suffer losses within the scope of coverage during carriage, the insurance company shall make economic compensation to the insured according to the provisions of the policy.

　　国际贸易中的货物一般都需经过长途运输，在整个运输过程中可能会遇到自然灾害或意外事故而使货物遭受损失。为了更好地将不可预知的风险转移给保险公司，使贸易得以顺利进行，货物装运前宜办理货运保险。

　　Carriage of goods in international trade generally involves long-distance transportation, and may encounter natural calamity or fortuitous accidents during the whole process of carriage, causing losses to the goods. In order to better transfer of unpredictable risks to the insurance company and facilitate smooth trade, cargo insurance shall be handled before shipment.

　　由于国际贸易中的货物可采取的运输方式有很多，如海洋运输、铁路运输、航空运输、公路运输和邮包运输等，国际货物运输保险也相应地分为海运货物保险、陆路运输货物保险、航空运输货物保险和邮包运输保险。

　　As there are many possible transportation modes for goods in international trade, such as ocean transportation, railway transportation, air transportation, road transportation and parcel post transportation, the international cargo insurance is correspondingly divided into marine cargo insurance, inland transit insurance, air cargo insurance and parcel post insurance.

第一节　海运货物保险的承保范围
Section 1　Coverage of Marine Cargo Insurance

海上运输货物风险很大，保险公司为了保证外贸业务的正常开展，根据海上运输的特点设置了海运货物保险承保的范围，包括保障的风险、保障的损失与保障的费用。

Carriage of goods by sea is very risky. In order to ensure the normal development of foreign trade business, the insurance company has set up the coverage of marine cargo insurance according to the characteristics of ocean transportation, including the risks, losses and expenses covered.

一、海运货物保险保障的风险
I. Risks Covered by Marine Cargo Insurance

对于海上货物运输，保险公司承保的风险有海上风险和外来风险两类。

For the carriage of goods by sea, there are two types of risks covered by the insurance company: perils of the sea and extraneous risks.

（一）海上风险 (Perils of the Sea)

海上风险也称为海难，包括自然灾害（natural calamity）和意外事故（fortuitous accidents）。自然灾害在这里是指因自然力量所造成的灾害，但并不泛指一切由自然界力量引起的灾害，而是具有特定的范围，如恶劣气候、雷电、海啸、地震、火山爆发、洪水、流冰等。意外事故在这里是指因意外原因造成的事故，但并不泛指海上发生的所有意外事故，而是具有特定的范围，如运输工具遭受搁浅、触礁、沉没、碰撞、失踪、失火、爆炸等。

Perils of the sea, also known as shipwrecks, include natural calamity and fortuitous accidents. Natural calamity here refers to disasters caused by natural forces, but does not generally refer to all disasters caused by natural forces. It has a specific scope, such as severe climate, lightning, tsunami, earthquake, volcanic eruption, flood and floating ice. Fortuitous accidents here refer to accidents caused by unexpected reasons, but do not generally refer to all Fortuitous accidents occurring at sea. They have specific scope, such as stranding, reef strike, sinking, collision, disappearance, fire and explosion of means of conveyance.

（二）外来风险 (Extraneous Risks)

外来风险包括一般外来风险（general extraneous risks）和特殊外来风险（special extraneous risks）。一般外来风险指被保险货物在运输途中由于一般外来原因所造成的风险，主要包括偷窃、玷污、渗漏、破碎、受热受潮、串味、生锈、钩损、淡水雨淋、碰损、短量、提货不着等。特殊外来风险指由于军事、政治、国家政策法令以及行政措施等特殊外来原因所造成的风险，主要包括战争、罢工、货物被有关当局拒绝进口或没收、船舶被扣导致交货不到等。

Extraneous risks include general extraneous risks and special extraneous risks. General extraneous risks refer to the risks caused by general external reasons during the carriage of the insured goods, mainly including theft, contamination, leakage, crushing, heating and dampness, odor mixing, rust, hook damage, fresh water & rain damage, collision damage, shortage, non-delivery, etc. Special extraneous risks refer to the risks caused by special external reasons such as military, political, national policies and decrees and administrative measures, mainly including war, strike, refusal of import or confiscation of goods by relevant authorities, detention of ships resulting in non-delivery, etc.

二、海运货物保险保障的损失
II. Losses Covered by Marine Cargo Insurance

海上货物运输损失,简称海损(average),是指被保险货物在海运途中,因遭受海上风险而产生的损失。在保险业务中海损一般还包括与海运相连接的陆上运输和内河运输过程中所发生的损失。按损失程度的不同,海损可分为全部损失和部分损失;按货物损失性质的不同,海损又可分为共同海损和单独海损。

Loss of goods transported by sea, referred to as "average", refers to the loss of the insured goods caused by perils of the sea in transit. Average in the insurance business generally includes losses incurred during land transportation and inland water transportation connected to ocean transportation. According to the degree of loss, average can be divided into total loss and partial loss; according to the nature of cargo loss, average can be further divided into general average and particular average.

(一)全部损失和部分损失 (Total Loss and Partial Loss)

(1)全部损失(total loss)又称全损,是指被保险货物全部遭受损失。按损失的情况,全部损失可以分为实际全损(actual total loss, ATL)和推定全损(constructive total loss, CTL)。实际全损是指物质性的消失,推定全损是指虽未达到全部货物的物质性灭失,但避免实际全损所需费用超过了其货值本身。需要注意的是,在海上保险业务中,全损的概念不是以一艘船上载运的全部货物的完全灭失为划分标准,保险人对全损范围的界定通常在保险条款中以文字加以说明。

(1) Total loss, or TL, means that all insured goods have suffered losses. According to the situation of loss, total loss can be divided into actual total loss (ATL) and constructive total loss (CTL). ATL refers to the physical disappearance of goods, while CTL refers to the cost of avoiding ATL exceeding the value of goods themselves although not all goods are physically destroyed. It should be noted that in the marine insurance business, the concept of total loss is not based on the complete loss of all goods carried on a ship. The insurer's definition of the scope of total loss is usually explained in writing in the insurance clause.

以下情况可以被认为是发生了实际全损:①被保险货物完全灭失,如船舶触礁后船货同时沉入海底;②货物实际上已经不可能归还被保险人,如货物被敌方扣押无法拿回;③货物丧失原有用途和价值,如水泥被海水浸泡成为硬块;④船舶失踪超过两个月仍无讯息。

ATL may be considered to have occurred under the following circumstances: ① complete loss of the insured goods, such as when the ship sinks deep into the sea at the same time after being hit by a reef; ② it is physically impossible for the goods to be returned to the insured, such as when the goods are detained by the enemy and cannot be taken back; ③ the goods lose their original use and value, such as when cement is soaked in seawater and becomes hard; ④ there is still no information about the ship missing for more than two months.

属于推定全损的情况包括:①货损后,修复费用超过货物修复后的价值;②货损后,整理和续运到目的地的费用超过货物到达目的地的价值;③实际全损已不可避免,或为避免全损所需的施救费用将超过获救后的价值;④被保险人失去货物所有权,而收回所有权所需支出的费用将超过收回后的货物价值。

Situations attributable to CTL include: ① after the goods are damaged, the repair cost exceeds the value of the goods after repair; ② after the goods are damaged, the cost of sorting out and subsequent transportation to the destination exceeds the value of the goods arriving at the destination; ③ ATL is unavoidable or sue & labor charges required to avoid total loss will exceed the value after salvage; ④ the insured loses the ownership of the goods, and the expenses required to recover the ownership will exceed the value of the recovered goods.

在推定全损的情况下，被保险人可以获得的损失赔偿有以下两种情况：①办理委付，获得全损的赔偿；②不办理委付，获得部分损失的赔偿。委付是海上货物运输保险中处理索赔的一种特殊做法，是指被保险人在保险标的处于推定全损时，向保险人声明愿意将保险标的的一切权益，包括财产权及一切由此产生的权利与义务转让给保险人，并要求保险人按全损给予赔偿的一种行为。在实务中的具体做法是，在推定全损发生后，被保险人如需获得全损的赔偿，应立即以书面或口头方式向保险人发出委付通知。

In case of CTL, the insured can obtain compensation for loss in the following two ways: ① compensation for total loss if entrusted; ② compensation for partial loss if not entrusted. Entrustment is a special method to deal with claim in marine cargo insurance, which means that the insured makes a statement to the insurer that he/she is willing to transfer all rights and interests of the subject matter insured, including bale property rights and all rights and obligations arising therefrom, to the insurer when the subject matter insured is under CTL, and requires the insurer to make compensation according to the total loss. In practice, the insured shall give written or verbal notices of abandonment to the insurer immediately after the occurrence of a CTL for which indemnity is sought.

（2）部分损失（partial loss）是指被保险货物的损失没有达到全部损失的程度。

(2) Partial loss refers to the extent that the loss of the insured goods does not reach total loss.

（二）共同海损和单独海损 (General Average and Particular Average)

1. 共同海损 (General Average)

共同海损是指载货的船舶在海上遇到灾害、事故，威胁到船、货各方的共同安全，为了解除这种威胁，维护船、货安全，或者使航程得以完成，由船方有意识地、合理地做出某些特殊牺牲或支出的某些特殊费用。例如，某海轮的舱面上装有 1000 台拖拉机，航行中遭遇大风浪袭击，450 台拖拉机被卷入海中，海轮严重倾斜，如不立即采取措施，则有翻船的危险。船长下令将余下的 550 台拖拉机全部抛入海中，船舶得以继续安全行驶。此时被抛入海的 550 台拖拉机的损失就是共同海损。共同海损的成立，必须具备一定的条件。

General average refers to some special sacrifices or expenses made by the shipowner consciously and reasonably to take measures in order to eliminate such threats, maintain the safety of the ship and cargo, or complete the voyage when the ship carrying cargo encounters disasters or accidents at sea. For example, there are 1,000 tractors on the deck of a seagoing ship. When it was hit by strong waves during navigation, 450 tractors were swept into the sea and the ship tilted seriously. If immediate measures were not taken, there would be a risk of overturning. The captain ordered all the remaining 550 tractors to be thrown into the sea, so that the ship could continue to navigate safely. The loss of the 550 tractors jettisoned at this time is the general average. The formation of general average must meet certain conditions.

（1）导致共同海损的危险必须是真实存在的，并危及船、货的共同安全；

(1) The hazards leading to general average must be real and endanger the common safety of ships and cargoes;

（2）共同海损措施必须是为了解除船、货的共同危险，人为地、有意识地采取的合理措施；

(2) General average measures must be reasonable measures taken artificially and consciously to eliminate the common danger of ships and cargoes;

（3）共同海损的牺牲是有特殊性质的，费用损失必须是额外支付的；

(3) The sacrifice of general average is special in nature, and the losses must be paid additionally;

（4）共同海损的损失必须是共同海损措施的直接的、合理的后果；

(4) The loss of general average must be a direct and reasonable consequence of the general average measures;

（5）共同海损措施最终必须有效。

(5) General average measures must ultimately be effective.

船舶在遭受共同海损后，凡属共同海损范围内的牺牲或费用均应由获救受益方（船方、货方和运费收入方）根据获救价值按比例分摊，这种分摊称为共同海损分摊。

Any sacrifices or expenses of a ship falling within the scope of general average shall be apportioned among the salved parties (shipowner, cargo owner and freight receiver) in proportion to the value salved after the ship has suffered general average. Such apportionment is referred to as GA contribution.

2. 单独海损 (Particular Average)

单独海损是指被保险货物遭受海损后，其损失未达到全部损失的程度，仅由受损方单独承担的部分损失。与共同海损相比，单独海损有以下三个特点：①它不是人为有意造成的部分损失；②它是保险标的本身的损失；③单独海损仅由受损失的被保险人单独承担，但其可根据损失情况从保险人处获得赔偿。

Particular average refers to the extent that the loss of the insured goods does not reach the total loss after suffering from average losses, and it is only a partial loss solely borne by the damaged party. Compared with general average, particular average has the following three characteristics: ① It is not a partial loss intentionally caused by human factors; ② It is a loss of the subject matter insured; ③ The particular average is solely borne by the insured suffering losses, but it can be indemnified from the insurer according to the circumstances of the loss.

三、海运货物保险保障的费用
III. Expenses Covered by Marine Cargo Insurance

海上运输风险导致的费用主要有以下两种。

There are mainly two types of expenses caused by the risks of sea carriage.

（一）施救费用 (Sue & Labor Charges)

施救费用又称营救费用或损害防止费用，是指当保险标的遭遇保险责任范围内的灾害事故时，被保险人或其代理人为防止损失的扩大而采取抢救措施所支出的费用。

Sue & labor charges, also known as salvage money, refers to the expenses paid by the insured or its agents for taking rescue measures to avoid aggravation of the loss when the subject matter insured encounters a disaster within the scope of cover.

各国保险法规或保险条款一般都规定：保险人对施救费用应承担赔偿责任，赔偿金额以不超过该批货物的保险金额为限。

Insurance laws or clauses in various countries generally stipulate that the insurer shall be liable for compensation of sue & labor charges, with an amount not exceeding the insured amount of this batch of goods.

（二）救助费用 (Salvage Charges)

救助费用是指保险标的遭遇承保范围内的灾害事故时，由保险人和被保险人以外的第三者采取救助措施并获成功，由被救助方支付给救助方的一种报酬。

Salvage charges refers to a kind of remuneration paid by the salved party to the salvor after the insurer and a third party other than the insured succeed in taking rescue measures when the subject matter insured encounters a disaster within the coverage.

救助费用一般都可以列为共同海损的费用项目。各国的保险法规或保险条款一般都规定：保险人对救助费用承担赔偿责任。

Salvage charges can generally be categorized as general average cost items. Insurance laws or clauses in various countries generally stipulate that the insurer shall be liable for compensation of salvage charges.

第二节 中国海运货物保险条款
Section 2　China Marine Cargo Insurance Clauses

为了适应国际货物海运保险的需要，中国人民保险公司（PICC）根据我国保险实际情况，并参照国际保险市场的习惯做法，分别制定了适用于各种运输方式的货物保险条款，总称"中国保险条款（China Insurance Clauses, CIC）"。其中，根据中国人民保险公司（PICC）制定的《海洋运输货物保险条款》（2009版）（Ocean Marine Cargo Clauses dated 2009），海洋运输货物保险条款包括基本险和附加险的保险范围、保险责任的起讫与除外责任等内容。

In order to meet the needs of international marine cargo insurance, PICC Property and Casualty Company Limited has formulated cargo insurance clauses applicable to various transportation modes according to the actual situation of China's insurance industry and with reference to the customary practices in the international insurance market, which are collectively referred to as "China Insurance Clauses (CIC)". According to the provisions of Ocean Marine Cargo Clauses dated 2009 formulated by PICC, China ocean marine cargo clauses include the coverage of the basic risks and additional risks, the commencement, termination and exclusion of insurance liability.

一、基本险
I. Basic Risks

基本险又称主险，可单独投保。根据我国海洋运输货物保险条款，基本险包括平安险、水渍险和一切险三种。

Basic risks, also known as main risks, can be covered separately. According to ocean marine cargo clauses, basic risks include free from particular average (FPA), with particular average (WPA/WA) and all risks.

（一）平安险 (FPA)

"平安险"一词是我国保险业的习惯叫法，其英文含义是单独海损不赔偿。平安险（free from particular average, FPA）的责任范围主要包括以下几种。

"FPA" is a common term in China's insurance industry, and it means "free of particular average". The scope of cover of FPA mainly includes the following.

（1）被保险货物在运输途中由于恶劣气候、雷电、海啸、地震、洪水等自然灾害造成整批货物的实际全损或推定全损。如果被保险货物用驳船运往或运离海轮，则每一艘驳船所装的货物可视为一个整批。

(1) ATL or CTL of the insured goods during carriage due to natural calamity such as severe weather, lightning, tsunami, earthquake and flood. If the insured goods are transported by barge to or from a seagoing vessel, the cargo loaded on each barge shall be deemed as one whole lot.

（2）运输工具搁浅、触礁、沉没、互撞、与流冰或其他物体碰撞，以及失火、爆炸等意外事故造成货物的全部或部分损失。

(2) Total or partial loss of goods caused by fortuitous accidents such as stranding, reef strike, sinking, mutual collision of means of conveyance, collision with floating ice or other objects, fire and explosion.

（3）在运输工具已经发生搁浅、触礁、沉没、焚毁等意外事故的情况下，货物在此前后又在海上遭遇恶劣气候、雷电、海啸等自然灾害所造成的部分损失。

(3) Partial loss caused by inclement weather, thunder and lightning, tsunami and other natural calamity before or after fortuitous accidents such as stranding, reef strike, sinking and burning of means of conveyance.

（4）在装卸或转船时，一件或数件甚至整批货物落海所造成的全部或部分损失。

(4) Total or partial loss caused by one or more piece(s) or even whole batch of goods falling into the sea during handling or transshipment.

（5）被保险人对遭受承保责任内危险的货物采取抢救、防止或减少货损的措施所支付的合理费用，但以不超过该批被救货物的保险金额为限。

(5) Reasonable expenses paid by the insured for taking measures to rescue, prevent or reduce damage to goods suffering from dangers within the scope of cover, but not exceeding the insured amount of this batch of salvaged goods.

（6）运输工具遭遇海难后，在避难港由卸货所引起的损失及在中途港、避难港由于卸货、存仓以及运送货物所产生的特别费用。

(6) Losses caused by unloading at the port of refuge and special expenses incurred in unloading, warehousing and transporting goods at intermediate ports or ports of refuge after a shipwreck.

（7）共同海损的牺牲、分摊和救助费用。

(7) Sacrifice, contribution and salvage charges of general average.

（8）运输合同中订有"船舶互撞责任"条款的，根据该条款规定应由货方偿还船方的损失。

(8) Where there is a "Both-to-Blame Collision (BTB)" clause in the contract of carriage, the cargo owner shall reimburse the shipowner for its losses according to this clause.

（二）水渍险 (WPA/WA)

"水渍险"也是我国保险业沿用已久的名称，其英文含义是负责单独海损的赔偿。水渍险（with particular average, WPA/WA）的责任范围主要包括以下两部分。

"WPA/WA" is also a long-standing term used in China's insurance industry, which means "With Particular Average". The coverage of WPA/WA mainly includes the following two parts.

（1）平安险所承保的范围。

(1) The scope covered by FPA.

（2）被保险货物由于恶劣气候、雷电、海啸、地震、洪水等自然灾害所造成的部分损失。

(2) Partial loss of the insured goods caused by natural calamity such as harsh climate, thunder and lightning, tsunami, earthquake and flood.

（三）一切险 (All Risks)

一切险是三种基本险别中承保责任范围最大的一种，其责任范围主要包括以下两部分。

All risks is the one with the largest coverage among the three basic types of insurance, and its coverage mainly includes the following two parts.

（1）水渍险所承保的范围。

(1) The scope covered by WPA/WA.

（2）被保险货物由于一般外来风险所造成的全部损失或部分损失。

(2) Total loss or partial loss of the insured goods due to general extraneous risks.

由此可见，一切险是水渍险和一般附加险的总和，但不包括特殊附加险。

It can be seen that all risks are the sum of WPA/WA and general additional risks, but does not include special additional risks.

二、附加险
II. Additional Risks

附加险是基本险的扩大和补充，不能单独投保，只能在投保一种基本险后加保，但是可以加保一种或数种附加险。根据我国"海洋运输货物保险条款（2009版）"，附加险可分为一般附加险、特殊附加险和特别附加险。

Additional risks are the extension and supplement of basic risks, which cannot be covered separately. It can only be added after insuring a basic risk, but one or more additional risks can be added. According to Ocean Marine Cargo Clauses dated 2009, additional risks can be divided into general additional risks, Special additional risks and specific additional risks.

（一）一般附加险 (General Additional Risks)

一般附加险承保的是一般外来风险造成的全部或部分损失。一般附加险主要有11种，具体的险别名称和承保范围如下。

General Additional Risks cover total or partial loss caused by General Extraneous Risks. There are mainly 11 general additional risks, and the specific risk names and coverage are as follows.

（1）偷窃、提货不着险（theft, pilferage and non-delivery, T.P.N.D），承保货物因遭偷窃，以及货物运抵目的地以后，货物的全部或整件提货不着的损失。

(1) Theft, pilferage and non-delivery (T.P.N.D), which covers the loss of goods due to theft and failure to pick up all or a whole package of goods after they arrive at their destination.

（2）淡水雨淋险（fresh water & rain damage, F.W.R.D），承保因淡水、雨水、融雪，包括舱汗、船舱淡水管漏水等造成货物浸水导致的损失。

(2) Fresh water & rain damage (F.W.R.D), which covers the losses caused by flooding of goods due to fresh water, rainwater, snowmelt, cabin sweat and leakage of cabin fresh water pipes.

（3）短量险（risk of shortage），承保袋装或散装货的数量或重量短少的损失。

(3) Risk of shortage, which covers the loss due to insufficient quantity or weight of cargo in bag or bulk.

（4）混杂、玷污险（risk of intermixture & contamination），承保货物因混入杂质或被玷污所造成的损失，如油漆污染了地毯、矿砂、矿石等混进了泥土、草屑等。

(4) Risk of intermixture & contamination, which refers to the loss caused by impurities or contamination of insured goods, such as paint polluting carpets, mineral sand and ore mixed with soil and grass cuttings.

（5）渗漏险（risk of leakage），承保流质或半流质货物因包装容器损坏发生渗漏造成货物短量的损失，或用液体浸泡的货物因液体流失而变质的损失。

(5) Risk of leakage, which covers the loss of liquid or semi-liquid goods due to leakage caused by damage to packing containers, or the loss of liquid soaked goods due to deterioration.

（6）碰损、破碎险（risk of clash breakage），承保易碎货物，如陶瓷器皿、玻璃花瓶、大理石等，因受压、碰撞和震动而出现破碎、凹瘪等的损失。

(6) Risk of clash breakage, which covers the loss of fragile goods such as ceramics, glass vases and marble due to pressure, collision and vibration.

（7）串味险（risk of odor），承保同舱装载的货物因受到异味的影响而使品质受到损坏，如茶叶、香料、药材等在运输过程中受到一起堆储的皮革、樟脑丸的影响而造成的串味损失。

(7) Risk of odor, which covers the damage to the quality of goods loaded in the same cabin due to the influence of peculiar smell, such as tea, spices and medicinal materials affected by leather and camphor pills stacked together during the carriage.

（8）受热、受潮险（damage caused by heating & sweating），承保航行途中，气温骤变或船上通风设备失灵使船上水汽凝结，货物受潮或受热所导致的损失。

(8) Damage caused by heating & sweating, which covers the loss caused by moisture condensation, dampness or heating of goods due to sudden temperature change or failure of ventilation equipment on board during voyage.

（9）钩损险（hook damage），承保装卸过程中使用钩子时，或因碰撞使货物遭受钩损，或因钩破包装使货物外漏、散失的损失，以及为修补、调换包装所支付的费用。

(9) Hook damage, which covers the loss of goods caused by hook damage during loading and unloading, or collision, or leakage or scattering of goods due to cracked packing, as well as the expenses paid for repairing or replacing packing.

（10）包装破裂险（loss or damage caused by breakage of packing），承保因运输或装卸不慎，包装破裂所造成的损失，以及为满足继续安全运输的需要而对包装进行修补或调换所支付的费用。

(10) Loss or damage caused by breakage of packing, which covers the loss caused by careless carriage or handling and packing breakage, as well as the expenses paid for repairing or replacing the packing to meet the needs of continued safe carriage.

（11）锈损险（risk of rust），承保运输途中因货物生锈造成的损失。

(11) Risk of rust, which covers the loss caused by rusting of goods in transit.

（二）特殊附加险 (Special Additional Risks)

特殊附加险承保的是由特殊外来风险造成的全部或部分损失，常见的有战争险和罢工险。

Special additional risks cover total or partial loss caused by special extraneous risks, commonly including war risk and strike risk.

（1）战争险（war risk），承保战争、类似战争、敌对行为、武装冲突或海盗引起的被保险货物的直接损失；由上述行为引起的捕获、拘留、扣留、禁制、扣押所造成的损失；各种常规武器，包括水雷、鱼雷、炸弹所致的损失；本条款责任范围内引起的共同海损的牺牲、分摊和救助费用。

(1) War risk, covering direct loss of the insured goods caused by war, warlike and hostile acts, armed conflicts or piracy; loss caused by capture, detention, restraint or seizure arising from the above acts; loss caused by conventional weapons, including mines, torpedoes and bombs; average general sacrifice, contribution and salvage charges arising within the scope of cover under this clause.

（2）罢工险（strike risk），承保由于罢工者、被迫停工工人或参加工潮、暴动、民众斗争的人员的行为，或任何人的恶意行为所造成的直接损失和上述行动或行为所引起的共同海损的牺牲、分摊和救助费用。

(2) Covering direct losses and average general sacrifice, contribution and salvage charges resulting from acts of strikers, forced lockout workers or persons participating in labor disturbances, riots, civil commotion or malicious acts of any person.

需要注意的是，按照国际保险市场的习惯做法，被保险货物如已投保战争险，再加保罢工险时，一般不再加收保险费。中国人民保险公司也采用该做法。

It should be noted that according to the customary practice in the international insurance market, if the insured goods have been covered against war risk and strike risk, no additional premium will be charged. This approach is also adopted by PICC.

（三）**特别附加险 (Specific Additional Risks)**

特别附加险的承保范围多与国家行政法令、政策措施及航海贸易习惯有关，包括交货不到险（failure to deliver risk）、进口关税险（import duty risk）、舱面险（deck risk）、拒收险（rejection risk）、黄曲霉素险（aflatoxin risk）、出口货物到中国香港（包括九龙）或中国澳门存储火险责任扩展条款（fire risk extension clause for storage of cargo at destination HK, including Kowloon, or Macao）。

The coverage of specific additional risks is mostly closely related to national administrative acts, policy measures and seafaring teade practices, including failure to deliver risk, import duty risk, deck risk, rejection risk, aflatoxin risk, fire risk extension clause for storage of cargo at destination HK, including Kowloon, or Macao.

三、保险责任的起讫与除外责任
III. Commencement, Termination and Exclusion of Insurance Liability

我国的"海洋运输货物保险条款（2009版）"除了规定上述基本险和附加险的承保范围外，还对保险责任的起讫和除外责任做了具体的规定。

Ocean Marine Cargo Clauses dated 2009 not only stipulate the coverage of the above-mentioned basic risks and additional risks, but also makes specific provisions on the commencement, termination and exclusion of insurance liability.

（一）**保险责任的起讫 (Commencement and Termination of Insurance Liability)**

保险责任的起讫又称承保责任期限，是指保险人承担责任的起讫时限。国际保险业惯用"仓至仓条款"（Warehouse-to-Warehouse Clause, W/W clause）来规定保险期限。我国海洋运输货物保险条款对"仓至仓条款"的规定如下。

The commencement and termination of insurance liability, also known as the period of liability covered, refers to the time limit for the Insurer to bear the liability. W/W clause is commonly used in the international insurance industry to specify the period of insurance. The provisions of "Warehouse-to-Warehouse Clause (W/W clause)" in Ocean Marine Cargo Clauses are as follows.

（1）仓至仓条款是指保险人对被保险货物所承担的保险责任，自被保险货物运离（此处的"运离"指货物在仓库或储存处所开始搬动时起算）保险单所载明的起运地仓库或储存处所开始运输时生效，包括正常运输过程中的海上、陆上、内河和驳船运输在内，直至该项货物到达（此处的"到达"是指运至并完成卸货）保险单所载明目的地收货人的最后仓库或储存处所，或被保险人用作分配、分派或非正常运输的其他储存处所为止。如未抵达上述仓库或储存处所，则以被保险货物在最后卸载港全部卸离海轮后满60天为止。如在上述60天内被保险货物需转运到非保险单所载明的目的地，则承保责任在该项货物开始转运时终止。

(1) W/W clause refers to the insurance liability assumed by the insurer for the insured goods. It shall take effect from the time when the insured goods are transported away ("transportation" here means the time when the goods start to move in the warehouse or storage facilities) and the carriage begins at the "from" warehouse

or storage facilities specified in the policy, including sea, land, river and barge transportation during regular carriage, until the goods arrive at the last warehouse or storage facilities of the consignee of destination specified in the policy ("arrival" here means completion of delivery and unloading), or other storage facilities used by the insured for distribution, assignment or irregular carriage. If the insured goods have not arrived at the above warehouse or storage facilities, the period shall be 60 days after they are completely discharged from the seagoing vessel at the final port of discharge. If transshipment of the insured goods to a destination other than that stated in the policy is required within the said 60 days, the coverage shall terminate at the commencement of such transshipment.

（2）被保险人无法控制的运输延迟、绕道、被迫卸货、重新装载、转载或承运人运用运输契约赋予的权限所做的任何航海上的变更或终止运输契约，致使被保险货物被运到非保险单所载明的目的地时，在被保险人及时将获知的情况通知保险人，并在必要时加交保险费的情况下，本保险仍继续有效，保险责任按下列规定终止：①被保险货物如在非保险单所载明的目的地出售，保险责任至交货时为止，但不论任何情况，均以被保险货物在卸载港全部卸离海轮后满 60 天为止；②被保险货物如在上述 60 天期限内继续运往保险单所载原目的地或其他目的地，保险责任仍按上述第 1 条的规定终止。

(2) If the insured goods are transported to a destination other than that stated in the policy due to delay, detour, forced unloading, reloading, transshipment beyond the control of the Insured or any nautical change made by the carrier using the authority given in the contract of carriage or termination of the contract of carriage, this insurance shall remain valid after the insured timely notifies the insurer of the situation and pays the premium if necessary. The insurance liability shall be terminated as follows: ① If the insured goods are sold at a destination other than that stated in the policy, the insurance liability shall continue until delivery but in no event later than 60 days after all of the insured goods have been discharged from the seagoing vessel at the port of discharge; ② If the insured goods continue to be transported to the original destination or other destinations specified in the policy within the above-mentioned 60 days, the insurance liability shall still terminate as stipulated in Article 1 above.

战争险的责任起讫不是"仓至仓"，而是以"水上危险"为限，即以货物装上保险单载明的装运港海轮或驳船开始，到货物卸离保险单载明的目的港海轮或驳船为止。如果被保险货物不卸离海轮或驳船，保险责任期限以海轮到达目的港当日午夜起算 15 天为止。

The liability for war risk is not "W/W" but limited to "marine perils", i.e. from the time when the goods are loaded onto the seagoing vessel or barge at port of shipment specified in the policy to the time when the goods are discharged from the seagoing vessel or barge at port of destination specified in the policy. If the insured goods are not discharged from the seagoing vessel or barge, the period of insurance liability shall be 15 days from midnight on the day when the seagoing vessel arrives at port of destination.

罢工险的保险责任起讫与基本险一致，采用"仓至仓"原则。

The commencement and termination of insurance liability for strike risk are consistent with those for basic risks, and the principle of "W/W" is adopted.

（二）除外责任 (Exclusion)

除外责任是指保险人不负赔偿责任的范围。根据我国海洋运输货物保险条款的规定，下列损失不在平安险、水渍险和一切险的承保范围内。

Exclusion refers to the scope within which the Insurer is not liable for compensation. According to the provisions of Ocean Marine Cargo Clauses, the following losses are not covered by FPA, WPA/WA and All risks.

（1）被保险人的故意行为或过失所造成的损失；

(1) Loss caused by intentional acts or negligence of the insured;

（2）属于发货人责任所引起的损失；

(2) Loss caused by the consignor;

（3）在保险责任开始前，被保险货物已存在的品质不良或数量短差所造成的损失；

(3) Loss caused by existing poor quality or quantity shortage of the insured goods before commencement of insurance liability;

（4）被保险货物的自然损耗、本质缺陷、特性以及市价跌落、运输延迟所造成的损失或费用；

(4) Natural wear and tear, inherent defects and characteristics of the insured goods, as well as loss or expense caused by falling market and delay in carriage;

（5）战争险和罢工险条款规定的责任范围和除外责任。

(5) Coverage and exclusion under war risk and strike risk clauses.

第三节　伦敦保险协会海运货物保险条款
Section 3　Institute Cargo Clauses

在世界海运保险中，英国是一个海运历史悠久和海运业务比较发达的国家，长期以来，它所制定的各种保险规章制度对世界各国有着广泛的影响，其中包括海运保险单格式和保险条款。目前，世界上有很多国家在海运保险业务中，直接采用伦敦保险协会制定的协会货物条款（Institute Cargo Clauses, ICC）或者在制定本国保险条款时参考或部分采用上述条款。

The United Kingdom is a country with a long history of shipping and relatively developed shipping business in the global marine insurance. For a long time, various insurance rules and regulations formulated by it have had wide influence on all countries in the world, including the format of marine insurance policy and insurance clauses. At present, many countries in the world directly adopt Institute Cargo Clauses (ICC) formulated by the Institute of London Underwriters or refer to or partially adopt them when formulating their own insurance clauses.

"协会货物条款"最早制定于1912年，为了适应不同时期法律、判例、商业、航运等方面的变化和发展，需要经常对条款进行补充和修订，最新一次修订完成于2009年1月1日。伦敦保险协会的"海运货物保险条款"主要有以下六种。

"Institute Cargo Clauses" was first formulated in 1912. In order to adapt to the changes and developments of laws, precedents, commerce, shipping and other aspects in different periods, it is necessary to supplement and revise the clauses frequently. The latest revision was completed on January 1, 2009. There are six main types of Marine Cargo Insurance Clauses issued by ILU.

（1）协会货物条款（A），简称ICC(A)；

(1) Institute Cargo Clauses(A);

（2）协会货物条款（B），简称ICC(B)；

(2) Institute Cargo Clauses(B);

（3）协会货物条款（C），简称ICC(C)；

(3) Institute Cargo Clauses(C);

（4）协会货物战争险条款（货物），简称IWCC；

(4) Institute War Clauses- Cargo;

（5）协会货物罢工险条款（货物），简称ISCC；

(5) Institute Strikes Clauses- Cargo;

（6）恶意损害险条款。

(6) Malicious Damage Clauses.

这里主要介绍ICC(A)、ICC(B)、ICC(C)三种基本险别。

Here, ICC(A), ICC(B) and ICC(C) are mainly introduced.

一、ICC(A)的承保范围和除外责任
I. Coverage and Exclusion of ICC (A)

ICC(A)承保的责任范围最大，承保责任以一切风险减"除外责任"的形式出现，即"除外责任"项下所列风险不予负责，其他风险保险人都予承保。

ICC(A) covers the largest scope of liability, which appears in the form of all risks less "exclusion", that is, except for the risks listed under "Exclusion", all other risks are covered by the insurer.

ICC(A)的除外责任主要包括以下三种。

Exclusion of ICC (A) can be classified into three main types.

（1）一般除外责任，包括归因于被保险人故意的不法行为造成的损失或费用；自然渗漏、自然损耗、自然磨损、包装不当或准备不足造成的损失或保险标的内在缺陷或特性造成的损失或费用；直接由于延迟所引起的损失或费用；由于船舶所有人、经营人、租船人经营破产或不履行债务造成的损失或费用；使用任何原子或核子裂变和（或）聚变或其他类似反应或放射性物质的武器或设备直接或间接造成的损失或费用。

(1) General exclusion, including loss or expense attributable to wilful misconduct of the insured; loss or expense due to natural leakage, natural wear and tear, improper packing or inadequate preparation or due to defects or features inherent in the subject matter insured; loss or expense directly caused by delay; loss or expense caused by bankruptcy or non-performance of debts of vessel owner, operator and charter party; loss or expense directly or indirectly caused by the use of any atomic or nuclear fission and/or fusion or other similar reaction or radioactive material weapon or equipment.

（2）不适航、不适货除外责任。所谓不适航、不适货除外责任，是指保险标的在装船时，若被保险人或其受雇人已经知道船舶不适航，以及船舶、装运工具、集装箱等不适货，保险人不负赔偿责任。

(2) Exclusion of unseaworthiness and cargo unsuitability. The so-called exclusion of unseaworthiness and cargo unsuitability means that the insurer shall not be liable for compensation if the insured or its servants have known that the ship is unseaworthy, and the ship, carrier, container, etc are unsuitable for cargo when the subject matter insured is loaded on board.

（3）战争除外责任和罢工除外责任。

(3) War exclusion and strike exclusion.

二、ICC(B)的承保范围和除外责任
II. Coverage and Exclusion of ICC(B)

ICC(B)的承保范围采用列明风险的形式，凡属于列出的就是承保的，没有列出的，不论何种情况均不负责。凡归因于下列情况者均予以承保：火灾、爆炸；船舶或驳船触礁、搁浅、沉没；陆上运输工具碰撞出轨；船舶、驳船或运输工具与水以外的外界物体碰撞；在避难港卸货；地震、火山爆发、雷电；共同海损牺牲；抛货或浪击落海；海水、湖水或河水进入运输工

具或储存处所；货物在装卸时落海或跌落造成的整件全损。

The coverage of ICC(B) is in the form of listed risks. Those that are listed are covered, and those that are not listed are not covered under any circumstances. Anything attributable to the following circumstances is covered: fire and explosion; vessel or barge struck, stranded, sunk; collision and derailment of onshore means of conveyance; collision of vessel, barge or means of conveyance with external objects other than water; unloading at port of refuge; earthquake, volcanic eruption and lightning; general average sacrifice; jettison or washing overboard; seawater, lake water or river water entering transportation or storage facilities; total loss of the whole package caused by falling into the sea or dropping during loading and unloading.

ICC(B)的除外责任，除对任何人故意损害或破坏、海盗等造成的损失或费用不负责外，其余与ICC(A)的除外责任相同。

Exclusion of ICC(B) is the same as exclusion of ICC(A), except that it shall not be liable for loss or expense caused by wilful damage or destruction to any person, marine accident, etc.

三、ICC(C)的承保范围和除外责任
III. Coverage and Exclusion of ICC(C)

ICC(C)的承保范围比ICC(A)、ICC(B)要小得多，它只承保重大意外事故，而不承保自然灾害及非重大意外事故的风险，其具体承保的风险是：火灾、爆炸；船舶或驳船触礁、搁浅、沉没；陆上运输工具倾覆或出轨；在避难港卸货；共同海损牺牲、抛货。ICC(C)的除外责任与ICC(B)完全相同。

The coverage of ICC(C) is much smaller than that of ICC (A) and ICC (B). It only covers major fortuitous accidents, rather than the risks of natural calamity and non-major fortuitous accidents. The specific scope of cover includes: fire and explosion; strike on reef, grounding and sinking of ship or barge; overturning or derailment of onshore means of conveyance; unloading at port of refuge; general average sacrifice and jettison. Exclusion of ICC(C) is exactly the same as that of ICC(B).

综上所述，ICC(A)的承保范围类似于我国的一切险，ICC(B)的承保范围类似于水渍险，ICC(C)的承保范围类似于平安险，但比平安险的责任范围要小些。

To sum up, the coverage of ICC(A) insurance is similar to that of all risks in China. The coverage of ICC(B) insurance is similar to that of with particular average, WPA/WA, and ICC(C) insurance is similar to that of free from particular average, FPA, but smaller than that of free from particular average, FPA.

ICC(A)、ICC(B)、ICC(C)的责任起讫也是"仓至仓"条款。ICC附加险的规定与中国保险条款的规定大致相同，但对战争险和罢工险专门制定了独立完整的条文，可以作为独立险别单独投保，而中国保险条款中的这两种特殊附加险是不能作为独立险别单独投保的。

The liability of ICC (A), ICC (B) and ICC (C) also starts and ends in accordance with "W/W clause". The provisions of ICC additional risks are roughly the same as those of China Insurance Clauses (CIC), but independent and complete provisions have been developed for war risk and strike risk, which can be covered separately as independent risks, while these two special additional risks in CIC cannot be covered separately as independent risks.

第四节　我国其他货运险别
Section 4　Other Cargo Risks in China

中国人民保险公司除了制定海洋运输货物保险条款外，还分别制定了适用于不同运输方式的货物保险条款，包括陆上运输货物保险、航空运输货物保险、邮包运输保险。

In addition to Ocean Marine Cargo Clauses, PICC has also formulated cargo clauses applicable to different transportation modes, including Inland Transit Insurance, Air Cargo Insurance and Parcel Post Insurance.

一、陆上运输货物保险
I. Inland Transit Insurance

陆上运输货物保险是承保铁路、公路货物运输损失的保险。

Inland Transit Insurance is an insurance policy that covers the loss of goods in carriage by railway or highway.

1. 陆运险 (Overland Transportation Risks)

陆运险负责对被保险货物在运输途中遭受暴风、雷电、洪水、地震等自然灾害，或运输工具遭受碰撞、倾覆、出轨，或在驳运过程中因驳运工具遭受搁浅、触礁、碰撞，或遭受隧道坍塌、崖崩、或失火、爆炸意外事故等情况造成的损失进行赔偿。

Overland transportation risks is liable for indemnifying the insured goods against losses caused by natural calamity such as storm, lightning, flood and earthquake during carriage, or collision, overturning and derailment of means of conveyance, stranding, reef striking and collision of lightering means during transfer, tunnel collapse, cliff collapse, fire and explosion accidents, etc.

陆运险的承保范围相当于海运货物保险中的水渍险。

The coverage of overland transportation risks is equivalent to WPA/WA in marine cargo insurance.

2. 陆运一切险 (Overland Transportation All Risks)

陆运一切险除包括陆运险的责任范围外，还负责对被保险货物在运输途中由于一般外来原因所致的全部或部分损失进行赔偿。

In addition to the scope covered by overland transportation risks, overland transportation all risks is also liable for indemnifying the insured goods for total or partial loss caused by general external reasons during carriage.

陆运一切险的承保范围相当于海运货物保险中的一切险。

The coverage of overland transportation all risks is equivalent to all risks in marine cargo insurance.

陆运险和陆运一切险的保险责任起讫按照"仓至仓"条款办理，但是，货物未进仓者，以该货物到达最后卸货车站满 60 天为止。

The commencement and termination of insurance liability for overland transportation risks and overland transportation all risks shall be handled in accordance with the "W/W clause". However, if the goods are not warehoused, it shall expire 60 days after the goods arrive at the final unloading station.

3. 陆上运输货物战争险 (Overland Transportation Cargo War Risks)

陆上运输货物战争险是陆上运输货物险的一种附加险，承保陆上运输途中由于战争、类似战争行为和敌对行为、武装冲突、各种常规武器所致的货物损失。

Overland transportation cargo war risks is an additional risk of land transportation cargo insurance, which covers the loss of goods caused by war, warlike and hostile acts, armed conflicts and various conventional weapons during land carriage.

4. 陆上运输冷藏货物险 (Overland Transportation Cargo Insurance-Frozen Products)

陆上运输冷藏货物险是陆上运输货物险的一种专门保险，承保范围除陆运险所列的损失外，还负责赔偿由于冷藏机器或隔温设备在运输途中损坏造成货物解冻融化而腐坏的损失。

Overland transportation cargo insurance-frozen products is a special insurance policy for onshore carriage of goods. In addition to the losses listed in overland transportation risks, it is also liable for compensating for the loss of spoilage caused by thawing and melting of goods due to damage to refrigerated machinery or thermal insulation equipment during carriage.

陆上运输冷藏货物险的保险责任起讫为自货物运离保单所载起运地点的冷藏仓库，装入运输工具开始运输时生效，直至运达目的地收货人仓库为止，但是最长保险期限以货物到达目的地车站后 10 天为限。

The insurance liability for overland transportation cargo insurance-frozen products shall be effective from the time when the goods leave the refrigerated warehouse at the place of departure specified in the policy and are loaded into the means of conveyance to start carriage until they arrive at the consignee's warehouse of destination, but the maximum period of insurance shall be limited to 10 days after the goods arrive at the station of destination.

二、航空运输货物保险
II. Air Cargo Insurance

航空运输货物保险是承保以飞机进行货物运输的保险。

Air cargo insurance is an insurance policy that covers the carriage of goods by aircraft.

1. 航空运输险 (Air Transportation Risks)

航空运输险的承保范围相当于海运货物保险中的水渍险。

The coverage of air transportation Risks is equivalent to WPA/WA in marine cargo insurance.

2. 航空运输一切险 (Air Transportation All Risks)

航空运输一切险的承保范围相当于海运货物保险中的一切险。

The coverage of air transportation all risks is equivalent to all risks in marine cargo insurance.

航空运输险和航空运输一切险的保险责任起讫按照"仓至仓"条款办理，但是，货物未进仓者，以该货物到达最后目的地卸离飞机满 30 天为止。

The insurance liability for air transportation risks and air transportation all risks shall be handled in accordance with "W/W clause". However, if the goods are not warehoused, it shall expire 30 days after the goods arrive at the final destination and are unloaded from the aircraft.

3. 航空运输货物战争险 (Air Transportation Cargo War Risks)

航空运输货物战争险是航空运输货物险的一种附加险，承保航空运输途中由于战争、类似战争行为和敌对行为、武装冲突以及各种常规武器所致的货物损失。

Air transportation cargo war risks is an additional risk of air transportation cargo insurance, which covers the loss of goods caused by war, warlike and hostile acts, armed conflicts and various conventional weapons during air carriage.

三、邮包运输保险
III. Parcel Post Insurance

邮包运输保险主要承保邮包在运输途中因自然灾害、意外事故和外来原因所造成的损失。

Parcel Post Insurance mainly covers the losses caused by Natural Calamity, Fortuitous Accidents and external causes during the carriage of parcel post.

1. 邮包险 (Parcel Post Risks)

邮包险的承保范围相当于海运货物保险中的水渍险。

The coverage of parcel post risks is equivalent to WPA/WA in marine cargo insurance.

2. 邮包一切险 (Parcel Post All Risks)

邮包一切险的承保范围相当于海运货物保险中的一切险。

The coverage of parcel post all risks is equivalent to all risks in marine cargo insurance.

邮包险和邮包一切险的保险责任起讫为自邮包离开保险单所载起运地点寄件人的处所，运往邮局时开始生效，直至邮包运达保险单载明的目的地邮局，发出通知书给收件人的当日午夜起算满 15 天为止，在此期限内，邮包一经交至收件人的处所，保险责任即行终止。

Insurance for parcel post risks and parcel post all risks shall commence when the parcel post leaves the sender's premises at the place of departure stated in the policy and is shipped to the post office, until 15 days have elapsed from midnight on the day the parcel post arrives at the post office of destination stated in the policy and notices are given to the recipient, during which period the insurance liability shall cease upon delivery of the parcel post to the recipient's premises.

3. 邮包战争险 (Parcel Post War Risks)

邮包战争险是一种附加险，承保邮包在运输途中由于战争、类似战争行为和敌对行为、武装冲突、海盗行为以及各种常规武器所致的邮包损失。

Parcel post war risks is an additional risk to cover the loss of parcel post caused by war, warlike and hostile acts, armed conflicts, piracy and various conventional weapons during carriage.

第五节　保险实务
Section 5　Insurance Practice

在进出口业务中，与运输保险相关的问题包括买卖双方如何办理保险手续、如何填写保险单据，以及在发生货损时如何办理保险索赔。

In the import and export business, problems related to cargo insurance include how the buyers and sellers complete the insurance formalities, how to fill out the insurance documents, and how to claim in case of cargo damage.

一、投保
I. Insurance

进出口双方签订合同后，在履约过程中，不管采用何种贸易术语成交，必须由出口方或进口方按合同的规定办理货运保险。

After the importer and exporter sign the contract, no matter what trade terms are adopted in the performance process, the exporter or importer must purchase cargo insurance according to the provisions of the contract.

（一）出口货物的投保手续 (Insurance Procedures for Export Goods)

我国出口货物如按 CIF 或 CIP 条件成交，由出口方办理货运保险手续。投保手续一般是：

投保人填写投保单→保险公司审核→投保人缴纳保险费→保险公司签署保险单据。

If China's export goods are concluded on a CIF or CIP basis, the exporter shall handle the cargo insurance procedures. The insurance procedures are generally as follows: the applicant fills in the application form → the insurance company reviews it → the applicant pays the premium → the insurance company signs the insurance documents.

1. 投保人填写投保单 (The Applicant Fills in the Application Form)

投保人根据合同或信用证的规定备齐货物并确定装船出运日期后，在货物尚未装船前，向保险公司填写一份"海运出口货物投保单"。

After the insured prepares all goods and determines the date of shipment according to the provisions of the contract or L/C, he shall fill in an "Application Form for Seaborne Exports" with the insurance company before the goods are shipped.

2. 保险公司审核 (Review by Insurance Company)

保险公司收到投保人递交的投保单后，根据有关规定对其进行审核，以决定是否承保。

After receiving the proposal submitted by the applicant, the insurance company shall review it in accordance with relevant regulations to decide whether to underwrite.

3. 投保人缴纳保险费 (Premium Paid by the Applicant)

投保人按约定方式缴纳保险费（premium）是保险合同生效的条件。保险费率（premium rate）是由保险公司根据一定时期、不同种类货物的赔付率，按不同险别和目的地确定的。保险费的计算公式为：

It is a condition for the insurance contract to come into effect that the applicant pays the premium in the agreed manner. The premium rate is determined by the insurance company according to different risks and destinations based on the loss ratio of different types of goods in a certain period. Premium is calculated as follows:

保险费＝保险金额×保险费率

Premium=Insured Amount × Premium Rate

其中，保险金额是被保险人的投保金额，是保险公司赔偿的最高限额，也是计算保险费的基础。按照国际保险市场的习惯做法，保险金额一般按CIF或CIP价加成计算，即按发票金额再加一定的百分率，此百分率称为投保加成率。投保加成率一般按10%计算。

Among them, insured amount is the insured amount of the insured, the maximum limit of compensation for the insurance company, and the basis for calculating the premium. According to the common practice in the international insurance market, the insured amount is generally calculated according to CIF or CIP addition, that is, adding a certain percentage to the invoice value, which is called percentage of addition. The percentage of addition is generally calculated at 10%.

4. 保险公司签署保险单据 (Insurance Documents Signed by Insurance Company)

投保人缴纳保险费后，保险公司则根据投保人的投保单内容缮制保险单据并签署投保单。保险单据是保险公司与投保人之间的保险合同，是保险公司对投保人的承保证明。

After the applicant pays the premium, the insurance company shall prepare and sign the insurance documents according to the contents of the application form. The insurance documents are the insurance contract between the insurance company and the applicant, as well as the undertaking certificate of the insurance company to the Applicant.

（二）进口货物的投保手续 (Insurance Procedures for Import Goods)

我国进口货物如按FOB或CFR条件成交，需由我国进口方办理保险。为了简化投保手续，以及防止漏保或来不及办理投保等差错，可以与保险公司签订预约保险合同。

Insurance shall be effected by the importer of our country if goods imported into our country are concluded under FOB or CFR conditions. To simplify the insurance procedures and prevent errors such as omission or late application, an open insurance contract can be signed with the insurance company.

按照海运进口货物预约保险合同的规定，投保人在获悉每批货物的起运消息后，给保险公司发出书面的装运通知，准确地将船名、开航日期、航线、货物品名及数量、货物价值等内容通知保险公司，就视为向保险公司办理了投保手续，无须再填写投保单。如被保险人未按预约保险合同的规定给保险公司发出书面的装运通知，则保险公司不负赔偿责任。

According to the provisions of open insurance contract for marine imported goods, after receiving the shipping information of each batch of goods, the applicant shall send a written shipping advice to the insurance company and accurately notify the insurance company of the name of the ship, Slg. on or abt., route, commodity and quantity of the goods, value of the goods, etc. It shall be deemed that it has gone through the insurance procedures with the insurance company and there is no need to fill in the application form again. If the insured fails to issue a written shipping advice to the insurance company as stipulated in the open cover insurance contract, the insurance company shall not be liable for compensation.

在进口业务中，按双方签订的预约保险合同规定，保险金额按以下公式计算，其中保险费率按"特约费率表"规定的平均费率计算。

In the import business, according to the provisions of the open insurance contract signed by both parties, the insured amount shall be calculated according to the following formula, and the premium rate shall be calculated at the average rate specified in the "Schedule of Special Rates".

保险金额＝[FOB价格×（1＋平均运费率）]÷（1－平均保险费率）
　　　　＝CFR价格÷（1－平均保险费率）

Insured Amount ＝ [FOB × (1 ＋ Average Rate of Freight)] ÷ (1－ Average Premium Rate)
　　　　　　　＝ CFR ÷ (1－ Average Premium Rate)

二、保险单据
II. Insurance Documents

保险单据是保险公司与投保人之间订立的保险合同，它反映了保险人与投保人之间的权利和义务关系，也是保险公司对投保人出具的承保证明。当发生保险责任范围内的损失时，它又是保险索赔和理赔的主要依据。常用的保险单据有以下几种。

Insurance documents is an insurance contract concluded between the insurance company and the applicant, which reflects the rights and obligations between the insurer and the insured and is also the undertaking certificate issued by the insurance company to the applicant. In case of any loss within the scope of cover, it serves as the primary basis for insurance claim and claim settlement. Common insurance documents are as follows:

（1）保险单（insurance policy）又称大保单，用于承保一个指定航程内某一批货物的运输保险。它是一种正规的保险合同，包括正面内容和背面条款。其正面内容一般包括被保险人的名称和地址、保险标的、运输标志、运输工具、起讫地点、承保险别、保险币别和金额、出单日期等项目，背面印有保险人和被保险人之间权利和义务方面的保险条款，保险单是使用最广的保险单据。

```
┌─────────────────────────────────────────────────────────────┐
│        PICC  中国人民财产保险股份有限公司                    │
│              PICC Property and Casualty Company limited     │
│   地址：                           邮编：100098              │
│   ADD:                             Postal Code: 100058      │
│   电话(TEL): 010-51577587          传真(FAX): 58471155      │
├─────────────────────────────────────────────────────────────┤
│                    货物运输保险投保单                        │
│         APPLICATION FORM FOR CARGO TRANSPORTATION INSURANE  │
│                                                             │
│  被保险人                                                    │
│  Insured: _____   │
│  发票号(INVOICE NO.)                                         │
│  合同号(CONTRACT NO.)                                        │
│  信用证号(L/C NO.)                                           │
│  发票金额(INVOICE AMORNT)          投保加成(PLUS)  110%     │
│                                                             │
│  兹有下列物品向中国人民保险公司北京市分公司投保。            │
│   (INSURANCE IS REQUIRED ON THE FOLLOWING COMMODITTES: )    │
│  ┌──────────┬──────────┬─────────────────┬──────────────┐  │
│  │  标记    │ 包装及数量│   保险货物项目  │  保险金额    │  │
│  │MARKS&NOS.│ QUANTITY │DESCRIPTION OF GOODS│AMOUNT INSURED│ │
│  ├──────────┼──────────┼─────────────────┼──────────────┤  │
│  │          │          │                 │              │  │
│  │          │          │                 │              │  │
│  └──────────┴──────────┴─────────────────┴──────────────┘  │
│                                                             │
│  启运日期：              装载运输工具：                      │
│  DATE OF COMMENCEMENT___ PER CONVEYANCE_____               │
│  自           经                     至                     │
│  FROM_____   VIA_____              TO_____               │
│  提单号：          赔款偿付地点：                            │
│  B/L NO.:_____     CLAIM PAYABLE AT_____                   │
│  投保险别：(PLEASE INDICATE THE CONDITIONS &/OR SPECIAL     │
│  COVERAGES:)                                                │
│                                                             │
│  请如实告知下列情况：(如 '是' 在 [ ] 中打 '√'，'不是' 打     │
│  '×') IF ANY, PLEASE MARK '√' OR '×':                       │
│  1、货物各类：  袋装[]   散装[]    冷藏[]  液体[]            │
│     GOODS:     BAG/JUMBO BULK    REEFERR LEQUID             │
│                 活动物[]   机器/汽车[]    危险品等级[]       │
│                 LIVE ANIMAL MACHINE/AUTO  DANGEROUS CLASS   │
│  2、集装箱种类：普通[]  开顶[]  框架[]  平板[]  冷藏[]       │
│     CONTAINER  ORDINARY OPEN    FRAME   FLAT   REFRIGERATOR │
│  3、转运工具：  海轮[]  飞机[]  驳船[]  火车[]  汽车[]       │
│     BY TRANSIT: SHIP    PLANE   BARGE   TRAIN   TRUCK       │
│  4、船舶资料：           船籍[           ] 船龄：[      ]    │
│     PARTICULAR OF SHIP:  RIGISTRY          AGE              │
│                                                             │
│  备注：被保险人确认本保险合同条款和内容已经完全了解。        │
│        THE ASSURED CONFIRMS HEREWITH THE TERMS              │
│        AND CONDITIONS OF THESE INSURANCE CONTRACTS          │
│        FULLY UNDERSTOOD.                                    │
│                            投保人(签名盖章)APPLICANT'S SIGNATURE│
│                            电话：(TEL)                       │
│   投保日期：(DATE)_____  地址：(ADD)                       │
│                                                             │
│               本公司自用(FOR OFFICE USE ONLY)               │
│   费率：          保费：                    备注：           │
│   RATE_____     PREMIUM_____            Remarks:        │
│   经办人：     核保人：          负责人：                    │
│   BY_____  — Underwriter:——  Person in Charge:——          │
└─────────────────────────────────────────────────────────────┘
```

图 9-1 涉外货物运输险投保单

Figure 9-1 Application Form for International Cargo Insurance

(1) Insurance policy, or big policy, is used to cover the carriage insurance of a certain batch of goods within a specified voyage. It is a formal insurance contract with front contents and back clauses. The contents on the front generally include the name and address of the insured, subject matter of insurance, shipping mark, means of conveyance, place of origin and destination, conditions, currency and amount of insurance policy, date of issue and other items. The back is printed with insurance clause on rights and obligations between the insurer and the insured. Insurance policy is the most widely used insurance document.

（2）保险凭证（insurance certificate）又称小保单，是一种简化的保险单。这种凭证除背面不载明保险人与被保险人的权利和义务条款外，其余内容与保险单相同。保险凭证与保险单具有同等效力。

(2) Insurance certificate, or small policy, is a simplified insurance policy. The contents of such certificate are the same as those in the policy, except that the reverse side does not specify the rights and obligations of the insurer and the insured. The insurance certificate has the same effect as the insurance policy.

（3）预约保单（open policy）又称开口保单，是保险公司承保被保险人一定时期内所有进出口货物使用的保险单。凡属于其承保范围内的货物一经起运即自动承保。被保险人在获悉每批货物起运时，必须及时将装运通知书送交保险公司。

(3) Open policy, or open cover, is an insurance policy used by the insurance company to cover all import and export goods of the insured within a certain period. All goods covered by it are automatically insured upon shipment. The insured must promptly send the shipping advice to the insurance company upon learning of each shipment.

（4）批单（endorsement），保险单签发以后，投保人如果需要对保险单的内容进行变更或修改，可以根据保险公司的规定，以书面形式向保险公司提出申请。经保险公司同意后可另外使用一种凭证，注明更改或补充的内容，这种凭证称为批单保险单。一经批改，保险公司即按批改后的内容承担责任。批单须粘贴在原保险单上，并加盖骑缝章，作为保险单不可分割的一部分。涉外货物运输险投保单如图 9-1 所示。

(4) Endorsement: After the insurance policy is issued, if the applicant needs to change or modify the contents of the policy, it can apply to the insurance company in writing according to the regulations of the insurance company. With the consent of the insurance company, an additional certificate indicating changes or additions may be used, which is called endorsement of insurance policy. Once corrected, the insurance company shall bear responsibilities according to the contents after correction. The endorsement shall be pasted on the original policy and stamped with a cross-page seal as an integral part of the policy. Application form for international cargo insurance see as figure 9-1.

三、投保金额和保险费
III. Insured Amount and Premium

投保金额也称保险金额（insured amount），是被保险人的投保金额，是保险公司赔偿的最高限额，也是计算保险费的基础。

Insured amount is the insured amount of the insured, the maximum limit of compensation for the insurance company and the basis for calculating the premium.

一般来说，保险金额是以商业发票的价值为基础的，确保对于货物进行充分的投保是非常有必要的。按照国际保险市场的习惯做法，出口货物的保险金额一般按 CIF 或 CIP 价加成计算，即按发票金额再加一定的百分率，此百分率称为投保加成率。投保加成率一般按 10% 计算。

Generally, the Insured Amount is based on the value of commercial invoice and it is essential to ensure adequate coverage for the goods. According to the common practice in the international insurance market, the Insured Amount of export goods is generally calculated according to CIF or CIP addition, that is, adding a certain percentage to the invoice value, which is called percentage of addition. The percentage of addition is generally calculated at 10%.

保险金额 = CIF 货价 × (1+投保加成率) = CIF 货价 × 投保加成

Insured Amount = CIF × (1 + Percentage of Addition) = CIF × Plus

保险费（premium）是根据投保金额和费率计算得到的。

Premium is calculated based on the insured amount and rate.

保险费＝保险金额×保险费率

Premium＝Insured Amount×Premium Rate

四、保险索赔
IV. Insurance Claim

保险索赔是指当被保险人的货物遭受承保责任范围内的风险损失时，被保险人向保险人提出的索赔要求。在国际贸易中，如由卖方办理投保，卖方在交货后将保险单背书转让给买方或其收货代理人，当货物抵达目的港（地）发现残损时，买方或其收货代理人作为保险单的合法受让人，可就地向保险人或其代理人要求赔偿。中国人民保险公司为方便中国出口货物运抵目的港（地）后能及时勘查损失、就地给予赔偿，已在100多个国家和地区建立了勘查或理赔代理机构。中国进口货物的出险勘查索赔，则由有关的专业进口公司或其委托的收货代理人在港口或其他收货地点，向当地的保险公司要求赔偿。

Insurance claim refers to the claim made by the insured against the insurer when the goods of the insured suffer from loss risks covered. In international trade, if the sellers purchase insurance, they shall transfer the insurance policy endorsement to the buyers or their receiving agents after delivery. When the goods arrive at the port (place) of destination and damage is found, the buyers or their receiving agents, as the legal assignee of the insurance policy, may claim compensation from the Insurer or its agent on site. PICC has established survey or claim settlement agencies in more than 100 countries and regions to facilitate the timely investigation of losses and local compensation after China's export goods arrive at foreign port of destination. Claim for compensation from the local insurance company at the port or other place of receipt shall be made by the relevant import company or its entrusted receiving agent.

被保险人或其代理人在向保险人索赔时，应做好下列几项工作。

When the insured or its agent makes a claim to the insurer, the following work shall be done.

（1）当被保险人得知或发现货物已遭受保险责任范围内的损失时，应及时通知保险公司并尽可能保留现场，由保险人会同有关方面查勘损失程度、调查损失原因、确定损失性质和责任、提出施救意见，并签发联合检验报告。检验报告是被保险人向保险人索赔的重要文件。

(1) When the insured knows or finds that the goods have suffered losses within the scope of cover, it shall promptly notify the insurance company and preserve the scene as far as possible. The insurer shall investigate the extent and cause of loss, determine the nature and liability of loss, put forward rescue opinions, and issue a joint inspection report together with relevant parties. The inspection report is an important document for the insured to claim against the insurer.

（2）当被保险货物运抵目的港（地）后，被保险人或其代理人提货时发现货物有明显的受损痕迹、整件短少或散装货物已经残损，应立即向理货部门索取残损或短少证明。如货损涉及第三者的责任，则首先应向有关责任方提出索赔或声明保留索赔权。在保留向第三者索赔权的条件下，可向保险公司索赔。被保险人在获得保险补偿的同时，须将受损货物的有关权益转让给保险公司，以便保险公司取代被保险人的地位或以被保险人的名义向第三者责任方进行追偿。保险人的这种权利，叫做代位追偿权（the right of subrogation）。

(2) When the insured cargo arrives at the port of destination, if the Insured or its agent finds that there are obvious signs of damage to the cargo, the whole package is missing or the bulk cargo has been damaged when

picking up the goods, it shall immediately ask for a certificate of damage or shortage from the tally department. If the damage involves the liability of a third party, it shall first lodge a claim with the relevant liable party or make a statement to reserve the right of claim. Claim against the insurance company under the condition of reserving the right to claim compensation from a third party. The insured shall transfer the relevant rights and interests of the damaged goods to the insurance company while obtaining the insurance compensation, so that the insurance company can replace the status of the Insured or recover from a third liable party in the name of the insured. This right of the Insurer is called the right of subrogation.

（3）采取合理的施救措施。当被保险货物受损后，被保险人和保险人都有责任采取可能的、合理的施救措施，以防止损失扩大。因抢救、阻止、减少货物损失而支付的合理费用，保险公司负责补偿。在被保险人能够施救而不履行施救义务时，保险人对于扩大的损失甚至全部损失有权拒赔。

(3) Take reasonable rescue measures. When the goods insured are damaged, both the insured and the insurer shall be liable for taking possible and reasonable remedial measures to avoid aggravation of the loss. The insurance company shall be liable for compensating the reasonable expenses incurred in rescuing, preventing or reducing the loss of goods. When the insured is able to salvage but fails to perform the obligation of salvage, the insurer has the right to refuse to compensate for the aggravated loss or even total loss.

（4）备妥索赔证据，在规定时效内提出索赔，并注意是否有免赔率的规定。在进行保险索赔时，通常应提供的证据有：保险单或保险凭证正本；运输单据；商业发票和重量单、装箱单；检验报告单；残损、短量证明；向承运人等第三者责任方请求赔偿的函电或其他证明文件，必要时还需提供海事报告；索赔清单，主要列明索赔的金额及其计算依据，以及有关的费用项目和用途等。

(4) Claim evidence shall be prepared and submitted within the specified time limit, and attention shall be paid to whether there is a franchise ratio. In making an insurance claim, the evidence that should be provided includes: original insurance policy or insurance certificate; transport documents; commercial invoice, weight list and packing list; certificate of analysis; certificate of damage and shortage; letters and telegrams requesting compensation from the carrier or other third liable parties or other supporting documents, and maritime reports if necessary; claim list, mainly stating the amount of claim and its calculation basis, as well as relevant cost items and purposes.

根据我国海洋运输货物保险条款的规定，当被保险货物遭受承保范围内的损失时，保险索赔时效，是从保险事故发生之日起算，最多不超过两年。

According to the provisions of ocean marine cargo clauses, when the insured goods have suffered a covered loss, the statute of limitations for insurance claims begins to run from the date of the insured incident and does not exceed a maximum of two years.

第六节　合同中的保险条款
Section 6　Insurance Clause in the Contract

一笔进出口业务由谁办理货运保险，主要看双方采用的是什么贸易术语，采用不同的贸易术语成交，合同中的保险条款内容会有所不同。

Who handles the cargo insurance for an import and export business mainly depends on what trade terms are adopted by the parties. The insurance clause in the contract will be different if different trade terms are adopted for transactions.

一、规定由买方办理保险手续
I. Insurance: to Be Effected by the Buyers

如以 FOB、CFR、FCA、CPT 贸易术语成交，则由买方办理保险，合同中只需规定：保险由买方负责办理（Insurance: to be effected by the buyers）。

If the transaction is concluded under FOB, CFR, FCA and CPT, it shall be covered by the buyers. It only needs to be specified in the contract that "Insurance: to be effected by the buyers".

如买方要求卖方代为办理保险，则需规定"由买方委托卖方按发票金额×× %代为投保××险，保险费由买方负担（Insurance to be covered by the sellers on behalf of the buyers for …% of the invoice value against … risks and premium is to be paid by the buyers）"。

If the buyers require the sellers to insure on their behalf, it shall be specified that "Insurance to be covered by the sellers on behalf of the buyers for …% of the invoice value against … risks and premium is to be paid by the buyers".

二、规定由卖方办理保险手续
II. Insurance: to Be Effected by the Sellers

如按 CIF、CIP 贸易术语成交，则由卖方办理保险。合同中的保险条款除约定险别、保险金额等内容外，还应标明条款版别，如"按中国人民保险公司海洋运输货物保险条款（2009版）投保"。保险条款如下：

If the transaction is concluded under CIF and CIP, it shall be covered by the sellers. In addition to the agreed risk and insured amount, the insurance clause in the contract shall also indicate the version, e.g. "Insurance according to Ocean Marine Cargo Clauses dated 2009, PICC". The insurance clause is as follows:

保险由卖方按发票金额的 110%投保一切险和战争险，以中国人民保险公司海洋运输货物保险条款（2009版）为准。

Insurance to be covered by the sellers for 110% of the invoice value against all risks and war risk as per Ocean Marine Cargo Clauses of the PICC dated 2009.

第九章拓展知识、专业词汇和练习

第十章　货款的支付
Chapter 10　Payment for Goods

导　读
Introduction

在国际贸易中，货款的收付直接影响双方的资金周转，采取何种结算方式，直接关系到买卖双方的利益。买卖双方在交易磋商时，都力争约定对自己有利的支付条件。国际支付方式又称国际结算方式，是指国与国之间通过结算工具，办理因债权债务所引起的货币资金收付所采取的方式。随着国际贸易和银行业务的发展，国际结算方式也从简单的交货付现的现金结算方式，转变为凭单付款的非现金结算方式；从买卖双方直接结算发展到通过银行进行结算。传统的国际结算方式主要有汇付、托收、信用证三大类，每一大类还可以分为若干小的类别。随着信用工具的多样化和银行业务的发展，银行保函、国际保理、福费廷等新的结算方式在结算中的应用逐渐增多。另外，各种结算方式还可以相互结合使用。外贸企业只有灵活运用各种结算方式才能在出口业务中安全收汇，提高经济效益。

In international trade, the receipt and payment of goods directly affects the capital turnover of both parties, and the settlement method adopted directly affects their interests. Both buyers and sellers strive to agree on terms of payment that are in their favor during business negotiation. International payment method, also known as international settlement method, refers to the method adopted by the international community to handle the receipt and payment of monetary funds caused by creditor's rights and debts through settlement tools. With the development of international trade and banking, the international settlement method has shifted from a simple cash settlement method of cash on delivery to a non-cash settlement method of cash against documents; from direct settlement between buyers and sellers to settlement through banks. Traditional international settlement methods mainly include remittance, collection and L/C, each of which can be divided into several sub-categories. With the diversification of credit instruments and the development of banking business, new settlement methods such as letter of indemnity, international factoring and forfaiting are increasingly applied in settlement. Also, various settlement methods can be used in combination with each other. Only when foreign trade enterprises flexibly use various settlement methods can they securely collect foreign exchange in export business and improve economic benefits.

第一节　支付工具
Section 1　Payment Instruments

国际贸易货款的收付，采用现金结算的较少，大多采用非现金结算，主要使用各类金融票据作为支付工具。金融票据是指可以流通转让的债券凭证，是国际上通行的结算和信贷工具。国际货款结算常用的金融票据有汇票、支票和本票三种，其中汇票在国际货款结算中最常见。

International trade is less settled by cash and mostly settled in non-cash, mainly using various financial instruments as payment tools. Financial instruments refer to bond certificates that can be negotiated and transferred, which are internationally accepted settlement and credit tools. Financial bills commonly used in international payment settlement mainly include draft, cheque and promissory note, among which draft is the most common one.

一、汇票（Bill of Exchange, Draft）

（一）汇票的含义 (Meaning of Draft)

根据1996年1月1日开始施行的《中华人民共和国票据法》(简称《票据法》) 第十九条规定："汇票是出票人签发的，委托付款人在见票时或者在指定的日期无条件支付确定金额给收款人或持票人的票据。"这里的票据指资金票据，是以支付一定金额为目的、用于债权债务关系清偿和结算的凭证。按照各国广泛引用或参照的英国1882年《票据法》的规定：汇票是一个人向另一个人签发的，要求即期或定期或在可以确定的将来时间，对某人或其指定人或持票人支付一定金额的无条件支付命令。

According to Article 19 of the Law of the People's Republic of China on Negotiable Instruments (hereinafter referred to as "Negotiable Instruments Law") which came into effect on January 1, 1996: "Draft is a bill issued by a drawer and entrusting a payer to unconditionally pay a certain amount to the payee or holder at sight or on a specified date." Bills here refer to fund bills, which are vouchers used for paying off and settling creditor-debtor relations with the purpose of paying a certain amount. Draft is an unconditional payment order issued by one person to another for the payment of a certain amount to a person or his nominee or holder at sight or periodically or at such future time as may be determined in accordance with the provisions of the British 1882 Law of Bills widely cited or referred to in various countries.

（二）汇票的当事人 (Parties to Draft)

一张汇票通常有三个基本当事人。

A draft usually has three basic parties.

1. 出票人 (Drawer)

出票人是签发汇票的人，商业汇票的出票人一般是出口商，银行汇票的出票人是银行。在汇票被承兑前出票人是主债务人，如果汇票遭到拒付，主债务人将保证偿付票款给持票人或被迫付款的任何背书人。

Drawer is the person who issues a draft. The drawer of trade bill is generally the exporter and that of banker's draft is the bank. Before acceptance of draft, the drawer is the principal debtor. If the draft is dishonored, the principal debtor will guarantee payment to the holder or any endorser who is forced to pay.

2. 受票人 (Drawee)

受票人是接受支付命令的人，又称付款人，一般是进口商或其指定银行。当受票人在汇票上签名（承兑）之前，不是汇票的主债务人，不承担付款之责；但当受票人在汇票上签名（承兑）之后，受票人作为承兑人成为汇票的主债务人，出票人退居从债务人。

Drawee is the person who accepts payment order, also known as payer, usually importer or its nominated bank. Before the drawee signs on draft (acceptance), it is not the principal debtor of the draft and shall not be liable for payment; however, after the drawee signs on draft (acceptance), the drawee becomes the principal debtor of the draft, and the drawer becomes a subordinate debtor.

3. 收款人 (Payee)

收款人是收取汇票上载明金额款项的人,一般为出口商或其指定银行。收款人作为汇票的第一持票人,因持有汇票而拥有所有的票据权利,如请求付款权、追索权和票据转让权等。

Payee is the person who receives the amount stated in the draft, usually the exporter or its nominated bank. As the first holder of draft, the payee owns all bill rights, such as right to request payment, right of recourse and right to transfer bill.

除以上基本当事人外,随着汇票的流通转让,又出现了背书人、被背书人、承兑人、保证人和持票人等其他当事人。

In addition to the above basic parties, with the circulation and transfer of draft, there are other parties such as endorser, endorsee, acceptor, guarantor and holder.

(三) 汇票的内容 (Contents of Draft)

汇票是要式证券,在汇票上依法记载的各种事项是汇票有效成立的要件。这些要件构成汇票的主要内容。各个国家的票据法对汇票的内容规定不一,根据我国《票据法》的规定,汇票应包括"汇票"字样,无条件的支付命令、确定的金额、付款人名称、收款人名称、出票日期、出票人签章等内容。据此,一张完整、合格的汇票应具备如下内容:

Draft is an important security. All items recorded on the draft according to law are elements for the valid establishment of the draft. These elements constitute the main contents of a draft. The bill laws of various countries has different regulations on the content of draft. According to the provisions of China's Negotiable Instruments Law, a draft shall include the words "Bill of Exchange/Draft", unconditional order to pay, determined amount, name of payer, name of payee, date of issue, signature of drawer, etc. Accordingly, a complete and qualified draft shall have the following contents:

1. 标明"汇票"字样 (Marked with "Bill of Exchange/Draft")

我国票据法和日内瓦《统一汇票本票法公约》都规定:汇票上必须表明"汇票"字样,以区别于本票和支票,同时也有利于明确各当事人的权利和责任。英国《票据法》无此要求,但在其结算实务中签发的汇票也大都有"汇票"字样。"汇票"一词在英文中有不同的表示,如"bill of exchange""exchange""draft"等。

Both China's Negotiable Instruments Law and the Geneva Convention on the Unification of the Law Relating to Bills of Ex-change and Promissory Notes stipulate that "Bill of Exchange/Draft" must be indicated on a draft o distinguish it from promissory note and cheque, and also help clarify the rights and responsibilities of all parties. There is no such requirement in the British Law of Bills, but most drafts issued in its settlement practice also have the words "Bill of Exchange/Draft". A draft can be expressed in English as "bill of exchange", "exchange" and "draft".

2. 无条件的支付命令 (Unconditional Order to Pay)

汇票是出票人给付款人的无条件支付命令,必须有无条件支付委托的文句,而且应该不受任何限制,不能将其他行为的履行或事件的发生作为其先决条件。如果汇票上规定诸如"于货物抵达目的地后才付款""出售某批货物所得价款中支付某人……万元"等附加条件或限制,则汇票无效。但是,在汇票上加注出票条款(draw clause)以表明汇票的起源交易,例如"按……信用证开立""按某合同装运某货物"等,并不构成支付的附加或限制条件。在我国,无条件的支付命令,通常用"凭票付"或"请于到期日无条件支付"等表示。英文中一般使用祈使句,如:"Pay to the order of ..."。

Draft is an unconditional payment order issued by the drawer to the payer. It must be a statement of unconditional payment entrustment and shall not be subject to any restriction. The performance of other acts or the occurrence of events cannot be taken as its prerequisite. If a draft specifies additional conditions or restrictions such as "Payment will be made after the goods arrive at the destination" and "Pay someone ... (RMB ×××) from the price of selling a certain batch of goods", it is invalid. However, adding a draw clause to the draft to indicate the origin transaction, such as "opening under an L/C" and "shipment of goods under a contract", does not constitute an additional or restrictive condition for payment. In China, unconditional order to pay is usually expressed by "pay against draft" or "please pay unconditionally on the due date". Imperative sentences are commonly used in English, such as "Pay to the order of ...".

3. 确定的汇票金额 (Certain in Money)

汇票是资金票据，所以汇票上必须明确记载支付款项的金额，不能用货物数量或其他需要换算的方式进行表示，不能模棱两可，如"About two hundred USD"，这种汇票是不能产生票据法律效力的。汇票金额同时以文字和数字表示的，两者应当相符。若有差异，按照英国《票据法》和日内瓦《统一汇票本票公约》的规定，应以文字表示的数额为准。但我国《票据法》第八条规定："票据金额以中文大写和数码同时记载，二者必须一致。二者不一致的，票据无效。"

Draft is a fund bill. Therefore, the amount of payment must be explicitly specified, which cannot be expressed in quantity of goods or other ways that need to be converted and cannot be ambiguous, such as "About two hundred USD". This kind of draft cannot produce legal effect of bills. If the amount of draft is expressed in words and figures at the same time, they shall be consistent. In the event of discrepancies, the amounts expressed in words shall prevail under the British Law of Bills and the Geneva Convention on the Unification of the Law Relating to Bills of Ex-change and Promissory Notes. However, Article 8 of China's Negotiable Instruments Law stipulates: "If the amount of a negotiable instrument is recorded in both Chinese capital and figures, the two must be consistent. If they are inconsistent, the instrument is invalid."

4. 付款人姓名、商号及地址 (Drawee)

各国票据法都要求汇票必须载明付款人的姓名或商号名称。汇票付款人名称和地址应当书写清楚，以便收款人或持票人向其提示付款或承兑。付款人的姓名、商号及地址通常写在汇票的左下方。

The bill laws of all countries require that a draft must contain the name or trade name of the payer. The name and address of the drawee shall be clearly written for presentation of payment or acceptance to it by the payee or holder. Payer's name, trade name and address are usually written at the bottom left of a draft.

5. 收款人姓名、商号及地址 (Payee)

英国《票据法》认为，汇票上可以指定收款人，也可以不指定收款人，而仅写付给持票人。但按我国《票据法》和日内瓦《统一汇票本票公约》，收款人名称是汇票必须记载的事项。我国《票据法》第二十二条规定，汇票必须记载收款人名称，未记载收款人名称的汇票无效。这种规定表明我国的汇票必须是记名汇票而不允许签发不记名汇票。这主要是从票据使用的安全性考虑，因为不记名汇票转让时，持票人不必在汇票上背书，仅凭交付即可转让，汇票的受让人如果再进行转让，也凭交付转让。由于汇票上既没有转让人的签章，也没有受让人的名称，票据转让的真实情况从汇票上无法反映出来，票据转让关系不明确。同时，转让人不在汇票上签字，也就不承担票据责任，这对保护持票人的票据权利是不利的。而记名式汇票则不同，收款人必须经过背书才能转让汇票，而不能仅凭交付进行转让。基于同样的安全考虑，我国《票据法》也规定背书必须是记名背书，被背书人如要转让汇票，也必须背书。我国《票据法》的这种规定确保了汇票转让关系可以从汇票的背书上加以认定。此外，背书人因在汇票上签了字，就要对持票人承担票据责任，这也可以增强票据的信用度，有利于保护持票人的票据权利。

The British Law of Bills states that a draft may or may not specify a payee and is payable only to the holder. However, according to China's Negotiable Instruments Law and the Geneva Convention on the Unification of the Law Relating to Bills of Ex-change and Promissory Notes, the name of payee is an item that must be specified in the draft. Article 22 of China's Negotiable Instruments Law stipulates that the name of payee must be specified in the draft, and a draft without the name of payee shall be invalid. This indicates that a draft in China must be an order bill, and it is not allowed to issue a bearer bill. This is based on security considerations of the use of bills, because when a bearer bill is transferred, the holder does not need to endorse the bill and can transfer it only by delivery. If the assignee of the bill transfers it again, it can also be transferred by delivery. As a draft has neither the signature and seal of the assignor nor the name of the assignee, the real situation of bill transfer cannot be reflected, and the transfer relationship of the bill is unclear. Besides, if the assignor does not sign the draft, he will not be liable for the bill, which is detrimental to protecting the holder's rights in the bill. An order bill is different. The payee must go through endorsement to transfer the bill, and it cannot be transferred by delivery alone. Based on the same security considerations, China's Negotiable Instruments Law also stipulates that "Endorsement must be endorsement in full. If the endorsee wants to transfer a draft, it must also be endorsed". This provision ensures that the transfer relationship of draft can be confirmed from the endorsement. In addition, the endorser will be liable to the holder for signing the draft, which can enhance the credibility of the bill and help protect the holder's rights on the bill.

汇票的收款人，又称为"抬头"，具体写法有三种：

Payee of draft, also known as "Title", can be written in three ways:

（1）限制性抬头。这种汇票不能经背书进行转让。

(1) Restricted order. This type of draft is not negotiable by endorsement.

例如：仅付给甲公司（Pay A Co. only.）

付给甲公司，不准转让（Pay A Co., not transferable.）

（2）指示式抬头。这种载有指示性抬头的汇票可以经过背书转让。

(2) Demonstrative order. This type of draft, bearing a demonstrative order, is negotiable by endorsement.

例如：付给甲公司或其指定人（Pay A Co. or order. / Pay to the order of A co.）

（3）来人抬头。按英国《票据法》，汇票可以做成来人抬头，即在汇票上不指定收款人名称，而只写明"付给持票人（Pay holder）"或"付给来人（Pay bearer）"字样。这种汇票可以仅凭交付汇票本身即可进行转让，而无须由持票人背书。

(3) To Bearer. According to the British Law of Bills, a draft can be made payable to bearer, that is, the name of payee is not specified on the draft and only the words "Pay holder" or "Pay bearer" are written. Such draft may be negotiable by delivery of the draft alone and without endorsement by holder.

收款人是汇票最初的权利人，也是主债权人，必须明确记载，一般写在汇票中间。

The payee is the original obligee and principal creditor of draft. It must be well defined, generally written in the middle of draft.

6. 出票日期 (Date of Issue)

我国《票据法》和日内瓦《统一汇票本票公约》规定，汇票应当记载出票日期，否则汇票有效。英国《票据法》则认为出票日期不是汇票必须记载的事项。如果汇票未填写出票日期，持票人可以将自己认为正确的日期填入。汇票记载出票日期的作用有三个：

According to China's Negotiable Instruments Law and the Geneva Convention on the Unification of the Law Relating to Bills of Ex-change and Promissory Notes, date of issue shall be specified in the draft; otherwise, the draft is valid. While the British Law of Bills states that the date of issue is not a mandatory item on a draft. If a draft does not include the date of issue, the holder may insert the date it deems correct. A draft records the date of issue for three purposes:

（1）决定票据的有效期。按票据法的一般规则，票据均有一定的有效期，持票人必须在有效期内向付款人提示要求付款或承兑。根据日内瓦《票据统一汇票本票公约》，即期汇票的有效期是出票日起的1年时间内。我国《票据法》规定见票即付的汇票有效期为出票日起的2年时间。出票人如果不在规定的有效期内要求票据权利，有效期满后票据权利自动消失。

(1) Determine the validity time of the bill. According to the general rules of bill law, there is a certain validity time for all bills, and the holder must present to the payer for payment or acceptance within the validity time. The validity time for sight bill is 1 year from the date of issue in accordance with the Geneva Convention on the Unification of the Law Relating to Bills of Ex-change and Promissory Notes. While China's Negotiable Instruments Law stipulates that the validity time for draft at sight is 2 years from the date of issue. If the drawer does not claim rights on the bill within the specified validity time, such rights will automatically disappear upon expiry of the validity time.

（2）决定付款到期日。以汇票出票日期推算付款到期日的远期汇票，就必须明示出票日期，否则无从计算付款日期，如"At 20 days after date pay to..."（出票后20天）。

(2) Determine the tenor. If the tenor of time bill is calculated based on the date of issue, the date of issue must be explicitly indicated. Otherwise, there is no way to calculate the date of payment, e.g. "At 20 days after date pay to...".

（3）判定出票人的行为能力。若出票人在出票时已被宣告破产、清理，则可判定出票人在出票时已经丧失行为能力，该汇票应为无效汇票。

(3) Determine the drawer's ability to act. If the drawer has been declared bankrupt and liquidated at the time of issue, it can be judged that the drawer has lost his ability to act at the time of issue, and the draft shall be invalid.

7. 出票人签章 (Signature of Drawer)

各国票据法都规定，汇票必须有出票人签名才能生效。签章是出票人承担出票责任的表示，出票人一旦在汇票上签了字，就确定了自己主债务人的地位。没有出票人签章的汇票是无效的。我国《票据法》第二十二条也把"出票人签章"作为汇票必须记载的事项之一。如果汇票的出票人是企业法人，则必须由其授权的代表签字。

It is stipulated in the bill laws of all countries that a draft must be signed by the drawer to take effect. Signature indicates that the drawer assumes the responsibility of to draw. Once the drawer signs on the draft, it determines its status as a principal debtor. A draft is invalid without the signature of drawer. Article 22 of China's Negotiable Instruments Law also takes "signature of drawer" as one of the items that must be specified in the draft. If the drawer of a draft is an enterprise legal person, it must be signed by its authorized representative.

以上七项为汇票的绝对应记载事项，未记载上述规定事项之一的，汇票无效。

The above seven items are absolutely necessary to be included in a draft. If one of the above specified items is not recorded, the draft will be invalid.

在实际业务中，汇票通常还需列明付款日期、付款地点和出票地点等内容。

In actual business, a draft shall also specify the date of payment, place of payment and place of issue.

8. 付款到期日 (Tenor)

汇票的付款到期日就是汇票所载金额的支付日期。按英国《票据法》，到期日不是汇票的必备项目，未载明到期日的汇票按见票即付处理。日内瓦《统一汇票本票公约》虽然规定汇票应载明付款时间，但也允许有例外，对未载明付款时间的汇票视为见票即付。我国《票据法》则规定：汇票上记载付款日期应当清楚、明确，未记载付款日期的视为见票即付。在实际业务中，汇票付款日期的记载形式主要有四种：

The tenor of draft is the date of payment for the amount stated in the draft. According to the British Law of Bills, due date is not a required item of draft, and a draft without due date shall be treated as at sight. Although the Geneva Convention on the Unification of the Law Relating to Bills of Ex-change and Promissory Notes stipulates that a draft shall specify the time of payment, an exception is allowed. If a draft does not specify the time of payment, it shall be deemed as at sight. According to the provisions of China's Negotiable Instruments Law, the date of payment stated on the draft shall be explicit and definite, and those without such date shall be deemed as at sight. In actual business, the payment date of draft is mainly recorded in four forms:

（1）见票即付（at sight/ on demand），是指持票人提示汇票的当天即为到期日，即期汇票无须承兑。如"见票即付（At sight pay to... ）"。

(1) At sight. It means the day on which the holder presents the draft is the due date and sight bill does not require acceptance. e.g. "At sight pay to...".

（2）见票后定期付款。如"见票后若干天/月付款（payable at ... days/months after sight）"，该汇票须由持票人向付款人提示，要求承兑，以便从承兑日（承兑人第一次见票日）起算，确定付款到期日，并明确承兑人的付款责任。

(2) Payable at a fixed period after sight. e.g. "payable at ... days/months after sight". The draft shall be presented by holder to payer for acceptance, so as to determine tenor from the date of acceptance (the date of first presentation by acceptor) and clarify the payment responsibility of acceptor.

（3）出票后定期付款。如"出票后若干天/月付款（payable at ... days/months after date）"。此种汇票也需由持票人事先向付款人提示汇票，以明确付款人的付款责任。

(3) Payable at a fixed period after date. e.g. "payable at … days/months after date". Such draft shall also be presented by holder to payer in advance to clarify the payment responsibility of payer.

（4）定日付款（fixed date）。如"定于2021年6月30日付款"（On 30th June, 2021 fixed pay to ... ）。这种汇票又称为板期付款汇票，需要提示承兑，以明确付款人的付款责任。

(4) Fixed date. e.g. "On 30th June, 2021 fixed pay to.". This draft, also known as bill payable at a fixed date, requires presentation for acceptance to clarify the payment responsibility of payer.

另外，在实践中还有使用"运输单据出单日期后定期付款"的做法，例如"提单日期后30天付款（at 30 days after date of bill of lading）"。

In addition, there is a practice of using "periodic payment after date of transport documents", e.g. "at 30 days after date of bill of lading".

远期汇票到期日的算法要遵循下列原则：

The due date of time bill shall be calculated according to the following principles:

（1）见票后、出票后若干天付款的汇票，算尾不算头，若到期日为节假日，可顺延。例如"At 60 days after sight"。见票日为5月16日，则此汇票的到期日为7月15日。

(1) For draft payable several days after sight and issue, the first day shall not be counted. If the due date falls on a holiday, it can be postponed accordingly. e.g. "At 60 days after sight". If the date of sight is May 16,

the due date of draft will be July 15.

（2）见票后、出票后若干月付款的汇票，其到期日为付款之月的相应日期，若无相应日期，则以该月最后一日为到期日。例如"At 2 months after sight"，见票日为7月31日，到期日为9月30日。

(2) For draft payable several months after sight and issue, the due date is the corresponding date in the month of payment, or if there is no corresponding date, the last day of that month shall be deemed as the due date. e.g. "At 2 months after sight". The date of sight is July 31 and the due date will be September 30.

（3）注明日期后若干天/月付款的汇票，其到期日应区分from和after。若付款时间为"At 60 days from 15th May, 2021"，则到期日按"算头不算尾"的原则确定，其到期日为7月13日。若付款时间为"At 60 days after 15th May, 2021"，则到期日按"算尾不算头"的原则确定，其到期日为7月14日。

(3) For draft payable several days/months after stated date, the due date shall be distinguished between "from" and "after". If the time of payment is "At 60 days from 15th May, 2021", the due date will be determined according to the principle that "the last day shall not be counted" and its due date is July 13. If the time of payment is "At 60 days after 15th May, 2021", the due date will be determined according to the principle that "the first day shall not be counted" and its due date is July 14.

9. 出票地点和付款地点 (Place of Issue, Place of Payment)

出票地点和付款地点的记载，对涉外汇票具有重要意义，因为按照国际惯例，汇票所适用的法律多采用行为地法律的原则。日内瓦《统一汇票本票法公约》明确规定："汇票应当记载出票地点和付款地点。未载明出票地点的，以出票人的营业场所、住所或居住地作为出票地点。"我国《票据法》虽未将出票地点和付款地点列为必要项目，但在第二十三条中也明确规定："汇票上记载的付款地、出票地等事项的，应当明确清楚；未记载付款地的，付款人的营业场所、住所或者经常居住地为付款地；汇票上未记载出票地的，出票人的营业场所、住所或经常居住地为出票地。"

The records of place of issue and place of payment are of great significance to a foreign draft, because according to international practice, the law applicable to draft often follows the principle of the law of the place of conduct. The Geneva Convention on the Unification of the Law Relating to Bills of Ex-change and Promissory Notes explicitly stipulates: "A draft shall specify the place of issue and the place of payment. If the place of issue is not stated, the place of business, domicile or residence of the drawer shall be taken as the place of issue." Although China's Negotiable Instruments Law does not list place of issue and place of payment as necessary items, Article 23 specifies that: "Where place of payment, place of issue and other items are recorded in a draft, they shall be clearly stated; if place of payment is not specified, the place of business, domicile or habitual residence of the payer shall be the place of payment; if place of issue is not specified, the place of business, domicile or habitual residence of the drawer shall be place of issue."

除上述项目外，汇票还可以有一些票据法允许的其他内容的记载，如：利息和利率、付一不付二、禁止转让、免做拒绝证明、汇票编号、出票条款等。

In addition to the above items, a draft can also have some other contents allowed by the bill law, such as interest and rate, second being unpaid, no transfer, exemption from protest, bill No., draw clause, etc.

汇票样本见图10-1。

See the figure 10-1 for a draft sample.

BILL OF EXCHANGE

凭 Drawn Under	CITIBANK N.A. HEAD OFFICE 111 WALL STREET NEW YORK, NY USA		不可撤销信用证 Irrevocable L/C No.	B590030622313	
日期 Date	2022-05-25	支取 Payable With interest @ %	按 息 付款		
号码 No.	I202203011	汇票金额 Exchange for USD71200.00	海口 Haikou	2022-06-25	

见票 at **** 日后（本汇票之副本未付）付交
sight of this FIRST of Exchange (Second of Exchange Being unpaid)

Pay to the order of **BANK OF CHINA HAINAN BRANCH**

金额 the sum of **U.S.DOLLARS SEVENTY-ONE THOUSAND TWO HUNDRED ONLY.**

此致 To **CITIBANK N.A. HEAD OFFICE**
111 WALL STREET NEW YORK, NY USA

Hainan Botong International Trade Co.
8 Guoxing Avenue, Meilan District, Haikou, China

陈雨

图10-1 汇票样本
Figure 10-1　Draft Sample

（四）汇票的种类 (Types of Draft)

汇票可以按照不同的分类标准分为不同的种类，常见的分类有以下几种。

Draft can be divided into different categories according to different classification standards. The common classifications are as follows.

1. 根据出票人不同划分 (By Drawer)

（1）银行汇票（banker's draft），其出票人和受票人都是银行。银行汇票的信用基础是银行信用，银行信用比一般的商业信用更加可靠，所以银行汇票的流通性较好。银行汇票主要用于汇款业务中的票汇。

(1) Banker's Draft, the drawer and drawee of which are both banks. The credit basis of banker's draft is bank credit, which is more reliable than general commercial credit, so banker's draft has good negotiability. It is mainly used for remittance by banker's demand draft (D/D) in remittance business.

（2）商业汇票（trade bill），其出票人是企业或个人，付款人可以是企业、个人，也可以是银行。商业汇票的信用基础是商业信用，其收款人或持票人承担的风险较大。不过，对商业汇票进行承兑，可在一定程度上降低收款人的风险；若由银行承兑，则能改变这张商业汇票的信用基础，提高该张汇票的身价。商业汇票在国际结算中的使用主要是出口商向国外进口商或银行收取货款时签发使用，如在商业托收、商业银行跟单信用证中通常会采用出口商签发的商业汇票。商业汇票通常一式两联，即同时签发两份正本，分别注明"付一不付二"和"付二不付一"的字样。

(2) The drawer of a trade bill is an enterprise or individual, and the payer can be an enterprise, individual or bank. The credit basis of trade bill is commercial credit and its payee or holder bears significant risk. Acceptance of the trade bill, however, will reduce the risk to the payee to some extent; if accepted by the bank, it will change the credit basis and increase the value of the bill. Trade bill is mainly used in international settlement when the exporter collects payment from foreign importers or banks. For example, trade bill issued by the exporter is

usually used in commercial collection and documentary credit of commercial banks. Trade bill is usually made in duplicate, i.e. two originals signed and issued at the same time, marked "second being unpaid" and "first being unpaid".

2. 根据承兑人不同划分 (By Acceptor)

（1）银行承兑汇票（banker's acceptance bill），是由银行承兑的远期汇票，建立在银行信用的基础上。银行可以对银行汇票承兑，也可以对商业汇票承兑，如果该张商业汇票的付款人是某家银行的话。银行对商业汇票加以承兑改变了汇票的信用基础，使商业信用转换为银行信用。汇票经过银行承兑后，持票人通常能按期取得票款，从而增强了该种汇票的可接受性和可流通性。

(1) Banker's acceptance bill is a time bill accepted by a bank, based on bank credit. Banks may accept banker's draft or trade bill if the payer of such trade bill is a bank. Bank acceptance of trade bill has changed the credit basis of bills, transforming commercial credit into bank credit. After accepted by the bank, the holder can usually get the payment on schedule, thus enhancing the acceptability and negotiability of such bills.

（2）商业承兑汇票（trader's acceptance bill），是由企业或个人承兑的远期汇票，建立在商业信用的基础上。

(2) Trader's acceptance bill is a time bill accepted by a company or individual, based on commercial credit.

3. 按付款时间不同来划分 (By Time of Payment)

（1）即期汇票（sight bill, demand draft），见票即付的汇票就是即期汇票。未载明具体付款日期的汇票按照票据法的规定视为即期汇票。

(1) Sight bill: a draft at sight is sight bill. A draft without specific payment date shall be deemed as sight bill in accordance with the bill law.

（2）远期汇票（time bill, usance draft），是在未来的特定日期或一定期限付款的汇票。根据付款期限的表示或确定方法不同，远期汇票又有定日付款（On...）、出票后定期付款（At...days after date of draft）、见票后定期付款（At ... days after sight）三种主要形式。其中见票后定期付款汇票使用较为普遍。国际上又习惯将 30 天以内付款的称为短期汇票（short bill），30 天以上付款的称为长期汇票（long bill）。

(2) Time bill is a draft payable on a fixed date or within a certain period in the future. According to the different expression or determination methods of payment term, Time bill have three main forms: fixed date (On...), payable at a fixed period after date (At…days after date of draft), payable at a fixed period after sight (At ... days after sight). Among them, draft payable at a fixed period after sight is widely used. Payment within 30 days is called short bill, and payment more than 30 days is called long bill.

4. 按有无附属单据划分 (By Additional Documents)

（1）光票（clean bill），是指不附带代表货物所有权的货运单据（如提单、保险单）的汇票，其流通完全依靠当事人（出票人、付款人、背书人）的信用，即全凭票面信用在市面上流通而无物资作保证。在国际贸易结算中较少使用光票，仅运费、保险费有时采用光票向对方收款。银行汇票多为光票。

(1) Clean bill refers to a draft without shipping documents representing the ownership of goods (such as B/L and insurance policy). Its circulation completely depends on the credit of the parties (drawer, payer and endorser), that is, it circulates in the market entirely by face credit without material guarantee. Clean Bill is seldom used in international trade settlement, and only freight charges and premium are sometimes collected from the other party by clean bill. Banker's draft is mostly clean Bill.

（2）跟单汇票（documentary bill），是指附带代表货物所有权的货运单据的汇票。跟单汇票的流通转让及资金融通，除与当事人的信用有关外，更取决于附属单据所代表货物的价值及单据质量。跟单汇票在国际贸易中被广泛使用，托收和信用证业务中通常都采用跟单汇票。商业汇票多为跟单汇票。

(2) Documentary bill refers to a draft attached with shipping documents representing the ownership of goods. The negotiation, transfer and accommodation of a documentary bill depend not only on the creditworthiness of the parties but also on the value and quality of the goods represented by additional documents. Documentary bill is widely used in international trade. It is usually adopted in collection and L/C business. Trade bills are mostly documentary bills.

5. 按流通领域的不同划分 (By Field of Circulation)

（1）国内汇票（inland bill, domestic bill），是指出票地和付款地同在一国之内，只在国内流通的汇票。

(1) Inland bill refers to a draft that is issued and paid in the same country and only circulated domestically.

（2）国外汇票（foreign bill, international bill），是指出票地和付款地有一方在国外，或双方均在国外，其流通涉及两国以上的汇票，在国际贸易结算中广泛使用。在使用国外汇票时，要特别注意票据记载事项及票据行为的法律适用。我国票据法规定，汇票出票时的记载事项，适用出票地法律。票据的背书、承兑、付款和保证行为，适用行为地法律。票据追索权的行使期限，适用出票地法律。票据的提示期限、有关拒绝证明的方式、出具拒绝证书的期限，适用付款地法律。

(2) Foreign bill refers to a draft with one or both of the place of issue and place of payment abroad, and its circulation involves two or more countries. It is widely used in international trade settlement. When using foreign bill, special attention shall be paid to the legal application of items recorded and acts on bill. According to China's Negotiable Instruments Law, the items recorded at the time of drawing a draft shall be governed by the law of the place of issue. Endorsement, acceptance, payment and guarantee of negotiable instruments shall be governed by the laws of the place where they are performed. The time limit for exercising the right of recourse shall be governed by the law of the place of issue. The time limit for presenting the bill, mode of protest and time limit for issuance of protest shall be governed by the law of the place of payment.

汇票按照上述标准的分类并不是绝对分类，并不意味着一张汇票只能限于某一种分类方式下的汇票，也就是说，一张汇票可能同时属于不同种类的汇票，如一张商业汇票与此同时又是银行承兑的远期商业跟单汇票。

The classification of draft according to the above standards is not absolute, which does not mean that a draft can only be limited to a certain classification. That is to say, a draft may belong to different categories at the same time. For example, a trade bill is also a time commercial documentary bill for bank acceptance.

（五）汇票的使用 (Use of Draft)

汇票使用过程中的各种行为，都由票据法加以规范，主要有出票、提示、承兑、付款等。如需转让，通常应经过背书行为转让。汇票遭到拒付，还要涉及发出拒付通知、做成拒绝证书和行使追索权等票据行为。

All kinds of acts during the use of draft are regulated by the bill law. The main ones are issue, presentation, acceptance and payment. A transfer shall normally be made by an act of endorsement. When a draft is dishonored, it involves acts such as giving notice of dishonor, making a protest and exercising the right of recourse.

1. 出票 (To Draw/Issue)

出票是出票人签发汇票并交付给收款人的行为。出票包括两个动作：一是出票人填写汇票并签字；二是将汇票交付给收款人。具备这两个行为，出票才有效。出票时必须逐一写明汇票各项必备内容。

Issue is the act of the drawer issuing a draft and delivering it to the payer. Issue involves two actions: one is for the drawer to fill in draft and sign; the other is to deliver the draft to payer. Issue is valid only if these two acts are present. All necessary contents of draft must be stated one by one when issuing.

2. 提示 (Presentation)

提示是指持票人向汇票的付款人或其他人出示汇票，要求其付款或承兑的行为。付款人看到汇票即为见票。提示可以分为两种：

Presentation refers to the act of holder presenting a draft to the payer or other persons for payment or acceptance. When the payer sees the draft, the draft is at sight. Presentation can be divided into two types:

（1）承兑提示（presentation for acceptance）。远期汇票应首先向付款人做承兑提示，即持远期汇票要求付款人承认到期付款的提示。

(1) Presentation for acceptance. A time bill shall first be presented to the payer for acceptance, i.e. a presentation requiring the payer to acknowledge due payment by holding the time bill.

（2）付款提示（presentation for payment）。即期汇票或已承兑的远期汇票应向付款人或承兑人做付款提示，即持即期汇票或已承兑的远期汇票要求付款人付款的提示。

(2) Presentation for payment. Sight bill or accepted time bill shall be presented for payment to the payer or acceptor, that is, a presentation to demand payment from the payer by holding the sight bill or accepted time bill.

可见，即期汇票只需一次付款提示，远期汇票则需两次提示，先提示承兑再提示付款。

It can be seen that sight bill only needs one presentation for payment, while time bill needs two presentations, first for acceptance and then for payment.

提示必须在规定的时限及规定的地点办理。英国《票据法》对于即期汇票要求付款的提示期限和远期汇票要求承兑的提示期限规定为合理时间内为之。日内瓦《统一汇票本票法公约》规定为一年。英国《票据法》规定对已承兑远期汇票的付款提示期限为在付款到期日提示。日内瓦《统一汇票本票法公约》规定要在付款到期日或其后的两个营业日内提示。如未在规定时限内提示，持票人即丧失对前手的追索权。

Presentation must be made within the prescribed time limit and at the prescribed place. The British Law of Bills stipulates that the presentation period of sight bill, and time bill for acceptance shall be a reasonable time. The Geneva Convention on the Unification of the Law Relating to Bills of Ex-change and Promissory Notes provides for one year. The British Law of Bills stipulates that the time limit for presentation for payment of an accepted time bill is within tenor. Presentation is required under the Geneva Convention on the Unification of the Law Relating to Bills of Ex-change and Promissory Notes within tenor or two business days thereafter. Failure to presentation within the specified time limit forfeits holder's right of recourse against remote holder.

我国《票据法》规定，见票即付的汇票，自出票日起1个月内向付款人提示付款。见票后定期付款的汇票，持票人应当自出票日起1个月内向付款人提示承兑。定日付款、出票后定期付款或见票后定期付款的汇票，自到期日起10日内向承兑人提示付款。

According to China's Negotiable Instruments Law, draft at sight shall be presented to payer for payment within 1 month from the date of issue. For draft payable at a fixed period after sight, the holder shall present to the payer for acceptance within 1 month from the date of issue. Draft payable on a fixed date, at a fixed period after date or sight shall be presented for payment to the acceptor within 10 days from due date.

持票人应在汇票载明的付款地点向付款人提示，如果汇票没有载明付款地点，则在付款人的营业场所或其住所提示。汇票上记载有担当付款人时，持票人应向担当付款人提示要求付款。

Presentation shall be made by holder to payer at the place of payment specified in the draft or, if no such place is specified in the draft, at payer's place of business or domicile. When the draft specifies a person designated as payer, the holder shall present to the person designated as payer for payment.

3. 承兑 (Acceptance)

承兑是指远期汇票的付款人承诺在汇票到期日支付汇票金额的票据行为。具体说，承兑是付款人在持票人向其提示远期汇票时，在汇票上签名，承诺于汇票到期时付款的行为。按照《票据法》的规定，付款人应当自收到提示承兑的汇票之日起3日内承兑或拒绝承兑未经承兑的远期汇票，在法律上对付款人没有强制效力。故远期汇票，一定要提示承兑，并经付款人承兑后再行付款。

Acceptance refers to the act on bill that payer of time bill promises to pay the amount on the due date of draft. Specifically, acceptance is the act of payer signing the bill and promising to make payment when the bill expires when the holder presents it with a time bill. According to the provisions of the Negotiable Instruments Law, the payer shall accept or reject an unaccepted time bill within 3 days from the date of receiving the bill presented for acceptance, which is not legally binding on the payer. Therefore, time bill must be presented for acceptance and accepted by the payer before payment can be made.

承兑包括两个动作：一是在汇票的正面写明"已承兑（ACCEPTED）"字样和承兑日期，并由承兑人签字；二是将已承兑的汇票交付持票人，或把承兑通知书交给持票人（国际银行业务习惯上由承兑行发出承兑通知书给持票人，来代替交付已承兑的汇票）。见票后定期付款的汇票，承兑日便是见票日，应当在承兑时记载付款到期日。

Acceptance involves two actions: one is to write the word "ACCEPTED" and acceptance date on the front of draft, which shall be signed by the acceptor; the other is to deliver the accepted draft to the holder, or hand over acceptance notices to the holder (Accepting bank customarily issues acceptance notices to the holder instead of delivering the accepted draft). For draft payable at a fixed period after sight, date of acceptance shall be the date of sight and tenor shall be recorded at the time of acceptance.

承兑汇票意味着承兑人对汇票的付款做了进一步的保证。当付款行承兑汇票后，按照英国《票据法》，该汇票可以当作持票人要求支取汇票金额的领款单。故一般银行愿意贴现买进银行承兑的远期汇票。远期汇票经承兑后，承兑人是汇票的主债务人，出票人退居从债务人位置。

Accepting a draft means that the acceptor has further guaranteed the payment of draft. After paying bank accepts a draft, such draft may be deemed as a receipt for the amount requested by holder in accordance with the British Law of Bills. Generally, banks are willing to buy banker's acceptance time bill at a discount. After a time bill is accepted, the acceptor becomes the principal debtor of bill, and the drawer becomes a subordinate debtor.

4. 付款 (Payment)

持票人在到期日提示汇票，经付款人或承兑人正当付款以后，汇票即被解除责任。所谓正当付款包括以下几种情况：①由付款人或承兑人支付足额票款，而不是由出票人或背书人支付；②要在到期日或以后支付而非在到期日以前支付；③要支付给持票人，即汇票如被转让，前手背书必须连续和真实；④善意的付款，指付款人按照专业惯例，利用专业信息不知道持票人权利有缺陷而付款者即为善意付款。付款人向持票人正当付款之后，全体汇票债务人的责任解除，即不仅解除付款人的付款义务，而且解除了所有票据债务人的债务责任。持票人获得付款的，应当在汇票上签收，并将汇票交给付款人。

When the holder presents the draft on the due date, it shall be discharged from liability upon payment in due course by payer or acceptor. The so-called payment in due course includes the following situations: ① full payment by payer or acceptor and not by drawer or endorser; ② to be paid on or after the due date and not before; ③ to be paid to the holder, i.e. if the draft is transferred, the prior endorsement must be continuous and true; ④ goodwill payment, which refers to the payment made in good faith by the payer who, in accordance with professional practice, utilizes professional information and is unaware that the holder's rights are defective. After the payer has made payment in due course to the holder, all bill debtors are discharged from liability, i.e. not only the payer's payment obligation but also the debt liability of all bill debtors is discharged. If the holder receives payment, it shall sign on the draft and hand it over to the payer.

5. 背书 (Endorsement)

背书是持票人在汇票背面签字并把它交给他人的票据转让行为。背书包括两个动作：一是签字；二是交付。只有两个行为同时具备，背书转让行为方才有效。背书人签字应包含他的签章并记载背书日期。

Endorsement is the act of transferring a draft signed by the holder on its back and handed over to another person. Endorsement involves two actions: signature and delivery. Endorsement for transfer is valid only if both acts are present. The endorser's signature shall include his signature and the date of endorsement.

背书是将汇票权利转让给他人的一种行为。经过背书，汇票权利由背书人转让给了受让人。通过背书转让，受让人不仅取得了该张汇票，而且取得了该张汇票上的权利；而背书人不仅转让了汇票，且要对该张汇票负有与出票人相同的连带责任。

Endorsement is the act of transferring draft rights to others. By endorsement, draft rights are transferred by the endorser to the assignee. Through transfer by endorsement, the assignee not only acquires the draft, but also acquires the rights on the draft; and the endorser not only transfers the draft, but also bears the same joint liability as the drawer.

在现代商品社会，一张指示性抬头的汇票往往可以经过多次背书转让，这样可能出现多名背书人和被背书人，如第一背书人和第一被背书人、第二背书人和第二被背书人，形成一种复杂连带的债权债务关系。第一背书人是汇票上载明的收款人。

In the modern commodity society, an draft bearing a demonstrative order can often be transferred by multiple endorsements, so there may be multiple endorsers and endorsees, such as the first endorser and the first endorsee, the second endorser and the second endorsee, forming a complex joint creditor-debtor relationship. The first endorser is the payer named on the draft.

背书人与被背书人称为前手（可以理解为前面经手的人，背书要签字，签字需要手签）和后手（是指在票据签章人之后签章的其他票据债务人）。前手对其任一后手负有担保该汇票一定为受票人承兑和付款的责任；同理，后手对其前手享有要求前手付款的权利。

The endorser and the endorsee are referred to as remote holder (which can be understood as those who have handled it before. Endorsement requires signature, and signature requires handwriting) and subsequent (referring to other bill debtors who sign after the signatory). The remote holder is liable for guaranteeing to any subsequent that the draft will be accepted and paid by the drawee; similarly, the subsequent has the right to demand payment from its remote holder.

6. 拒付/退票 (Dishonor)

持票人提示汇票要求付款时，遭到拒绝付款，或持票人提示汇票要求承兑时，遭到拒绝承兑，或付款人避而不见、死亡或宣告破产，以致付款已事实上不可能时，均称为拒付，也叫退票。遭到拒付后，持票人应立即向前手追索，否则会丧失追索权。

When the holder presents a draft for payment or acceptance and is rejected, or when the payer evades, dies or declares bankruptcy, making payment virtually impossible, it is called dishonor. The holder shall immediately seek recourse from its remote holder upon dishonor, otherwise such right of recourse will be forfeited.

7. 拒付通知 (Notice of Dishonor)

拒付通知的作用是要汇票的债务人及早知道拒付，以便做好准备。持票人若不及时制作拒付通知，并及时发出，即丧失追索权。汇票遭到拒付后，一般情况下，持票人应在1个营业日内将拒付的事实通知其前手背书人，前手应于接到拒付通知后的1个营业日内再通知其前手背书人，一直通知到出票人为止。如后手未及时通知其前手背书人，而使前手遭受损失，后手应负赔偿之责。也可由持票人同时向各汇票债务人发出拒付通知，这样每个前手就无须继续向前手通知了。

The purpose of notice of dishonor is to make the bill debtors aware of the dishonor in advance so that they can prepare for it. If the holder fails to make a notice of dishonor in time and send it out in time, it shall lose its right of recourse. Where a draft is dishonored, the holder shall generally notify its prior endorser of such dishonor within 1 business day and the prior endorser shall give further notices to its prior endorser within 1 business day after receipt of the notice of dishonor, until the notice reaches the drawer. The endorser shall be liable for any loss suffered by the prior endorser as a result of his failure to give timely notices. Notice of dishonor may also be given by the holder to each bill debtor at the same time so that no further notices are required from each remote holder.

8. 拒绝证书 (Protest)

拒绝证书是由拒付地点的法定公证人做出证明拒付事实的文件。持票人请求公证人做出拒绝证书时，应将汇票交出，由公证人再次向付款人提示，遭到拒付时按规定做出拒绝证书。持票人凭退回的汇票和拒绝证书向前手背书人行使追索权。

Protest is a document issued by the legal notary at the place of protest certifying the fact of non-payment. When the holder requests a notary to protest, it shall surrender the draft for further presentation by the notary to the payer and in case of dishonor make such protest as prescribed. The holder shall exercise the right of recourse against the returned draft and protest to the prior endorser.

持票人要求公证人做成拒绝证书时所付的公证费用，在追索票款时，一并向出票人算收。有时出票人为了免除此项费用，可在汇票上加注"放弃拒绝证书"字样，则持票人不需做成拒绝证书即可行使追索权。

The notarial fee paid by the holder when requesting the notary to make a protest shall be calculated and collected from the drawer at the time of recourse. Sometimes, in order to waive this fee, the drawer may write "Waiver of Protest" on a draft, so that the holder can exercise its right of recourse without making a protest.

我国《票据法》规定，持票人不能出示拒绝证明（可由承兑人或付款人出具，也可由公证人出具）、退票理由书或者未按规定期限提供其他合法证明的，丧失对其前手的追索权。但是，承兑人或者付款人仍应当对持票人承担责任。

According to China's Negotiable Instruments Law, if a holder fails to show a protest (which may be issued by an acceptor or payer or notary), reasons for dishonor or other legal evidence within the prescribed time limit, it will lose its right of recourse against its remote holder. However, the acceptor or payer shall remain liable to the holder.

9. 追索 (Recourse)

追索指汇票遭到拒付时持票人对其前手背书人或出票人要求偿还汇票金额及费用的行为。持票人是汇票的债权人，如在法定期限内向付款人提示承兑或付款遭到拒付，可向其任一前手背书人、出票人和承兑人行使追索权，要求偿还汇票金额及费用。持票人行使追索权之前，必须及时发出拒付通知，将其遭到拒付的事实书面通知其前手，并及时做成拒绝证书。另外，持票人必须在法定期限内行使其追索权，否则权利丧失。我国《票据法》规定，持票人对前手的追索权，自被拒绝承兑或拒绝付款之日起6个月。

Recourse refers to the act of holder claiming reimbursement for the amount and costs of draft against its prior endorser or drawer in case of dishonor. Holder is a creditor of draft and may exercise the right of recourse against any of its prior endorsers, drawers and acceptors for reimbursement of the amount and costs of draft if presentation to payer for acceptance or payment is dishonored within the statutory time limit. Before exercising the right of recourse, the holder must promptly give notice of dishonor, notify its remote holder in writing of the fact that it has been dishonored and make a protest without delay. In addition, the holder must exercise its right of recourse within the statutory period or it will be forfeited. China's Negotiable Instrument Law stipulates that the holder's right of recourse to remote holder shall be 6 months from the date of refusal of acceptance or payment.

（六）汇票的贴现 (Discount of Draft)

1. 贴现业务 (Discount Business)

贴现（discount）是指远期汇票承兑后尚未到期，由银行或贴现公司从票面金额中扣除按一定贴现率计算的贴现息后，将余额（净款）支付给持票人从而取得汇票的行为。

Discount refers to the act that the bank or discount company deducts the discount interest calculated at a certain discount rate from the face amount of a time bill that has not yet matured after acceptance and pays the balance (net proceeds) to the holder to obtain the bill.

贴现后，汇票将被贴现行持有。贴现行持贴进汇票直至到期日，提示给承兑人要求付款，承兑人支付票面金额，相当于归还了贴现行的垫款，并令贴现行赚取了贴现利息。所以贴现业务既是票据买卖业务，也是资金融通业务。

After discount, draft will be held by the discount bank. The discount bank holds the draft discounted until its expiry date, and presents it to the acceptor for payment. the acceptor pays the face amount, which is equivalent to repaying the advance made by the discount bank and enabling the discount bank to earn discount interest. Discount business is not only a bill trading business, but also a financing business.

2. 贴现息和汇票净款的计算 (Calculation of Discount Interest and Net Proceeds)

贴现息是按照贴现天数，即距到期日的天数乘以每天贴现率来计算的。但因贴现率多用年率来表示，所以要先将其折成日率，英镑按一年365天作为基本天数，美元按一年360天作为基本天数。

Discount interest is calculated as the number of days to due date multiplied by the daily discount rate. However, since the discount rate is mostly expressed by an annual rate, it should be converted into a daily rate first. GBP is based on 365 days a year while USD is based on 360 days a year.

$$贴现息 = 票面金额 \times \frac{贴现天数}{365 \text{ 或 } 360} \times 年贴现率$$

$$\text{Discount Interest} = \text{Nominal Amount} \times \frac{\text{Discount Days}}{365 \text{ or } 360} \times \text{Annual Discount Rate}$$

净款（net proceeds）又称汇票现值，它是汇票票面金额与贴现息的差额。

Net Proceeds, also known as the present value of draft, is the difference between the face amount and discount interest.

$$净款 = 票面金额 - 贴现息$$
$$\text{Net Proceeds} = \text{Face Amount} - \text{Discount Interest}$$

$$净款 = 票面金额 \times (1 - \frac{贴现天数}{365 \text{ 或 } 360} \times 年贴现率)$$

$$\text{Net Proceeds} = \text{Nominal Amount} \times (1 - \frac{\text{Discount Days}}{365 \text{ or } 360} \times \text{Annual Discount Rate})$$

例1：一张见票后90天付款，票面金额8000美元的承兑汇票，承兑日为4月1日，持票人要求承兑行于承兑当日贴现，该行按年贴现率6%计算，应付多少净款给持票人？

Example 1: An acceptance bill with a face amount of USD 8000, payable 90 days after sight, is accepted on April 1. The holder requires the accepting bank to discount on the acceptance date. If the bank calculates at an annual discount rate of 6%, how much net proceeds should be paid to the holder?

贴现息 = 8000×90/360×6% = 120（美元）

Discount Interest = 8000×90%/360×6% = USD 120

净款 = 8000 - 120 = 7880（美元）

Net Proceeds = 8000 - 120 = USD 7880

二、支票（Cheque/Check）

（一）支票的含义 (Meaning of Cheque)

支票是存款人对其开户行签发的，授权该银行对某人或其指定人或持票人即期支付一定金额的无条件的书面支付命令。简单地说，支票就是以银行为付款人的即期汇票。

A Cheque is an unconditional order to pay in writing issued by the depositor to its bank authorizing it to pay a certain amount of money to someone or their nominee or holder at sight. In short, cheque is a sight bill with the bank as payer.

支票与汇票一样有三个基本当事人：出票人、付款人和收款人。支票的出票人必须在付款银行开设有存款账户。实际上，支票是存款人用以从存款银行支取存款而开出的票据，它首先被交给收款人，或者出票人本身就是收款人，再由收款人凭票提示取款，或由收款人转让给别人，再由持票人向银行提示取款。所以，支票也是可流通的凭证。

A cheque, like a draft, has three basic parties: drawer, payer and payee. Drawer of cheque must have a deposit account the paying bank. In practice, a cheque is an instrument drawn by the depositor to withdraw funds from the deposit bank. It is first handed over to the payee or the drawer as payee, and then withdrawn by the payee through presentation of cheque, or transferred by the payee to someone else for withdrawal by the holder from bank presentation. Therefore, a cheque is also negotiable.

支票的功能在于"支（取）"，持票人应尽快去提示支款，所以支票总是见票即付的，不能开出远期支票。根据我国《票据法》的相关规定，支票的持票人应自出票日起10日内向付款人提示付款；异地使用的支票，其提示付款的期限由中国人民银行另行规定。另外，持票人对支票出票人的权利，自出票日起6个月。其他凡适用于见票即付的即期汇票的各项规定，都适用于支票。

The function of a cheque is "payment (withdrawal)" and the holder should make a presentation as soon as possible, so the cheque is always at sight and we cannot issue a post-dated cheque. According to the relevant provisions of China's Negotiable Instrument Law, the holder of a cheque shall present to the payer for payment within 10 days from the date of issue; for a cheque used in other places, the time limit for presentation for payment shall be separately stipulated by the People's Bank of China. In addition, the holder's right to a cheque drawer is 6 months from the date of issue. All other provisions of sight bill applicable to at sight apply to cheque.

（二）支票的内容 (Contents of Cheque)

根据日内瓦《统一支票法公约》的规定，支票必须记载以下各项：① 写明"支票"字样；② 无条件支付一定金额的命令；③ 付款银行名称；④ 付款地点（未写明的，以付款银行所在地为付款地点）；⑤ 写明"即期"字样（如未写明，仍视为见票即付）；⑥ 收款人或其指定人；⑦ 出票日期、地点（未写明的，出票人所在地为出票地点）；⑧ 出票人的签字。

In accordance with the Geneva Convention Providing a Uniform Law of Cheques, a cheque must include: ① marked with "cheque"; ② an unconditional order to pay a certain amount; ③ name of paying bank; ④ place of payment (if not specified, the location of the paying bank shall be place of payment); ⑤ marked with "At sight" (if not, it shall still be deemed as at sight); ⑥ the payee or its nominee; ⑦ date of issue and place (if not specified, the location of the drawer shall be place of issue); ⑧ signature of the drawer.

我国《票据法》第八十四条规定，支票必须记载下列事项：表明"支票"字样、无条件支付的委托、确定的金额、付款人名称、出票日期、出票人签章。支票上未记载上述事项之一的，支票无效。

Article 84 of China's Negotiable Instruments Law stipulates that the following items are essential to a cheque: the word "cheque", unconditional payment entrustment, a sum certain in money, name of payer, date of issue and drawer's signature shall be indicated in cheque. If one of the above particulars is included in the cheque, the cheque will be invalid.

（三）支票的种类 (Types of Cheque)

1. 记名支票和不记名支票 (Order Cheque and Bearer Cheque)

所谓记名与不记名，是指支票上收款人这一栏的行文。凡记名支票者，必须在这一栏写明某人或某人的指定人为收款人，如"Cheque payable to A or order"；凡不记名支票者，这一栏就写成"来人（bearer）"，如"Cheque payable to bearer"。

The term "order" or "bearer" refers to the wording in the payee column of a cheque. Where a cheque is payable to order, it must be stated in this column that the person or their nominee is the payee, e.g. "Cheque payable to A or order"; where a cheque is payable to bearer, it must be written in this column as "Bearer", e.g. "Cheque payable to bearer".

2. 一般支票和划线支票 (Open Cheque and Crossed Cheque)

所谓划线支票（crossed cheque）就是在支票的证明画上两条平行线，以此表明该支票不能付款行的柜台提现，而只能付到收款人的账户入账。划线支票因为不能提现而只能入账，就相当于一张转账支票，这样可以防止支票失落后被冒领。与此相反的是未划线支票（uncrossed cheque），即一般支票（open cheque），它既能转账也能提现。

Crossed cheque refers to drawing two parallel lines on the certificate of a cheque, indicating that the cheque cannot be withdrawn at the counter of the paying bank and can only be credited to the account of the payee. A crossed cheque, which cannot be withdrawn and can only be credited, is equivalent to a transfer cheque, which can prevent it from being falsely claimed after being lost. On the contrary, an uncrossed cheque, also known as an open cheque, can be used for both transfer and withdrawal.

3. 保付支票 (Certified Cheque)

保付支票是付款行加盖"保付"戳记并签字，表明在支票提示时一定付款的支票。支票一经保付，付款责任即由付款银行承担。发票人、背书人都可免于追索。付款银行对支票保付后，即将票款从出票人账户转入一个专户，以备付款。支票保付后，付款银行就成为主债务人。另外，持票人可以不受付款提示期的限制。倘若持票人遗失保付支票，一般不能做出止付通知。

A certified cheque is a cheque stamped and signed by the paying bank to indicate that payment will be made when the cheque is presented. Payment responsibility is assumed by the paying bank once the cheque has been certified for payment. Recourse may be waived by the drawer or endorser. After the paying bank certifies the cheque, it will transfer the money from the drawer's account to a special account for payment. When the cheque is certified, the paying bank becomes the principal debtor. In addition, the holder may not be limited by the presentation period for payment. Stop order is generally not available if the holder loses a certified cheque.

4. 银行支票 (Banker's Cheque)

银行支票是指由银行签发的，并由银行付款的支票，也就是银行即期汇票。银行支票的出票人和付款人都是银行。

Banker's cheque refers to a cheque issued and paid by the bank, i.e. a bank sight bill. Both the drawer and payer of banker's cheque are banks.

5. 空头支票 (Bad Cheque)

按照各国票据法规定，支票的出票人必须按照签发的支票金额承担保证向持票人付款的责任。据此，支票的出票人所签发的支票金额不得超过其付款时在付款人处实有的存款金额。如果出票人签发的支票金额超过其付款时在付款人处实有的存款金额的，称为空头支票。我国票据法禁止签发空头支票，并规定签发空头支票或者故意签发与其预留的本名签名式样或者印鉴不符的支票，骗取财物的属于票据诈骗行为，依法追究刑事责任。

The drawer of a cheque must be responsible for securing payment to the holder in accordance with the bill laws of all countries for the amount of the cheque issued. Accordingly, the amount of a cheque issued by the drawer shall not exceed the amount actually on deposit with the payer at the time of payment. If the amount of the cheque issued by the drawer exceeds the actual deposit amount with the payer at the time of payment, it is called a bad cheque. China's Negotiable Instruments Law prohibits the issuance of a bad cheque, and stipulates that issuing a bad cheque or deliberately issuing a cheque that is inconsistent with its reserved signature style or seal belongs to bill fraud and shall be investigated for criminal responsibility according to law.

（四）支票与汇票的区别 (Differences between Cheque and Draft)

支票是由汇票演变而来的，故它们有许多相同之处：同是一项无条件的书面支付命令；同是委托式票据；基本当事人相同。但支票与汇票也有区别，主要有以下几方面：

Cheque evolved from draft, so they have a lot in common: both are an unconditional order to pay in writing; both are entrusted bills; and the basic parties are the same. However, cheque is different from draft in the following aspects:

（1）付款期限不同。支票都是即期的，而汇票有即期和远期之分。

Payment term. Cheque is at sight, while draft is divided into sight bill and time bill.

（2）资金关系不同。支票的签发必须以出票人与付款人之间存在资金关系为前提，而汇票在签发时，出票人和付款人之间不必先有资金关系。

Financial relationship. Cheque must be issued on the premise that there is a financial relationship between drawer and payer, while draft does not require a financial relationship between drawer and payer before issuance.

（3）提示期限不同。根据我国《票据法》，支票的提示期限是自出票日起 10 日内，即期付款和见票后定期付款的汇票是自出票日后 1 个月内提示。

Presentation period. According to China's Negotiable Instruments Law, the presentation period for a cheque is within 10 days from the date of issue. For draft payable at sight or at a fixed period after sight, the presentation period is within 1 month from the date of issue.

（4）可否止付不同。支票可以止付，如发生支票的遗失或毁坏，出票人可以要求银行止付；又如出票人出票后发现收款人没有按合同履约，也可通知银行止付。但汇票在承兑后即不可止付。

Whether the payment can be stopped. The cheque can be stopped. In case of loss or destruction of the cheque, the drawer may require the bank to stop payment; in case that the payee fails to perform according to the contract after the drawer issues a cheque, the drawer may also notify the bank to stop payment. However, payment cannot be stopped for an accepted draft.

（5）用途不同。支票只能作为结算工具使用；而汇票除结算工具外，还可作为押汇工具，远期汇票还是一种信贷工具。

Purpose. Cheque can only be used as a settlement tool, while draft can serve as a documentary tool in addition to a settlement tool. Time bill is also a credit instrument.

三、本票（Promissory Note）

（一）本票的含义 (Meaning of Promissory Note)

英国《票据法》对本票的定义为：本票是一人向另一人签发的，保证于见票时或定期或在可以确定的将来时间，支付一定金额给某人或其指定人或持票人的一张无条件的书面支付承诺。

A promissory note is defined in the British Law of Bills as an unconditional promise in writing by one person to another to pay a certain amount at sight or at regular intervals or at such future time as may be determined to that person or his nominee or holder.

我国《票据法》第七十三条规定，本票是出票人签发的，承诺自己在见票时无条件支付确定的金额给收款人或持票人的票据。我国票据法所称的本票，是指银行本票，且只有即期付款一种付款时间。

Article 73 of China's Negotiable Instruments Law stipulates that promissory note is a note issued by the drawer, promising to unconditionally pay a sum certain in money to the payee or holder at sight. The term "Promissory Note" as mentioned in China's Negotiable Instruments Law refers to banker's promissory note, and there is only "by sight payment".

（二）本票的内容 (Contents of Promissory Note)

日内瓦《统一汇票本票法公约》规定，本票应具备以下几项内容：① 表明"本票"字样；② 无条件支付一定金额的承诺；③ 付款期限；④ 付款地点；⑤ 收款人名称；⑥ 出票地点与日期；⑦ 出票人签字。

The Geneva Convention on the Unification of the Law Relating to Bills of Ex-change and Promissory Notes stipulates that a promissory note shall set out the following particulars: ① marked with "Promissory Note"; ② a commitment to pay a certain amount unconditionally; ③ payment term; ④ place of payment; ⑤ name of payee; ⑥ place and date of issue; ⑦ signature of the drawer.

我国《票据法》第七十五条规定，本票必须记载下列事项：表明"本票"的字样；无条件支付的承诺；确定的金额；收款人名称；出票日期；出票人签章。本票上未记载前款规定事项之一，本票无效。我国《票据法》第七十六条规定，本票上记载付款地、出票地等事项的，应当清楚、明确。本票上未记载付款地的，出票人的营业场所为付款地。本票上未记载出票地的，出票人的营业场所为出票地。并且，我国《票据法》明确规定"本票自出票日起，付款期限最长不得超过2个月。"

Article 75 of China's Negotiable Instruments Law stipulates that the following items are essential to a promissory note: the word "Promissory Note"; unconditional promise to pay; a sum certain in money; name of payee; date of issue; drawer's signature. A promissory note shall be invalid if any one of the particulars mentioned in the preceding paragraph is not specified thereon. Article 76 of China's Negotiable Instruments Law stipulates that where the place of payment, place of issue and other particulars are recorded on a promissory note, they shall be explicit and definite. If place of payment is not specified on the promissory note, the business place of drawer shall be the place of payment. If place of issue is not specified on the promissory note, the business place of drawer shall be the place of issue. Moreover, China's Negotiable Instrument Law explicitly stipulates that "the payment period of promissory note shall not exceed 2 months from date of issue."

（三）本票的种类 (Types of Promissory Note)

根据我国《票据法》关于本票的规定和国际上关于本票种类划分方法，我国《票据法》所调整的本票有以下种类。

According to the provisions of China's Negotiable Instrument Law on promissory note and international classification methods for promissory note, the types of promissory note adjusted by China's Negotiable Instrument Law as follows.

1. 即期本票 (Sight Note)

根据本票付款期限的不同，国际上本票可分为即期本票和远期本票。所谓即期本票是见票即付的本票；远期本票包括定日付款本票、出票后定期付款的本票和见票后定期付款的本票。我国《票据法》第七十三条第一款只规定了"本票是出票人签发的，承诺自己在见票时无条件支付确定的金额给收款人或者持票人的票据"，因此，我国《票据法》只调整"见票时无条件支付"的即期本票，而不调整远期本票。

According to the different payment terms of promissory notes, international promissory notes can be divided into sight note and time note. The so-called sight note is a promissory note at sight; time note includes promissory note payable on a fixed date, at a fixed period after date and at a fixed period after sight. Paragraph 1 of Article 73 of China's Negotiable Instruments Law only provides that "A promissory note is an instrument issued by a drawer and promises to unconditionally pay a sum certain in money to the payee or holder at sight". Therefore, China's Negotiable Instruments Law only adjusts sight note instead of time note.

2. 银行本票 (Banker's Promissory Note)

根据签发本票的主体不同，国际上本票可分为企事业单位和个人签发的商业本票与银行签发的银行本票。我国《票据法》第七十三条第二款规定"本法所称本票，是指银行本票"，所以，我国《票据法》只调整银行本票，而不调整商业本票。

According to the different subjects of issuing promissory note, promissory note can be divided into trader's promissory note issued by enterprises, institutions and individuals and banker's promissory note issued by banks. Article 73 (2) of China's Negotiable Instruments Law provides that "Promissory note used in this law refers to banker's promissory note". Therefore, our negotiable instruments law only adjusts banker's promissory note, not trader's promissory note.

3. 记名本票 (Order Note)

根据本票上是否记载收款人的名称，国际上本票可分为记名本票和无记名本票。我国《票据法》第七十五条规定，本票必须记载收款人名称，否则，本票无效；所以，我国票据法只调整记名本票。

According to whether the name of payee is specified on promissory note, international promissory note can be divided into order note and bearer note. Article 75 of China's Negotiable Instrument Law stipulates that a promissory note must specify the name of payee, otherwise, the promissory note is invalid; therefore, China's Negotiable Instruments Law only adjusts order note.

（四）本票与汇票的区别 (Differences between Promissory Note and Draft)

本票与汇票都属于票据，具有一些相同的票据特性和票据行为，也都需要记载一些相同的必要项目，它们的区别主要体现在以下几点。

Promissory note and draft are both bills. They share the same characteristics and acts on bill and need to include some necessary items. Their differences are mainly reflected in the following aspects.

1. 票据性质不同 (Nature of Bill)

本票是一种无条件的书面支付承诺，而汇票是一种无条件的书面支付命令。

Promissory note is an unconditional promise to pay in writing, while draft is an unconditional order to pay in writing.

2. 基本当事人不同 (Basic Parties)

本票只有两个基本当事人，即出票人和收款人；而汇票有三个基本当事人，即出票人、付款人和收款人。

Promissory note has only two basic parties, namely drawer and payee; whereas draft has three basic parties, namely drawer, payer and payee.

3. 付款方式不同 (Payment Method)

本票的出票人同时就是付款人，所以出票人向收款人承诺自己付款，它是承诺式票据。汇票的出票人委托或命令付款人无条件支付一定金额给收款人的票据，付款人没有义务必须支付票款，除非他承兑了汇票，所以汇票是命令式或委托式的票据。

The drawer of a promissory note is also the payer, so the drawer promises to make payment to the payee, which is a promissory note. The drawer of a draft entrusts or orders the payer to unconditionally pay a certain amount to the payee, and the payer is not obligated to pay the bill unless he has accepted it. Therefore, a draft is an ordered or entrusted bill.

4. 票据行为不同 (Acts on Bill)

本票不需要承兑提示、承兑、遭拒付后做成拒绝证书等，而汇票则需要这些行为。因为本票无须承兑，所以英国《票据法》主张远期本票只有after date，没有after sight。但日内瓦《统一汇票本票法公约》认为其可有after sight付款，需要持票人向出票人提示"签见"，从签见日起算，确定到期日。如出票人拒绝签见，则从提示签见日起算。

Promissory note does not require presentation for acceptance, acceptance, protest after dishonor, etc., while draft requires these acts. Since a promissory note does not require acceptance, the British Law of Bills maintains that a time note is only after date and not after sight. However, according to the Geneva Convention on the Unification of the Law Relating to Bills of Ex-change and Promissory Notes, after sight payment may be made, and the holder needs to present a "Sight" to the drawer for determination of due date from the date of sight payment. If the drawer refuses "Sight", it shall be counted from the date of presentation for sight payment.

5. 主债务人不同 (Principal Debtor)

本票的主债务人是出票人，且自始至终都是出票人；汇票的主债务人在承兑前是出票人，承兑后是承兑人。

The principal debtor of promissory note is the drawer and shall be the drawer from beginning to end; the principal debtor of draft is the drawer before acceptance and the acceptor after acceptance.

6. 当事人能否重叠不同 (Whether the Parties Can Be the Same)

本票不允许出票人和收款人做成同一个当事人，而汇票允许出票人与收款人做成同一个当事人。

Promissory note does not allow drawer and payee to be the same party, while draft allows drawer and payee to be the same party.

7. 签发的份数不同 (Number of Copies Issued)

本票出票时只开出一式一份，而汇票一般是开出一套，即一式两份或数份。

Promissory note is only issued in one copy, while draft is usually issued in one set, that is, two or more copies.

第二节　信用证支付
Section 2　L/C Payment

信用证方式是银行信用介入国际货物买卖货款结算的产物。它的出现不仅在一定程度上解决了买卖双方互不信任的矛盾，而且还能使双方在使用信用证结算货款的过程中获得银行资金融通的便利，从而促进了国际贸易的发展，因此被广泛地应用于国际贸易之中，成为当今国际贸易中的一种主要的结算方式。

L/C method is the product of bank credit intervention in international settlement of payment. It not only solves the contradiction of mutual distrust between buyers and sellers to a certain extent, but also makes it convenient for them to obtain bank financing in the process of using L/C to settle payment for goods, thus promoting the development of international trade. Therefore, it is widely used and has become a main settlement method in today's international trade.

一、信用证的含义与有关的国际贸易惯例
I. Meaning of L/C and Relevant International Trade Customs

（一）信用证的含义 (Meaning of L/C)

信用证（letter of credit, L/C），指由银行（开证行）依照（申请人）的要求和指示或自己主动，在符合信用证条款的条件下，凭规定单据向第三者（受益人）或其指定方进行付款的文件。简言之，信用证是银行出具的一种有条件的付款保证文件。

Letter of Credit (L/C) refers to a document issued by the opening bank to the beneficiary or its nominated party according to the requirements and instructions of the applicant or on its own initiative, subject to the terms of L/C. In short, L/C is a conditional payment guarantee issued by the bank.

《跟单信用证统一惯例》（UCP600）对信用证的定义是：信用证意指一项不可撤销的约定，无论其名称或描述如何，该项约定构成开证行对相符交单予以承付的确定承诺。

UCP600 defines L/C as an irrevocable agreement, however named or described, which constitutes a definitive commitment by the opening bank to honor conforming documents.

（二）信用证相关的国际贸易惯例 (L/C-related International Trade Customs)

信用证是国际贸易中常用的一种结算方式，但在处理相关业务时，各国银行没有一个统一的解释和公认的准则，往往按照各自的习惯和规定办事，当事人之间常发生争议和纠纷。国际商会为了减少信用证各当事人间的争议，推出了《跟单信用证统一惯例》（UCP600）和《关于审核跟单信用证项下单据的国际标准银行实务》（ISBP）两个重要惯例。

L/C is a settlement method commonly used in international trade. However, when dealing with related businesses, banks all over the world do not have a unified interpretation and recognized standards, and often act according to their own customs and regulations. Dispute and controversy often occur between parties. In order to reduce the dispute between parties of L/C, International Chamber of Commerce (ICC) has introduced two important conventions: UCP600 and ISBP.

UCP600 的英文全称是 Uniform Custom and Practice for Documentary Credits, 2006 revision, ICC Publication No. 600，是关于跟单信用证业务处理最新和最为详细、全面的版本。它是在 UCP500 的基础上，为适应各国银行、运输、保险业务的发展，而修订产生的，并于 2007 年 7 月 1 日起正式实施。

The full English name of UCP600 is Uniform Custom and Practice for Documentary Credits, 2006 revision, ICC Publication No. 600, which is the latest and most detailed and comprehensive version regarding the processing of documentary credit business. It was revised on the basis of UCP500 to adapt to the development of banking, carriage and insurance business in various countries and officially implemented from July 1, 2007.

ISBP 的英文全称是 International Standard Banking Practice for the Examination of Documents under Documentary Credits，目前采用的 ISBP 是国际商会于 2007 年在新加坡通过的适用于 UCP600 的最新修订本。ISBP 是一个供单据审核员在审核跟单信用证项下提交的单据时使用的审查项目清单，作为 UCP 的必不可少的补充，得到了各界广泛的接纳。

The full English name of ISBP is International Standard Banking Practice for the Examination of Documents under Documentary Credits. Currently, ISBP is the latest revision applicable to UCP600 adopted by ICC in Singapore in 2007. ISBP is a list of review items for use by document reviewers when reviewing documents submitted under documentary Credit and has been widely accepted as an essential supplement to UCP.

二、信用证支付的特点
II. Characteristics of L/C Payment

作为银行的一种有条件的付款承诺，信用证支付具有如下特点。

As a conditional payment commitment of the bank, L/C payment has the following characteristics.

（一）信用证支付是一种银行信用 (L/C Payment Is a Type of Bank Credit)

信用证是以银行信用为基础的一种支付方式，开证行以其自身的信用对有关当事人做出付款承诺。该付款承诺独立于开证申请人以外，即便开证申请人出现不愿意或没有能力付款，或资金状况恶化甚至破产倒闭的情况，开证行也必须按照信用证的规定履行付款义务。信用证的开证行承担第一性的、独立的、终局性的付款责任。开证行一旦同意开证申请人的请求，开出以出口商为受益人的信用证，便与受益人形成了一种以信用证为基础的契约关系，即开证行承担了付款的责任，该责任只有在受益人提交的单据与信用证条款不符的情况下才能被免除。

L/C is a payment method based on bank credit. The opening bank makes payment commitment to relevant parties with its own credit. The payment commitment is independent of the applicant. Even if the applicant is unwilling or unable to make payment, or its financial situation deteriorates or even goes bankrupt, the opening bank must fulfill the payment obligation in accordance with the provisions of L/C. The opening bank of L/C shall bear the primary, independent and final payment responsibility. Once the opening bank agrees with the applicant's request and issues an L/C in favor of the exporter, it forms a contractual relationship based on L/C with the beneficiary, that is, the opening bank assumes the responsibility for payment, which can only be exempted if the documents submitted by the beneficiary are inconsistent with the terms of L/C.

（二）信用证是一项独立于合同的自足文件 (L/C Is a Self-contained Document Independent from the Contract)

在国际贸易结算中，银行开立的信用证虽然以进出口双方的贸易合同为基础，但信用证一经开出，就成为独立于贸易合同以外的具有法律效力的文件。信用证下的银行只受信用证及相关惯例的约束，不受买卖合同或其他合同的约束。贸易合同是进出口双方之间的契约，通常仅仅对进出口双方具有约束力。而信用证是开证行与受益人之间的约定，并按照信用证指定的国际贸易惯例来规范各当事人的权利与义务。UCP600明确规定："信用证与可能作为其依据的销售合同或其他合同，是相互独立的交易。即使信用证中提及该合同，银行亦与该合同完全无关，且不受其约束。"据此，信用证的银行只受信用证及相关惯例的约束，不受买卖合同或其他合同的约束，这样规定的意图是使银行不至于陷入买卖双方之间复杂的合同纠纷之中。

In international trade settlement, although the L/C issued by a bank is based on the trade contract between importer and exporter, once issued, it will become a legally effective document independent from the trade contract. Banks under L/C are only subject to L/C and related customs, not sales contract or other contracts. A trade contract is a contract between importer and exporter, usually only binding on both parties. L/C is an agreement between the opening bank and the beneficiary, which regulates the rights and obligations of all parties in accordance with the international trade customs nominated by the L/C. UCP600 explicitly provides that "L/C and the Sales Contract or other contracts on which it may be based are independent transactions. Notwithstanding the reference to this Contract in L/C, the bank is wholly independent from and not bound by this Contract." Accordingly, the bank of L/C is only subject to L/C and related customs, not sales contract or other contracts. The intent of this provision is to prevent the bank from being involved in a complex contract dispute between buyers and sellers.

（三）信用证支付是一种纯粹的单据买卖 (L/C Payment Is a Purely Documentary Transaction)

信用证支付遵循凭单付款的原则。银行仅处理单据，只要受益人提供符合信用证要求的单据，做到"单证相符、单单相符、单内相符"，开证行就必须履行付款责任，而无须过问单据所代表的货物。UCP600明确规定："在信用证业务中，各有关当事人处理的只是单据，而不是单据所涉及的货物、服务或其他行为。"据此，信用证结算方式是一种纯单据业务，银行关心和处理的仅仅是单据，只要受益人提供符合信用证要求的全套合格的单据，开证行就必须履行付款责任，而无须过问单据所代表的货物是否符合合同规定，是否已经装船发运，是否已完好抵达目的地。如果货物确有问题，进口商只能根据买卖合同或运输、保险合同，向有关责任方索赔，而不能向银行要求损失赔偿。

L/C payment follows the principle of cash against documents. The bank only handles the documents. As long as the beneficiary provides the documents that meet the requirements of L/C, so as to achieve "consistency between bills and documents, between documents and documents, and within the same document", the opening bank must fulfill its payment responsibility without asking about the goods represented by the documents. UCP600 explicitly states: "In L/C business, the parties concerned only deal with documents and not the goods, services or other acts involved in the documents." Accordingly, the L/C settlement method is a pure document business. The bank only cares about and processes documents. As long as the beneficiary provides a full set of qualified documents that meet the requirements of L/C, the opening bank must fulfill its payment responsibility without asking whether the goods represented by the documents conform to the provisions of the contract, have been shipped and arrived at the destination in good condition. If there is a problem with the goods, the importer can only claim compensation from the responsible party according to the sales contract or carriage and insurance contract, but not from the bank.

另外，根据UCP600的相关规定，银行虽有义务"合理小心地审核一切单据"，但这种审核，只是用以确定单据表面上是否符合信用证条款，开证行只根据表面上符合信用证条款的单据付款。因此，银行对任何单据的形式、完整性、准确性、真实性以及伪造或法律效力，或单据上规定的或附加的一般和/或特殊条件概不负责，对单据在邮递过程中的遗失也不负责任。由此可见，信用证业务是一种纯粹的单据买卖，它既不涉及贸易合同和货物，也不管单据的真伪。这使得银行能够有效避免由于货物原因而引起的贸易合同争端，有利于银行工作效率的提高。

More importantly, according to UCP600, although banks are obliged to "review all documents with reasonable care", such review is only used to determine whether the documents appear to conform to L/C terms. The opening bank shall only make payment based on the documents that appear to conform to L/C terms. Therefore, the bank shall not be responsible for the form, completeness, accuracy, authenticity and forgery or legal effect of any documents, nor for the general and/or special conditions specified on or attached to them, nor for their loss during the mailing process. It can be seen that L/C business is a purely documentary transaction involving neither trade contract nor goods, nor the authenticity of documents. This enables the bank to effectively avoid trade contract disputes caused by goods, which is conducive to improving the work efficiency of the bank.

三、信用证业务的当事人
III. Parties to L/C Business

（一）开证申请人 (Applicant)

开证申请人，又称开证人（opener），指向银行申请开立信用证的人，一般是进口商。开证申请人根据与出口商的买卖合同，在规定的时间内向银行申请开证、交纳开证保证金并及时付款赎单。

Applicant, also known as opener, refers to the person who applies to a bank for opening L/C, usually the importer. The applicant shall, in accordance with the sales contract signed with the exporter, apply to the bank for L/C opening, payment of deposit for L/C opening and timely documents against payment within the specified time.

（二）开证行 (Opening/Issuing Bank)

开证行是接受开证申请人的委托和指示开立信用证的银行，通常为进口地银行。开证行承担第一性的付款责任，有权收取开证手续费，应及时正确开证，一旦付款，一般无追索权。

Opening bank is a bank entrusted and instructed by the applicant to open L/C, usually at the place of import. The opening bank bears the primary liability for payment, has the right to collect opening charges, and shall issued L/C in a timely and correct manner. Once payment is made, there is generally no right of recourse.

（三）受益人 (Beneficiary)

受益人是指信用证上指定的有权使用信用证，并可按照信用证条款签发汇票或提交单据、收取信用证所列金额的人，通常为出口商。受益人有按时交货并提交符合信用证规定单据的义务，也有凭单索取货款的权利。

Beneficiary means the person named on L/C who is entitled to use L/C and may issue draft or present documents, receive the amount listed in L/C in accordance with the terms of L/C, usually the exporter. The beneficiary is obliged to deliver the goods on time and submit documents conforming to the provisions of L/C. It also has the right to claim payment against such documents.

（四）通知行 (Advising/Notifying Bank)

通知行是指接受开证行的委托，将信用证或信用证修改书通知受益人的银行。通知行一般在出口地，且通常是开证行的代理行或分支机构。通知行除应合理审慎地鉴别所通知的信用证及其修改书的表面真实性并及时、准确地将信用证及其修改书通知受益人以外，无须承担其他义务。

Advising bank refers to the bank entrusted by opening bank to notify the beneficiary of the L/C or amendment to the L/C. The advising bank is generally located at the place of export and is usually a correspondent or branch of the opening bank. The advising bank shall not be obliged to undertake any other obligations except that it shall reasonably and prudently verify the apparent authenticity of the L/C and timely and accurately notify the beneficiary of the L/C and its amendment.

以上四个当事人为信用证业务的四个基本当事人，在实际业务中，可能还会涉及以下其他当事人。

The above are the four basic parties of L/C business, and in actual business, the following other parties may also be involved.

（五）议付行 (Negotiating Bank)

所谓"议付"是指指定银行在相符交单的条件下，在其应获偿付的银行工作日当天或之前向受益人预付或同意预付款项，购买信用证项下汇票及/或单据的行为。议付行就是执行议付的银行。议付行向受益人买单垫款后有权凭单据向开证行索偿，如遭拒付，有权向受益人追索。

The so-called "available by negotiation" refers to the act that the nominated bank makes or agrees to make an advance payment to the beneficiary on or before the banking day when it should be reimbursed, and purchases draft and/or documents under L/C, subject to the conditions of conforming documents. Negotiating bank is the bank that executes "available by negotiation". The negotiating bank has the right to claim compensation from the opening bank against the documents after making advances to the beneficiary for purchasing documents, and has the right of recourse to the beneficiary in case of dishonor.

（六）付款行 (Paying Bank)

付款行是被开证行指定的，担任信用证项下付款人或充当汇票付款人的银行，又称受票行（drawee bank）。付款行可以是开证行自己，也可以是开证行的付款代理，由其代开证行审单无误后付款，付款后无追索权。

Paying bank is a bank designated by the opening bank to act as payer or drawee under L/C, also known as drawee bank. The paying bank can be the opening bank itself or the paying agent of the opening bank. Payment will be made on behalf of the opening bank after the documents are verified to be correct, and there is no right of recourse after payment.

（七）保兑行 (Confirming Bank)

保兑行是接受开证行的委托或请求，对开证行开出的信用证以本行名义予以保证兑付的银行。保兑行通常是受益人所在地的通知行，也可是开证行指定或受益人约定的其他银行。保兑行对信用证加具保兑后，就独立地对受益人承担起第一性的、无追索权的审单付款责任。因此，保兑行与开证行处于同样的付款地位，受益人或议付行可以在开证行和保兑行之间任意选择一家提交单据。保兑行收到符合信用证规定的单据后，必须按信用证规定付款或延期付款或承兑到期付款。

The confirming bank is a bank that accepts the entrustment or request of the opening bank and guarantees to honor the L/C issued by the opening bank in the name of the bank. The confirming bank is usually the advising bank in the location of the beneficiary or such other bank as may be specified by the opening bank or agreed to by the beneficiary. After the confirming bank confirms the L/C, it shall independently assume the primary and non-recourse payment responsibility for document review to the beneficiary. Therefore, confirming bank and opening bank are in the same payment status, and either the beneficiary or the negotiating bank can choose any one to present documents between the opening bank and the confirming bank. Confirming bank must make payment as per L/C or by deferred payment or acceptance for due payment after receiving the documents conforming to L/C.

（八）偿付行 (Reimbursing Bank)

偿付行又称清算银行（clearing bank），是指接受开证行在信用证上委托的，代开证行对议付行或付款行清偿垫款的银行。信用证指定偿付行时，开证行开出信用证后应立即向偿付行发出偿付授权书，通知授权付款的金额及有权索偿银行的名称等内容。议付行或付款行付款后，在把单据直接寄给开证行的同时，向偿付行发出索偿书。偿付行在收到索偿书后，不需要凭单据，即可向议付行或付款行清偿垫款。偿付行不负责审核信用证项下单据，如事后开证行发现单证不符，只能向索偿行而不能向偿付行追索。

Reimbursing bank, also known as clearing bank, refers to the bank entrusted by opening bank in L/C to pay off advances to negotiating bank or paying bank on behalf of the opening bank. When the L/C specifies a reimbursement bank, the opening bank shall issue an authorization for reimbursement to the reimbursing bank immediately after L/C, notifying the amount of authorized payment and the name of the bank entitled to claim compensation. After payment by the negotiating bank or paying bank, a claim is issued to the reimbursing bank at the same time as the documents are sent directly to the opening bank. Upon receipt of the claim, the reimbursing bank shall settle the advance to the negotiating bank or paying bank without presenting the documents. The reimbursing bank is not responsible for reviewing the documents under L/C. if the opening bank finds that the documents are inconsistent afterwards, it can only have recourse to the claiming bank instead of the reimbursing bank.

四、信用证支付的业务流程
IV. Business Process of L/C Payment

信用证种类繁多，其业务流程也较为复杂。以常见的跟单议付信用证为例，介绍信用证的业务流程。

There are various types of L/C, and their business processes are also complex. Taking common documentary negotiation credit as an example, the business process of L/C is described as follows.

（一）进出口双方签订合同 (Contract Signed by Importer and Exporter)

进出口双方在买卖合同中对信用证的种类和开证时间等做出明确规定。

The importer and exporter shall explicitly specify the type and opening time of L/C in the sales contract.

（二）进口商申请开立信用证 (Importer's Application for Opening L/C)

进口商填写开证申请书，提供开证保证金或担保，支付开证手续费，委托开证行向出口商开立信用证。

The importer fills in the L/C application form, provides an opening deposit or guarantee, pays the opening charges and entrusts the opening bank to open an L/C with the exporter.

（三）开证行开立信用证并送达通知行 (Opening Bank Issues an L/C and Delivers it to Advising Bank)

开证行如接受申请人的开证委托，就必须按照开证申请书及时开出信用证，并将信用证送达通知行通知受益人。

If the opening bank accepts the entrustment of the applicant, it must issue an L/C in time according to the L/C application and notify the beneficiary by delivering it to the advising bank.

（四）通知行将信用证通知受益人 (Advising Bank Notifies Beneficiary of the L/C)

通知行收到信用证，在核验其真实性无误后，将信用证通知或转递给出口商。

After receiving the L/C and verifying its authenticity, the advising bank will notify or forward the L/C to the exporter.

（五）受益人审证、发货、交单 (Beneficiary Verifies the L/C, Delivers Goods and Presents Documents)

1. 受益人审证 (Beneficiary Verifies the L/C)

受益人即出口商收到信用证后应认真审核信用证，其对信用证主要审查三个方面：检查信用证内容是否完整，检查信用证内容是否与合同规定一致，检查信用证条款是否存在自相矛盾或欺骗之处。受益人审证后发现信用证与合同不符的，或某些条款无法办到的，或由于政治、经济上的原因不能按照来证条款规定办理的，受益人可以提出修改信用证，但必须经过有关当事人的同意。

The beneficiary, i.e. the exporter, shall carefully review the L/C after receiving it, mainly including three aspects: check whether the contents of L/C are complete; check whether the contents of L/C are consistent with the provisions of the contract; check whether there is any contradiction or deception in the terms of L/C. If the beneficiary, after verifying the L/C, finds that it is inconsistent with the contract, or some terms cannot be fulfilled, or cannot be handled according to the terms of L/C due to political and economic reasons, the beneficiary may propose to amend the L/C, but it must obtain the consent of the parties concerned.

2. 受益人发货、交单 (Beneficiary Delivers Goods and Presents Documents)

受益人审核信用证或修改书无误后，应在信用证规定的装运期限内，按照信用证规定的装运方式将货物装船出运。受益人装运货物后，应按照"正确、完整、简明、整洁"的原则及时取得和缮制信用证所规定的单据，如发票、汇票、检验证书、提单或其他运输单据、保险单，连同信用证正本、修改通知书，送交信用证指定银行要求付款或承兑。

After the beneficiary checks that L/C or amendment is correct, the goods shall be shipped within the date of shipment specified in L/C according to the shipping method specified in L/C. The beneficiary shall obtain and prepare the documents specified in L/C (such as invoices, draft, inspection certificate, B/L or other transport documents, insurance policy) together with L/C original and Amendment Notices in a timely manner according to the principle of "correctness, completeness, conciseness and neatness" and submit them to the nominated bank of L/C for payment or acceptance.

受益人取得和缮制好各种单据后，应按照"单证、单单、单内一致"的原则，对所交单据进行认真审核。在确认无误后，应在信用证规定的交单期限内到规定的交单地点提交全套单据。

After obtaining and preparing various documents, the beneficiary shall carefully review the submitted documents in accordance with the principle of "consistency between bills and documents, between documents and documents, and within the same document". After confirm that there is no error, the full set of documents shall be submitted to the specified presentation place within the period for presentation stipulated in L/C.

（六）议付行审单垫款并向开证行索偿 (Negotiating Bank Reviews Documents, Makes Advances and Claims from Opening Bank)

1. 议付行审单垫款 (Negotiating Bank Reviews Documents and Makes Advances)

议付是指议付行买入受益人提交的跟单汇票，议付行扣除手续费和贴现息后将汇票净额垫付给受益人，在我国俗称出口押汇。议付的实质是议付行对受益人的垫款，其前提是受益人交单符合信用证的规定。议付行议付后成为信用证项下汇票的善意持票人，如遇开证行拒付，有向其前手即受益人追索的权利。受益人也可能向其他被指定银行交单，如付款行、承兑行、保兑行。无论受益人向上述哪家银行交单，被指定银行都必须审核单据并确定单证相符后，根据自己的义务付款、承兑或议付。

Available by negotiation means that the negotiating bank buys the documentary bill submitted by the beneficiary, and advances the net amount of draft to the beneficiary after deducting the handling fee and discount interest. It is commonly known as outward bill in China. The essence of available by negotiation is the advance made by the negotiating bank to the beneficiary, provided that the beneficiary's presentation complies with the provisions of L/C. After negotiation, the negotiating bank becomes a bona fide holder of draft under L/C. In case of refusal to pay by the opening bank, it has the right of recourse against its remote holder, namely the beneficiary. The beneficiary may also present the documents to other nominated banks such as paying bank, accepting bank and confirming bank. Regardless of which bank the beneficiary presents the documents to, the nominated bank must review the documents and confirm that they comply with bills before making payment, acceptance, or negotiation according to its obligations.

2. 议付行索偿 (Negotiating Bank Claims)

议付行议付后，一边将单据分次直接寄给开证行，一边向偿付行发出索偿书，请求偿付。偿付行收到索偿书后，只要索偿金额不超过授权书金额，就立即根据索偿书的指示向议付行付款。凡信用证有电汇索偿条款的，议付行就需以电报、电传或SWIFT方式向开证行、付款行或偿付行索偿。

After negotiation, the negotiating bank will send the documents directly to the opening bank in batches while issuing a claim to the reimbursing bank for reimbursement. Payment shall be made by the reimbursing bank to the negotiating bank in accordance with the instructions of the claim, provided that the amount claimed does not exceed the authorization. Where the L/C has a T/T claim clause, the negotiating bank shall make a claim to the opening bank, paying bank or reimbursing bank by cable, telex or SWIFT.

（七）开证行或偿付行审单无误后偿付 (Reimbursement by Opening Bank or Reimbursing Bank after Documents are Verified to be Correct)

1. 开证行审单 (Opening Bank Reviews Documents)

开证行收到议付行寄来的单据后，必须在交单次日起的至多5个银行工作日内审核单据，以确定交单是否相符。开证行应按照单证、单单、单内表面严格相符的原则，根据国际惯例

UCP和ISBP的规定，审核单据。

After receiving the documents from the negotiating bank, the opening bank must review them within a maximum of 5 banking days from the next day of presentation to determine whether they are in conformity. The opening bank shall review the documents in accordance with the principle of strict compliance between bills and documents, between documents and documents, and within the same document, and in accordance with international practices such as UCP and ISBP.

2. 开证行偿付或拒付 (Reimbursement or Refusal by Opening Bank)

开证行经审核认为单证相符后，应将款项和银行费用付给议付行。若开证行发现单证不符，可以拒绝付款，但必须在交单次日起的5个银行工作日内通知议付行，表示拒绝接受单据，并告知不符点。开证行一旦付款，即为终局性付款，对有关各方均无追索权，即不能因事后发现不符点而要求退款。

The opening bank shall pay the amount and bank charges to the negotiating bank after reviewing and confirming that bills complied with documents. Payment may be refused if the opening bank finds discrepancies in the documents, provided that it notifies the negotiating bank within 5 banking days from the next day of presentation that it rejects the documents and advises the discrepancy. Payment by the opening bank is final and has no right of recourse to the parties concerned, i.e. refund cannot be claimed for discrepancies found afterwards.

（八）开证行通知开证申请人付款赎单 (Opening Bank Notifies Applicant of Documents Against Payment)

开证行履行付款义务后，应立即通知开证申请人付款赎单。开证行一般会向申请人发出赎单通知并将全套单据的副本附在其后供申请人审核。

The opening bank shall promptly notify the applicant of documents against payment after fulfillment of its payment obligations. The opening bank will normally issue redemption notices to the applicant and attach a copy of the full set of documents for review by the applicant.

（九）开证申请人付款赎单 (Documents against Payment by Applicant)

开证申请人收到赎单通知后，应审核单据以决定是否付款赎单。如申请人接受单据，应将货款及应付手续费交给开证行；若申请人发现不符点，可在规定时间内提出拒付，但拒付的理由必须是单证、单单或单内不符，其他如货物质量等非单据表面问题，不能作为拒付的理由，只能向有关责任方索赔。信用证支付流程如图10-2所示。

Upon receipt of redemption notices, the applicant shall review the documents to determine whether or not to effect payment. If the applicant accepts the documents, it shall pay the payment for goods and handling fee payable to the opening bank. If the applicant finds any discrepancy, it may refuse to pay within the specified time, but the reason for refusal must be the inconsistency between bills and documents, between documents and documents, and within the same document. Other non-documentary problems such as the quality of the goods cannot be used as reasons for refusal. Claim can only be made against the relevant responsible party. Flow of L/C payment shows as figure 10-2.

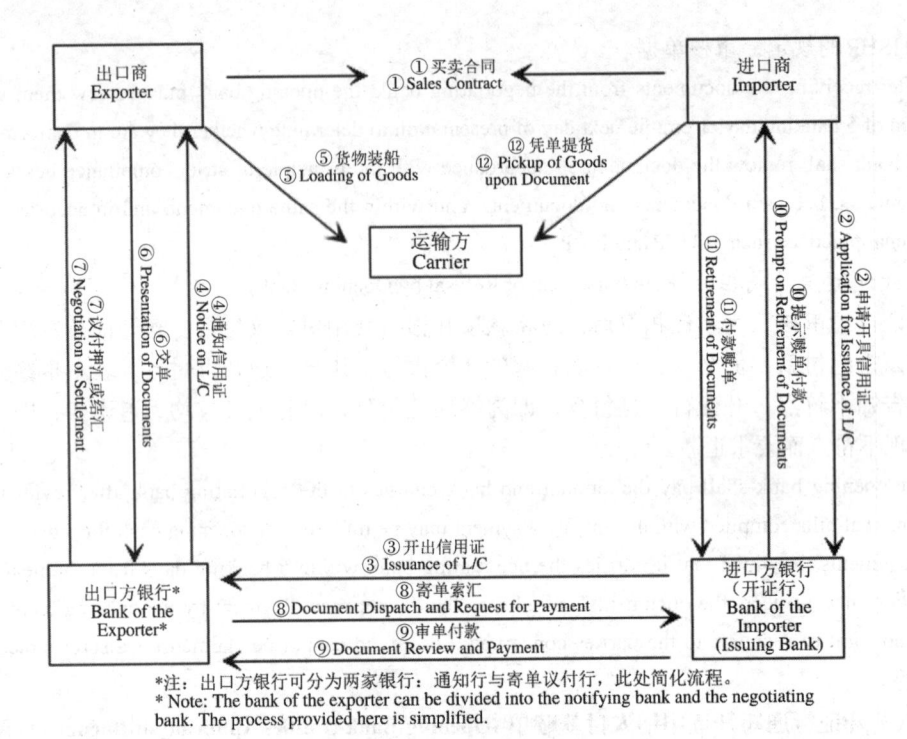

图 10-2 信用证支付流程

Figure 10-2 Flow of L/C Payment

五、信用证的形式与内容
V. Form and Contents of L/C

（一）信用证的形式 (Form of L/C)

信用证的开立形式有信开和电开两种。电开还可分为简电通知、全电开证和SWIFT开证三种。

L/C can be opened by airmail or by cable. To open by cable can also be divided into three types: with brief advice by teletransmission, by full cable and SWIFT.

（1）信开信用证（mail credit），是以信函邮寄的方式开立的信用证。开证行将信用证正本邮寄给通知行，请其通知受益人。

(1) Mail Credit is an L/C issued by airmail. The opening bank will mail the L/C original to the advising bank requesting it to notify the beneficiary.

（2）电开信用证（tele transmission credit），是指开证行以电子文本的形式开立信用证的有效文本，并以电信方式（电投、电传或SWIFT系统）传递给通知行的信用证。SWIFT是Society for Worldwide Interbank Financial Telecommunications（环球同业银行金融电信协会或环球银行间金融通信协会）的缩写，是于1973年在比利时成立的一个国际银行间非营利性的合作组织，现在已有200个国家的10000多家银行、证券机构和企业用户参加。需要明确的是SWIFT也不是支付清算机构，而是一个标准化的报文传输机构，即金融机构间进行金融信息传递的通道，银行之间以及银行与支付机构之间的信息传输，包括支付指令、信息确认等均是通过SWIFT报文完成。协会成员银行可以通过国际金融电信网办理开立信用证、汇款、托收、外汇买卖、证券交易等业务。SWIFT的使用，为银行结算提供了安全、可靠、快捷、标准化、自动化的通信业务，从而大大提高了银行的结算速度。

(2) A tele tansmission letter of credit is a letter of credit in which the issuing bank opens a valid text of the letter of credit in the form of an electronic text and transmits it to the advising bank by the telecommunication (telegram, telex or SWIFT system). or Society for Worldwide Interbank Financial Telecommunications, is an international inter-bank non-profit cooperative organization founded in Belgium in 1973 and now has more than 10,000 banks, securities institutions and corporate users from 200 countries. It should be made clear that SWIFT is not a payment and settlement institution, but a standardized message transmission institution, i.e. a channel for financial information transmission between financial institutions. Information transmission between banks and between banks and payment institutions, including payment instructions, information confirmation, etc., is completed through SWIFT messages. The member banks of SWIFT can handle businesses such as opening L/C, remittance, collection, foreign exchange trading and securities transaction through the international financial telecommunication network. The use of SWIFT provides secure, reliable, fast, standardized and automated communication services for bank settlement, greatly improving the efficiency of bank settlement.

SWIFT信用证，指通过SWIFT系统开立的信用证。SWIFT有自动开证格式，在信用证开端标着MT700，MT701代号。SWIFT成员银行均参加国际商会，遵守SWIFT规定，使用SWIFT格式开立信用证，其信用证则受国际商会UCP600条款约束。所以通过SWIFT格式开证，实质上已相当于根据UCP600开立信用证。

SWIFT L/C refers to the L/C issued through SWIFT system. SWIFT has an automatic L/C format, with MT700 and MT701 marked at the beginning of L/C. All SWIFT member banks participate in the ICC and abide by SWIFT regulations. They use SWIFT format to open L/C, which is subject to the provisions of UCP600. Therefore, the issuance of L/C in SWIFT format is essentially equivalent to the issuance of L/C under UCP600.

（二）信用证的内容 (Contents of L/C)

信用证的内容主要包括以下几个方面。

The contents of L/C mainly include the following aspects.

1. 信用证本身的说明 (L/C Description)

（1）信用证的类型：说明可否撤销、转让；是否经另一家银行保兑；偿付方式等。

(1) Type of L/C: indicate whether it can be revoked or transferred; whether it is confirmed by another bank; reimbursement method, etc.

（2）信用证号码和开证日期。

(2) L/C No. and Date of Issue.

2. 信用证的当事人 (Parties to L/C)

（1）必须记载的当事人：申请人、开证行、受益人、通知行。

(1) Parties that must be specified: applicant, opening bank, beneficiary and advising bank.

（2）可能记载的当事人：保兑行、指定议付行、付款行、偿付行等。

(2) Parties that may be specified: confirming bank, nominated negotiating bank, paying bank, reimbursing bank, etc.

3. 信用证的金额和汇票 (Amount of L/C and Draft)

（1）信用证的金额：币别代号、金额、加减百分率。

(1) Amount of L/C: currency code, amount and percentage credit amount.

（2）汇票条款：汇票的金额、到期日、出票人、付款人。

(2) Draft: draft amount, date of expiry, drawer and payer.

4. 货物条款 (Cargo Clause)

货物条款包括货物名称、规格、数量、包装、单价以及合约号码等。

Cargo clause includes the name, specification, quantity, packing, unit price and contract No. of the goods, etc.

5. 运输条款 (Carriage Clause)

运输条款包括运输方式、装运地和目的地、最迟装运日期、可否分批装运或转运。

Carriage clause includes transportation mode, place and destination of shipment, latest date of shipment, partial shipments or transshipment.

6. 单据条款 (Document Clause)

单据条款说明要求提交的单据种类、份数、内容要求等。基本单据包括商业发票、运输单据和保险单。其他单据有检验证书、产地证、装箱单或重量单等。

Document clause explains the type, number of copies and content requirements of documents required to be submitted. Basic documents include commercial invoice, transport documents and insurance policy. Other documents include inspection certificate, certificate of origin, packing list or weight list.

7. 其他规定 (Miscellaneous)

（1）对交单期的说明。

(1) Description of period for presentation.

（2）对银行费用的说明。

(2) Description of bank charges.

（3）对议付行寄单方式、议付背书和索偿方法的指示。

(3) Instructions to the negotiating bank on dispatch of documents, endorsement for negotiation and claim method.

8. 责任文句 (Statement of Responsibility)

通常说明根据UCP600开立以及开证行保证付款的承诺，但SWIFT信用证可以省略。

Usually, it indicates the commitment to issue and guarantee payment from the opening bank in accordance with UCP600, but SWIFT L/C can be omitted.

六、信用证的种类
VI. Types of L/C

按照UCP600的规定，信用证是一项不可撤销的安排，构成开证行对相符交单予以承付的确定承诺。所以，根据UCP600开立的信用证都是不可撤销的。不可撤销信用证指开证行一旦开立信用证，在信用证有效期内，未经受益人及有关当事人同意，任何人不得片面修改和撤销的信用证。

The L/C is an irrevocable arrangement under UCP600 and constitutes a firm commitment by the opening bank to honor conforming documents. Therefore, letters of credit issued under UCP600 are irrevocable. Irrevocable L/C means that once the opening bank issues an L/C, no one is allowed to unilaterally modify or revoke it without the consent of the beneficiary and relevant parties within the validity time of L/C.

（一）按是否随附单据，分为跟单信用证和光票信用证 (According to Whether Documents Are Attached or Not, It Is Divided into Documentary Credit and Clean Credit)

1. 跟单信用证 (Documentary Credit)

跟单信用证指开证行凭规定的单据或跟单汇票付款的信用证。此处的单据主要指代表物权的货运单据，即海运提单，还包括其他货运单据。国际贸易结算中使用的大多是跟单信用证，其核心是单据，银行通过控制单据以掌握货权，通过转移单据以转移物权，并可凭单据抵押提供融资。

Documentary credit refers to L/C for payment by the opening bank against specified documents or documentary bill. Documents here mainly refer to shipping documents representing real rights, i.e. Ocean B/L, and also include other shipping documents. Most of the documents used in international trade settlement are documentary credit, with the core being documents. Banks control documents to hold title to goods, transfer real rights by transferring documents, and provide financing against document mortgage.

2. 光票信用证 (Clean Credit)

光票信用证是不随附单据、受益人可以凭开立收据或汇票分批或一次在通知行领取款项的信用证。在贸易中，它可以起预先支取货款的作用。

Clean credit is an L/C in which the beneficiary can receive payment from advising bank in batches or at one time against receipt or draft. In trade, it can act as an advance on goods.

（二）按有无开证行以外其他银行对信用证加以保证兑付，分为保兑信用证和不保兑信用证 (According to Whether There Are Banks other than Opening Bank that Guarantee to Honor the L/C, It Is Divided into Confirmed Credit and Unconfirmed Credit)

1. 保兑信用证 (Confirmed Credit)

保兑信用证指根据开证行的授权或要求，另一家银行对不可撤销信用证加具保兑，只要信用证规定的单据按期提交到保兑行，并与信用证条款相符，则构成保兑行在开证行以外的确定付款承诺。在保兑信用证下，保兑行对信用证所负的责任与开证行相同，也是第一性的、独立的、终局性的。并非在开证行由于某种原因无法付款或拒付的情况下，才向保兑行要求付款。保兑信用证有开证行和保兑行的双重付款承诺，对受益人的收款更有保障。保兑信用证一般在以下两种情形中出现。

Confirmed credit means that another bank confirms the irrevocable L/C according to the authorization or requirement of the opening bank. As long as the documents specified in the L/C are submitted to the confirming bank on time and consistent with the terms of the L/C, it constitutes a firm payment commitment of the confirming bank other than the opening bank. Under confirmed credit, the responsibility of confirming bank for L/C is the same as that of opening bank and is also primary, independent and final. Payment will not be required from the confirming bank unless the opening bank is unable to make or refuse payment for any reason whatsoever. Confirmed credit has a dual payment commitment from both the opening bank and the confirming bank, which is more secure for the beneficiary's collection. Confirmed credit generally occurs in the following two situations.

（1）当受益人对开证行的资信不了解、不满意或对进口国（地区）的政治经济形势有所顾虑时，往往要求由另一家银行对开证行开出的信用证加保兑。

(1) When the beneficiary does not know or is dissatisfied with the credit standing of the opening bank or has concerns about the political and economic situation of the importing country (region), it often requires another bank to confirm the L/C issued by the opening bank.

（2）开证行担心自己开出的信用证不能被受益人接受或不易被其他银行议付，主动要求由另一家银行对信用证加具保兑。

(2) The opening bank is concerned that the L/C it has issued may not be accepted by the beneficiary or may not be easily negotiated by other banks, and actively requires another bank to confirm the L/C.

2. 不保兑信用证 (Unconfirmed Credit)

不保兑信用证指没有另一家银行加以保证兑付的信用证，仅有开证行承担付款责任。国际上使用的信用证绝大多数是不保兑信用证，因为只要开证行资信好，付款是有保证的。保兑是非正常情况下的变通做法。而且保兑费用为数不菲，一般为信用证金额的1%～5%，与0.1%～0.125%的议付费相比，高出数十倍。因此，高昂的保兑费往往使受益人望而却步。

Unconfirmed Credit refers to the L/C that has not been guaranteed by another bank for payment. Only the opening bank is responsible for payment. L/C used internationally is mostly unconfirmed credit, because payment is guaranteed as long as the opening bank has good credit standing. Confirmation is an alternative under abnormal circumstances. Moreover, the confirmation fee is quite expensive, generally between 1%~5% of the L/C amount, which is dozens of times higher than the negotiation fee of of 0.1%~0.125%. Beneficiaries are therefore often discouraged by the high confirmation fee.

（三）按信用证下指定银行付款期限和兑付方式不同，分为即期信用证和远期信用证 (According to Different Payment Terms and Methods of Nominated Banks under L/C, It Is Divided into Sight L/C and Usance L/C)

1. 即期付款信用证 (Sight Credit)

即期付款信用证指受益人一旦提交了符合信用证要求的即期汇票及单据，开证行或付款行就必须立即付款的信用证。即期付款信用证规定受益人开出即期汇票，或不需即期汇票仅凭单据即可向指定银行提示请求付款。银行付款后，对受益人没有追索权。信用证明确规定有"适于即期付款"（available by payment at sight）。

Sight credit refers to an L/C that must be paid immediately by the opening bank or paying bank once the beneficiary submits the sight bill and documents meeting the requirements of L/C. Sight credit stipulates that the beneficiary can issue a sight bill or request payment from the nominated bank by presentation of documents only without no sight bill required. After the bank makes payment, there is no right of recourse against the beneficiary. "Available by payment at sight" is explicitly stated in the L/C.

2. 远期付款信用证 (Usance Credit)

远期付款信用证指开证行或付款行收到符合信用证条款的单据时不立即付款，而是按信用证规定的付款期限到期付款的信用证。它包括延期付款信用证、承兑信用证。

Usance credit refers to an L/C in which the opening bank or paying bank does not make immediate payment upon receipt of documents that meet the terms of L/C, but makes due payment according to the payment term specified in L/C. It includes deferred payment credit and acceptance credit.

（1）在延期付款信用证下，受益人不开汇票，仅将符合信用证要求的单据交到指定银行，指定银行在审单无误后接受单据，待付款到期日再行付款。其特点在于受益人不开汇票，仅凭单据索款，其实质是不用汇票的远期信用证。此类信用证中明确规定有"Available by deferred payment at..."。

(1) Under deferred payment credit, the beneficiary will not issue draft and only submit the documents that meet the requirements of L/C to the nominated bank. The nominated bank will accept the documents after reviewing them and make payment after tenor. It is characterized in that the beneficiary does not issue a draft and only claims payment by documents. It's essentially a usance L/C without the need for a draft. "Available by deferred payment at ..." is expressly stated in such L/C.

延期付款信用证有利于进口商不利于出口商。对进口商而言，不仅得到了远期付款的优惠，还在出现纠纷时，由于没有汇票而不受票据法的约束，容易在处理中占主动地位。对出口商，由于没有开出汇票，无法获得贴现汇票提前收款的便利，且一旦出现纠纷，也无法根据票据法获得应有的保护。

Deferred payment credit is beneficial for importers but not for exporters. For importers, they not only get the after sight preference, but also are easy to take an active position in handling disputes due to the absence of draft and not being bound by the bill law. For exporters, since no draft has been issued, it is impossible to obtain the convenience for early collection of discounted draft, and in case of any dispute, due protection will not be available under the bill law.

（2）承兑信用证指开证行或指定银行收到符合信用证要求的远期汇票和单据后，不立即付款，而是承兑汇票，待汇票到期后才履行付款责任的信用证。它是需要受益人开出汇票的远期信用证，明确规定有"Available by acceptance of draft at…"。

(2) Acceptance credit refers to an L/C in which the opening bank or nominated bank does not make payment immediately after receiving the time bill and documents that meet the requirements of L/C, but accepts the draft. It is a usance L/C that requires the beneficiary to issue a draft, expressly stating that it is "Available by acceptance of draft at...".

相比于延期付款信用证，承兑信用证对受益人较为有利。一方面，受益人得到银行承兑的汇票，就等于获得了银行确定的付款保证，并受法律保护。另一方面，受益人可通过办理有追索权的融资（押汇或贴现，即议付）或无追索权的融资（买断票据，即福费廷），而提前取得信用证下的款项。

The acceptance credit is more favorable to the beneficiary than the deferred payment credit. On the one hand, if the beneficiary receives a bank accepted draft, it is equivalent to obtaining a payment guarantee determined by the bank and protected by law. On the other hand, the beneficiary can obtain payment under L/C in advance through financing with right of recourse (documentary or discount, i.e. Available by negotiation) or financing without right of recourse (forfaiting).

3. 议付信用证 (Negotiation Credit)

议付信用证指开证行在信用证中邀请其他银行买入汇票及/或单据的信用证。当受益人提交的单据符合信用证规定的条款时，议付行扣除利息后将余款付给受益人。然后，议付行将汇票和单据向开证行索偿。若不能从开证行处取得偿付，议付行有权向受益人追索。议付信用证中明确规定有 Available by negotiation。根据受益人对议付行的选择权不同，议付信用证可分为两种：

Negotiation credit refers to an L/C in which the opening bank invites other banks to buy draft and/or documents. The negotiating bank shall pay the balance to the beneficiary after deducting interest when the documents submitted by the beneficiary comply with the terms stipulated in L/C. The negotiating bank will then claim from the opening bank against draft and documents. If reimbursement cannot be obtained from the opening bank, the negotiating bank shall have the right of recourse to the beneficiary. Available by negotiation is expressly stated in the negotiation credit. According to the beneficiary's choice of negotiation bank, negotiation credit can be divided into two types:

（1）限制议付信用证（restrict negotiation credit），指只能由开证行在信用证中指定的银行进行议付的信用证，受益人不能向其他银行议付款项。一般规定有：This credit is restricted with ×× bank by negotiation。限制议付信用证使受益人丧失了自由选择议付行的权利，对受益人较为不利。若开证行指定的议付行远离受益人所在地，则会增加受益人的成本费用，带来更多不便。

(1) Restrict Negotiation credit refers to an L/C that can only be negotiated by the bank specified by the opening bank in the L/C, and the beneficiary cannot negotiate payments with other banks. Generally: This

credit is restricted with ×× bank by negotiation. Restrict negotiation credit makes the beneficiary lose the right to freely choose the negotiating bank, which is more unfavorable to the beneficiary. If the negotiating bank nominated by the opening bank is far away from the location of the beneficiary, it will increase the costs and expenses of the beneficiary and cause more inconvenience.

（2）自由议付信用证（freely/open negotiation credit），又称公开议付信用证，指受益人可以在任何银行议付的信用证。开证行一般在信用证中规定：This credit is available with any bank by negotiation。

(2) Freely negotiation credit, also known as open negotiation credit, refers to an L/C that the beneficiary can negotiate with any bank. The opening bank generally stipulates in the L/C that "This credit is available with any bank by negotiation".

4. 买方远期信用证/假远期信用证 (Buyer's Usance Credit)

有一种信用证，规定受益人开立远期汇票，但又同时规定"远期汇票可即期付款，贴现息和承兑费由买方负担"（Usance drafts to be negotiated at sight basis and discounted by us, discount charges and acceptance commission are for applicant's account.)，因兼具即期付款信用证和远期付款信用证的某些特定，而被称为假远期信用证。其表面上看是远期付款，而实质上受益人可以无偿获得即期付款。

There is an L/C, which stipulates that the beneficiary shall issue a usance draft, but at the same time stipulates that "Usance drafts to be negotiated at sight basis and discounted by us, discount charges and acceptance commission are for applicant's account." It is called a usance credit payable at sight because it combines certain characteristics of both a sight credit and a usance credit. It is ostensibly a usance payment, whereas in essence the beneficiary can receive sight payment free of charge.

在假远期信用证下，受益人开出远期汇票，然后在开证行或其他银行处办理贴现，由此可以像即期信用证那样立即取得货款，而开证申请人却不必立即付款，但必须承担贴现息和费用。此类信用证对进出口双方都有一定的吸引力，在国际贸易中常被采用。对受益人来说，它是即期付款，不会对其资金周转产生不利影响；对进口商来说，它是远期付款，可以得到银行的资金融通；对银行来说，虽然它为受益人的远期汇票办理了贴现，但可收取费用和利息，且只要进口商资信好，银行也没有太大风险。

Under the usance credit payable at sight, the beneficiary issues a usance draft and applies for discount at the opening bank or other banks so that immediate payment can be obtained, similar to a sight credit. the applicant does not need to make immediate payment but must bear the discount interest and expenses. This type of L/C has certain attraction for both importers and exporters and is often used in international trade. For the beneficiary, it is a sight payment, which will not adversely affect its capital turnover; for the importer, it is a usance payment, which can be financed by the bank; for the bank, although it has discounted the beneficiary's time bill, it can charge fees and interests, and as long as the importer has good credit standing, the bank does not have much risk.

（四）按受益人对信用证的权利是否可转让，分为可转让信用证和不可转让信用证
(According to Whether the Beneficiary's Rights in L/C Are Transferable or Not, It Is Divided into Transferable Credit and Non-transferable Credit)

1. 可转让信用证 (Transferable Credit)

可转让信用证指受益人（第一受益人）可将信用证全部或部分转让给一个或数个受益人（第二受益人）使用的信用证。在国际贸易中，可转让信用证的第一受益人往往是中间商，第二受益人常为实际供货商。转让中应注意：

Transferable credit refers to an L/C that the beneficiary (the first beneficiary) can transfer in whole or in part to one or more beneficiaries (the second beneficiary) for use. In international trade, the first beneficiary of Transferable credit is often the intermediary, and the second beneficiary is often the actual supplier. It should be noted in the transfer that:

（1）可转让信用证的确认。根据UCP600的规定，只有明确注明可转让字样的信用证才可被转让。信用证若未有该明确注明，则不可被转让。

(1) To confirm the transferable credit. According to UCP600, L/C can only be transferred when it is indicated as transferable. L/C is not transferable unless expressly stated otherwise.

（2）转让的次数。除非信用证另有规定，可转让信用证可由第一受益人一次转让给多个第二受益人，第二受益人不得要求将信用证转让给其后的第三受益人，但可以再转回给第一受益人。（只能转让一次，但转回不在此限）

(2) Number of transfers. Unless otherwise specified in the L/C, the transferable credit may be transferred by the first beneficiary to more than one second beneficiary at a time, and the second beneficiary shall not require the transfer of the L/C to subsequent third beneficiaries but may transfer it back to the first beneficiary. (Transfer can only be made once, except reversal)

（3）转让时内容的变更第一受益人在转让信用证时，除信用证的以下内容可变更外，转让证的其他内容必须与原证内容相同：①减少信用证金额；②降低信用证单价；③提前信用证的到期日和最迟装运期；④提高投保金额或加成率；⑤第一受益人可以自己的名字代替原证开证申请人的名字。

(3) Changes in content during transfer: When transferring an L/C, the first beneficiary must have the same content as the original L/C, except that the following content of L/C can be changed: ① reduce the amount of L/C; ② reduce the unit price of L/C; ③ advance the expiry date and latest shipment date L/C; ④ increase the insured amount or percentage of addition; ⑤ The first beneficiary may substitute his own name for that of the original Applicant.

（4）转让程序：第一受益人必须通过转让行办理信用证转让业务，而不能自行将信用证转让给第二受益人。

(4) Transfer procedures: The first beneficiary must handle the L/C transfer business through the transferring bank, and cannot transfer the L/C to the second beneficiary by itself.

（5）受让人的数量。可转让信用证能否分割转让给数个第二受益人，应视信用证是否允许分批装运而定。若信用证允许分批装运，便可分割转让给数个第二受益人。

(5) Quantity of assignee. Whether a transferable credit can be divided and transferred to several second beneficiaries depends on whether the L/C allows partial shipments. If the L/C allows partial shipments, it may be divided and transferred to several second beneficiaries.

2. 不可转让信用证 (Non-transferable Credit)

不可转让信用证指受益人不能将信用证权利转让给他人的信用证。凡未注明可转让的信用证均属此类。

Non-transferable credit means that the beneficiary cannot transfer the rights of L/C to others. Where no transferable credit is indicated, L/C falls into this category.

（五）其他特殊跟单信用证 (Other Special Documentary Credits)

1. 背对背信用证 (Back to Back Credit)

背对背信用证指信用证受益人以进口商开来的原证做抵押，要求通知行或其他银行以原证为基础，向实际供货商开出一张以其为申请人，以实际供货商为受益人的本地信用证。其中的原始信用证又称主要信用证，而背对背信用证是第二信用证。此种信用证主要用于中间商的贸易活动。

Back to back credit refers to the beneficiary of an L/C using the original L/C issued by the importer as mortgage, requiring the advising bank or other banks to issue a local L/C based on the original L/C to the actual supplier, with the beneficiary as the applicant and the actual supplier as the beneficiary. Original credit is also known as the primary credit, while back to back credit is the secondary credit. This type of L/C is mainly used for trading activities of intermediaries.

使用背对背信用证的贸易背景与可转让信用证很相似，即出口商是中间商的转口贸易，但两者之间仍有明显差异。可转让信用证下，原证与新证的关系紧密；背对背信用证下的两张信用证相互独立。

The trade background of using back to back credit is very similar to that of transferable credit, where the exporter is an intermediary in entrepot trade, but there are still significant differences between the two. Under transferable credit, there is a close relationship between original and new credits; under back to back credit, two credits are independent from each other.

2. 预支信用证 (Anticipatory Credit)

预支信用证是允许出口商在装货交单前可以支取全部或部分货款的信用证。在该证下，受益人在货物装运前，可凭汇票或其他有关证件向指定付款行（通知行）提前支取全部或部分货款。待受益人交单议付时，付款行在扣除预支金额及利息和相关费用后，将余款付给受益人。由于在早期的信开信用证中，开证行授权付款行预支的条款适用红色油墨打印的，故预支信用证又被称为红条款信用证。

Anticipatory credit is an L/C that allows the exporter to draw down all or part of the payment for goods before shipment. Under this L/C, the beneficiary can withdraw all or part of the payment from the nominated paying bank (advising bank) in advance by presenting draft or other relevant documents before shipment. When the beneficiary presents the documents for negotiation, the paying bank shall pay the balance to the beneficiary after deducting the advance amount and interest and related expenses. Anticipatory credit is also known as red clause L/C because in the early mail credit, the terms authorized by opening bank to paying bank for advance were printed with red ink.

预支信用证实质上是一种进口商预付货款的信用证。进口商愿意提前付款的原因在于争取低廉的价格和稳定的货源。因为有时出口商由于资金缺乏，无法组织货源出口，进口商便允许其预支全部或部分款项，以便其组织货源出口。由于进口商给予了出口商资金融通，故一般要求出口商接受较低价格。此外，当市场属于卖方市场时，由于出口货源紧俏，进口商为能更早争取货源，也会采用此种信用证。如20世纪初，从澳大利亚或南非购买羊毛时，进口商常使用预支信用证。但预支信用证对进口商有一定的风险。

Anticipatory credit is essentially an importer's L/C for payment in advance. The reason why importers are willing to pay in advance is due to the low price and stable supply. Sometimes the exporter is unable to organize the export of goods due to lack of funds, and the importer allows him to advance all or part of the payment so that he can organize the export of goods. Due to the financial assistance provided by the importer to the exporter, it is generally required that the exporter accept a lower price. Furthermore, when the market is in a seller's market, due to the shortage of export supplies, importers will also use this L/C in order to obtain supplies earlier. For example, in the early 20th century, importers often used Anticipatory Credit when buying wool from

Australia or South Africa. But Anticipatory Credit has certain risks for importers.

3. 循环信用证 (Revolving Credit)

循环信用证指信用证被全部或部分使用后，又恢复到原金额继续使用，直至用完规定的使用次数或累计达到原总金额为止的信用证。循环信用证按运用的方式可分为按时间循环和按金额循环两种。

Revolving credit refers to an L/C that is restored to its original amount after being used in whole or in part and continues to be used until it has been used up for a specified number of times or cumulatively reaches the original total amount. Revolving credit can be divided into revolving by time and revolving by amount according to the application mode.

（1）按时间循环的信用证，规定了受益人每隔多长时间可以循环使用信用证规定金额。

(1) L/C revolving by time, which specifies how often the beneficiary can reuse the amount specified in L/C.

（2）按金额循环的信用证，信用证金额议付后，仍可恢复到原金额再次使用，直到用完规定的总金额为止。

(2) L/C revolving by amount: After the negotiation of the L/C amount, it can still be restored to the original amount and reused until the specified total amount is used up.

循环信用证的优点在于：买卖双方订立长期合同，在准备均衡分批交货的情况下，进口商开出此种信用证可节省手续费、邮电费、保证金等，降低业务费用和成本；而出口商也可省去等待进口商开证及催证、审证的麻烦。

Advantages of revolving credit: A buyer and a seller enter into a long-term contract. Under the circumstance of preparing for balanced delivery in batches, the importer can open such an L/C to save handling charges, postal and telecommunications fees, deposits, etc., and reduce business expenses and costs; while the exporter can also save the trouble of waiting for the importer to issue L/C, urging the L/C and verifying the L/C.

4. 对开信用证 (Reciprocal Credit)

指在国际贸易中，通过相互向对方开立信用证进行结算。其主要特点是：双方同时开证，第一张信用证的受益人是第二张信用证的申请人，第一张信用证的通知行是第二张信用证的开证行，反之亦然。两张信用证的金额可以相等或不同，可以同时生效或分别生效。

It refers to the settlement by opening L/C with each other in international trade. Its main characteristics are: both parties open the L/C simultaneously, the beneficiary of the first L/C is the applicant of the second L/C, the advising bank of the first L/C is the opening bank of the second L/C, and vice versa. The amounts of the two may be equal or different and may take effect simultaneously or separately.

对开信用证在来料加工、来件装配贸易中使用较为广泛。特别是在我国，作为原料的进口方和成品的出口方，使用此类信用证较多。

Reciprocal credit is widely used in the processing of supplied materials and assembly trade. Especially in China, as the importer of raw materials and the exporter of finished products, such L/C is often used.

第三节　汇付
Section 3　Remittance

汇付（remittance），又称汇款。汇付是指付款人主动通过银行或其他途径将款项汇交收款人。对外贸易的货款如采用汇付，一般是由买方按合同约定的条件（如收到单据或货物）和时间，将货款通过银行，汇交给卖方。在国际贸易业务中，汇付主要用于小额货款的支付。

至于大额款项的支付，一般采用托收、L/C信用证等其他结算方式。

Remittance, also known as remitting money. Remittance refers to the voluntary remittance of funds by the payer to the payee through a bank or other means. Remittance of payment for goods in foreign trade is generally made by the buyers to the sellers through banks according to the conditions (such as receipt of documents or goods) and time agreed in the contract. Remittance is mainly used for the payment of small amount of goods in international trade. As for the payment of large amounts, other settlement methods such as collection and L/C are generally adopted.

一、汇付的当事人
I. Parties to Remittance

在汇付业务中，通常有四个当事人：

Remittance business usually involves four parties:

（1）汇款人（remitter）：汇出款项的人，在进出口交易中，汇款人通常是进口商。

(1) Remitter: refers to the person who remits money. In import and export business, the remitter is usually the importer.

（2）收款人（payee/beneficiary）：收取货款的人，在进出口交易中通常是出口商。

(2) Payee: The person who receives the payment for goods, usually the exporter in import and export business.

（3）汇出行（remitting bank）：受汇款人的委托、汇出款项的银行，通常是在进口地银行。

(3) Remitting bank: It refers to the bank entrusted by the remitter to remit money, usually at the place of import.

（4）汇入行（paying bank）：受汇出行委托解付汇款的银行，又称解付行，在对外贸易中，通常是出口地银行，并为汇出行的分行或代理行。

(4) Paying bank: It refers to the bank entrusted by the remitting bank to settle the remittance, also known as the receiving bank. In foreign trade, it is usually a bank t the place of export and is the branch or correspondent of the remitting bank.

二、汇付的种类及其业务流程
II. Types and Business Processes of Remittance

按照汇出行向汇入行发送解付授权书的方式（亦即银行发送支付命令方式），汇付可以分为电汇、信汇和票汇。

Remittance can be divided into T/T, M/T and D/D according to the way in which the remitting bank sends a payment authorization letter to the paying bank (i.e. the way in which the bank sends a payment order).

（一）电汇 (Telegraphic Transfer, T/T)

电汇是指汇出行用SWIFT（环球同业银行金融电信协会）或其他电信手段（如电报、电传）向汇入行发出付款委托的一种汇款方式。采用电汇方式交付款项的速度快、安全性高，且随着电信技术的发展其成本逐渐降低，因此，电汇成为使用最多的汇款方式。

T/T refers to a remittance method in which the remitting bank sends payment entrustment to the paying bank by SWIFT (Society for Worldwide Interbank Financial Telecommunications) or other telecommunication means (such as cable and telex). Payment by T/T is fast and safe. With the development of telecommunication technology, its cost gradually decreases. Therefore, T/T has become the most commonly used remittance method.

电汇业务的具体流程为：

The specific procedures of T/T services are as follows:

（1）汇款人填写汇款申请书，交款付费给汇出行，申请书上说明使用电汇方式；

(1) The remitter shall fill in the remittance application form and pay to the remitting bank, indicating that T/T is used;

（2）汇款人取得电汇回执；

(2) The remitter obtains the T/T receipt;

（3）汇出行发出 SWIFT 或加押电报、电传给汇入行，委托汇入行解付汇款给收款人；

(3) The remitting bank sends SWIFT or tested cable or telex to the paying bank, and entrusts the paying bank to settle the remittance to the payee;

（4）汇入行收到 SWIFT 或加押电报、电传，核对密押无误后，缮制电汇通知书，通知收款人收款；

(4) After receiving SWIFT or tested cable and telex, the paying bank shall prepare T/T Notices after checking that test key is correct. Notices shall be sent to the payee for collection;

（5）收款人收到通知书后在收据联上盖章，交汇入行；

(5) After receiving the notices, the payee shall stamp the receipt copy and submit it to the paying bank;

（6）汇入行借记汇出行账户，取出头寸，解付汇款给收款人；

(6) The paying bank debits the remitting bank account, withdraws the position and settles the remittance to the payee;

（7）汇入行将付讫借记通知寄汇出行，通知它汇款解付完毕，资金从债务人流向债权人，完成一笔电汇汇款。电费支付流程如图 10-3 所示。

(7) The paying bank sends the debit advice to the remitting bank, notifying that the remittance is completed, and funds flow from the debtor to the creditor to complete a T/T remittance. Flow of T/T payment see sa figure 10-3.

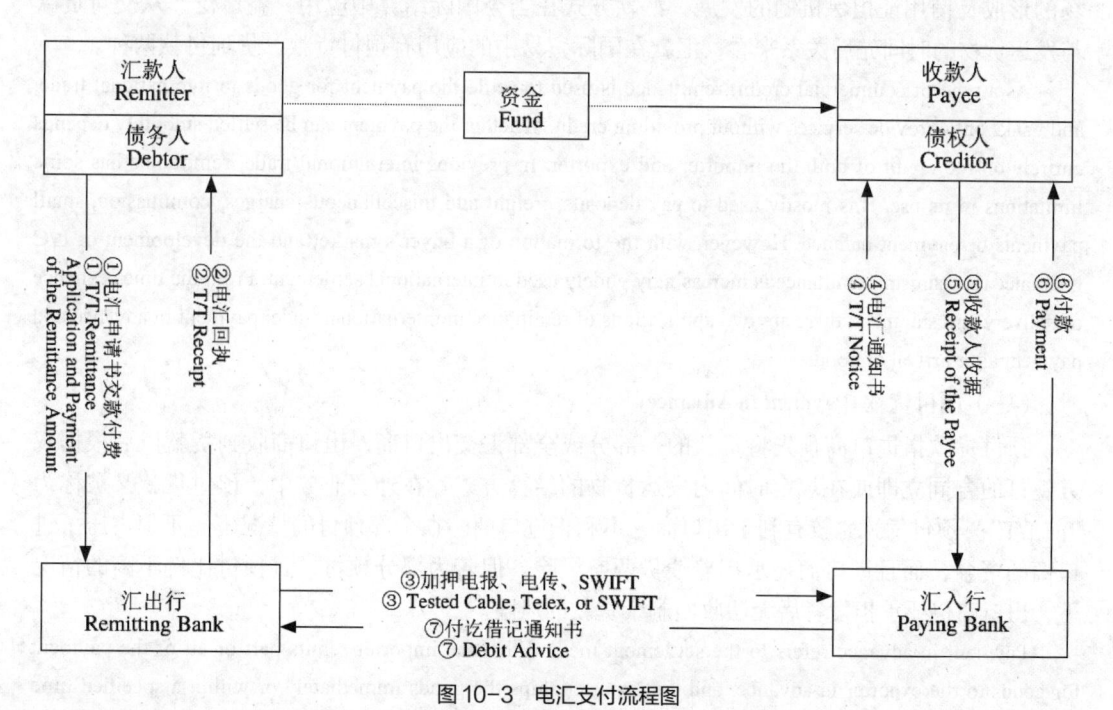

图 10-3 电汇支付流程图

Figure 10-3 Flow Chart of T/T Payment

（二）信汇 (Mail Transfer, M/T)

信汇是应汇款人的申请，由汇出行通过航邮（by airmail）信汇委托书（M/T advice）或支付委托书（payment order）指示汇入行，解付一定金额给收款人的一种汇款方式。采用信汇方式，资金转移速度较慢，收款迟缓，安全性较差，目前很多国家的银行已经不再使用。

M/T is a remittance method in which the remitting bank instructs the paying bank to settle a certain amount to the payee at the request of the remitter by airmail M/T advice or payment order. M/T features slow fund transfer, slow collection and poor security. At present, it is no longer used by banks in many countries.

（三）票汇 (Remittance by Banker's Demand Draft, D/D)

票汇是汇出行应汇款人的要求，开立一张有指定付款行（一般为其联行或账户行）的银行即期汇票给汇款人，由汇款人自行邮寄或直接交给收款人，凭票取款的一种汇款方式。票汇因环节多、耗时长，且安全性较差，资金转移速度也较慢，在实际国际结算业务中使用不多。

Remittance by banker's demand draft (D/D) is a remittance method in which the remitting bank issues a bank sight bill with nominated paying bank (usually its affiliate or account bank) at the request of the remitter, and the sight bill is mailed by the remitter itself or directly delivered to the payee for withdrawal against the bill. D/D is rarely used in actual international settlement business due to multiple stages, long time consumption, poor security and slow fund transfer.

三、汇付在国际贸易中的应用
III. Application of Remittance in International Trade

汇付属于商业信用，使用汇付方式进行国际贸易货款结算，银行只提供服务，不提供信用，货款能否顺利结清完全取决于进出口双方的信用。在以往的国际贸易中，汇付的使用有一定的局限性，多用于订金、运杂费用、佣金、小额货款或货款尾数的支付。但随着买方市场的形成及信用证担保机制的发展，汇款方式在当今国际结算中应用日益广泛。从交付货款与发运货物的时间先后关系来看，汇款在国际贸易中的应用有预付货款、货到付款两种。

As a type of commercial credit, remittance is used to settle the payment for goods in international trade, and banks only provide services without providing credit. Whether the payment can be settled smoothly depends entirely on the credit of both the importer and exporter. In previous international trade, remittance has some limitations in its use. It is mostly used to pay deposits, freight and miscellaneous charges, commission, small payments or payment balance. However, with the formation of a buyer's market and the development of L/C guarantee mechanism, remittance is increasingly widely used in international settlement. From the time sequence of delivery and shipment, there are two applications of remittance in international trade: payment in advance and payment after arrival of goods.

（一）预付货款 (Payment in Advance)

预付货款指进口商预先将货款的一部分或全部汇交出口商，出口商收到货款以后根据双方签订的合同立即或在规定时间内发运货物的结算方式。在外贸业务中，预付货款又被称为"前T/T"。预付货款比较有利于出口商，不利于进口商。在全部预付的情况下，不但占压了进口商的资金，而且进口商还承担着钱货两空风险。但若为部分预付，且预付比例不高的情况下，出口商仍要承担发货后无法收回剩余货款的风险。

Payment in advance refers to the settlement method that the importer remits part or all of the payment for goods to the exporter in advance, and the exporter ships the goods immediately or within a specified time according to the contract signed by both parties after receiving the payment. In international trade, payment in advance is also known as "T/T in advance". Payment in advance is more favorable to the exporter than to the importer. In the case of full prepayment, not only does it occupy the importer's funds, but the importer also bears the risk of losing everything. In case of partial prepayment and low prepayment ratio, the exporter still bears the risk that the remaining payment cannot be recovered after delivery.

（二）货到付款 (Payment after Arrival of Goods)

指出口商先发货，进口商收到货物后再付款的一种汇款结算方式。货到付款在外贸业务中有时也被称为"后T/T"。记账赊销（open account, O/A）为货到付款的一种，即卖方发货，自寄单据给买方，暂不收取货款，而是记在账户上，待一定时期按账面金额结算一次。货到付款对出口商非常不利，他不仅要迟收货款，影响资金周转，而且承担着货物已发出，但进口商拒收或收货后不付款的风险。这种方式传统上只用于新产品或滞销品的出口，以便在国外市场打开销路。但在当今以买方市场为主导的趋势下，被广泛使用。

It refers to a remittance settlement method in which the exporter delivers the goods first and the importer pays after receiving the goods. Payment after arrival of goods is sometimes called "T/T at sight" in international trade. Open account (O/A) is a type of payment after arrival of goods, i.e. Sellers deliver goods and send documents to the buyers without receiving payment for the time being, but it will be recorded in the account and settled according to the book amount within a certain period. Payment after arrival of goods is very unfavorable to the exporter, as it not only delays payment, but also affects capital turnover. Payment is also made at the risk of rejection or non-receipt by the importer of goods that have been dispatched. This approach has traditionally been used only for the export of new or slow-moving products in order to sell abroad. However, it is widely used in the current trend of buyer-oriented market.

第四节　托收
Section 4　Collection

随着国际市场竞争日益激烈，买方市场逐渐形成。为在激烈的国际竞争中取胜，扩大商品出口，出口商有时会采用托收支付方式，作为在付款条件上给予进口商的一种优惠。

With increasingly fierce competition in the international market, a buyer's market has gradually taken shape. In order to compete in the fierce international competition and expand the export of goods, the exporter sometimes adopts collection payment as a preferential payment method for the importer.

一、托收的含义及其当事人
I. Meaning of Collection and the Parties

（一）托收的含义及其国际贸易惯例 (Meaning of Collection and Its Application in International Trade)

托收（collection）指由卖方开具汇票并随附单据，把它交给当地银行并提出申请，委托该银行通过它在进口地的代理行代向进口商收款的方式。

Collection refers to the method in which sellers issue draft and accompanying documents, submit it to local bank for application, and entrust the bank to collect payment from importers through its correspondent at the place of import.

国际贸易中各国银行在办理托收业务时，往往由于当事人各方对权利、义务和责任的解释不同，各个银行的具体业务做法有差异，导致矛盾和纠纷的产生。国际商会为协调和统一各有关当事人在托收业务中的做法，于 1958 年草拟了《商业单据托收统一规则》。目前采用的是 1996 年 1 月 1 日正式生效的 URC522。该惯例自公布实施以来，被各国银行广泛采纳和使用，我国银行在办理托收时，一般都参照该规则办理。但应指出，惯例本身不是法律，因而对当事人没有约束力，只有在有关当事人事先约定采用惯例的情况下，才受该惯例的约束。此外，当惯例与一国或地区的法律法规相抵触时，惯例应服从于法律。

In international trade, when banks deal with collection business, they often have different interpretations of rights, obligations and responsibilities, which leads to contradictions and disputes. In 1958, ICC drafted Uniform Rules for the Collection of Commercial Paper in order to coordinate and unify the practices of all interested parties in collection business. Currently, URC 522, which came into effect on January 1, 1996, is used. Since its promulgation and implementation, this practice has been widely adopted and used by banks all over the world. Banks in China generally refer to this rule when handling collection. It should be noted that a practice itself is not a law and therefore does not bind the parties but is bound by it only if the parties concerned have agreed in advance to use it. Additionally, when the practice conflicts with the laws and regulations of a country or region, the practice shall be subject to law.

（二）托收业务的当事人 (Parties to Collection Business)

托收方式有四个基本当事人，分别是委托人、托收行、代收行和付款人。有时还要涉及提示行和需要时的代理，它们是托收方式的其他当事人。

There are four basic parties involved in the collection method, namely principal, remitting bank, collecting bank and payer. the presenting bank and the principal's representative in case of need, which are other parties to the collection method, may also be involved.

1. 委托人 (Principal)

委托人是托收业务中委托银行办理托收的债权人。由于委托人通常开具汇票委托银行向国外债务人收款，所以又被称为出票人，在国际贸易中，一般是指出口商。

Principal is the creditor who entrusts the bank to handle the collection in the collection business. The principal usually issues a draft to entrust the bank to collect money from a foreign debtor, so it is also known as the drawer, and in international trade, it is generally the exporter.

2. 托收行 (Remitting Bank)

托收行又称寄单行，指接受委托人的委托办理托收的出口地银行。

Remitting bank, also known as sending bank, refers to the bank at the place of export entrusted by the principal for collection.

3. 代收行 (Collecting Bank)

代收行指接受托收行的委托，向付款人收款，并将单据交给付款人的银行。代收行通常是托收行在付款人所在地的联行或代理行，在国际贸易中，一般为进口地银行。

Collecting bank refers to the bank that accepts the entrustment of remitting bank, collects money from payer and delivers documents to payee. the collecting bank is usually an affiliate or correspondent bank of the remitting bank in the place where the payer is located. In international trade, it is generally the bank at the place of import.

4. 付款人 (Payer)

付款人是根据托收委托书向其提示单据和汇票，并要求其付款的人。也是委托人开出汇票上的受票人。一般是国际贸易中的进口商。

Payer is the person to whom documents and draft are presented under a collection advice and to whom payment is requested. It is also drawee on the draft issued by the principal. Generally, they are importers in international trade.

5. 提示行 (Presenting Bank)

指负责向付款人提示单据及汇票的银行，通常由代收行兼任。但若代收行与付款人不在同一个地方，或无账户往来关系，为便于付款人的往来银行向其融通资金，便利收款，代收行可主动或应付款人的请求，委托与代收行有账户关系的银行充当提示行。

It refers to the bank responsible for presentation of draft to the payer, which is usually concurrently held by collecting bank. However, if the collecting bank and the payer are not located in the same place or have no account relationship, the collecting bank may entrust a bank with which the collecting bank has an account relationship to act as the presenting bank on its own initiative or at the request of the payer in order to facilitate the financing and collection by the correspondent bank of the payer.

6. 需要时的代理 (Principal's Representative in Case of Need)

它是委托人为避免在付款人拒付时，无人照料货物的情况发生，而在付款地事先指定的代理人。该代理负责在付款人拒付时，办理货物的存仓、投保、转售或运回等事宜。按照URC522的规定，如果委托人在其申请书中有指定该代理，它应同时完整明确地注明该代理人的权限。若无此注明，银行将不接受该代理人的任何指示。

It is the agent appointed in advance by principal at the place of payment to avoid leaving goods unattended when the payer refuses payment. The agent is responsible for the warehousing, insurance, resale or return of goods in case of non-payment by the payer. In accordance with URC522, if the principal designates such an agent in its application, it shall also indicate fully and expressly the authority of such agent. In the absence of such indication, the bank will not accept any instructions from that agent.

二、托收的种类及其业务流程
II. Types and Business Processes of Collection

按是否附带货运单据，托收方式分为光票托收和跟单托收两大类。

Collection methods are divided into clean collection and documentary collection according to whether shipping documents are attached or not.

（一）光票托收 (Clean Collection)

光票托收指不附带商业单据的金融单据的托收。这里的金融单据指票据中的汇票，这里的商业单据包括商业发票、装箱单或重量证明、所有权单据、保险单及其他单据。光票托收主要适用于小额贸易货款、贸易从属费用（如运费、保险费、佣金等）、非贸易费用的托收。

Clean collection refers to the collection of financial documents without commercial documents. The financial document here refers to draft in the bill. The commercial document here includes commercial invoice, packing list or certificate of weight, ownership document, insurance policy and other documents. Clean collection is mainly applicable to the collection of small trade payments, trade ancillary charges (such as freight charges, premium and commission) and non-trade charges.

（二）跟单托收 (Documentary Collection)

跟单托收指附带商业单据的金融单据的托收，或不附带金融单据的商业单据托收。金融单据附带商业单据的托收，一般都是商业汇票后面随附发票、提单、装箱单、品质证以及有需要时的保险单和其他单据的托收。这种跟单托收是凭汇票付款，托收的标的物是汇票，其他单据是汇票的附件，起支持汇票的作用。这类托收的目的就是收取汇票的票款，在托收实务中是大量而常见的。

Documentary collection refers to the collection of financial documents with or without commercial documents. Collection of financial documents with commercial documents is generally the collection of invoices, bill of lading, packing list, quality certificate and insurance policy and other documents when necessary. This type of documentary collection is based on payment against draft. The subject matter of the collection is draft, and other documents are attachments to it, which play a role in supporting draft. The purpose of this type of collection is to collect the fare of draft. It is large and common in collection practice.

在跟单托收业务中,银行代收货款时通常掌握有包括物权凭证在内的全套商业单据。银行应按何种条件向付款人(进口商)交付商业单据,特别是具有物权凭证性质的运输单据,对国际货物买卖双方的利益关系重大。跟单托收的交单方式,应由委托人在托收申请书上确定,由托收行、代收行、付款人按照执行。跟单托收按银行向付款人交单的条件不同,可分为付款交单和承兑交单两种。

In documentary collection business, banks usually have a complete set of commercial documents, including documents of title, when collecting payment on behalf of others. The conditions under which the bank should deliver commercial documents to the payer (importer), especially transport documents with the nature of documents of title, are of great importance to the interests of both international buyers and sellers of goods. The presentation method of documentary collection shall be determined by the principal in the application for collection, and executed by the remitting bank, collecting bank and payer. Documentary collection can be divided into documents against payment (D/P) and documents against acceptance (D/A) according to different conditions of presentation from the bank to the payer.

1. 付款交单 (Documents against Payment, D/P)

付款交单是委托人指示银行,在付款人付清款项后方能将单据交给付款人。付款交单按付款时间可分为即期付款交单和远期付款交单。

D/P refers to the principal instructing the bank to hand over the documents to the payer after the payer has paid the full amount. According to the payment time, D/P can be divided into D/P at sight and D/P after sight.

(1) 即期付款交单(Documents against payment at sight, D/P at sight) 是付款交单最常见的方式,它是委托人向托收行提交即期汇票并随附商业单据,委托托收行寄交代收行并指示代收行提示即期汇票,要求付款人付款,付款人审核有关单据无误后立即付款赎单。如付款人拒绝接受单据,付款人应提出拒付理由,单据由代收行暂代保管,代收行将拒付情况及理由电告托收行,等候其进一步答复。

(1) D/P at sight is the most common way of documents against payment. It refers to that the principal submit sight bill and attached commercial documents to the remitting bank, entrust the remitting bank to send them to the collecting bank and instruct the collecting bank to present sight bill, requesting the payer for payment. After reviewing the relevant documents, the payer immediately effect payment. If the payer refuses to accept the documents, the payer shall give reasons for dishonor, and the documents shall be temporarily kept by the collecting bank. the collecting bank shall inform the remitting bank of the dishonor and the reasons by telegram, waiting for its further reply.

若买卖双方签订进出口合同,合同规定以即期付款交单方式结算货款,即期付款交单的业务流程为:①出口商按合同规定装运后,填写托收申请书,开立即期汇票,连同货运单据交托收行,委托代收货款;②托收行根据托收申请书缮制托收委托书,连同跟单汇票交进口地代收行委托代收货款;③代收行按委托书指示向进口商提示即期跟单汇票;④付款人审单无误后立即付款;⑤代收行交单;⑥代收行办理转账并通知托收行款已收妥;⑦托收行向出口商交款。

即期付款交单流程如图 10-4 所示。

If the buyer and the seller sign an import and export contract, which stipulates that the payment for goods shall be settled by D/P at sight, the business process of D/P at sight is as follows: ① After shipment according to the contract, the exporter shall fill in the application for collection, issue a sight bill, submit it together with shipping documents to the remitting bank, and entrust the collection of payment for goods; ② The remitting bank shall prepare the collection advice according to the application for collection, and submit it together with the documentary bill to the collecting bank at the import place for entrusted collection of payment for goods; ③ The collecting bank shall present the sight documentary bill to the importer according to the instructions in the advice; ④ The payer shall make payment immediately after the documents are verified to be correct; ⑤ Presentation by the collecting bank; ⑥ The collecting bank shall handle the transfer and notify the remitting bank that the payment has been received; ⑦ The remitting bank shall pay the exporter. Flow of D/P at sight see as figure 10-4.

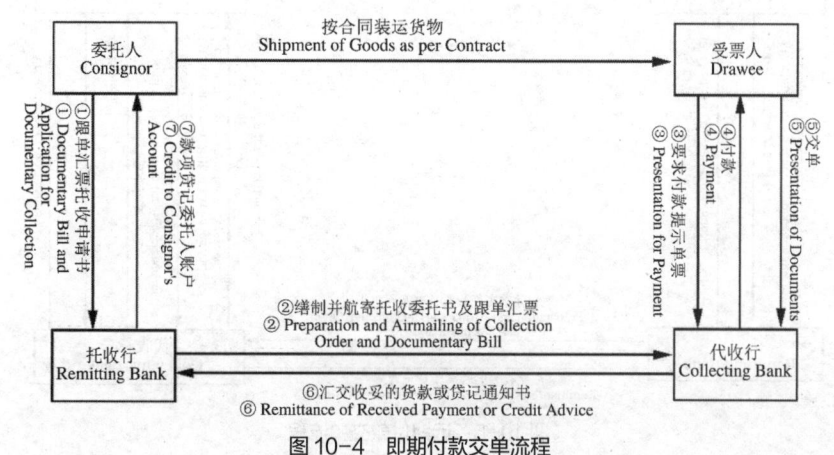

图 10-4　即期付款交单流程
Figure 10-4　Flow of D/P at sight

（2）远期付款交单（D/P at ...days after sight），指进口商在银行提示远期跟单汇票时先承兑，待汇票到期日再付款，付款人付清货款后银行才交单。远期付款交单方式的目的是给进口商以准备资金的时间，在到期付款之前，单据由代收行掌握。

(2) D/P after sight refers to the importer accepting the time documentary bill upon presentation by the bank, and making payment on the due date of the bill. The bank will not present the documents until the payer has paid the full amount. The purpose of D/P after sight is to give the importer time to prepare funds, and the documents will be held by the collecting bank before payment becomes due.

若买卖双方签订进出口合同，合同规定以远期付款交单方式结算货款，远期付款交单的业务流程为：①出口商按合同规定装运后，填写托收申请书，开立远期汇票，连同货运单据交托收行，委托代收货款；②托收行根据托收申请书缮制托收委托书，连同跟单汇票交进口地代收行委托代收货款；③代收行按委托书指示向进口商提示远期跟单汇票要求其承兑；④付款人审单无误后，对远期汇票予以承兑；⑤汇票到期日代收行再次向付款人提示要求其付款；⑥进口商付清货款；⑦代收行交单；⑧代收行办理转账并通知托收行款已收妥；⑨托收行向出口商交款。远期付款交单流程如图 10-5 所示。

If the buyer and the seller sign an import and export contract, which stipulates that the payment for goods shall be settled by D/P after sight, the business process of D/P after sight is as follows: ① After shipment as stipulated in the contract, the exporter shall fill in the application for collection, issue a time bill, submit it to the remitting bank together with shipping documents, and entrust collection of payment for goods; ② The remitting bank shall prepare the collection advice according to the application for collection, and submit it together with the documentary bill to the collecting bank at the import place for entrusted collection of payment for goods; ③ The collecting bank shall present the time documentary bill to the importer according to the instructions in the advice; ④ The payer shall accept the time bill after the documents are verified to be correct; ⑤ On the expiry date of draft, the collecting bank shall make presentation again to the payer for payment; ⑥ The importer shall pay the full amount for the goods; ⑦ Presentation by the collecting bank; ⑧ The collecting bank shall handle the transfer and notify the remitting bank that the payment has been received; ⑨ The remitting bank shall pay the exporter. Flow of D/P after sight see as figure 10-5.

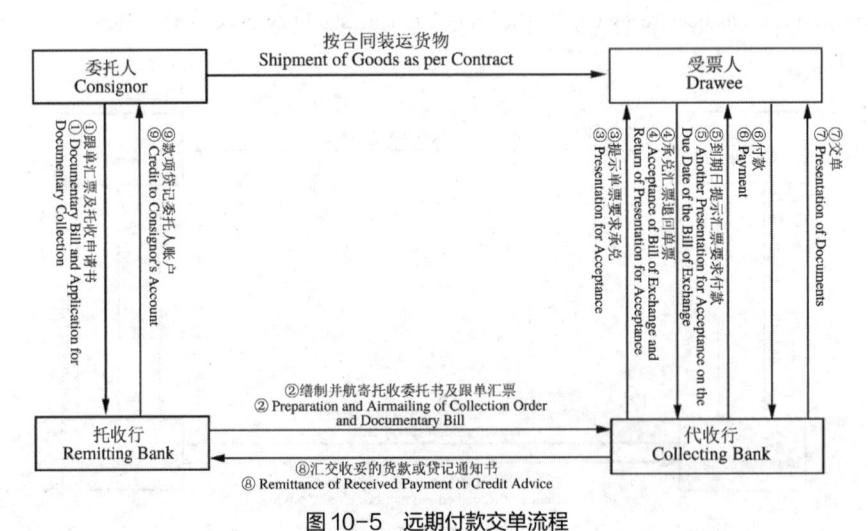

图 10-5　远期付款交单流程
Figure 10-5　Flow of D/P after sight

　　如果远期付款的期限较长，而货物运抵目的地的时间较短，进口商如要等到到期日才能付款赎单，将影响它提货，不利于与市场时机紧密相连。所以，远期期限的规定最好能跟运输航程相匹配，以避免出现"到货不到期"的情况发生。如货物海运到美国需要 30 天，那么远期付款交单的期限不宜超过 30 天，最好规定成"Documents against Payment at 30 days after sight"。

　　Documents against payment by the importer until its due date will affect his ability to take delivery of the goods, which is not in line with market timing, if the time limit for usance payment is long and the arrival time of the goods at destination is short. Therefore, the stipulation of forward time limit should be matched with the voyage to avoid "non-due delivery". If it takes 30 days for the goods to be shipped by sea to the United States, the period of D/P after sight should not exceed 30 days and it is better to specify "Documents against Payment at 30 days after sight".

　　在远期付款交单下，若出现"到货不到期"，进口商想在付款到期日前取得单据提取货物，有两种办法。一是提前付款赎单。这样不但可即时取得货运单据，提货应市，而且可以要求出口商偿还提前付款的利息。二是凭"信托收据"（trust receipt, T/R）向银行借单，现行提货，于汇票到期日再向银行付款。这实际上是代收行对进口商的一种资金融通。所谓信托收据，是指进口商向代收行借取货运单据时提供的一种书面担保文件，表示愿意以代收行的委托人身份代为提货、报关、存仓、保险、出售，并承认货物的所有权仍属于代收行，在货物售出后所得款项应交银行。但采取第二种做法时，若出现付款人到期拒付的情况应如何处理呢？这就要看授权借单给进口商的人是谁。若是代收行自行决定的，由代收行对出口商负责；若是出口商主动授权代收行向进口商提供该种便利的（D/P·T/R），则由出口商承担全部风险。

In case of "non-due delivery" under D/P after sight, the importer has two options if he wants to obtain documents and pick up the goods before tenor. First, to effect payment in advance. This not only allows for immediate access to shipping documents and pick-up, but also allows the exporter to be required to reimburse interest on advance payment. Second, to borrow shipping documents from the bank against "Trust Receipt (T/R)", take delivery of goods and make payment to the bank on the due date of draft. This is actually a type of financing for importers by the collecting bank. The so-called T/R refers to a written guarantee document provided by the importer when borrowing shipping documents from the collecting bank, indicating that he is willing to take delivery, customs declaration, warehousing, insurance and sale as the principal of the collecting bank, and acknowledging that the ownership of the goods still belongs to the collecting bank, and the proceeds shall be turned over to the bank after the goods are sold. But what if the payer refuses to pay when due under the second approach? It depends on who authorizes the lending of documents to the importer. If the collecting bank decides at its own discretion, it shall be responsible to the exporter; if the exporter actively authorizes the collecting bank to provide such convenience (D/P·T/R) to the importer, the exporter shall bear all risks.

2. 承兑交单 (Documents against Acceptance, D/A)

承兑交单指银行以付款人承兑汇票作为交付单据的条件，具体来说就是委托人提交远期跟单汇票，并提示银行只需付款人在远期汇票上承兑即可将单据交付给他。单据凭承兑汇票一经交出，则银行对这样交出的单据就不承担进一步的责任了。承兑交单是出口商给予进口商的一种真正意义上的资金融通，允许进口商仅凭承兑汇票就取得单据提取货物，待到付款到期日再付款。

D/A means that the bank takes the payer's acceptance bill as the condition for delivery of documents. Specifically, the principal submits a time documentary bill and prompts the bank to deliver the documents to the payer simply by accepting the time bill. Once the documents are presented against the acceptance bill, the bank shall not be held further responsible for the documents so presented. D/A is a type of real financing given by the exporter to the importer. It allows the importer to take delivery of the goods with documents only based on the acceptance bill. Payment will be made after tenor.

若买卖双方签订进出口合同，合同规定以承兑交单方式结算货款，承兑交单的业务流程为：①出口商按合同规定装运后，填写托收申请书，开立远期汇票，连同货运单据交托收行，委托代收货款；②托收行根据托收申请书缮制托收委托书，连同跟单汇票交进口地代收行委托代收货款；③代收行按委托书指示向进口商提示远期跟单汇票要求其承兑；④付款人审单无误后，对远期汇票予以承兑；⑤代收行交单；⑥汇票到期日代收行再次向付款人提示要求其付款；⑦进口商付清货款；⑧代收行办理转账并通知托收行款已收妥；⑨托收行向出口商交款。承兑交单流程如图10-6所示。

If the buyer and the seller sign an import and export contract, which stipulates that the payment for goods shall be settled by D/A, the business process of D/A is as follows: ① After shipment as stipulated in the contract, the exporter shall fill in the application for collection, issue a time bill, submit it to the remitting bank together with shipping documents, and entrust collection of payment for goods; ② The remitting bank shall prepare the collection advice according to the application for collection, and submit it together with the documentary bill to the collecting bank at the import place for entrusted collection of payment for goods; ③ The collecting bank shall present the time documentary bill to the importer according to the instructions in the advice; ④ The payer shall accept the time bill after the documents are verified to be correct; ⑤ Presentation by the collecting bank; ⑥ On the expiry date of draft, the collecting bank shall make presentation again to the payer for payment; ⑦ The importer shall pay the full amount for the goods; ⑧ The collecting bank shall handle the transfer and notify the remitting bank that the payment has been received; ⑨ The remitting bank shall pay the exporter. Flow of D/A see as figure 10-6.

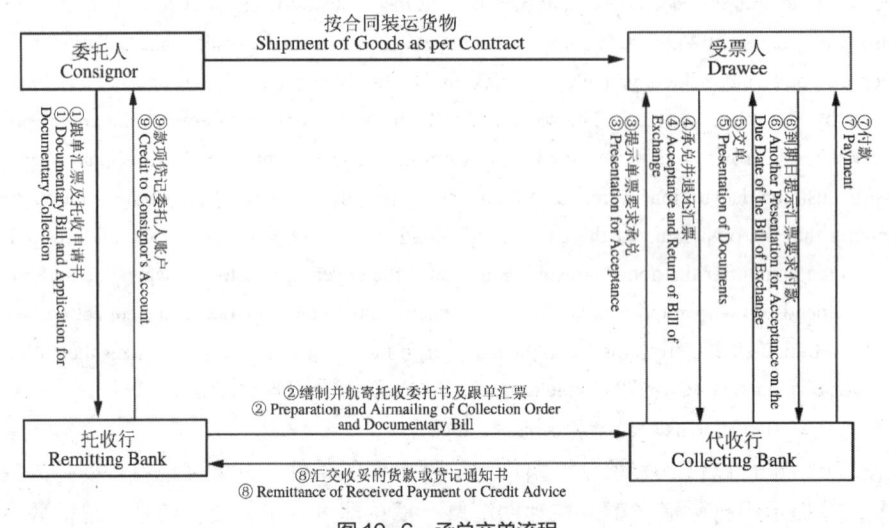

图 10-6　承兑交单流程
Figure 10-6　Flow of D/A

承兑交单与付款交单最大的区别就是交单的条件不同。对出口商来说，承兑交单比付款交单的风险大，因其在取得货款前就已经把包括物权凭证在内的单据交给了买方，到期如果买方以各种理由推脱拒不付款，出口商就有可能钱货两空。

The biggest difference between D/A and D/P is the different conditions for presentation. For the exporter, D/A is more risky than D/P, as he has already handed over documents, including documents of title, to the buyer before obtaining the payment. If the buyer refuses to make payment due to various reasons, the exporter may lose everything.

三、托收的风险与防范
III. Risks and Prevention of Collection

跟单托收属于商业信用，业务中的银行仅提供服务，而不提供任何信用担保。托收中的出口商在订立合同后，就需垫付自己的资金进行备货、装运，然后通过银行收款。总体而言，托收是一种有利于进口商，不利于出口商的支付方式。但当出口产品滞销并处于买方市场，或新产品需要促销时，采用这种结算方式，不失为一种提高自身竞争力、扩大营业额和利润的手段。出口商如何在跟单托收结算方式下趋利避害、安全收汇，可以做好以下几点。

Documentary collection is a commercial credit in which the bank only provides services and does not provide any credit guarantee. Exporter in Collection is required to advance his own funds for stocking, shipment and collection through bank after signing the contract. Collection is generally a method of payment that is beneficial for importers but not for exporters. When export products are unsold and in a buyer's market, or new products need to be promoted, this settlement method can be regarded as a means to improve its own competitiveness and expand turnover and profits. The exporter can do well in the following aspects to seek benefits and avoid harms under the documentary collection settlement method.

（一）事先调查进口商的资信状况和经营作风 (Investigate the Credit Status and Business Style of Importers in Advance)

跟单托收业务中，出口商收款人能否顺利收回货款，完全依赖于进口商付款人的信誉，因此，出口商必须认真调查进口商的资信情况，估计进口商对进口货物的承受能力，以便妥善掌握成交和具体发货的数量、品种、金额等。当然，企业或个人的信用状况不是一成不变的，商场犹如战场，全世界几乎每天都有企业的产生、破产或消亡，因此也要及时了解进口商的动态信息，防患于未然。

In documentary collection business, whether the exporter (payee) can successfully recover the payment for goods depends entirely on the reputation of the importer(payer). Therefore, the exporter must carefully investigate the credit status of the importer, estimate the importer's tolerance for imported goods, and properly grasp the quantity, variety, and amount of transactions and specific shipments. Of course, the credit status of enterprises or individuals is not static. Shopping malls are like battlefields, and enterprises emerge, go bankrupt or die out almost every day in the world. Therefore, it is also necessary to keep abreast of the dynamic information of importers in time to prevent problems before they happen.

（二）了解出口商品在进口国（地区）的市场行情 [Understand the Market Conditions of Export Goods in the Importing Country (Region)]

出口商在交易前必须了解该出口商品在进口国（地区）的市场行情，根据不同的情况做出决策。如当出口商品在进口国（地区）属于滞销品，出口商又急于使商品进入进口国（地区）市场，在进口商资信和经营作风良好的条件下，为了鼓励进口商经营该商品的积极性，给予进口商一定的优惠，可考虑使用远期承兑交单；反之，当出口商品在进口国（地区）属于畅销品，进口商又急于要货的情况下，在进口商资信和经营作风一般的条件下，可考虑使用即期付款交单。

The exporter must understand the market conditions of export goods in importing countries (regions) before trading, and make decisions based on different circumstances. If the export goods are unsold in the importing country (region) and the exporter is eager to bring the goods into the importing country (region), in order to encourage the importer's enthusiasm for operation and provide them with certain discounts, D/A after sight may be considered if the importer has good credit and business style; on the contrary, when the export goods are best-selling products in the importing country (region) and the importer is eager to purchase the goods, D/P at sight may be considered under the conditions of general credit and business style of the importer.

（三）熟悉出口国（地区）的贸易管制和外汇管理法规 [Be Familiar with the Trade Control and Foreign Exchange Administration of Exporting Countries (Regions)]

对于有进口管制的国家（地区），应确定进口商已获得有关法定部门的进口许可证明或类似文件；对于进口商所在国（地区）是有外汇管制的国家（地区），或本国货币为不可自由兑换货币时，应确定进口商已取得相关的外汇额度，或该国（地区）外汇管理法规需要的证明文件。否则，一般不宜贸然发货，以免发生货到目的地后发生由于不准进口或没有许可证明不能进口，导致货物长期滞留港口或被处罚没收的情况；或由于缺乏外汇额度，进口商无法付出外汇的情形。

For countries (regions) with import control, it shall be confirmed that the importer has obtained the import permit or similar documents from relevant statutory departments; for countries (regions) where the importer is located that have foreign exchange controls or where the domestic currency is non convertible, it shall be confirmed that the importer has obtained the relevant foreign exchange quota, or the supporting documents required by the country's (region's) foreign exchange administration. Otherwise, it is generally not advisable to deliver the goods hastily, so as to avoid the situation that the goods are detained in the port for a long time or confiscated due to impermissibility of import or non-importability without permit after arrival at the destination; or the situation that the importer cannot pay foreign exchange due to lack of foreign exchange quota.

（四）了解进口国（地区）银行的习惯做法 [Understand the Customary Practices of Banks in Importing Countries (Regions)]

在跟单托收实务中，无论是银行还是企业，各当事人对即期付款交单和远期承兑交单的操作、各自应承担的义务和责任都趋于一致，没有多大的争议。但在远期付款交单下，各当事人对各自应承担的义务和责任、具体的业务操作均有较大分歧，银行，特别是代收行往往喜欢按自己的习惯操作业务。例如一些南亚和拉美国家的代收行，基于当地的法律和习惯，对来自别国（地区）的远期付款交单条件的托收业务，通常在进口商承兑汇票后就立即将单据交给进口商，就是把远期D/P擅自改为D/A处理。这种做法虽然是超越了委托人的授权，却符合当地法律的对价原则，其结果是使出口商的风险大为增加。在这种情况下，如进口商信守合同和票据法的规定，按时付款，则出口商尚能安全收汇；若进口商信誉不佳、市场疲软，或遇进口商居心不良甚至心存欺诈，出口商就有可能钱货两空。

In the practice of documentary collection, no matter banks or enterprises, all parties concerned tend to be consistent in their operations and respective obligations and responsibilities for D/P at sight and D/A after sight, without much controversy. However, under D/P after sight, all parties have great disagreements on their respective obligations and responsibilities and specific business operations. Banks, especially collecting banks, often prefer to operate businesses according to their own habits. For example, some collection banks in South Asian and Latin American countries, based on local laws and customs, usually hand over documents to importers immediately after the importer accepts the bill for collection business under D/P after sight from other countries (regions), which means changing D/P after sight to D/A without authorization. This practice, although beyond the authority of the principal, was consistent with the principle of consideration under local law and resulted in a significant increase in risk for the exporter. In this case, if the importer abides by the contract and bill law and makes payment on time, the exporter can still collect foreign exchange securely. If the importer has poor reputation, weak market, bad intentions or even fraud, the exporter may lose everything.

（五）使用适当的贸易术语，争取出口商办理保险 (Use Appropriate Trade Terms for Export Insurance)

在跟单托收业务中，出口商应使用适当的贸易术语，争取自己办理出口货物的保险，以便应对日后的不利情况。在出口托收业务中，出口商应争取按CIF或CIP条件达成协议或签订合同，出口货物的保险由出口商负责办理。万一货物出险，又遇进口商拒付，由于出口商掌握保险单，就可以据此向保险公司索赔。

In documentary collection business, the exporter shall use appropriate trade terms to purchase his own insurance for export goods in order to cope with future adverse circumstances. In export collection business, the exporter shall strive to reach an agreement or sign a contract on a CIF or CIP basis. Insurance for export goods shall be handled by the exporter. If the goods are in danger and the importer refuses to pay, as the exporter has the insurance policy, he can claim from the insurance company accordingly.

（六）办理出口信用保险 [Apply for Export Credit Insurance (ECI)]

出口信用保险是我国政府为了推动、鼓励出口贸易，保障出口企业的收汇安全而制定的一项由国家财政提供保险准备金的政策性保险业务，一般适用于付款期限不超过180天的D/

A、O/A等结算方式下的保险。这种保险，是将进口商的信用风险转由保险公司承担，因此，出口商办理出口信用保险不失为目前规避进口商风险的相对有效地手段之一。当然，出口信用保险收费较高，一般在1%～2%，风险越高的国家或地区，手续费越高，相对于银行费用的千分之一，多出10倍以上。因而，出口商也应权衡利弊后再做打算。

ECI is a policy-based insurance business formulated by the Chinese government to promote and encourage export trade and ensure the safety of foreign exchange collection of export enterprises. It is generally applicable to insurance under D/A, O/A and other settlement methods with payment terms not exceeding 180 days. This type of insurance is to transfer the importer's credit risk to the insurance company. Therefore, it is one of the relatively effective means for the exporter to apply for ECI at present to avoid the risks of the importer. Of course, ECI charges are relatively high, generally 1%~2%. The higher the risk is in countries or regions, the higher the handling fee will be, which is more than 10 times of one thousandth of bank charges. Therefore, the exporter should weigh the pros and cons before making plans.

第五节　合同中的支付条款
Section 5　Payment Terms in the Contract

一、信用证支付条款
I. Payment Terms of L/C

在信用证支付时，合同中的支付条款应包括受益人、开证行、开证日期、信用证的种类、金额、有效期和到期地点，以及信用证的兑用方式等内容。

When making payment under an L/C, the payment terms in the contract shall include beneficiary, opening bank, date of issue, type, amount, validity time and place of expiry, as well as availability mode of L/C.

例1：即期信用证支付条款。

Example 1: Payment terms of sight L/C.

买方应通过卖方可接受的银行开立不可撤销的即期信用证并在装运月份前××天送达卖方，此证装运日后15天内在中国议付有效。

The buyer shall open through a bank acceptable to the seller an irrevocable sight letter of credit to reach the seller ×× days before the month of shipment, and valid for negotiation in China until the 15th day after the date of shipment.

例2：远期信用证支付条款。

Example 2: Payment terms of usance L/C.

买方应于2022年8月6日前通过××银行开立以卖方为受益人的不可撤销的见票后××天付款的银行承兑信用证，信用证承兑有效期为装运后15天内。

The buyer shall arrange with ×× bank for opening an irrevocable letter of credit in favor of the seller before August 6th, 2022. The said letter of credit shall be available by draft at ×× days after sight and remain valid for acceptance until the 15th day after the aforesaid time of shipment.

二、汇款支付条款
II. Payment Terms of Remittance

采用汇款支付方式时，买卖双方应在合同中规定采用何种汇款方式，以及买方何时付款。

When remittance payment is adopted, the buyers and sellers shall specify in the contract which remittance method to adopt and when to make payment.

例 3：买方应于 2022 年 9 月 20 日前将 30% 的货款电汇至卖方，其余 70% 的货款在收到正本提单传真后两日内支付。

Example 3: The buyer shall pay 30% of the sales proceeds by T/T not later than September 20th, 2022. The remaining 70% of the amount should be paid within 2 days against faxed B/L.

例 4：买方应不迟于 2022 年 10 月 31 日将 100% 的货款用电汇方式预付给卖方。

Example 4: The buyer shall pay 100% of the sales proceeds in advance by T/T to reach the seller not later than October 31st, 2022.

三、托收支付条款
III. Payment Terms of Collection

采用跟单托收支付时，买卖双方应规定托收的交单条件，若为远期付款交单或承兑交单，还应规定具体的付款期限等。

When documentary collection is used for payment, the buyers and sellers shall specify the presentation conditions of documentary collection. In case of D/P after sight or D/A, the payment period shall also be specified.

例 5：即期付款交单。

Example 5: D/P at sight.

买方应根据卖方开出的即期跟单汇票，于见票时立即付款，付款后交单。

Upon first presentation, the buyer shall pay against documentary draft drawn by the seller at sight. The shipping documents are to be delivered against payment only.

例 6：远期付款交单。

Example 6: D/P after sight.

买方根据卖方开出的见票后 60 天付款的跟单汇票，于提示时承兑，并在汇票到期时付款，付款后交单。

The buyer shall duly accept the documentary draft drawn by the seller at 60 days after sight upon first presentation and make payment on its maturity. The shipping documents are to be delivered against payment only.

例 7：承兑交单。

Example 7: D/A.

买方根据卖方开出的见票后 90 天付款的跟单汇票，于提示时承兑，并在汇票到期时付款，承兑后交单。

The buyer shall duly accept the documentary draft drawn by the seller at 90 days after sight upon first presentation and make payment on its maturity. The shipping documents are to be delivered against acceptance.

第十一章　商品检验、索赔、不可抗力与仲裁
Chapter 11　Commodity Inspection, Claim, Force Majeure and Arbitration

导　读
Introduction

在国际货物买卖中，买卖双方分处不同的国家或地区，一般不能当面交接货物，往往容易在交货的质量和数量等问题上发生争议。并且，货物通常要经过长途运输，在运输过程中可能发生残损、短少甚至灭失的现象。所以，需要一个公正的第三者，即商品检验机构，对货物进行检验或鉴定，以查明货损的原因，确定责任的归属，以利于货物的交接和交易的顺利进行。此外，由商品检验检疫机构出具的检验证书，一般都是凭以报关及交单的必备单证之一。因此，商品检验是国际贸易中不可缺少的重要环节之一，商品检验也与交易中违约与争议的产生，以及争议的预防与处理密切相关。

In the international trade of goods, buyers and sellers are located in different countries or regions. Generally, they cannot hand over the goods face to face. Dispute often arises on the quality and quantity of delivery. Carriage of goods usually involves long-distance transportation, which may cause damage, shortage or even loss. Therefore, an impartial third party, i.e. the commodity inspection agency, is required to inspect or identify the goods so as to find out the cause of damage and determine the attribution of responsibility for smooth delivery and transaction of goods. In addition, the inspection certificate issued by the commodity inspection and quarantine authority is generally one of the necessary documents for customs declaration and presentation. Therefore, commodity inspection is an integral stage in international trade. It is also closely related to the occurrence of defaults and disputes in transactions, as well as the prevention and handling of disputes.

第一节　商品检验
Section 1　Commodity Inspection

一、商品检验的含义及作用
I. Meaning and Function of Commodity Inspection

商品检验（commodity inspection），是指专门的进出口商品检验机构和其他指定的机构，依照法律、法规或进出口合同的规定，对进出口商品的品质、规格、数量、包装及安全性能等进行各种分析和测量，并出具检验证书的活动。

Commodity inspection refers to the activities carried out by import and export commodity inspection authorities and other specified agencies in accordance with laws, regulations or provisions of the import and export contract to analyze and measure the quality, specification, quantity, packing and safety performance of import and export goods and issue an inspection certificate.

由于商品检验直接关系到买卖双方在货物交接方面的权利与义务，某些进出口商品的检

验工作，还关系到国民经济发展、生态环境平衡、人民健康和动植物生长、国家安全及生产、建设的顺利进行。因此，各国法律和国际公约都对商品的检验问题作了明确规定。例如，英国《货物买卖法》（1979年修订）规定，除非双方另有约定，当卖方向买方交付货物时，买方有权要求有合理的机会检验货物。《联合国国际货物销售合同公约》规定，卖方对货物风险转移到买方时所存在的任何与合同不符的情形，均负有责任，即使这种不符在风险转移后才开始变得明显也不例外。上述各种规定都体现了一个共同原则，即除买卖双方另有规定外，买方在接受货物之前应有权对其购买的货物进行检验。但买方对货物的检验权并不是买方接受货物的前提条件。如果买方未利用合理的机会检验货物，那么他就自动放弃了检验货物的权利。另外，若合同中的检验条款规定"以卖方的检验为准"时，同样排除了买方对货物的检验权。

Commodity inspection directly impacts the rights and obligations of buyers and sellers in delivery of goods. The inspection of some import and export commodities is also related to national economic development, ecological environment balance, people's health, animal and plant growth, national security and smooth production and construction. The laws and international conventions of various countries have made clear provisions on the inspection of goods. For example, the Sales of Goods Act (as amended in 1979) provides that unless otherwise agreed by both parties, when the sellers deliver goods to the buyers, the buyers shall have the right to demand a reasonable opportunity to inspect the goods. United Nations Convention on Contracts of International Sales of Goods (CISG) stipulates that the sellers shall be liable for any non-conformity with the contract existing at the time of transfer of risks to the buyers, even if such non-conformity becomes apparent only after the transfer of risks. The above provisions embody a common principle that, unless otherwise specified by both parties, the buyers shall have the right to inspect the goods they purchase before accepting them. However, the buyers' right to inspect the goods is not a prerequisite for them to accept the goods. The buyers automatically waive their right to inspect the goods if they do not take a reasonable opportunity of doing so. Moreover, if the inspection clause in the contract specifies that "the sellers' inspection shall prevail", it also excludes the buyers' right to inspect the goods.

二、商品检验的时间和地点
II. Time and Place of Commodity Inspection

合同中对检验时间和地点的规定直接关系到买卖双方的权利与义务，因为它涉及检验权、检验机构以及有关的索赔问题。而检验时间和地点的规定又与合同中使用的贸易术语、商品特性、包装方式以及当事人所在国（地区）的法律法规等有着密切联系。在实践中，关于检验时间和地点的规定方法主要有下列四种。

The provisions on the time and place of inspection in the contract directly impact the rights and obligations of both parties, as they involve inspection rights, inspection agencies and related claims. The provisions on the time and place of inspection are closely related to the trade terms, commodity characteristics, packing methods used in the contract and the laws and regulations of the country (region) where the parties are located. In practice, there are four main methods for specifying the time and place of inspection.

（一）在出口国（地区）检验 [Inspection in the Exporting Country (Region)]

在出口国（地区）检验，又称为装船前或装船时检验，指在产地检验出口商品。在出口国检验包括产地（工厂）检验和装运港（地）检验两种。

Inspection in the exporting country (region), also known as pre-shipment or shipment inspection, refers to the inspection of export goods at the place of origin. It includes origin/factory inspection and shipping port/place inspection.

产地（工厂）检验（origin/factory inspection）是指由产品制造工厂或买方的验收人员在产品出厂前进行检验或验收。在这种情况下，卖方只承担产品在离厂前的责任，至于运输途中的品质、数量变化的风险概由买方负担。在采用这种做法时，有的还允许买方代表在产地或发货地监造或监装，这是国际贸易中普遍采用的习惯做法，已为我国的《商检法》所肯定和采纳。

Origin/factory inspection refers to the inspection or acceptance carried out by the inspectors of the product manufacturers or the buyers before the products leave the factory. In this case, the sellers shall only bear the responsibilities of the products before leaving the factory. The buyers shall bear the risks of changes in quality and quantity during carriage. Some buyers' representatives are allowed to supervise the manufacture or loading at the place of origin or shipment. This is a common practice in international trade and has been affirmed and adopted by the Law of the PRC on Inspection of Import and Export Commodities.

装运港（地）检验（shipping port/place inspection）是指出口货物在装运港装船前，以双方约定的商检机构检验货物后出具的品质、重量、数量和包装等检验证明，作为决定商品品质和重量的最后依据。买方在货物到达目的港后，可以进行复验，但无权再对货物的品质、重/数量提出异议。这一规定显然对卖方有利。

Shipping port/place inspection (SPI) refers to the inspection certificate of quality, weight, quantity and packing issued by the commodity inspection agency agreed by both parties after inspecting the export goods before loading at the port of shipment as the final basis for determining the quality and weight of the commodities. The buyers may re-inspect the goods after their arrival at port of destination, but shall have no right to raise any objection to quality and weight/quantity. This provision evidently favors the sellers.

（二）在进口国（地区）检验 [Inspection in the Importing Country (Region)]

在进口国（地区）检验是指货物到目的港后由双方约定的目的港商检机构检验货物，并出具商检证书作为最后依据。在出口国（地区）检验包括目的港（地）检验和最终用户所在地检验。

Inspection in the importing country (region) means that after the goods arrive at the port of destination, the commodity inspection agency agreed by both parties shall inspect the goods and issue a commodity inspection certificate as the final basis. It includes destination port/place inspection (DPI) and end user location inspection (EULI).

目的港（地）检验，又称"到岸品质、到岸数量"(landed quality and weight)，是指货物运达目的港或目的地后，由双方约定的检验检疫机构在合同规定的时间内对货物进行检验，并出具检验检疫证书作为卖方交货品质、数量等的最后依据。

DPI, also known as "landed quality and weight", means that after the goods arrive at the port/place of destination, the inspection and quarantine authority agreed by both parties shall inspect the goods within the time specified in the contract, and issue inspection certification as the final basis for the sellers' delivery quality and quantity.

检验地点可因商品性质的不同而异，一般货物可在码头仓库进行检验，易腐货物通常应于卸货后在关栈或码头尽快进行检验，并以其检验结果作为货物质量和数量的最后依据。

The place of inspection may vary depending on the nature of the commodity. Generally, goods can be inspected at the shipping terminal, while perishable goods shall be inspected as soon as possible after unloading at the customs warehouse or yard, and their inspection results shall be taken as the final basis for the quality and quantity of goods.

最终用户所在地检验（end user location inspection）通常是指在货物运抵最终用户所在地（买方营业处所）后，由合同规定的检验检疫机构对货物进行检验，并由该机构出具检验检疫证书作为卖方交货品质、数量等的最后依据。

EULI usually refers to the inspection of goods by an inspection and quarantine authority specified in the contract after they arrive at the place where the buyers are located, and the inspection and quarantine authority shall issue an inspection certification as the final basis for the sellers' delivery quality and quantity.

对于一些不便在目的港卸货时检验的货物，例如采用密封包装、在使用之前打开有损于货物质量或会影响使用的货物，或是规格复杂、精密程度高、需要在一定操作条件下用精密仪器或设备检验的货物，一般不能在卸货地进行检验，需要将检验延迟到用户所在地进行。使用这种条件时，货物的品质和重量（数量）是以用户所在地的检验结果为准。

For some goods that are inconvenient to be inspected at the port of destination, such as those with sealed packing and opening before use will damage the quality or affect the use of the goods, or those with complex specification and high precision, which need to be inspected by precision instruments or equipment under certain operating conditions, generally they cannot be inspected at the discharge place, and it is necessary to postpone the inspection to the user's site. When using this condition, the quality and quantity of the goods shall be subject to the inspection results at the place where the user is located.

（三）出口国（地区）检验、进口国（地区）复验 [Export Country (Region) Inspection, Import Country (Region) Reinspection]

出口国（地区）检验、进口国（地区）复验，即货物检验两次，出口国（地区）的检验证书用于交单索汇，进口国（地区）的检验证书用于证明货物是否符合合同的规定。由于这种方法同时考虑了出口商和进口商实际操作的需要，所以受到行业中的普遍欢迎，现在大多数国际货物买卖合同在检验条款上都采用这个方法。在合同中写上"出口国（地区）检验、进口国（地区）复检"的检验条款就确定了出口地和进口地的检验机构出示的证书都是有效的。

Export country (region) inspection, import country (region) reinspection, i.e. the goods are inspected twice. The inspection certificate of the exporting country (region) is used for presentation of documents for foreign exchange, and the inspection certificate of the importing country (region) is used to prove whether the goods comply with the provisions of the contract. Since this method takes into account the practical needs of both exporter and importer, it is popular in the industry. Nowadays, most contracts for international sale of goods adopt this method in terms of inspection clauses. The inspection clause of "Export Country (Region) Inspection, Import Country (Region) Reinspection" in the contract confirms that the certificates issued by the inspection agencies at both exporting and importing places are valid.

（四）装运港（地）检验重量、目的港（地）检验品质 (Inspection Weight at Shipping Port/Place and Inspection Quality at Destination Port/Place)

装运港（地）检验重量、目的港（地）检验品质是交货重量以装运港约定的检验机构出具的重量检验证明作为最后依据，交货品质以目的港约定的检验机构出具的品质检验证明作为最后依据，也称为"离岸重量、到岸品质"（shipping weight, landed quality）。该条款多用于大宗商品的检验中，以调和双方在商检问题中存在的矛盾。

Inspection weight at shipping port/place and inspection quality at destination port/place refer to the delivery weight being based on the weight inspection certificate issued by the agreed inspection agency at port of shipment as the final basis, and the delivery quality being based on the quality inspection certificate issued by the agreed inspection agency at port of destination as the final basis, also known as "shipping weight, landed quality". This clause is mostly used in the inspection of bulk commodities to reconcile the contradiction between both parties in commodity inspection.

三、商品检验的内容及标准
III. Contents and Standards of Commodity Inspection

进出口商品实施检验的内容，包括商品的质量、规格、数量、重量、包装，以及是否符合安全、卫生要求。检验的依据为买卖合同及相关的国家法律法规。

The inspection of import and export commodities shall include the quality, specification, quantity, weight, packing, and compliance with safety and hygiene requirements. The basis for inspection is the sales contract and relevant national laws and regulations.

进出口商品法定检验是国家出入境检验检疫部门根据国家法律法规规定，对规定的进出口商品或有关的检验检疫事项实施强制性的检验检疫，未经检验检疫或经检验检疫不符合法律法规规定要求的，不准输入输出。法定检验检疫的目的是保证进出口商品、动植物（或产品）及其运输设备的安全、卫生符合国家有关法律法规规定和国际上的有关规定；防止次劣有害商品、动植物（或产品）以及危害人类和环境的病虫害和传染病源输入或输出，保障生产建设安全和人类健康。

Statutory inspection of import and export commodities refers to the compulsory inspection and quarantine carried out by CIQ on specified import and export commodities or related inspection and quarantine particulars in accordance with national laws and regulations. Those that have not been inspected and quarantined or do not meet the requirements of laws and regulations after inspection and quarantine are not allowed to be imported or exported. The purpose of statutory inspection and quarantine is to ensure that the safety and hygiene of import and export commodities, animals and plants (or products) and their carriage equipment comply with relevant national laws and regulations as well as relevant international provisions; prevent the import or export of inferior harmful commodities, animals and plants (or products), diseases and pests endangering mankind and the environment, and infectious disease sources, so as to guarantee the safety of production and construction and human health.

国家出入境检验检疫部门对进出口商品实施法定检验检疫的范围包括：
CIQ shall carry out statutory inspection and quarantine on the import and export commodities, including:

（1）列入《出入境检验检疫机构实施检验检疫的进出境商品目录》（简称《检验检疫商品目录》）；
(1) Those listed in the Catalogue of Import and Export Commodities Subject to Inspection and Quarantine by Entry-Exit Inspection and Quarantine Authority (hereinafter referred to as the Catalogue of Inspection and Quarantine Commodities);

（2）《中华人民共和国食品安全法》规定，应实施卫生检验检疫的进出口食品；
(2) Import and export food subject to health inspection and quarantine as stipulated in the Food Safety Law of the People's Republic of China;

（3）危险货物的包装容器、危险货物运输设备和工具的安全技术条件的性能和使用鉴定；
(3) Performance and use appraisal of safety technical conditions for packing containers, equipment and tools for the carriage of dangerous goods;

（4）装运易腐烂变质食品、冷冻品的船舱、货舱、车厢和集装箱等运载工具；

(4) Ship hold, cargo hold, cargo compartment, container and other means of delivery for transporting perishable foods and frozen products;

（5）国家其他有关法律法规规定必须经出入境检验检疫机构检验的进出口商品、物品、动植物等。

(5) Import and export commodities, articles, animals and plants that must be inspected by entry-exit inspection and quarantine authorities according to other relevant national laws and regulations.

四、商品检验的机构
IV. Commodity Inspection Agencies

（一）国际上商品检验机构的类型 (Types of International Commodity Inspection Agencies)

国际上的商品检验机构种类繁多，名称各异，但大体可归纳为官方、半官方和非官方三种检验机构。官方检验机构是由国家或地方政府投资、按照国家有关法令对进出口商品实施检验、检疫和监督的机构，如美国的食品药物管理局（FDA）。半官方检验机构是指一些有一定权威的、由国家政府授权、代表政府行使某项商品检验或某一方面检验管理工作的民间机构，如美国保险人实验室（Underwriter's Laboratory）。非官方检验机构主要是指由私人创办的、具有专业检验鉴定技术能力的公证行或检验公司，如英国劳埃氏公证行（Lloyd's Surveyor），瑞士日内瓦通用公证行（Societe Generale de Surveillance, SGS）。

There are various types of international commodity inspection agencies with different names, but they can be generally classified into three types: official, semi-official, and non-official inspection agencies. Official inspection agency is an agency invested by the state or local government, such as Food and Drug Administration (FDA), that conduct inspections, quarantine and supervision of import and export goods in accordance with relevant national laws and regulations. Semi-official inspection agencies refer to some non-governmental organizations with certain authority, such as Underwriter's Laboratory, which are authorized by the national government to carry out a certain commodity inspection or inspection management work in a certain aspect, on behalf of the government. Non-official inspection agencies refer to private founded surveyors or inspection companies with professional inspection and appraisal technical capabilities, such as Lloyd's Surveyor, Societe Generale de Surveillance (SGS).

（二）中国的商品检验机构 (China's Commodity Inspection Agencies)

中国的商检机构原为国家出入境检验检疫局及其设在全国各口岸的出入境检验检疫局。2001年4月，国家质量监督检验检疫总局成立，简称国家质检总局（AQSIQ），成为我国主管质量监督和检验检疫工作的最高行政执法机构，其设在各地的直属机构即各地出入境检验检疫局管理其所辖地区的进出口商品检验工作。

China's commodity inspection agencies were originally China Entry-Exit Inspection and Quarantine Bureau and its entry-exit inspection and quarantine bureaus located at various ports throughout the country. In April 2001, the General Administration of Quality Supervision, Inspection and Quarantine of the People's Republic of China (AQSIQ) was established as China's highest administrative law enforcement agency in charge of quality supervision, inspection and quarantine. Its directly affiliated agencies, namely local entry-exit inspection and quarantine bureaus, are responsible for commodity inspection under their jurisdiction.

2018年3月，根据第十三届全国人民代表大会第一次会议批准的国务院机构改革方案，将国家质量监督检验检疫总局的出入境检验检疫管理职责和队伍划入海关总署。海关总署主管全国进出口商品检验工作。海关总署设在省、自治区、直辖市以及进出口商品的口岸、集散地、的出入境检验检疫局及其分支机构，管理所负责地区的进出口商品的检验工作。

In March 2018, according to the institutional reform plan of the State Council approved at the first session of the 13th National People's Congress, the entry-exit inspection and quarantine management responsibilities and teams of AQSIQ were transferred to the General Administration of Customs. The General Administration of Customs shall be responsible for commodity inspection nationwide. The General Administration of Customs shall be located in the entry-exit inspection and quarantine bureaus and their branches at provinces, autonomous regions, municipalities directly under the central government, as well as import and export commodity ports and distribution centers, responsible for managing the inspection work of import and export commodities in their respective regions.

五、商品检验证书
V. Commodity Inspection Certificate

检验证书（inspection certificate）是检验机构对进出口商品进行检验、鉴定后出具的书面证明文件。它是证明卖方所交货物的品质、数量、包装等项内容是否符合合同规定的依据，是海关凭以验关放行和卖方凭以办理贷款结算的一种单据，也是买方对货物的不符点向卖方索赔和卖方理赔的主要依据。在实际业务中，究竟需要提供何种检验证书，应根据交易商品的种类、特性、进出口国（地区）的贸易习惯及有关政策法令而定，并在合同中予以明确规定。

Inspection certificate is a written document issued by the inspection agency after inspecting and appraising the import and export goods. It is the basis for proving whether the quality, quantity and packing of the goods delivered by the Sellers conform to the provisions of the contract. It is also a type of document based on which the customs can check and release the goods and the sellers can handle loan settlement. It also serves as the primary basis for claim and claim settlement for non-conformity of the goods. In actual business, the type of inspection certificate required shall be determined according to the types and characteristics of traded goods, trade practices of importing and exporting countries (regions) and relevant policies and decrees, and specified in the contract.

目前，常见的检验证书有以下几种：

At present, the following types of Inspection Certificate are commonly used:

（1）品质检验证书（inspection certificate of quality），是出口商品交货结汇和进口商品结算索赔的有效凭证；法定检验商品的证书，是进出口商品报关、输出输入的合法凭证。商检机构签发的放行单和在报关单上加盖的放行章有与商检证书同等通关效力；签发的检验情况通知单同为商检证书性质。

(1) Inspection certificate of quality is a valid certificate for the delivery and settlement of foreign exchange for export goods and for the settlement of claims for import goods; the certificate of statutory inspection of goods is a legal certificate for customs declaration, output and input of import and export goods. The release note issued by the commodity inspection agency and the release seal affixed to the customs declaration form shall have the same effect of customs clearance as the commodity inspection certificate; the notices on inspection conditions issued shall be of the same nature as the commodity inspection certificate.

（2）重量检验证书（inspection certificate of weight），是证明进出口商品重量的证明文件。

(2) Inspection certificate of weight is a document certifying the weight of import and export goods.

（3）数量检验证书（inspection certificate of quantity），是证明进出口商品数量的证明文件。

(3) Inspection Certificate of Quantity is a document certifying the quantity of import and export goods.

（4）兽医检验证书（veterinary inspection certificate），是证明出口动物产品或食品经过检疫合格的证件。适用于冻畜肉、冻禽、禽畜罐头、冻兔、肠衣等出口商品。是对外交货、银行结汇和进口国（地区）通关输入的重要证件。

(4) Veterinary inspection certificate is a document certifying that the exported animal products or food have passed quarantine. Applicable to export goods such as frozen meat, frozen poultry, canned livestock, frozen rabbits and casings. It is an important document for external delivery, bank settlement of foreign exchange and customs clearance in the importing country (region).

（5）卫生/健康检验证书（sanitary inspection certificate），是证明可供人类食用的出口动物产品、食品等经过卫生检验或检疫合格的证件。适用于肠衣、罐头、冻鱼、蛋品、乳制品、蜂蜜等，是对外交货、银行结汇和通关验放的有效证件。

(5) Sanitary inspection certificate is a document certifying that the export animal products and food for human consumption have passed health inspection or quarantine. Applicable to casings, canned goods, frozen fish, eggs, dairy products, honey, etc. It is a valid certificate for external delivery, bank settlement and customs clearance.

（6）消毒检验证书（disinfection inspection certificate），是证明出口动物产品经过消毒处理，保证安全卫生的证件。适用于猪鬃、马尾、羽毛、头发等商品，是对外交货、银行结汇和国外通关验放的有效凭证。

Disinfection inspection certificate is a document certifying that export animal products have been disinfected to ensure safety and hygiene. It is suitable for pig bristles, horsetails, feathers, human hair and other commodities. It is a valid certificate for external delivery, bank settlement of foreign exchange and foreign customs clearance.

（7）产地检验证书（inspection certificate of origin），是出口商品在进口国（地区）通关输入和享受减免关税优惠待遇和证明商品产地的凭证。如果合同规定出具原产地证明，按给惠国的要求，出口方开具原产地证明，商检机构签发原产地证书。

Inspection certificate of origin is a document certifying the origin of export goods, which are imported through customs in the importing country (region) and enjoy preferential treatment for tariff reduction and exemption. If the contract stipulates that a certificate of origin shall be issued, the exporter shall issue a certificate of origin and the commodity inspection agency shall issue a CERTIFICATE OF ORIGIN as required by the preference-giving country.

（8）价值检验证书（inspection certificate of value），证明产品的价值或发票所载商品价值正确的文件。

(8) Inspection certificate of value is a document certifying that the value of products or goods contained in invoices is correct.

其他检验证书还包括熏蒸证书、残损检验证书、积载鉴定证书、财产价值鉴定证书、船舱检验证书、生丝品级及公量检验证书、舱口检视证书、货载衡量检验证书、集装箱租箱交货检验证书等。

Other inspection certificates also bale inspection certificate of fumigation, inspection certificate on damaged cargo, inspection certificate on hatch and/or cargo, certificate of valuation, inspection certificate on tank/hold, inspection certificate for spun silk yarn quality, certificate of hatch survey, inspection certificate on cargo weight & measurement, inspection certificate on container leasing & delivery, etc.

六、合同中的商品检验条款
VI. Commodity Inspection Clause in the Contract

（一）合同商品检验条款商订的内容 (Contents Agreed in the Commodity Inspection Clause of the Contract)

订立商品检验条款的目的在于确定商品的质量、数量（重量）和包装等是否符合要求，用以验证卖方是否履行了合同规定的交货义务。特别是，有关商品检验权的规定是直接关系到买卖双方切身利益的重要问题，因此，交易双方应在买卖合同中对于商品检验有关的问题做出明确的规定。

The purpose of the commodity inspection clause is to verify that the sellers have fulfilled their delivery obligations under the contract by determining whether the quality, quantity (weight) and packing of the goods meet the requirements. Especially, the stipulation of commodity inspection right is an important issue directly impact the vital interests of both parties. Therefore, the buyers and sellers should make clear provisions on issues related to commodity inspection in the sales contract.

交易双方商订商检条款时，应结合商检工作与商品自身特点、国家相关规定及贸易惯例等因素，综合考虑，合理规定。一般商检条款的主要内容应包括检验的时间与地点、检验机构、检验的标准与方法、复验的期限与地点、商品检验的内容、检验证书的种类。

When both parties negotiate commodity inspection clause, they should make reasonable provisions after comprehensive consideration in combination with the commodity inspection work and its own characteristics, relevant national regulations and trade practices. The main contents of commodity inspection clauses shall include time and place of inspection, inspection agency, standard and method of inspection, period and place of reinspection, content of commodity inspection and type of commodity inspection certificate.

此外，订立商检条款应注意以下几点：应坚持独立自主、平等互利的原则；应明确规定出口商品复验期限及复验机构；商检条款的内容应与合同其他条款内容相符合，不能互相矛盾。

Moreover, please note the following when formulating commodity inspection clauses: The principle of independence, equality and mutual benefit shall be adhered to; Exporter's re-inspection period and re-inspection agency shall be specified; The contents of commodity inspection clauses shall conform to those of other clauses in the contract without contradicting each other.

（二）国际货物买卖合同的商品检验条款实例 (Examples of Commodity Inspection Clause in Contract for International Sale of Goods)

以最常用的"出口国（地区）检验、进口国（地区）复验"做法下合同商检条款为例。如：

Take the most commonly used "Export Country (Region) Inspection, Import Country (Region) Reinspection" as an example. For example,

卖方在发货前由检验机构对货物的品质、规格和数量进行检验，并出具检验证明书。货物到达目的口岸后，买方可委托当地的商品检验机构对货物进行复检。如果发现货物有损坏、残缺或规格、数量与合同规定不符，买方须于货到目的口岸的30天内凭检验机构出具的检验证明书向卖方索赔。

The sellers shall have the qualities, specifications, quantities of the goods carefully inspected by the inspection authority, which shall issue inspection certificate before shipment. The buyers have right to have the goods inspected by the local commodity inspection authority after the arrival of the goods at the port of destination. If the goods are found damaged/short/their specifications and quantities not in compliance with that specified in the contract, the buyers shall lodge claims against the sellers based on the inspection certificate issued by the commodity inspection authority within 30 days after the goods arrival at the destination.

第二节 索赔
Section 2 Claim

一、争议与违约
I. Dispute and Breach of Contract

（一）争议的含义及其产生的原因 (Meaning of Dispute and Causes)

争议（dispute）是指交易一方认为另一方没有履行或没有完全履行合同规定的责任而引起的纠纷。在国际货物买卖合同的履行过程中，争议产生的原因主要有以下几方面。

Dispute refers to a dispute arising from one party's belief that the other party has not fulfilled or fully fulfilled its contractual obligations. The main reasons for disputes arising during the performance of contracts for international sale of goods are as follows.

1. 卖方违约 (Seller's Breach of Contract)

按照《联合国国际货物销售合同公约》的规定，卖方的基本义务是向买方交付货物，移交单据并转移货物所有权。而如果卖方不同程度地违反了其承担的基本义务，如不交货，或未按合同规定的时间、品质、数量、包装交货，或移交的单证不全或单证之间不符等，都会导致争议的产生。在实践中，卖方违约是产生争议和索赔案件的主要原因。

According to CISG, the basic obligations of sellers are to deliver goods, hand over documents and transfer ownership of goods to the buyers. Dispute will arise if the sellers violate their basic obligations to varying degrees, such as non-delivery of goods or failure to deliver goods according to the time, quality, quantity and packing specified in the contract, or incomplete or inconsistent documents handed over. In practice, the seller's breach of contract is the main reason for disputes and claims.

2. 买方违约 (Buyer's Breach of Contract)

按照《公约》的规定，买方的基本义务是向卖方支付货款，受领货物。而如果买方不同程度地违反了其承担的基本义务，如不开或迟开信用证，不支付或不按时支付货款，无理拒收货物，或在 FOB 条件下不派船或不按期派船等，都有可能导致争议的产生。

According to CISG, the basic obligation of the buyers is to pay the sellers for the goods and receive them. Disputes may arise if the buyers violate their basic obligations to varying degrees, such as failing to open or delaying in opening L/C, failing to pay or not paying on time for goods, unreasonably rejecting the goods, or failing to dispatch ships under FOB or not dispatching ships on schedule.

3. 合同中的某些条款规定不当 (Inappropriate Provisions in Certain Clauses of the Contract)

买卖合同条款规定不当，会导致合同的履行失去可操作性，造成双方当事人对合同条件理解上的不一致，从而引发争议。如贸易术语选用不当，交货时间规定的过于笼统，对远期 D/P 的理解不一致，规定了"软条款"，或是对合同是否有效成立也有不同看法等。

Inappropriate provisions in the terms of a sales contract can lead to loss of operability in the performance of the contract, resulting in inconsistent understanding of contract conditions between both parties, and thus causing disputes. e.g. Improper selection of trade terms, over general delivery time, inconsistent understanding of D/P after sight, provision of "soft clause", or differing opinions on the validity of the contract, etc.

4. 引用不可抗力事故条款争议 (Disputes over Citing Force Majeure)

在合同的履行过程中，合同一方当事人认为发生了某种合同规定的不可预见或无法预防、无法控制的突发事件，需要引用相关条款予以免责，而合同另一方当事人对此的解释又不一致时，也会导致争议的产生。

During the performance of the contract, if one party believes that an unforeseeable, unpreventable or uncontrollable emergency has occurred as specified in the contract, relevant provisions need to be cited to exempt them from liability. If the other party to the contract interprets this differently, it will also lead to a dispute.

5. 与运输合同当事人、保险合同当事人的争议 (Dispute with Parties to Contract of Carriage or Insurance Contract)

国际货物买卖合同的履行过程中，涉及运输合同、保险合同相关当事人的责任。若相关当事人违反了运输或保险合同的规定，未尽到自己应尽的责任，或合同双方对有关问题认定不清，也是产生争议的常见原因。

During the performance of contract for international sale of goods, responsibilities of relevant parties to contract of carriage or insurance contract are involved. If the relevant parties violate the provisions of carriage or insurance contract, fail to fulfill their responsibilities, or the parties to the contract are unclear about the relevant issues, it is also a common reason for disputes.

（二）违约的法律责任 (Legal Liability for Breach of Contract)

因为争议产生的主要原因是违约（breach of contract），而违约行为不同，所导致的法律后果和违约方应承担的责任也不同，对此，各国法律及公约有着不同的规定。英国《货物买卖法》将违约分为违反要件和违反担保两种，并规定：如果一方违反要件，受损方有权解除合同并要求损害赔偿；而如果违约方违反担保，受损方只能要求损害赔偿，无权解除合同。一般认为与交易标的物直接相关的品质、数量、包装、交货期条件属于要件，与标的物不直接联系的为担保。

The main reason for disputes is breach of contract, and the legal consequences and responsibilities of the defaulting party vary depending on the breach of contract. Therefore, laws and conventions of different countries have different provisions regarding this. The Sale of Goods Act divides breach of contract into two types: breach of condition and breach of warranty, and stipulates that if one party violates the conditions, the injured party has the right to terminate the contract and claim damages; while if the other party violates the warranty, the injured party can only claim damages and has no right to terminate the contract. It is generally believed that the quality, quantity, packing and time of delivery directly related to the subject matter of transaction are conditions, while those not directly related to the subject matter are warranty.

《联合国国际货物销售合同公约》把违约分为根本性违约和非根本性违约两类，并规定，如果一方根本性违约，另一方有权撤销合同并要求损害赔偿，否则只能要求损害赔偿，不能撤销合同。虽然根据违约的法律责任不同，受损方可以有不同的救济措施，但最基本也是最主要的违约救济措施就是索赔。

CISG divides breach of contract into two categories: fundamental breach of contract and non-fundamental breach of contract, and stipulates that if one party commits a fundamental breach of contract, the other party has the right to revoke the contract and claim damages; otherwise, only damages can be claimed, and the contract cannot be revoked. Although the injured party may have different remedies based on the legal liability for breach of contract, the most basic and primary remedy for breach of contract is claim.

二、索赔与理赔
II. Claim and Settlement

索赔（claim）是指遭受损害的一方向违约方提出赔偿的要求，在法律上是指主张权利；理赔（claim settlement）是指违约一方对受损害方所提赔偿要求的受理与处理。索赔和理赔是一个问题的两个方面，对受损方而言，称为索赔；对违约方而言，称为理赔。

Claim refers to a claim made by the party who has suffered damage to the defaulting party for compensation, which legally refers to claiming rights; settlement refers to the acceptance and handling of compensation claims made by the defaulting party to the injured party. Claim and settlement are two aspects of the same problem, which is called claim for the injured party and claim settlement for the defaulting party.

索赔要有充分的索赔依据，且应在索赔期限内提出，否则即丧失索赔权。若合同规定有索赔期的，应在合同规定的期限内提出索赔要求；若无，则应按有关法律或公约的规定办理。《联合国国际货物销售合同公约》第三十九条第二款规定："如果买方不在实际收到货物之日起两年内将货物不符合合同的情形通知卖方，他就丧失声称货物不符合合同的权利。"

Claim shall be based on sufficient basis and submitted within the claim period, otherwise the right of claim will be lost. If the contract stipulates a claim period, the claim shall be submitted within the period specified in the contract; if not, it shall be handled according to relevant laws or CISG. Article 39 (2) of CISG stipulates: "If the buyers do not notify the sellers of the nonconformity of the goods within two years from the date of actual receipt, they lose the right to claim that the goods do not comply with the contract."

根据损失的原因和责任不同，索赔有三种不同情况：凡属承保范围内的货物损失，向保险公司索赔；若系承运人的责任所造成的货物损失，向承运人索赔；如系买卖合同当事人的责任造成的损失，则向责任方提出索赔。

According to the different causes and responsibilities of losses, there are three types of claim: claim against the insurance company for the loss of goods within the scope of cover; claim against the carrier for the loss of goods caused by the responsibility of the carrier; claim against the responsible party for the loss caused by responsibility of the parties to the sales contract.

买卖合同当事人在向对方索赔时，应注意查明责任，遵守索赔期限，正确确定索赔款项，并备齐索赔所需的单证。在理赔时，则应认真分析对方所提索赔理由是否充分、情况是否属实、是否符合合同及法律规定，仔细审核对方的索赔单证和文件，合理确定赔付办法。

When the parties to a sales contract claim against the other party, they shall pay attention to ascertaining responsibilities, complying with the claim period, correctly determining the amount of claim and preparing all documents required for claim. When settling a claim, it is necessary to carefully analyze whether the reasons for the claim put forward by the other party are sufficient, whether the situation is true, and whether it complies with the contract and legal provisions, carefully review the claims documents and files of the other party, and reasonably determine the compensation method.

三、合同中的索赔条款
III. Claim Clause in the Contract

在国际货物买卖合同中，索赔条款有两种规定方式：一是只规定异议与索赔条款（discrepancy and claim clause）；二是在规定异议与索赔条款的基础上再加订一个罚金条款（penalty clause）。在一般合同中，只订异议与索赔条款，只有在大宗商品或重大交易合同中，要再加订罚金条款。

In the contract for international sale of goods, there are two ways to stipulate claim clause: one is to only stipulate discrepancy and claim clause; the other is to add a penalty clause on the basis of discrepancy and claim clause. In the general contract, only discrepancy and claim clause is stipulated; while in the bulk commodity or major transaction contract, a penalty clause shall be added.

（一）异议与索赔条款 (Discrepancy and Claim Clause)

1. 索赔依据 (Claim Basis)

索赔依据指索赔必须具备的证据和出证机构。包括法律依据（贸易合同和有关国家的法律规定），事实依据（违约的事实真相及其书面证明）。贸易索赔一般以商检证书为主。国际货物买卖中，商检时间和地点的规定通常采用"出口国（地区）检验，进口国（地区）复验"的做法。因此，进口商收到货物后，应在合同规定的复验期内向当地商检机构申请货物检验。如经检验，发现货物的品质、规格与合同不符，原装数量短少，目的地商检机构出具的检验证书就是主要的索赔证据。同时，应根据不同情况随附其他必要证明：

Claim basis refers to the evidence and issuing authority that must be present for a claim, including legal basis (trade contracts and relevant national laws and regulations), factual basis (the truth of the breach of contract and its written proof). Trade Claim is generally based on commodity inspection certificate. In international sales of goods, the time and place for commodity inspection are usually stipulated as "Export Country (Region) Inspection, Import Country (Region) Reinspection". Therefore, after receiving the goods, the importer shall apply to the local commodity inspection agency for goods inspection within the reinspection period specified in the contract. If it is found through inspection that the quality and specification of the goods are not in conformity with the contract, or the original quantity is insufficient, the inspection certificate issued by the commodity inspection agency at the destination shall be the main evidence for claim. At the same time, other necessary certificates shall be attached as appropriate:

（1）运输证明，如海运提单、铁路运单、航空运单等；

(1) Proof of carriage, such as B/L, railway bill and airway bill;

（2）货物证明，包括商业发票、装箱单、重量单等；

(2) Certificate of goods, including commercial invoice, packing list and weight list;

（3）港务局理货员签证的理货报告；

(3) Tally report signed by the tally clerk of the port authority;

（4）承运人或其代理人签发的货损货差证明；

(4) Certificate of damage or shortage issued by the carrier or its agent;

（5）索赔清单等。

(5) Claim list, etc.

2. 索赔期限 (Claim Period)

索赔期限指索赔方向违约方提赔的有效时限，逾期提赔，违约方可不予受理。索赔期限的规定要根据商品性质以及检验所需时间等因素确定。如果合同中没有规定索赔期限，可以参考有关法律及公约。

Claim period refers to the effective time limit for a claimant to make a claim to the defaulting party. If the claim is overdue, the defaulting party may not accept it. Claim period shall be determined according to the nature of goods and the time required for inspection. If the contract does not specify a claim period, relevant laws and CISG can be referred to.

（1）贸易索赔：《联合国国际货物销售合同公约》规定，向卖方索赔的期限为买方实际收到货物后两年内。

(1) Trade claim: CISG stipulates that the time limit for claim against the sellers is two years after the buyers actually receive the goods.

（2）运输索赔：向船公司索赔的期限为货物到达目的港交货后1年内。

(2) Carriage claim: The time limit for claim against the shipping company is within 1 year after the goods arrive at the port of destination.

（3）保险索赔：向保险公司提出索赔的期限为自保险事故发生之日起算，最多不超过2年。

(3) Insurance claim: The time limit for claim against the insurance company is a maximum of 2 years from the date of the insured accident.

业务中的习惯做法是：一般货物的索赔期限为货到目的港30～45天；食品、农产品等易腐商品的索赔期限可以再短些；机器设备的索赔期限分数量和品质做不同的规定，数量方面的索赔期限一般为货到目的港后60天，品质方面的索赔期限一般为1年或1年以上，并通常规定其为质量保证期。

The common practice in business includes: the claim period for general goods is 30~45 days after the goods arrive at port of destination; the claim period for perishable goods such as food and agricultural products may be shorter; the claim period for machinery and equipment varies depending on the quantity and quality. The claim period for quantity is generally 60 days after the goods arrive at port of destination, while the claim period for quality is generally 1 year or more, which is usually specified as warranty period.

3. 处理索赔的办法和索赔金额 (Claim Processing and Amount Claimed)

通常在合同中只作一般笼统性规定。具体发生违约时，根据双方商定和有关法律规定来确定。

Generally, only general provisions are made in the contract. The specific breach of contract shall be determined according to the agreement between both parties and relevant laws and regulations.

4. 异议与索赔条款的规定方法实例 (Examples of Provision Methods for Discrepancy and Claim Clause)

如果买方发现货物的质量（数量）不一致，则在货物到达目的港之后，买方可在30天之内向卖方提出索赔，并以卖方认可的公证机构出具的检验证书为依据。卖方应在收到索赔后30天内答复买方。对索赔货物所提任何异议应由保险公司、运输公司或邮递机构负责的，卖方不负任何责任。

In case discrepancy on the quality or quantity (weight) of the goods is found by the buyer, the buyer may within 30 days, after arrival of the goods at the port of destination, lodge with the seller a claim which should be supported by an inspection certificate issued by a public surveyor approved by the seller. The seller shall reply to the buyer within 30 days after receipt of the claim. The sellers shall not take any responsibility if any claims concerning the shipping goods is up to the responsibility of insurance company/transportation company/post office.

（二）罚金或违约金条款 (Penalty Clause)

罚金或违约金条款是指当一方未履行合同义务时，应向对方支付一定数额的约定金额，以补偿对方的损失。

Penalty clause means that when one party fails to perform its obligations under the contract, it shall pay a certain amount of agreed amount to the other party to compensate for its losses.

罚金或违约金条款一般适用于卖方延期交货或买方延迟开立信用证或延期接货、拖欠货款等情况下。在买卖合同中规定罚金或违约金条款，是促使合同当事人履行合同义务的重要措施，能起到避免和减少违约行为发生的预防性作用。

Penalty clause is applicable to the sellers' delay in delivery or the buyers' delay in opening L/C or delayed receipt of goods, arrears of payment for goods, etc. The provision of penalty clause in the sales contract is an important measure to urge the parties to fulfill their contractual obligations, and can play a preventive role in avoiding and reducing the occurrence of breach of contract.

罚金或违约金的数额一般由当事人约定，以违约时间的长短为转移，并规定最高限额。罚金或违约金的支付并不解除违约方继续履行的义务。

The amount of penalty is generally agreed by the parties, and is transferred based on the duration of the breach, with a maximum limit specified. The payment of penalty shall not relieve the party from its obligations to continue to perform.

合同中的罚金条款示例：

Example of penalty clause in the contract:

除不可抗力外，如果发生延迟交货，卖方必须支付罚款，买方有权向卖方提出索赔。罚款率每天收取0.1%，罚款总额不得超过货物价值的5%。

Except for Force Majeure, if late delivery occurs, the seller must pay a penalty, and the buyer shall have the right to lodge a claim against the seller. The rate of penalty is charged at 0.1% for every day. The total penalty amount will not exceed 5% of the shipment value.

需要注意的是，按违约金是否具有惩罚性，可分为惩罚性违约金和补偿性违约金。世界上大多数国家（地区）都以违约金的补偿性为原则，以惩罚性为例外。因此应注意违约金的合法性问题。

It should be noted that according to whether the penalty is punitive, it can be divided into punitive penalty and compensatory penalty. Most countries (regions) in the world take the compensatory nature of penalty as their principle, with exceptions to punitive nature. Therefore, attention shall be paid to the legality of penalty.

罚金或违约金与赔偿损失的区别：①罚金或违约金不以造成损失为前提条件，即使违约的结果，并未发生任何实际损害，也不影响对违约方追究违约金责任。②违约金数额与实际损失是否存在及损失的大小没有关系，法庭或仲裁庭也不要求请求人就损失举证，故在追索程序上比要求赔偿损失简便得多。

Difference between penalties and compensation for losses: ① Penalties or liquidated damages shall not be premised on causing losses, and even if no actual damage has occurred as a result of the breach, it does not affect the accountability of the defaulting party for liquidated damages. ② The amount of liquidated damages has nothing to do with the existence or size of the actual loss, and the court or arbitral tribunal does not require the claimant to prove the loss. Therefore, the recourse procedure is much simpler than requesting compensation for the loss.

第三节　不可抗力
Section 3　Force Majeure

一、不可抗力的含义

I. Meaning of Force Majeure

不可抗力（force majeure），又称人力不可抗拒，是指在货物买卖合同签订以后，不是由于订约者任何一方当事人的过失或疏忽，而是由于发生了当事人既不能预见和预防，又无法避免和克服的意外事故，以致不能履行或不能如期履行合同，遭受意外事故的一方可以免除履行合同的责任或延期履行合同。

Force majeure means that after the signing of the contract for sales of goods, the party suffering from fortuitous accidents may be exempted from liability for performance or delay in performing the contract due to the occurrence of fortuitous accidents which are neither foreseeable nor preventable by the parties concerned and cannot be avoided.

二、不可抗力事故的范围及认定条件
II. Scope and Determination Conditions of Force Majeure

一般来讲，导致不可抗力事故发生的因素主要有两种：一种是地震、火灾、水灾、冰灾、雪灾、暴风雨、雷电等"自然力量"；另一种是战争、罢工、政府禁令、禁运、封锁等"社会力量"。对上述事故范围，各国对"自然力量"引起的事故解释比较一致，但对"社会力量"引起的事故解释往往不同。例如，美国习惯上认为不可抗力事故仅指由于"自然力量"引起的事故，而不包括由于"社会力量"引起的事故。故美国一般也不用"不可抗力"这一术语，而称为"意外事故条款"（Contingency Clause）。

Generally speaking, there are two main factors leading to force majeure: one is "natural forces" such as earthquakes, fires, floods, ice disasters, snow disasters, storms and lightning; the other is "social forces" such as wars, strikes, government bans, urgent transportation and blockades. Regarding the scope of above-mentioned accidents, countries have relatively consistent explanations for accidents caused by "natural forces", but explanations for accidents caused by "social forces" are often different. For example, it is customary in the United States to assume that force majeure refers only to accidents caused by "forces of nature" and does not include accidents caused by "social forces". Therefore, the United States generally does not use the term "Force Majeure", which is referred to as the "Contingency Clause".

另外，值得注意的是，并非所有阻碍合同履行的意外事故都可以归为不可抗力事故，综合国际上不同法律法规对不可抗力的解释，构成不可抗力事故必须同时具备以下三个条件。

In addition, it is worth noting that not all fortuitous accidents hindering the performance of the contract can be classified as force majeure. Based on the interpretation of force majeure in different international laws and regulations, the following three conditions must be met at the same time to constitute force majeure.

（1）事故必须发生在买卖合同签订之后。

(1) The accident must occur after the sales contract is signed.

在合同订立时，这种意外事故并没有发生。假如在订立合同时，这种事故已经存在的话，那么，当事人在签订合同时就应该考虑到该事故对合同的影响，这种事故就不具备偶然性和突发性，就不属于不可抗力事故。

Such fortuitous accidents did not occur at the time of contract signing. If such an accident already exists at the time of signing the contract, then the parties shall consider the impact of the accident on the contract when signing the contract. This type of accident does not have contingency or suddenness, and is not considered a force majeure.

（2）事故不是当事人的疏忽或故意行为造成的。

(2) The accident was not caused by the negligence or intentional act of the party concerned.

即当事人对意外事故的发生并无责任。如果是由于当事人的过失或故意行为而导致意外事故的发生，从而致使合同不能履行或不能如期履行，那么该事故就不能被看作不可抗力。

That is, the parties are not responsible for fortuitous accidents. If fortuitous accidents occur due to the negligence or intentional acts of the parties, which makes it impossible to perform or delay the performance of the contract, such accidents shall not be regarded as force majeure.

（3）事故是当事人不能预见、无法控制的。

(3) The accident is unforeseeable and beyond the control of the party concerned.

在意外事故发生之前，当事人根本无法预料到会发生这种事故，或者即使预测到可能会发生该事故，但也无法阻止它的发生。

Fortuitous accidents could not have been foreseen by the parties before they occurred, or prevented from occurring even if they were anticipated to occur.

在实际业务中，应正确区分不可抗力事故与价格、汇率等因素所致的正常的商业风险之间的区别，以防止当事人随意扩大不可抗力事故的范围，推卸应承担的合同责任。根据国际贸易惯例的解释，货价的变动、运价的变动、汇率的变动等不属于不可抗力，是正常的商业风险。

In actual business, the difference between force majeure and normal commercial risks caused by factors such as price and exchange rate shall be correctly distinguished to prevent the parties from arbitrarily expanding the scope of force majeure and shirking their liabilities under the contract. According to the interpretation of international trade customs, changes in price, rate and exchange rate are not force majeure but normal commercial risks.

三、不可抗力事故的法律后果
III. Legal Consequences of Force Majeure

不可抗力事故所造成的法律后果主要有两种，一种是解除合同，另一种是变更合同。所谓变更合同是指由一方当事人提出并经另一方当事人同意，对合同的内容作适当的修改，包括延期履行、分期履行、替代履行和减量履行，其中延期履行是较常见的一种变更合同方式。

There are mainly two kinds of legal consequences caused by force majeure, one is to terminate the contract and the other is to change the contract. The so-called change of contract refers to the appropriate modification of the contents of the contract proposed by one party and agreed by the other party, including deferred performance, installment performance, substitute performance and reduced performance. Delayed performance is a common way of changing the contract.

究竟什么情况下可以解除合同，什么情况下不能解除合同，而只能变更合同，要看买卖双方在合同中是如何对不可抗力条款予以规定的。如果双方未在合同中做出明确规定，则应根据所发生事故的性质及其对合同履行的影响程度而定。一般的原则是：如果不可抗力事故的发生使履行合同成为不可能，则可以解除合同；如果不可抗力事故只是暂时阻碍了合同的履行，待不可抗力事故消失后，仍可以继续履行合同，那么，就只能变更合同，而不能解除合同。

Under what circumstances can the contract be terminated, and under what circumstances cannot the contract be terminated but can only be changed, it depends on how the buyer and seller stipulate force majeure in the contract. If both parties fail to make clear provisions in the contract, it shall be determined based on the nature of the accident and its impact on the performance of the contract. The general principle is as follows: If the occurrence of force majeure makes it impossible to perform the contract, the contract can be terminated; if force majeure only temporarily hinders the performance of the contract and the contract can still be performed after the force majeure disappears, then the contract can only be changed but not terminated.

四、合同中的不可抗力条款
IV. Force Majeure in the Contract

（一）不可抗力条款的主要内容 (Main Contents of Force Majeure)

由于世界各国（地区）在对不可抗力的认定及不可抗力所引起的法律后果的解释不完全一致，为了避免不必要的纠纷，防止当事人任意扩大或缩小不可抗力事故的范围，买卖双方需要在合同中对不可抗力条款做出明确具体的规定。

As the definition of force majeure and the interpretation of legal consequences caused by force majeure are not completely consistent in all countries (regions) around the world, in order to avoid unnecessary disputes and prevent the parties from arbitrarily expanding or narrowing the scope of force majeure, both parties need to make clear and specific provisions on force majeure in the contract.

尽管国际上不同的货物买卖合同对不可抗力条款的规定不尽相同，有的烦琐，有的简单，但一般的货物买卖合同中的不可抗力条款主要包括四个方面的内容：不可抗力事故的范围，不可抗力事故的法律后果，不可抗力事故的证明机构，不可抗力事故发生后通知对方的期限与方法。

Although the provisions on force majeure vary among different international contracts for the sale of goods, some are cumbersome and some are simple, the force majeure in general contracts for the sale of goods mainly include four aspects: scope of force majeure, legal consequences of force majeure, certification organization of force majeure, deadline and method for notifying the other party after force majeure.

（二）合同中不可抗力条款示例 (Examples of Force Majeure in the Contract)

买卖合同中的不可抗力条款，如：由于战争、地震、火灾、雪灾、暴风雨或其他不可抗力事故，致使卖方不能全部或部分装运或延迟装运合同货物，卖方对于这种不能装运或延迟装运本合同货物不负有责任。但卖方须用电报或电传方式通知买方，并应在15天内以航空挂号信向买方提供中国国际贸易促进委员会出具的证明此类事故的证明文件。

Force majeure in the sales contract, such as:If the shipment of the contracted goods is prevented or delayed in whole or in part by reason or war, earthquake, fire, flood, heavy snow, storm or other causes of force majeure, the sellers shall not be liable for non-shipment or late shipment of the goods of this contract. However, the sellers shall notify the buyers by cable or telex and furnish the letter within 15 days by registered airmail with a certificate issued by the China Council for Promotion of International Trade attesting such event or events.

（三）援引不可抗力条款处理事故应注意的事项 (Precautions for Citing Force Majeure to Handle Accidents)

（1）发生事故的一方当事人应按合同规定的期限和方式将事故情况通知对方，对方也应及时答复，如有异议要及时提出。关于通知方式和时限，一般规定：一方遭遇不可抗力事故以后，应以电报或电传通知对方，并在15天内提供事故的详情及影响合同履行的程度的证明文件。

(1) The party involved in the accident shall notify the other party within the time limit and in the manner specified in the contract, and the other party shall also reply in a timely manner. if there is any objection, it shall be raised in a timely manner. Notices and time limit: In case of force majeure, one party shall notify the other party by cable or telex, and provide details of the accident and supporting documents for the extent of impact on the performance of the contract within 15 days.

（2）发生事故的一方当事人应出具有效的证明文件，以作为发生事故的证据。进出口合同一般都明确规定了出证机构。在国外，一般是由当地的商会或合法公证机构出具，在我国，是由中国国际贸易促进委员会及其设在口岸的贸促会分会出证。

(2) The party involved in the accident shall issue valid supporting documents as evidence of the accident. Import and export contracts generally specify the issuing authority. In foreign countries, it is generally issued by the local chamber of commerce or legal notaries. In China, it is issued by CCPIT and its sub-councils set up at ports.

（3）双方当事人都要认真分析事故的性质，看其是否属于不可抗力事故的范围，并就不可抗力的后果，按约定的处理原则和办法进行协商处理。

(3) Both parties shall carefully analyze the nature of the accident to see whether it falls within the scope of force majeure, and negotiate and handle the consequences of force majeure according to the agreed principles and methods.

第四节　仲裁
Section 4　Arbitration

由于政治、经济、自然条件等诸方面的变化和影响，买卖双方在履行合同的过程中，难免会有不履约或不完全履约的情况发生，以致双方产生争议。国际贸易中解决争议的方式有很多，仲裁是其中之一。由于采用仲裁方式解决争议具有诸多优点，因此它在国际贸易中常被广泛采用，并作为条款被列入买卖合同中。

Due to the changes and influence of political, economic and natural conditions, it is inevitable that non or incomplete performance of the contract may occur between the buyer and seller, leading to disputes between the two parties. Arbitration is one of the many ways to settle disputes in international trade. Dispute settlement by arbitration has many advantages, so it is widely used international trade and included in the sales contract as a clause.

一、国际贸易中解决争议的方式
I. Dispute Resolution in International Trade

在国际贸易中，一旦买卖双方发生争议，一般可以通过协商、调解、诉讼或仲裁四种途径来解决。可以说，这四种解决争议的方式各有利弊。

In international trade, once a dispute arises between the buyer and the seller, it can generally be resolved through consultation, conciliation, litigation or arbitration. It can be said that each of these four ways of dispute resolution has its own advantages and disadvantages.

（一）协商 (Consultation)

协商（consultation，negotiation），又称友好协商，是指在争议发生后，买卖双方本着友好、协作的精神，在互谅、互让的基础上，不借助外界力量，自行协商解决纠纷，必要时双方或其中一方做出让步，消除分歧，达成一致。采用协商方式解决争议的好处主要体现在：

Consultation, also known as friendly negotiation, refers to the negotiation and resolution of disputes between the buyer and seller in a spirit of friendship and cooperation, based on mutual understanding and compromise, without the help of external forces. If necessary, both parties or one of them make concessions to eliminate differences and reach an agreement. The advantages of dispute resolution through consultation are mainly reflected in:

（1）双方可在较为平和的气氛中自主解决问题，进一步加深对彼此的了解，不伤害彼此的感情，有利于日后双方贸易关系的发展；

(1) Both parties can independently solve problems in a relatively peaceful atmosphere, further deepening their understanding of each other, without harming each other's emotions, which is conducive to the development of future trade relations;

（2）由于是自行协商解决争议，没有任何第三方参与，可在很大程度上保守商业机密；

(2) As the dispute is resolved through consultation without any third-party involvement, it has a high degree of commercial confidentiality;

（3）不受程序和手续的限制，可节省时间、费用和精力。

(3) Not limited by procedures and procedures, it can save time, cost and effort.

由于协商方式不受任何形式上的限制，具有很大的灵活性，所以当买卖双方发生争议时，一般都愿意最先选择协商方式来解决纠纷。但这种方式也有一定的局限性，因为有时协商的结果并不能使双方消除分歧、达成协议。此时，就需要寻求其他途径以解决争议。

Due to the flexibility of consultation, which is not subject to any formal restrictions, when disputes arise between the buyer and seller, they are generally willing to choose consultation first to resolve the dispute. However, this method also has some limitations. Consultation sometimes fails to resolve the differences and reach an agreement between the two parties. At this point, it is necessary to seek other ways to resolve the dispute.

（二）调解 (Conciliation)

调解（conciliation），也称第三方调解，就是指买卖双方发生争议时，在自愿的基础上请第三方从中调和矛盾，以解除双方间的分歧，达成和解协议。

Conciliation, also known as third-party conciliation, means that when a dispute arises between the buyer and seller, a third party is invited to mediate the contradiction on a voluntary basis so as to resolve the differences between the two parties and reach a settlement agreement.

调解从本质上讲与协商并无太大的区别，它最重要的特点是，该方式的运用是以双方当事人的自愿为前提，一方当事人或调解员无权强迫另一方当事人接受调解。因此，当事人可以通过调解员在平和的气氛中比较灵活快捷的方式解决问题，调解的成功与否都不会让买卖双方已经建立起来的业务关系造成太大的不利影响。

Conciliation is essentially the same as consultation. Its most important feature is that its application is based on the voluntariness of both parties, and one party or conciliator has no right to force the other party to accept conciliation. Thus, the parties can resolve their issues in a flexible and efficient manner through conciliation in an atmosphere of peace that does not adversely affect much of the business relationship already established between the buyer and seller.

但是，由于调解是以当事人自愿为原则，所以，它的使用也有一定的局限性。当争议所涉及的金额巨大、性质严重或当事人对和解无诚意以致调解失败时，一般只能在诉讼或仲裁这两种方式中再做选择。

However, because conciliation is based on the principle of voluntariness of the parties, its use also has certain limitations. Litigation or arbitration is generally the only choice when a dispute involves a huge amount of money, its nature is serious, or the parties have no good faith in conciliation and thus fail.

（三）诉讼 (Litigation)

诉讼（litigation），俗称打官司，是指发生争议的一方当事人依据一定的法律程序，要求有管辖权的法院对有关的争议予以审理，并依据法律做出裁决。

Litigation, commonly known as filing a lawsuit, refers to a party to a dispute who, in accordance with certain legal procedures, requests a court with jurisdiction to hear the relevant dispute and make a ruling in accordance with the law.

诉讼与协商及调解最本质的区别是，诉讼具有强制性。诉讼的强制性表现在法院的强制管辖和判决的强制执行两个方面。

The essential difference between litigation and consultation and conciliation is that litigation is mandatory. Litigation is compulsory in two aspects: the compulsory jurisdiction of courts and the enforcement of judgments.

由于采用诉讼方式解决争议程序复杂、耗时久、费用高，常常造成当事人关系紧张，不利于贸易关系的发展。而且跨国判决，执行起来也较为困难。所以，目前国际贸易中越来越多地采用仲裁解决争议。

Dispute resolution by litigation is complicated, time-consuming and costly, which often causes tension between the parties and is not conducive to the development of trade relations. Moreover, transnational judgements are difficult to enforce. So arbitration is increasingly used in international trade to resolve disputes.

（四）仲裁 (Arbitration)

仲裁（arbitration），俗称公断，指买卖双方按照在争议发生前或发生后签订的协议，自愿将合同争议交给双方同意的仲裁机构进行裁决。

Arbitration refers to the voluntary submission of contract disputes to an arbitration institution agreed upon by both parties in accordance with an agreement signed before or after the occurrence of the dispute.

仲裁既不同于诉讼，也不同于协商和调解，它比诉讼更强调自愿性，而较之协商和调解更强调强制性。仲裁的自愿性主要表现在，向仲裁机构提起仲裁必须有双方达成的协议。它的强制性则体现在仲裁裁决是终局性的，双方当事人必须遵照执行。此外，与诉讼相比，采用仲裁方式解决争议还有如下好处：

Arbitration is different from litigation and consultation and conciliation. It emphasizes voluntariness more than litigation and enforceability more than consultation and conciliation. Arbitration is mainly voluntary in that there must be an agreement between the parties to initiate arbitration before the arbitration institution. Arbitration award is final and must be executed by both parties. Moreover, dispute resolution by arbitration has the following advantages over litigation:

（1）当事人双方可以选择仲裁员，仲裁员通常是各相关行业资深专家、学者，裁决案件较为中肯和合情合理；

(1) Both parties may choose an arbitrator, who is usually a senior expert or scholar from relevant industries, and is more pertinent and reasonable in adjudicating the case;

（2）仲裁机构是非官方机构，审理案件不受外界干预，可以有效地保证裁决的公正性，这就进一步增强了当事人对采用仲裁方式解决争议案件的愿望；

(2) Arbitration institutions are non-official institutions, which can effectively ensure the impartiality of awards without external interference, thus further enhancing the parties' desire to resolve dispute cases by arbitration;

（3）仲裁案件的审理一般不公开，可以有效地保守商业机密，维护当事人商业信誉；

(3) Arbitration cases are generally heard in private, which can effectively keep trade secrets and maintain

the business reputation of the parties;

（4）仲裁程序比诉讼程序简单，而且仲裁裁决一般都是终局性的，因此，采用仲裁方式解决争议通常比采用诉讼要迅速、及时，而且当事人所支出的仲裁费也较低。

(4) Arbitration proceedings are simpler than litigation, and arbitration awards are generally final. Dispute resolution by arbitration is therefore usually more expeditious and timely than by litigation, with lower costs to the parties.

（5）跨国仲裁的裁决，执行起来相对于诉讼较有保障。1958年6月10日在纽约召开的联合国国际商业仲裁会议上签署的《承认及执行外国仲裁裁决公约》(the New York Convention on the Recognition and Enforcement of Foreign Arbitral Awards，简称《纽约公约》)，是处理外国仲裁裁决的承认和仲裁条款执行问题的公约，为承认和执行外国仲裁裁决提供了一定的保证和便利，推动了国际商事仲裁活动的发展。目前世界上已有包括我国在内的130多个国家和地区加入了《纽约公约》。

(5) The award of cross-border arbitration is more secure in execution compared to litigation. The New York Convention on the Recognition and Enforcement of Foreign Arbitral Awards (hereinafter referred to as the "New York Convention"), signed at the United Nations Conference on International Commercial Arbitration held in New York on June 10, 1958 is a convention dealing with the recognition and enforcement of foreign arbitration awards, which provides certain guarantee and convenience for the recognition and enforcement of foreign arbitration awards and promotes the development of international commercial arbitration activities. At present, more than 130 countries and regions including China have joined the New York Convention.

由于以上原因，当争议双方通过友好协商或调解不能消除分歧、达成一致时，一般都愿意通过仲裁方式解决。

Due to the above reasons, when both parties to the dispute cannot resolve their differences or reach an agreement through friendly consultation or conciliation, they are generally willing to resolve the dispute through arbitration.

二、仲裁协议的形式及作用
II. Form and Role of Arbitration Agreement

仲裁协议（arbitration agreement）是有关当事人自愿将已经发生或即将发生的争议提交双方同意的仲裁机构进行裁决的一种意思一致的表示，同时也是仲裁机构和仲裁员受理争议案件的依据。

Arbitration agreement is a consistent expression of the voluntariness of relevant parties to submit the dispute that has occurred or is about to occur to an arbitration institution agreed by the parties for adjudication, and also serves as the basis for arbitration institutions and arbitrators to accept dispute cases.

（一）仲裁协议的形式 (Form of Arbitration Agreement)

包括我国在内的绝大多数国家的仲裁规则及一些国际公约均规定，仲裁协议必须以书面方式订立。书面仲裁协议的形式主要有三种。

The arbitration rules of most countries, including ours, and some international conventions stipulate that the arbitration agreement must be concluded in writing. There are three main forms of written arbitration agreement.

（1）双方当事人在争议发生之前订立的，表示愿意将可能发生的争议提交仲裁裁决的协议。这种协议一般作为合同条款包含在买卖合同之中，即合同的"仲裁条款"(Arbitration Clause)。

(1) An agreement signed by both parties prior to the occurrence of a dispute, expressing their willingness to refer such dispute as may arise to arbitration. This type of agreement is generally included as a clause in the sales contract, i.e. "Arbitration Clause" of the contract.

（2）由双方当事人在争议发生后订立的，表示同意将已经发生的争议提交仲裁裁决的协议。这种协议既可以采用协议书的形式，也可以通过双方的往来函件、电报或电传表示，被称为"提交仲裁的协议"（Submission）。

(2) An agreement signed by both parties after the occurrence of a dispute, expressing their consent to refer the dispute that has already arisen to arbitration. Such an agreement may be in the form of an agreement or by way of correspondence, cable or telex between the parties and is referred to as "Submission".

（3）由双方当事人在争议发生之前或发生之后，通过援引方式签订的仲裁协议，即当事人不直接拟定协议的具体内容，而只是同意有关争议按照某公约、双边条约、多边条约的仲裁条款所述的内容进行仲裁。

(3) An arbitration agreement concluded by reference between the parties before or after the dispute arises, i.e. the parties do not directly formulate the specific contents of the agreement, but only agree to conduct arbitration in accordance with the arbitration clause of a certain convention, bilateral treaty or multilateral treaty.

（二）仲裁协议的作用 (Role of Arbitration Agreement)

以上三种仲裁协议虽然在形式上有所不同，但它们的法律效力是相同的，其作用表现在三个方面：首先，约束双方当事人按照协议的规定以仲裁方式解决争议，而不得向法院起诉；第二，排除法院对有关争议案件的管辖权；第三，授予仲裁机构和仲裁员对有关争议案件的管辖权。这三方面的作用既相互联系、又相互制约，其中最关键的第二条，即排除法院对有关争议案件的管辖权，也就是说，只要双方当事人签有仲裁协议，就意味着只能采取仲裁方式解决争议，而不得将有关案件提交法院审理。如果一方违反仲裁协议，自行向法院提起诉讼，另一方即可根据协议要求法院停止司法诉讼程序，把争议案件发还仲裁庭审理。

Although the above three arbitration agreements are different in form, they have the same legal effect, which is manifested in three aspects: firstly, binding both parties to resolve disputes through arbitration according to the provisions of the agreement without bringing a lawsuit to the court; secondly, excluding the court's jurisdiction over dispute cases; thirdly, conferring jurisdiction on the arbitration institution and the arbitrator over relevant dispute cases. These three roles are both interrelated and mutually restrictive, the most crucial of which is the second, exclusion of the court's jurisdiction over dispute cases. In other words, as long as both parties sign an arbitration agreement, it means that disputes can only be resolved through arbitration and the relevant case cannot be referred to the court. If one party violates the arbitration agreement and brings a lawsuit to the court on its own, the other party can request the court to discontinue the judicial proceedings and return the dispute case to the arbitration tribunal according to the agreement.

三、合同中的仲裁条款
III. Arbitration Clause in the Contract

（一）仲裁条款的主要内容 (Main Contents of Arbitration Clause)

仲裁协议通常采用的形式是仲裁条款，即双方当事人在其签订的买卖合同中的约定将日后可能发生的争议提交仲裁的条款，它通常包括仲裁地点、仲裁机构、仲裁程序与规则、仲裁裁决的效力等方面内容。

The arbitration agreement is usually in the form of an arbitration clause, i.e. a clause that both parties agree to submit a dispute that may occur in the future to arbitration in the sales contract signed by them. It usually includes place of arbitration, arbitration institution, arbitration procedures and rules, validity of arbitration Award, etc.

1. 仲裁地点 (Place of Arbitration)

仲裁地点是指仲裁所选择的地点，一般是指仲裁机构的所在地。在什么地点进行仲裁是买卖双方十分关心的问题，因而也是仲裁条款中一项重要的内容。

Place of arbitration refers to the place chosen for arbitration, generally referring to the location of the arbitration institution. Place of arbitration is a matter of great concern to the buyer and seller, so it is also an important element in the arbitration clause.

在商定仲裁条款时，交易双方一般都愿意在本国仲裁，其原因主要是当事人对本国的仲裁机构和有关程序规则比较了解，而且没有语言障碍，还可以节省费用。除此之外，还有一个不容忽视的重要原因，那就是仲裁地点与仲裁所使用的程序法，甚至与买卖合同所适用的实体法都有着密切关系。根据许多国家法律的解释，凡属程序方面的问题，一般都适用审判地法律，即在哪个国家仲裁，如果没有相反的约定，就适用哪个国家的仲裁法规。

When negotiating the arbitration clause, both parties to the transaction are generally willing to conduct arbitration in their home country mainly because they have better knowledge of the local arbitration institutions and relevant procedural rules, and there is no language barrier, which can save costs. Furthermore, there is another important reason that cannot be ignored, which is that place of arbitration is closely related to the procedural law used in arbitration, and even to the substantive law applicable to the sales contract. According to the legal interpretations of many countries, procedural issues are generally governed by the law of the forum, i.e. for arbitration in a certain country, if there is no contrary agreement, the arbitration statute of that country shall apply.

我国对外签订的贸易合同，在规定仲裁地点时，应首选在我国仲裁。如果争取不到在我国仲裁，可与对方协商，选择在被诉方所在国仲裁，或是规定在我方较为信任的第三国进行仲裁。

When specifying the place of arbitration for trade contracts signed by China with foreign countries, arbitration in China shall be the first choice. If arbitration in China is not possible, we can negotiate with the other party and choose to arbitrate in the country where the defendant is located, or stipulate that arbitration be conducted in a third country that we trust more.

2. 仲裁机构 (Arbitration Institution)

明确了仲裁地点，买卖双方还应同时在合同中对仲裁机构加以确定。所谓仲裁机构是指受理仲裁案件并做出裁决的机构。

In addition to specifying the place of arbitration, both parties should also determine the arbitration institution in the contract. Arbitration institution refers to the institution that accepts arbitration cases and makes awards.

目前，国际商事方面的仲裁机构有两种，一种是常设机构，如我国的国际经济贸易仲裁委员会和海事仲裁委员会、巴黎的国际商会仲裁院、英国伦敦国际仲裁院、瑞典斯德哥尔摩仲裁院、瑞士苏黎世商会仲裁院、日本商事仲裁协会、美国仲裁协会、意大利仲裁协会、香港国际仲裁中心。这种常设机构因其组织稳定、制度健全、人员齐备、选用方便，有利于仲裁的顺利进行，而被国际上绝大多数仲裁争议案件所选用。另外一种是临时性的仲裁机构，是指专门为审理某一争议案件而临时组成的仲裁庭。组成仲裁庭的仲裁员由双方当事人指定，案件审理完毕后，仲裁庭即自动解散。在仲裁地点无常设仲裁机构，或当事人双方为解决特定争议而愿意指定仲裁员专审案件时，常选择临时性的仲裁机构进行仲裁。在选用临时性仲裁机构仲裁时，双方当事人应在合同的仲裁条款中就所选仲裁程序与规则，选定仲裁员的办法、人数、是否需要首席仲裁员等问题做出明确规定。

At present, there are two types of arbitration institutions in international commercial affairs. One is permanent institution, such as CIETAC and CMAC, ICC, LCIA, SCC, ZCC, JCAA, AAA, AIA and HKIAC. This permanent institution is chosen by the vast majority of international arbitration disputes due to its stable organization, sound system, complete personnel and convenient selection, which is conducive to the smooth progress of arbitration. The other is ad hoc arbitration, which is an arbitration tribunal specially formed to hear a certain dispute case. Arbitrators constituting the arbitration tribunal shall be appointed by both parties, and the arbitration tribunal shall be automatically dissolved upon completion of the hearing of the case. When there is no permanent institution in the place of arbitration, or when both parties are willing to appoint arbitrators to conduct special cases to resolve specific disputes, an ad hoc arbitration is often chosen. When selecting an ad hoc arbitration, both parties shall clearly specify in the arbitration clause of the contract regarding the selected arbitration procedures and rules, the method of selecting arbitrators, the number of arbitrators, and whether a chief arbitrator is required.

3. 仲裁程序与规则 (Arbitration Procedures and Rules)

仲裁程序规则是指进行仲裁的程序和具体做法，包括如何提交仲裁申请，如何进行答辩，如何指定仲裁员，如何组成仲裁庭，如何进行仲裁审理，如何做出裁决及如何交纳仲裁费等。

Arbitration procedures and rules refer to the procedure and specific practice of arbitration, including how to submit an arbitration application, how to defend, how to appoint arbitrators, how to form an arbitration tribunal, how to conduct arbitration proceedings, how to make an award, and how to pay arbitration fees.

仲裁程序与规则的作用主要在于能为当事人和仲裁员提供一套仲裁时必须遵守的行为准则。为了便于仲裁的顺利进行，常设的仲裁机构一般都制定了自己的仲裁规则，如中国国际经济贸易仲裁委员会制定的《中国国际经济贸易仲裁委员会仲裁规则》、国际商会仲裁院制定的《国际商会仲裁规则》，此外，一些区域性和国际性组织也定有仲裁规则，如《联合国欧洲经济委员会仲裁规则》、《联合国远东及亚洲经济委员会仲裁规则》、《联合国国际贸易法委员会仲裁规则》。

Arbitration procedures and rules are mainly to provide the parties and arbitrators with a set of code of conduct that must be observed during arbitration. To facilitate the smooth progress of arbitration, permanent arbitration institutions have formulated their own arbitration rules, such as Arbitration Rules of CIETAC, and ICC Rules of Arbitration. In addition, some regional and international organizations also have arbitration rules, such as UNECE Arbitration Rules, ECAFE Arbitration Rules and UNCITRAL Arbitration Rules.

仲裁规则与仲裁机构有着密切的关系，通常情况下，合同的仲裁条款中规定在哪个仲裁机构进行仲裁，就应该按照哪个机构制定的仲裁规则办理。但是，也有不少国家允许当事人选择仲裁地点以外的其他国家仲裁机构的仲裁规则，但以不违反仲裁地国家仲裁法中的强制性规定为前提条件。临时仲裁机构所适用的仲裁规则由双方当事人自行约定。

Arbitration rules are bound up with arbitration institutions. Usually, the arbitration clause of a contract stipulates that the arbitration shall be conducted in accordance with the arbitration rules formulated by the arbitration institution. There are also a number of countries that allow parties to choose the arbitration rules of an arbitration institution other than the place of arbitration provided that they do not violate the mandatory provisions of the arbitration law of the country where arbitration takes place. The arbitration rules applicable to ad hoc arbitration shall be agreed upon by both parties themselves.

4. 仲裁裁决的效力 (Validity of Arbitration Award)

仲裁裁决的效力是指仲裁机构对争议案件审理后所作的裁决对双方当事人是否有约束力，是不是终局性的，以及能否向法院上诉，要求变更裁决。

The validity of arbitration award refers to whether the award made by the arbitration institution after hearing the dispute case is binding on both parties and final, as well as whether it can appeal to the court for revision.

在国际上，包括中国在内的绝大多数国家都规定，仲裁裁决具有终局效力，对当事人均具有约束力，双方必须遵照执行，任何一方都不得向法院起诉要求变更。也有少数国家允许不服裁决的当事人向法院上诉，但法院一般只审查程序，不审查实体，即只有在发现仲裁员未按仲裁程序规则审理案件时，法院才可以撤销裁决。为了明确仲裁裁决的效力，避免引起上诉情况的发生，当事人在订立合同中的仲裁条款时，应明确规定。仲裁条款中还可写明仲裁费用应由哪一方负担。多数合同规定仲裁费用由败诉方负担，但也有的合同规定由仲裁庭酌情掌握。

Internationally, the vast majority of countries, including China, stipulate that the arbitration award is final and binding on both parties and must be complied with by both parties, and neither party may bring a lawsuit to court for change. A few countries allow parties who do not agree with the award to appeal to the court, but the court generally only reviews procedures and not merits, i.e. they may set aside an award only if it is found that the arbitrator has failed to comply with arbitration procedures and rules. To clarify the validity of arbitration award and avoid the occurrence of appeals, the parties shall specify the arbitration clause in the contract. The arbitration clause may also specify which party shall bear the costs of arbitration. Most contracts stipulate that the costs of arbitration shall be borne by the losing party, but some contracts stipulate that it is at the discretion of the arbitration tribunal.

（二）合同中仲裁条款示例 (Examples of Arbitration Clause in the Contract)

下面列举我国对外贸易合同中规定仲裁条款的三种范例。

Below are three examples of arbitration clause specified in China's foreign trade contracts.

1. 合同中规定在我国仲裁的条款 (Contract Clauses Providing for Arbitration in China)

凡因本合同所引起的或与本合同有关的任何争议，双方应通过友好的协商解决。如果协商不能解决，应提交中国国际经济贸易仲裁委员会按该会仲裁规则，在北京进行仲裁。仲裁裁决是终局的，对双方都有约束力。

Any dispute arising from or in connection with this contract shall be settled amicably through negotiation. In case no settlement can be reached through negotiation, the case shall then be submitted to the China International Economic and Trade Arbitration Commission for arbitration which shall be conducted by the Commission in Beijing in accordance with the Commission's arbitration rules. The arbitration award is final and binding upon both parties.

2. 合同规定在被诉方所在国仲裁的条款 (Contract Clauses Providing for Arbitration in the Defendant's Country)

凡因本合同所引起的或与本合同有关的任何争议，双方应通过友好协商解决。如果协商不能解决，应该提交仲裁，仲裁在被诉一方所在国进行。如在中国，由中国国际经济贸易仲裁委员会根据该会仲裁规则在北京进行仲裁。如在××（被诉一方所在国家的名称），则由××（被诉一方所在国的仲裁机构的名称及所在城市）根据该仲裁机构的仲裁规则进行仲裁。仲裁裁决是终局的,对双方都有约束力。

Any dispute arising from or in connection with this contract shall be settled amicably through negotiation. In case no settlement can be reached through negotiation, the case shall then be submitted for arbitration. The location of arbitration shall be in the country of domicile of the defendant. If in China, the arbitration shall be conducted by the China International Economic and Trade Arbitration Commission in Beijing in accordance with it's arbitration rules by … (name of the country of domicile of the defendant), the arbitration shall be conducted by … (name of the arbitration organization) in … (name of the place) in accordance with it's arbitration rules. The arbitration award is final and binding upon both parties.

3. 合同规定在第三国或对方所在国仲裁的条款 (Contract Clauses Providing for Arbitration in a Third Country or the Other Party's Country)

凡因本合同所引起的或与本合同有关的任何争议,双方应通过友好协商解决。如果协商不能解决,应提交……(某第三国或对方所在国仲裁机构的名称及所在城市)根据该仲裁机构的仲裁规则进行仲裁。仲裁裁决是终局的,对双方都有约束力。

Any dispute arising from or in connection with this contract shall be settled amicably through negotiation. In case no settlement can be reached through negotiation, the case shall then be submitted to … (name of the arbitration organization in the third country or the other country) in (name of the place) in accordance with it's arbitration rules. The arbitration award is final and binding upon both parties.

第十二章 进出口合同的履行
Chapter 12　Performance of Import and Export Contract

导　读
Introduction

对于一个外贸业务上的生手来讲，接到第一个客户的询盘或发盘，与客户进行具体的磋商、订立合同是令人振奋的好事，但接下来面临的履行合同阶段常常让外贸新手感觉摸不着头脑，不知道具体的业务流程是如何展开的。因此，熟悉外贸业务流程及掌握各个环节的具体操作，对于外贸业务员顺利进行业务操作及履行合同至关重要。

For a novice in international trade, it is exciting to negotiate with the customer and sign the contract after receiving the inquiry or offer from the first customer. However, the next stage of performing the contract often makes them feel confused and unsure of how the specific business process is carried out. Therefore, being familiar with the international trade process and mastering the specific operation of each stage is crucial for foreign trade salespersons to smoothly carry out business operations and perform the contract.

本章主要介绍出口业务流程和进口业务流程，各业务环节的具体操作在前序相关章节中已经进行了详细的介绍，同学们可以根据本节内容将前序章节的学习进行有机串联，进一步掌握和理解各业务环节在进出口商品合同履约过程中的意义和作用。

This chapter mainly introduces the export business process and import business process. The specific operations of each stage have been detailed in the previous relevant chapters. Students can organically connect the learning of the previous chapters based on the content of this section, so as to further grasp and understand the significance and role of each stage in the performance of import and export commodity contracts.

第一节　出口合同的履行
Section 1　Performance of Export Contract

一、出口业务流程
I. Export Business Process

一笔出口交易大体上可分为三个阶段：①交易前的准备阶段；②对外洽谈阶段；③履行合同阶段。

An export transaction can be roughly divided into three stages: ① Pre-transaction preparation stage; ② External negotiation stage; ③ Contract performance stage.

交易前的准备工作，即寻找客户、做好客户资信调查、与潜在的客户建立业务联系。若收到客户的询盘或发盘，则意味着双方可进入具体的洽谈阶段。图12-1是CIF（成本、保险费加运费，指定目的港）条件下的出口业务流程，对外洽谈阶段就是与客户就各交易条件进行具体磋商的阶段，一般要经过询盘、发盘、还盘直至接受，接受意味着双方对所有的交易条件达成了一致，双方可着手签订一份书面合同。签订书面合同后，有关当事人必须履行合同规定的各项义务，履行合同时，有关当事人都应重合同、守信用，否则，违约的一方必须承担法律责任。

Pre-transaction preparation, i.e. looking for customers, doing a good job in customer credit investigation and establishing business contacts with potential customers. Receipt of an inquiry or offer from a customer means that both parties can proceed to a specific negotiation stage. Figure 12-1 shows the export business process under CIF (cost insurance and freight, named port of destination). The external negotiation stage is a specific negotiation stage with customers on various transaction conditions. Generally, it goes through inquiry, offer, counter-offer until acceptance. Acceptance means that both parties have reached an agreement on all transaction terms, and can proceed to sign a written contract. After signing a written contract, the parties involved must fulfill all the obligations stipulated in the contract. During the performance of the contract, relevant parties shall abide by the contract and keep their promises; otherwise, the party who breaches the contract must bear legal liabilities.

对于出口方来讲，出口合同的履行就是要按照合同的规定履行交货并安全收回货款等一系列的工作。在前面章节的学习中，我们已经学习了出口业务中合同履行阶段所涉及的各项业务流程，在这里我们需要注意，不同的结算方式下工作的流程会有所不同，特别是后期的交单结汇工作流程，新业务员需要特别注意，图12-1所示的流程图为在使用信用证作为支付方式条件下的出口业务流程。

For the exporter, the performance of an export contract involves performing a series of tasks such as delivering goods and safely recovering payment in accordance with the provisions of the contract. In the previous chapters, we have learned various business processes involved in the contract performance stage of export business. Here we need to note that the workflow will be different under different settlement methods, especially the document presentation and foreign exchange settlement workflow in the later period. New salespersons need to pay special attention to this. The flow chart shown in Figure 12-1 is the export business process when L/C is used as the payment method.

以下简要介绍出口合同的履行程序：

The following is a brief description of the procedures for performing an export contract:

（1）备货（stocking）与报验。为了保证按时、按质、按量交付约定的货物，在订立合同之后，卖方必须及时落实货源，备妥应交的货物，并做好出口货物的报验工作。

(1) Stocking and inspection application. In order to ensure that the agreed goods are delivered on time, with good quality and quantity, after signing the contract, the Sellers must promptly determine the source of goods, prepare the goods to be delivered, and do a good job in applying for inspection of export goods.

（2）催证、审证和改证（urging the L/C, verifying the L/C, amending the L/C）。在履行凭信用证付款的出口合同时，应注意做好催证、审证和改证工作。

(2) Urging the L/C, verifying the L/C, amending the L/C. During the performance of an export contract with L/C Payment, attention shall be paid to Urging the L/C, Verifying the L/C and Amending the L/C.

（3）租船订舱（charter and booking）。按CIF或CFR条件成交时，卖方应及时办理租船订舱工作，如系大宗货物，需要办理租船手续。

(3) Charter and booking. When the transaction is concluded on a CIF or CFR basis, the sellers shall handle charter and booking in a timely manner. In case of bulk goods, charter procedures shall be handled.

（4）办理报关（customs clearance）。出口货物在装船出运之前，需向海关办理报关手续，出口货物办理报关时必须填写出口货物报关单，必要时还需要提供出口合同副本，发票，装箱单，重量单，商品检验证书，以及其他有关证件。

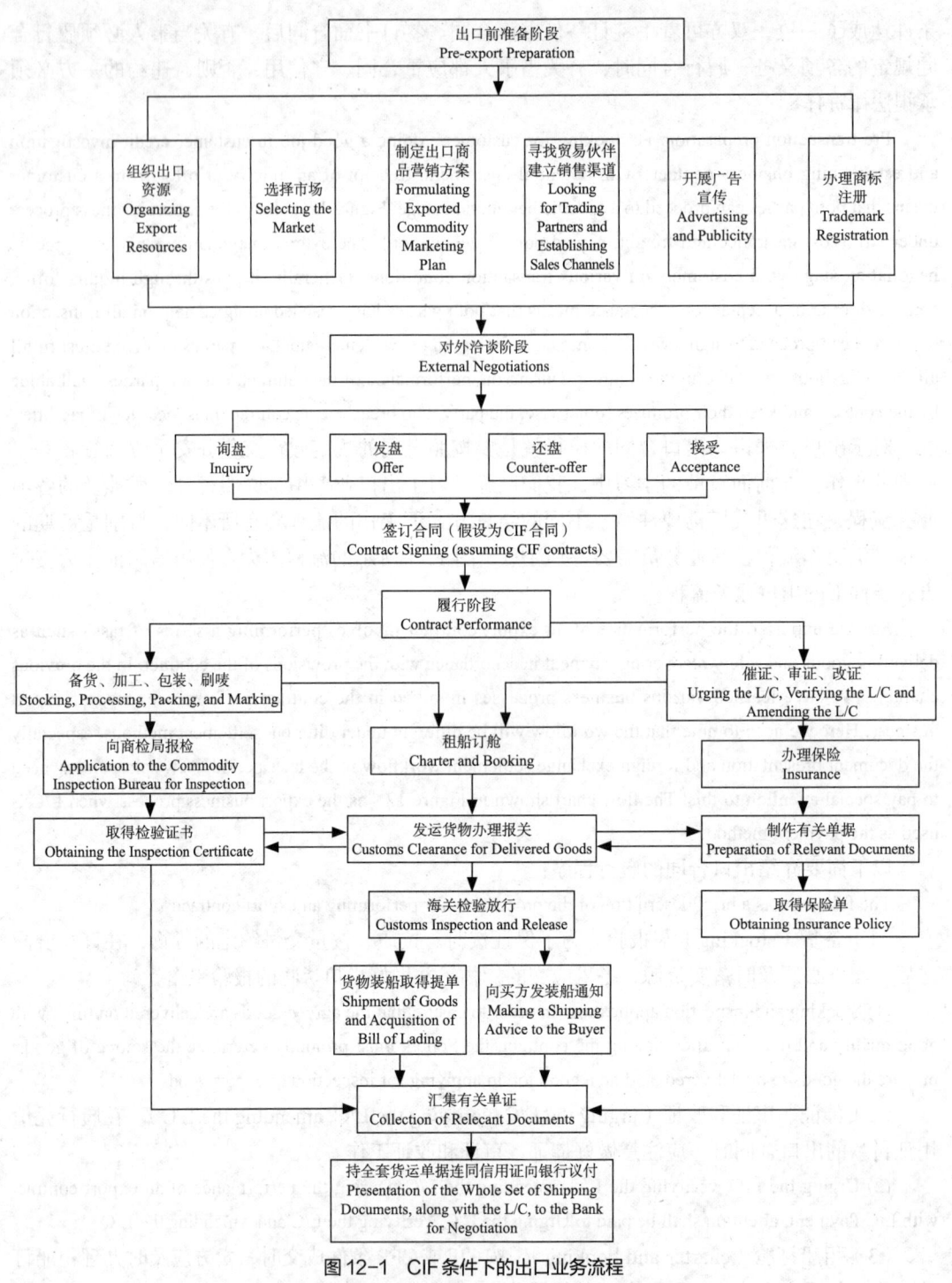

```
                        出口前准备阶段
                    Pre-export Preparation
                              │
  ┌──────────┬──────────┬─────┼─────┬──────────┬──────────┐
  │          │          │           │          │          │
组织出口    选择市场   制定出口商   寻找贸易伙伴  开展广告    办理商标
资源       Selecting   品营销方案   建立销售渠道  宣传       注册
Organizing  the        Formulating  Looking     Advertising Trademark
Export     Market      Exported     for Trading and         Registration
Resources              Commodity    Partners and Publicity
                       Marketing    Establishing
                       Plan         Sales Channels

                        对外洽谈阶段
                    External Negotiations
                              │
       ┌──────────┬──────────┼──────────┬──────────┐
      询盘        发盘        还盘        接受
      Inquiry    Offer       Counter-offer Acceptance

              签订合同（假设为CIF合同）
           Contract Signing (assuming CIF contracts)

                        履行阶段
                   Contract Performance
```

Figure 12-1　Export Business Process under CIF

图 12-1　CIF 条件下的出口业务流程

(4) Customs clearance. Before the export goods are shipped, it is necessary to go through customs clearance. During customs clearance of export goods, a customs declaration form for export goods must be filled in. Copy of export contract, invoice, packing list, weight list, commodity inspection certificate and other relevant certificates shall also be provided when necessary.

（5）办理保险（insurance）。凡按CIF条件成交的出口合同，在货物装船前，卖方应及时向中国人民保险公司办理投保手续，出口货物投保都是逐笔办理，投保人应填制投保单，将货物名称，保险金额，运输路线，运输工具，开航日期，投保险别等一一列明。

(5) Insurance. For export contracts concluded under CIF, the sellers shall go through the insurance procedures with PICC before loading the goods. The insurance for export goods is handled on a case-by-case basis. The applicant shall fill out the application form and list the name of the goods, insured amount, route of carriage, means of conveyance, Slg. on or abt., type of insurance, etc.

（6）装箱单和重量单（packing list and weight list）。装箱单又称花色码单，它列明每批货物的逐件花色搭配；重量单则列明每件货物的净重和毛重，这两种单据可用来补充商业发票内容的不足，便于进口国（地区）海关检验和核对货物。

(6) Packing list and weight list. the packing list shows the design and color matching of each batch of goods one by one; the weight list shows the net weight and gross weight of each piece of goods. These two documents can be used to supplement the contents of the commercial invoice for the convenience of customs inspection and verification of the goods in the importing country (region).

（7）持全套业务单据，通常有汇票、发票、提单等，连同信用证一起，向银行议付（Available by negotiation）。

(7) Hold a full set of business documents, usually including draft, invoice, B/L, etc. and negotiate with the bank together with L/C.

第二节　进口合同的履行
Section 2　Performance of Import Contract

一笔进口交易大体上也可以分为三个阶段：①交易前的准备阶段；②对外洽谈阶段；③履行合同阶段。

An import transaction can also be roughly divided into three stages: ① Pre-transaction preparation stage; ② External negotiation stage; ③ Contract performance stage.

以FOB（装运港船上交货，指定装运港）条件成交、信用证方式结算为例，进口业务各阶段的具体工作内容如图12-2所示。主要介绍如下几个业务环节：申请开立信用证、安排运输和保险、审查文件和付款、申请清关和检查进口货物。

Taking FOB (free on board, named port of shipment) transaction and L/C settlement as an example, the specific work contents at each stage of import business are shown in Figure 12-2. The following stages are mainly introduced: Application for L/C, arrangement of carriage and insurance, review of documents and payment, application for customs clearance and inspection of import goods.

1. 申请进口许可证 (Application for Import Permit)

通常，进口公司应向主管部门申请进口许可证，并获得海关和相关部门的许可。

Generally, the importing company shall apply to the competent authority for an import permit and obtain permission from customs and relevant authorities.

2. 开立信用证 (Opening L/C)

进口商应按合同规定开立信用证，并在需要时做出适当的修改。进口商应遵守合同中的期限。如果信用证太早开立，进口商会增加开支，浪费时间筹措资金，如果信用证太晚开立，会导致进口商履行合同义务的失败，进而延误出口商的运输操作。

```
进口前的准备工作
Pre-import Preparation
```

- 编制进口计划报表 / Development of Import Planning Report
- 用货部门填制进口订货卡片 / The User Department Fills in the Import Order Card
- 进出口公司审查订货卡片 / The Import and Export Company Reviews the Order Card
- 安排订购货物和选择交易对象 / Arrangement of Goods Ordering and Selection of the Trading Partner
- 制定具体的进口商品经营方案 / Formulation of Specific Business Plan for Imported Commodities

```
对外洽谈阶段
External Negotiations
```

- 询盘 Inquiry
- 发盘 Offer
- 还盘 Counter-offer
- 接受 Acceptance

```
签订合同（假设为FOB合同、L/C支付）
Contract Signing (assuming FOB contracts and L/C payment)
```

```
履约阶段
Contract Performance
```

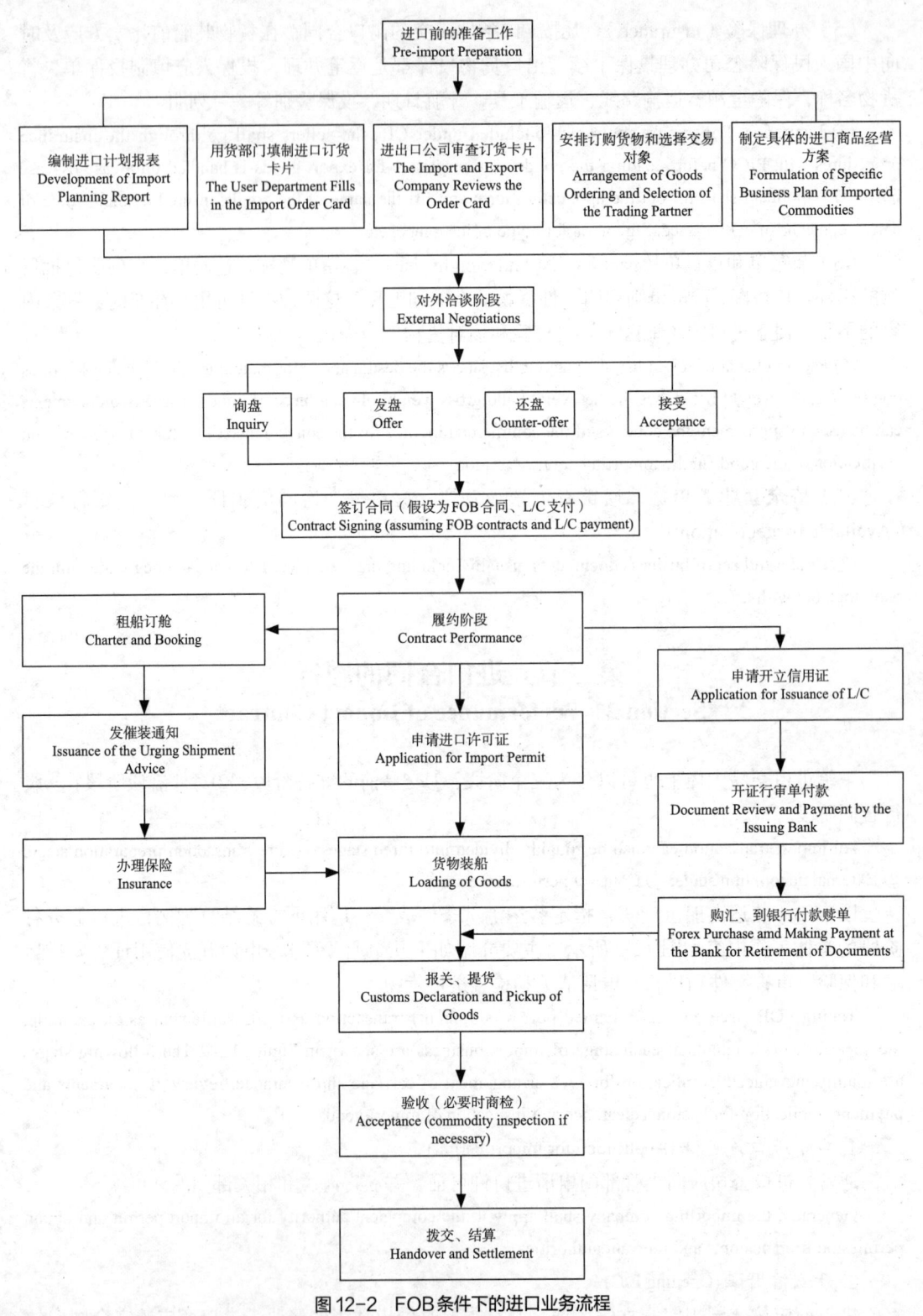

- 租船订舱 / Charter and Booking
- 发催装通知 / Issuance of the Urging Shipment Advice
- 办理保险 / Insurance
- 申请进口许可证 / Application for Import Permit
- 货物装船 / Loading of Goods
- 报关、提货 / Customs Declaration and Pickup of Goods
- 验收（必要时商检） / Acceptance (commodity inspection if necessary)
- 拨交、结算 / Handover and Settlement
- 申请开立信用证 / Application for Issuance of L/C
- 开证行审单付款 / Document Review and Payment by the Issuing Bank
- 购汇、到银行付款赎单 / Forex Purchase and Making Payment at the Bank for Retirement of Documents

图 12-2　FOB条件下的进口业务流程

Figure 12-2　Import Business Process under FOB

The importer shall open an L/C as stipulated in the contract and make appropriate amendments if required.

The importer shall comply with the terms specified in the contract. If the L/C is opened too early, the importer will incur additional expenses and waste time raising funds. If the L/C is opened too late, it will lead to the failure of the importer to fulfill its obligations under the contract, thus delaying the exporter's carriage operation.

3. 安排发运 (Arrange Shipment)

在FOB进口合同下，进口商应履行在指定地点收货、装船或订舱的义务。进口商应根据进口货物数量填写订舱单，并将订舱单与合同副本一起交船代。进口商应在安排船后的45天内通知出口商及时交货和装货，以免延误整个业务流程。

Under the FOB import contract, the importer shall perform its obligation to receive, ship or book at a named place. The importer shall fill in the Booking Note according to the quantity of goods imported and submit it to the shipping agent together with a copy of the contract. The importer shall notify the exporter of timely delivery and loading within 45 days after arranging the shipment to avoid delaying the entire business process.

4. 海运保险 (Marine Insurance)

在FOB或CFR合同项下，进口商在收到出口商的装船通知后，应为船上货物办理海运保险。

Under FOB or CFR contracts, the importer shall effect marine insurance for the cargo on board after receiving a shipping advice from exporter.

5. 支付 (Payment)

进口商银行根据信用证审核单据和汇票，决定银行是付款还是承兑。

The importer's bank reviews the documents and draft according to L/C, and decides whether the bank will make payment or accept them.

如果银行确认单据正确，并将单据寄给进口商作进一步检查。如果进口商承认单据的完整性，银行就会按照信用证的条款付款。如果发现不符点，银行将告知进口商，如果进口商接受不符合规定的货物，进口商可以指示银行付款或承兑。

If the bank confirms that the documents are correct, they will be sent to the importer for further inspection. Payment will be made in accordance with the terms of L/C if the importer accepts the completeness of the documents. If a discrepancy is found, the bank will advise the importer. If the importer accepts goods that do not meet the requirements, they may instruct the bank for payment or acceptance.

第十二章拓展知识、专业词汇和练习

参考文献
References

[1] 黎孝先，王健. 国际贸易实务[M]. 7版. 北京：对外经济贸易大学出版社，2020.

[2] 田运银. 国际贸易实务精讲[M]. 7版. 北京：中国海关出版社，2018.

[3] 张燕芳，刘梓豪. 国际贸易实务（附微课）[M]. 北京：人民邮电出版社，2023.

[4] 吴百福，徐小薇，聂清. 进出口贸易实务教程[M]. 8版. 上海：格致出版社，2020.

[5] 傅龙海，吴慧君，陈剑霞. 国际贸易实务[M]. 4版. 北京：对外经贸大学出版社，2021.

[6] 中国国际贸易商会/国际商会中国国家委员会. 国际贸易术语解释通则2020[M]. 北京：对外经济贸易大学出版社，2020.

[7] 周瑞琪，王小鸥，徐月芳. 国际贸易实务（英文版）[M]. 5版. 北京：对外经济贸易大学出版社，2020.

[8] 田运银，胡少甫，史理，等. 国际贸易操作实训精讲[M]. 2版. 北京：中国海关出版社，2015.

[9] 易露霞，陈新华，尤彧聪. 国际贸易实务双语教程[M]. 5版. 北京：清华大学出版社，2020.

[10] 冷柏军，李洋. 国际贸易实务双语教程[M]. 北京：中国人民大学出版社，2021.

[11] 孙智慧. 国际贸易实务（双语）[M]. 北京：对外经济贸易大学出版社，2018.

[12] 徐凡. 国际贸易实务（双语版）[M]. 北京：对外经济贸易大学出版社，2013.